Lame Brains & LUNATICS

Lame Brains & LUNATICS

The Good, The Bad, and the Forgotten of SILENT COMEDY

by Steve Massa

BearManor Media

2013

Lame Brains & Lunatics:
The Good, the Bad, and the Forgotten of Silent Comedy

For information, address:

BearManor Media
P. O. Box 71426
Albany, GA 31708

bearmanormedia.com

Typesetting and layout by John Teehan

Published in the USA by BearManor Media

ISBN—978-1-62933-941-2

To Susan and David

"Well... nobody's perfect."
– Joe E. Brown, *Some Like It Hot* (1959)

Table of Contents

Foreword by Eileen Bowser

ABOUT TWENTY-FIVE YEARS AGO, I got a phone call in my office at the Museum of Modern Art from a young man who had heard that we were planning to hold a Slapstick Symposium and Identification Seminar and he asked whether he could attend. I explained that the event was part of the annual congress of FIAF, the International Federation of Film Archives, and that it was intended for the members, not the general public. He pleaded a special interest in slapstick films. I tried to discourage him by saying we were emphasizing little-known films instead of the usual Charlie Chaplin, Buster Keaton, and Harold Lloyd. He said, "Oh, you mean like the Three Fat Men, Fox Sunshine Comedies, The Hallroom Boys, films like that?" I paused for a moment. I told him I would call him back. After thinking about it, I did invite him. That man was Steve Massa, the author of the essays in this volume. He says that I am responsible for his lifelong dedication to the rediscovery of this genre. I will gladly take the blame. Steve got together with musician Ben Model, who frequently accompanies silent films at the Museum of Modern Art, to organize showings of slapstick films in a variety of locations. Ben told me that he grew up in the same town as Walter Kerr, author of *The Silent Clowns*, who invited Ben to join his home screenings of slapstick films.

The two of them have been identifying unknown comedy titles in the Museum of Modern Art collection and out of that ongoing work, they, joined by Ron Magliozzi of the MoMA staff, have organized a series called *Cruel and Unusual Comedies*. The concept of this series is to show the astounding things they found in this long-neglected genre. The idea, the same as the one we had for that long-ago Slapstick Symposium, is not so much to celebrate the well-known comics, but to examine the genre as a whole in its heyday and its place in American film history and in American life in the teens and twenties.

According to my theory that these silent short slapstick films subverted the conventions of the feature films with which they were shown, these films were a reverse mirror of the conventions of society. Where many feature films in this period taught a moral lesson, the short slapstick films mocked authority figures and family values, they were amoral and politically incorrect, and they tell us a lot about American life at the time. Filled with dynamic energy of the age of invention and the machine, they still amuse and shock us today.

Steve Massa's obsessions with the slapstick films have continued to motivate his research, the screenings he has organized to share his discoveries with the public, and his writings about them. His research is careful and his facts may be trusted. He has what seems to me to be total recall, recognizing the least significant actors on the screen, giving the correct names even to the cats, dogs, and monkeys that populate these films. I don't know, maybe he has found names even for those mangy lions that roamed Los Angeles streets in the films of the twenties. In this collection of essays, he tells us many more things he has found out about the fantastic figures that populated the lost world of silent slapstick films.

Eileen Bowser is a noted film historian and archivist. She was the curator of the Department of Film at the Museum of Modern Art, now retired, and served on the executive committee of the International Federation of Film Archives (FIAF). During her tenure at MoMA, she repatriated and preserved scores of silent comedies and in 1985 organized the FIAF Slapstick Symposium, where scholars and archivists from around the world convened to identify films and document the genre. She is the author of The Transformation of Cinema: 1907—1915, The Slapstick Symposium, A Handbook for Film Archives, *and other publications on film history and film archiving.*

Introduction and Acknowledgments

My love for silent comedy began at an early age and I'm sure that my experiences are very similar to anyone who's reading this volume. I remember seeing my very first silent short when I was four and it was at an end-of-the-year festival at the elementary school where my aunt worked. Besides booths with prizes, cartoons were shown in the auditorium and after Woody Woodpecker, a one-reeler came on about a little Neely Edwards-type of guy with a moustache trying to park his car and the cop who was lying in wait to give him a ticket. No matter what elaborate machinations the little guy went through, the cop was always there with ticket ready. Although I can still hear our laughter echoing in the auditorium, I've never seen that short again, nor been able to identify what it was.

Growing up, my mantra was "movies, monsters, and comic books." I soon discovered silent comedies on television and became completely hooked. These were programs such as *Funny Manns* and *Comedy Capers*, where silent comedies were edited down and repackaged for kids. This was my initial exposure to Harry Langdon, Billy Bevan, the Smith Family, A Ton of Fun, and many others, and although there was no information given on the performers or the films, I began to recognize faces and routines. At the same time, I was getting a steady diet of *Laurel and Hardy*, *The Three Stooges*, and *The Little Rascals* sound shorts, where I spotted many of the same silent performers.

When I got old enough to have some disposable income, the first film-related material I bought was *Famous Monsters of Filmland* magazine and from there I worked my way up to an actual book: Daniel Blum's *A Pictorial History of the Silent Screen*. Basically an oversized picture book crammed with a gazillion photographs, I was finally putting names with faces and quickly moved on to William K. Everson's *The Films of Laurel and Hardy*, John McCabe's *Mr. Laurel & Mr. Hardy*, and Rudy Blesh's *Keaton*.

There was also a lot of information to be gotten from the Blackhawk Films catalogues, not to mention their films. Repeats of Paul Killiam series, such as *Silents Please*, and Robert Youngson's compilation features became my steady diet as a teenager. A real breakthrough came when I was in college and the campus library had a copy of Kalton C. Lahue and Sam Gill's *Clown Princes and Court Jesters*. I was galvanized by all the information and continually renewed it for the entirety of my junior and senior years. When graduation came, I xeroxed the entire thing to take with me into the great beyond.

All of the above took place in Ohio, where there was not much in the way of art museums, revival cinemas, or film societies. Reading *The New Yorker* magazine would give me heart failure when I saw everything that was being shown in New York at the Elgin Theatre or the Museum of

The author under the influence of silent comedy at an early age (I'm the one on the right).

Modern Art. Since my interest in films had inspired me to become an actor, after college, I moved to New York, where all my time not spent pursuing my career or scrambling to make a living was given over to watching movies. New York in the late 1970s and into the 1980s was teeming with revival houses, such as the Bleecker Street Cinema, The Thalia, Theatre 80 St Marks, The Metro, and many more that routinely offered double-bills that changed daily. Although I immersed myself in all kinds of films, my love for silent comedies remained constant and I sought out as many of the films and as much information on the era as I could find.

1985 was a turning point. By then, I had become a working actor, having appeared on Broadway with Eva Le Gallienne and regularly employed in television commercials. Between gigs, I also worked as an assistant manager at The Regency, one of the biggest revival cinemas in the city. If you've read Eileen Bowser's foreword, you've heard the story of how I got myself invited to her FIAF Slapstick Symposium, a two-day and -evening smorgasbord of silent comedy at the Museum of Modern Art. Eileen assembled an eye-opening selection of films that covered the entire spectrum of the genre and inspired me to move beyond keeping this as a private obsession. I decided to go public—to get involved in creating programs and writing about the films. Although I wasn't entirely sure on how to go about this, I was lucky that I was working at the Regency, as I got started by contributing titles for their screenings and was eventually able to co-curate some of the shows.

After sending out proposals to cinemas and archives, Richard Kozarski, then head curator of the Museum of the Moving Image, gave me the opportunity to do my first solo program—*Laughing out Loud*, which focused on comedy shorts from 1925 to 1935. From there, I moved on to programs for other venues and eventually had the great fortune to hook up with Ben Model and Bruce Lawton at the very beginning of the Silent Clown Film Series, where we're still presenting silent comedies with live accompaniment fifteen years later. Ben and I also teamed up with Ron Magliozzi at the Museum of Modern Art for a Roscoe Arbuckle retrospective in 2006 and have followed that up with an annual series titled *Cruel and Unusual Comedy*, which showcases some of the more outrageous and politically incorrect examples of the genre. Along the way, while trying to throw some light in the darker corners of silent comedy, I've also had the good luck to have been able to work on programs for other institutions and festivals, be involved in a number of DVD collections, help identify many unidentified comedies, and spend time at various archives.

Many of the pieces in this collection began as program notes, DVD booklet essays, or film journal items. Each covers a specific topic, but some of my favorite books on silent comedy, such as Sam Gill and Kalton Lahue's aforementioned *Clown Princes and Court Jesters*, Rob Stone's *Laurel or Hardy*, and Brent Walker's recent *Mack Sennett's Fun Factory*, all focus on specific topics and themes, but still give a comprehensive look at the genre. It's my hope that all these pieces together will give a similar overview of the world of silent comedy.

There are so many people to thank—so many good friends and colleagues who love silent comedy and have shared information and films over the years—that it's hard to know where to begin.

First, I want to thank my regular partner in crime, film historian and accompanist Ben Model, for really encouraging me to sit down and put this volume together. We've had great times over the last fifteen years putting shows together for the Silent Clown Film Series, the Museum of Modern Art, Library of Congress, and others, and I hope we have the opportunity to continue for many more.

In addition to generously loaning photos from his collection, my good friend Robert Arkus volunteered to supervise the transferral and organization of this book's images. His superb eye, good ideas, and diligent work gave me much-needed support and a strong base for assembling all the various elements.

Sam Gill, besides the inspiration and friendship he's provided over the years, got the ball rolling on the photographs with the beautiful cover shot of Hank Mann doing his best Lillian Gish and continued with copious offerings from his mind-blowing collection. This was soon joined by incredible selections from the collections of my generous friends Robert Arkus, Robert S. Birchard, Louie Despres, Cole Johnson, Mark Johnson, Jim Kerkhoff, Bruce Lawton, Steve Rydzewski, James Snaden and family, and Elif Rongen-Kaynakci at the Eye Film Institute, Netherlands.

I'd like to give special thanks to Eileen Bowser for her kind foreword in addition to her inspiration and friendship over the years. The work of Serge Bromberg, Robert Farr, Ron Magliozzi, David Robinson, Elif Rongen-Kaynakci, Rob Stone, and Brent Walker, not to mention their friendship and support, have also been major inspirations. Debts of gratitude go to Stefan Droessler, Paul E. Gierucki, David Kalat, Hooman Mehran, Richard M. Roberts, Steve Rydzewski, Frank Schiede, and Dave Stevenson for giving me the opportunity to express my thoughts in print and for allowing me to rework some of those ideas here.

In addition to everyone mentioned above, there are the friends, fellow researchers, and comedy lovers Michael Abadi, Marlene Weisman Abadi, Joe Adamson, Mana Allen, Norbert Aping, Alice Artzt, Matt Barry, Bo Berglund, Lisa Bradberry, Geoff Brown, Michael Campino, Bill Cassara, Robert Costello, Rick DeCroix, David Eickemeyer, Frank Flood, Richard Finnegan, Bob Greenberg, Chuck Harter, Geraldine Hawkins, Michael J. Hayde, Mark Heller, Tommie Hicks, Ron Hickson, Lisa Stein Haven, Chad Hunter, Dan Kamin, Dave Kehr, Rob King, Richard Kozarski, Annette D'Agostino Lloyd, Pandora Lupino, Bruno Mestdagh, Glenn Mitchell, Molly Model, Joe Moore, Tom Reeder, Jack Roth, Frank Rowley, Uli Ruedel, Jeni Rymer, David Schwartz, Linda Shah, Rick Sheckman, David Shepard, Andrew Sholl, Randy Skretvedt, Marilyn Slater, Melinda Solan, Yair Solan, Bill Sprague, Tom Stathes, Cathy Surowiec, Karl Tiedemann, Patty Tobias, Ed Watz, Bill Weber, Stephen Winer, Joseph Yranski, Steve Zalusky, and Henry Zorn. I'd also like to give a respectful nod to mentors and friends, such as William K. Everson, Jay Leyda, James Kostilibus Davis, Richard Lupino, and Russ Riley, who have passed on.

A good deal of the material on silent comedy—information and surviving films—are held by the libraries, archives, and research facilities that have done yeoman work to preserve them. I've had the good fortune to have been welcomed by various archives and I'm grateful to their respective staff members, who have always provided tireless help and over the years have become friends and colleagues. First, I'd like to mention the Billy Rose Theatre Collection at the New York Public Library for the Performing Arts, since six years ago I joined the staff after retiring from performing and having practically lived there doing research. I'd like to thank all my fellow NYPL librarians, but especially Tom Lisanti, Jeremy MeGraw, David Callahan, Charlie Morrow, and Imogen Smith. I also want to give big thanks to:

- The Museum of Modern Art: Ron Magliozzi, Charles Silver, Larry Kardish, Anne Morra, Rajendra Roy, Josh Siegel, Katie Trainor, Peter Williamson, Mary Corliss, and Terry Geesken.
- The Library of Congress: Rob Stone, Mike Mashon, Madeline Matz, Rosemary Hanes, Rachel Parker, Jenny Paxson, Zoran Sinobad, Larry Smith, Kim Tomadjolou, and George Willeman.
- Eye Film Institute, Netherlands: Elif Rongen-Kaynakci, Catherine Cormon, Rixt Jonkman, Marlene Labijt, Mark Paul Meyer, Dorrette Schootemeijer, and Frederique Urlings.

- George Eastman House: Anthony L'Abbate, Jared Case, and Nancy Kaufman.

Thank you to Ben Ohmart, Sandra Grabman, John Teehan, editors Wes Britton, Michael Hayde, and everyone else at Bear Manor Media for the opportunity to make this volume a reality.

My most important and heartfelt thanks go to my wonderful wife, son, and mother. Their love, support, patience, good counsel, and even nagging have enriched my life and kept me this side of sanity (although I won't say which side).

Finally, to the reader, I'm primarily interested in documenting the era—who did what and when and where—so I leave the theoretical analysis and studies to others. A friend once said, "You're more interested in the peel than the fruit." Not sure I agree with that, but there are a lot of facts and information in these "peelings," which I hope are presented in an entertaining way that reflects the films themselves.

Silent Partners: Comedy Teams of the Teens and Twenties Part One: The Teens

On the subject of silent movie comedy teams, Laurel and Hardy immediately come to mind and, while they're certainly the most famous, they're only the tip of the iceberg, the culmination of a long tradition. American silent comedy was full of teams of all shapes and sizes, most of whom are forgotten today but deserve a fresh reexamination.

The first film comedies were basically little one-joke vignettes: a country rube reacting to his first motion picture; a cook lighting a stove with kerosene and being blown out of the film frame. But soon filmmakers tapped into material and traditions from other popular arts, such as vaudeville and comic strips, and eventually began utilizing stories that depended on the characters and performances of the actors to create the comedy. By 1910, things really started to develop.

COMEDY'S CAINS AND ABELS

At the end of that year, what appears to be the U.S. screen's first physically mismatched comedy duo—Hank and Lank—debuted at Essanay. Inspired by Bud Fisher's popular newspapercomic *Mutt and Jeff*, producer Gilbert M. "Broncho Billy" Anderson discovered string bean Victor Potel dressing windows at Marshall Field's department store in Chicago and grafted him to stunted Essanay stock company member and former vaudevillian Augustus Carney. Together, they were hungry hoboes in only nine shorts made from late 1910 into January 1911, where they were always involved in schemes that had Lank ending up getting the worst of things. Mutt and Jeff themselves soon turned up in a series of live-action comedies from David Horsley's Nestor Films. Shot on the east coast by Al Christie, the films were very primitive, made up of mostly long-shot

Nestor Films' exhibitor ads for their live-action *Mutt and Jeff* series featured generous helpings of Bud Fisher artwork.

tableaux. The characterizations were pretty indistinct, too, with various people (including Bud Duncan) stepping in to play the leads from short to short. While both of these early series were short-lived and crude, they were popular and they opened the floodgates for other teams to follow.

BIG, DYSFUNCTIONAL FAMILIES

At the same time, Mack Sennett had begun directing comedies for the Biograph Company. Starting with the studio in 1908 as a bit player and occasionally selling a scenario, Sennett worked in the films directed by D.W. Griffith and Frank Powell. In mid-1911, when Powell left Biograph for Paris and the Pathé Studio, Mack moved up to direction and put together a group of performers made up of himself, Mabel Normand, Fred

Mace, Del Henderson, Eddie Dillon, and occasionally Ford Sterling.

They would be mixed and matched as the stories dictated, but in shorts like *A Spanish Dilemma*, *Tragedy of a Dress Suit*, and *The Furs* (all 1912), they became an identifiable comedy ensemble. The teamwork became more pronounced when Keystone was formed and released its first films in September of 1912. There the group boiled down to Normand, Mace, Sterling, and Sennett, who became known as "the largest aggregation of famous comedians in the world."

This tight unit continued until mid-1913 when Fred Mace left to go out on his own and Sennett began limiting his appearances to concentrate on the administrating duties of his booming fun factory. In the ensuing years, Mack would continue to build his stable of comedy performers and bring together a number of comedy duos, but nothing matched the intensive teamwork of his early films.

In the meantime, another comedy ensemble came together quickly at Essanay's West Coast company. After the quick demise of Hank and Lank, Victor Potel and Augustus Carney had remained in the studio's stock company and became regulars in a series of western comedies set

The Keystone quartet of Mack Sennett (far right), Fred Mace (as King), Mabel Normand (as Page), and Ford Sterling (Court Jester) are joined by Nick Cogley (front left), Dot Farley (seen between Mabel and Mace's shoulders), and Laura Oakley as the Queen in *Those Good Old Days* (1913). Photo courtesy of Cole Johnson.

in the mythical town of Snakeville, joined by real-life husband and wife Harry Todd and Margaret Joslin. The series really got off the ground with the smash hit *Alkali Ike's Auto* (May 20, 1911). This made Carney one of the first American comedy stars and he headlined in the films until his defection to Universal in November of 1913. His exit put the series' focus on the trio of Sophie Clutts (Joslin), Mustang Pete (Todd), and Slippery Slim (Potel) and strengthened the ensemble nature of the shorts. During the next two years, performers such as Ben Turpin, Lloyd Bacon, Robert McKenzie, and David Kirkland were added to the mix.

Most of the Snakevilles were helmed by Roy Clements and were so popular that they were alternating weekly with Anderson's dramatic productions, although occasionally Broncho Billy himself joined in the fun. In the charming *Broncho Billy Steps In* (August 3, 1915), Billy is engaged to Snakeville schoolteacher Marguerite Clayton. Her students (Potel, Todd, Turpin, etc., as a sort of western adult special ed. class) secretly take up a donation and surprise her by producing her aged mother at the wedding.

In the six years the series ran, nearly one hundred comedies were produced, but only a mere handful exist today. At the end of 1915, Clements and Potel left to go to Universal and Wallace Beery was brought

Augustus Carney (left) and Harry Todd (right) eye each other over the affections of Margaret Joslin in *Alkali Ike's Auto* (1911). Photo courtesy of Sam Gill.

in from Essanay's Chicago studio to direct what would be the last leg of the series. Ben Turpin was given the lead in this group and was paired with Lloyd Bacon as Bloggie and Hotch. Although production finished in 1916, the shorts lived on, reissued with "new titles, new tints and careful editing," according to *Moving Picture World*, on the states' rights market until the end of the decade.

Comedy ensembles began popping up at other studios. Nestor Films had moved to California in 1911 and put together a comedy unit under the supervision of Al Christie. The regular stock company soon consisted of Eddie Lyons, Lee Moran, Victoria Forde, Billie Rhodes, Jack Dillon, Stella Adams, Betty Compson, Neal Burns, Harry Rattenbury, Ray Gallagher, and little Gus Alexander. These easygoing one-reelers were distributed by Universal, with the behind-the-scenes talent including direction by Christie and Horace Davy and scripts by Robert F. McGowan. In 1916, Christie left Nestor to set up his own independent concern and by the late Teens, Nestor's stars had splintered off into their own series for different companies.

Joker Comedies, started by Universal in 1913 to compete with Keystone, were one-reel knockabouts and burlesques that were cranked out at an incredible rate. Max Asher was the big cheese, with the rest of the group made up of Harry McCoy, Billy Franey, Louise Fazenda, and Bobby Vernon under the direction of Allen Curtis. Gale Henry joined the squad in 1914 and when McCoy, Fazenda, and Vernon defected to Sennett, they were replaced by Milburn Moranti, Lillian Peacock, and Charles "Heinie" Conklin.

Another unit was formed in 1915 with Ernie Shields, Eddie Boland, and Bertha Burnham. Their director was Archer McMackin. A third group, which also released on Universal's Imp and Victor labels, came together under Roy Clements with Victor Potel, Jane Bernoudy, and Eileen Sedgwick before Joker closed its doors, probably from sheer exhaustion, at the end of 1917.

Over at Harry Aitken's Reliance/Majestic organization, a comedy company was put together under the supervision of D.W. Griffith. Their brand name was Komic Comedies and the performers were Fay Tincher, Tod Browning, Max Davidson, Tammany Young, Joseph "Baldy" Belmont, and Eddie Dillon, who also directed. Maintaining a schedule of one release a week, they alternated a one-shot Komic with a Bill the Office Boy comedy, their series that made Fay Tincher a household favorite. Later, during Komic's 1914 and 1915 run, Chester Withey, Bobby Feuhrer

The group dynamics of Gale Henry (front left), Billy Franey (middle), Lillian Peacock (back right), and Milburn Moranti (front right) in the 1916 Joker Comedy *His Highness the Janitor*. Photo courtesy of Robert Arkus.

(a.k.a. Bobby Ray), and Elmer Booth joined the regular crew. And finally, as success breeds imitation, the Selig Company came up with their own version of the Snakeville comedies titled *The Chronicles of Bloom Center*. Selig was an old pirate from the earliest days of filmmaking and this short-lived series about the denizens of a rural small town starred Ralph McComas, Lee Morris, William Hutchinson, Lillian Brown Leighton, John Lancaster, and a young Sid Smith.

NICE AND POLITE

For the beginnings of the more genteel comedy teams, we have to return to 1910 when, according to legend, a rotund stage actor presented himself at the Vitagraph studio in Brooklyn looking for work. In a career that had encompassed twenty-two years, John Bunny had appeared in minstrel shows, circuses, and vaudeville and had worked with legends like William Brady, Lew Fields, and Raymond Hitchcock. Despite this long track record, he had decided that movies were the coming thing and that "he would rather be behind the guns than in front of them." Bunny, who looked like Shakespeare's Falstaff and Sir Toby Belch come to life, made an immediate impression on moviegoers and became a favorite. In February of 1911, he first worked with Flora Finch. The combination of the expansive Bunny with the severe Finch created an instant combative chemistry (which may have been helped by the fact that they're said to have had an active mutual dislike for each other). Finch was born in England in 1867 and began her career on stage. After coming to the U.S., she started working in films while trying to establish herself on the American stage. Starting at Biograph in 1908, she caught the attention of D.W. Griffith and made an impression in the "Jones Family" shorts and other comedies like *All on Account of the Milk* (1910). In 1910, she moved over to Vitagraph.

Although Bunny appeared in only a bit more than half of his total output of films with Ms. Finch, the "Bunnyfinches" were his most popular. The pair often played husband and wife, as in the famous *A Cure for*

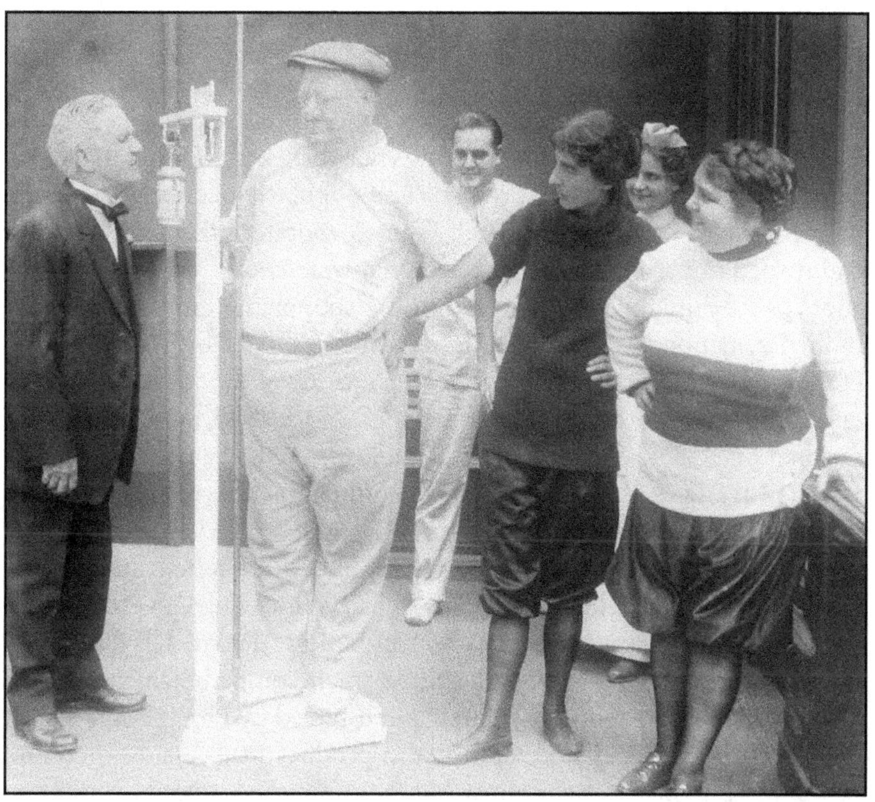

Charles Eldridge gives John Bunny the bad news in *Bunny Backslides* (1914) as Flora Finch and Josie Sadler look on. Photo courtesy of Billy Rose Theatre Division, The New York Public Library for the Performing Arts, Astor, Lenox and Tilden Foundations.

Pokeritis (1912) and *Polishing Up* (1914), but not always. In *Her Crowning Glory* (1911), Bunny plays a widower with a young daughter that he indulges, so she's growing up wild and spoiled. His sister (Kate Price) hires a governess to put some discipline into the household. The governess (Finch) turns out to be a scrawny, hatchet-faced tyrant, but Bunny is infatuated with her long, beautiful hair and she wraps him around her little finger. Bunny proposes to her and things look dire, but the baby's nurse gets an idea when the governess is taking a nap and gives the kid a pair of scissors. With the governess' attractive hair chopped off, Bunny's ardor cools and she's sent packing.

Although physically filling the stereotype of the jolly fat man, it's rumored that Bunny was bad-tempered and egotistical and, due to his extreme weight, narcoleptic, even able to snooze away in a complete standing position. In 1914, despite declining health, the comedian began doing double duty in films and on stage. Overwork, combined with kidney disease, caused his death on May 1, 1915. Tributes eulogized Bunny around the world, predicting that he and his films would be cherished by future generations, but within only a few years the memory of him dimmed and most of the films disappeared.

The peak of Flora Finch's career was her years with Bunny; afterward, she was never able to recapture the same popularity. Leaving Vitagraph in 1916, she set up the Flora Finch Film Corporation the following year and turned out a series of two-reelers that were coolly received by audiences and exhibitors. She returned to the supporting ranks, turning up in the live-action *Carrie of the Chorus* comedies made by Max and Dave Fleischer and in high profile features such as *Quality Street* and *The Cat and the Canary* (both 1927). By the time sound arrived, outside of an occasional bit like her funny cameo at the opening of Laurel and Hardy's *Way Out West* (1937), she was mostly confined to anonymous extra work until her death in 1940.

In early polite comedy, there are a number of forgotten combos. Before becoming "Queen of the Serials," Pearl White starred with Chester Barnett in a huge number of split-reel and one-reel comedies from 1912 to 1914. These were made by Crystal, a small company which released through Universal, and were written and directed by Phillips Smalley. At the same time, Smalley and Crystal also produced the "Baldy" Belmont series. Joseph "Baldy" Belmont was a longtime stage veteran who often wore a toupee and would lose his flip top for comic effect. After supporting White and Barnett in a number of their comedies, Belmont was given his own series, which teamed him with Vivian Prescott and ran in 1913 and 1914. From here, "Baldy" took himself and his toupee over to Komic Comedies, leaving Ms. Prescott to be teamed with stage refugee and former comedian for Imp Charlie De Forrest until the end of 1914.

The longest-lasting of these duos was Harry Myers and Rosemary Theby. Myers, chiefly remembered today as the drunken millionaire in Chaplin's *City Lights* (1931), made his stage debut in 1900 and spent ten years playing in stock companies and touring road shows. He entered

This 1916 Vim exhibitor ad gives a good illustration of Harry Myers and Rosemary Theby's type of domestic comedies.

films with the Lubin Company in 1910 as a leading man, but soon turned to comedy and directing his own films. Rosemary Theby, although trained for the stage, never appeared there professionally. Instead, a friend took her to Vitagraph, where she worked from 1910 to 1913, and from there was a leading lady for the Reliance Film Co. In 1914, she and Myers became a team at Lubin in a series of one- and two-reel comedies. The couple moved over to Universal's Victor brand to continue their shorts, then jumped around quite a bit, going to Vim in 1916, then back to Universal, and to Pathé in 1917.

Myers directed their films, which are virtually impossible to see, but this quote from a 1917 exhibitor ad seems to sum up their series nicely: "Refined comedy of a high order—The Myers-Theby Comedies. The humorous adventures of a newlywed couple are shown in each release. All who intend to be, are, have been or don't want to be married, will enjoy them."

Eventually, the pair married and in the late teens dissolved their formal screen partnership, although they appeared together in *A Connecticut Yankee in King Arthur's Court* (1921), each moving into starring roles in features. But ten years later, their careers had waned and, after his brief regeneration in *City Lights*, Myers descended to walk-ons in sound films until his death on December 25th, 1938. Theby was working as an extra and after Myers's death remarried and left Hollywood. She died on June 10th, 1973.

Back at Vitagraph, filling the gap left by the death of John Bunny, were the films of Mr. and Mrs. Sidney Drew. Sidney Drew was a member of the famous Drew and Barrymore theatrical clan and an uncle to Ethel, Lionel, and John Barrymore. After many years on stage as a light comedian, Drew originally entered films at Kalem in 1911; then he and his first wife, Gladys Rankin, joined the Vitagraph family in 1913. Mrs. Drew died soon after and Sydney married Lucille McVey, a young actress and writer in the company who worked under the name Jane Morrow. Together, they found fame with the 1914 launching of their series chronicling the misadventures of an average married couple that became known as Henry and Polly. Mrs. Drew contributed most of the scripts, together they directed, while Mr. Drew's performances put them over on the screen.

A number of their light and witty shorts survive and one of the best is *Boobley's Baby* (April 26, 1915). It concerns Sydney having to stand on the crowded trolley every day to and from work. He notices that anyone carrying a baby always gets a seat and, inspired, he buys a doll, wraps it in a blanket, and carries it on the next trolley ride. Everyone, from men to old ladies, makes room for him and the "baby" to sit, so he uses it every day, keeping it in a small bag while he's at work. In the meantime, he's started a romance with a young woman in his office (Mrs. Drew). Just as things are getting serious between them, she happens to ride home on the same trolley and sees Sidney with "the baby." Thinking he's a married man, she confronts him, saying that she never wants to see him again. Angry at the situation he's gotten himself into, Sidney gets off the trolley and vents his frustrations on the doll. The woman has gotten off also and in a wonderful long shot, filmed from her point of view, we see Sydney throttle and tear the arms and legs off the doll (which really looks like he's murdering

Mr. and Mrs. Sidney Drew in a publicity photo for their series of shorts for Metro Pictures.

a baby). Aghast, she gets the police, but of course the misunderstanding is cleared up to provide the happy ending.

The immensely popular Drews left Vitagraph in 1916, continuing their film series for Metro and Paramount, and appeared together on stage. Sadly, Sidney Drew's health rapidly declined after the death of his son in World War I and he died at the peak of his fame on April 9, 1919. Mrs. Drew soldiered on, finishing their Paramount contract and then writing, directing, and starring in some shorts for Pathe, not to mention directing the feature *Cousin Kate* (1921) before her own premature death on November 3, 1925.

A COUPLE OF "DUTCH" UNCLES

Returning to the slapstick couplings, a stage tradition that took root in silent comedy was that of "Dutch" comedians. Vaudeville made fun of every ethnic group in America and "Dutch" acts were parodies of German/Jewish immigrants, full of rough knockabout and dialogue which fractured the English language. Joe Weber and Lew Fields were the most famous stage practitioners and despite the lack of sound, it became popular on the screen. Ford Sterling is best remembered with his characters of Chief Teheezal, Cohen, and Snookie. After Sterling came Max Asher, a former vaudeville magician and "Dutch" comic who led the ensemble at Joker Comedies. In 1913-1914, Asher was teamed with Harry McCoy for a series of "Mike and Jake" one-reelers. Titles like *Mike and Jake Among the Cannibals* (1913) and *Mike and Jake Close to Nature* (1914) suggest that the operating motif was sending the pair where they would be the most fish out of water. Joker made about fifteen of their adventures before McCoy moved over to Keystone and although Bobby Vernon replaced him, the series ended.

Weber and Fields themselves were soon lured to the screen. After a 1913 debut for Kinemacolor, the May 8, 1915, Motion Picture News announced:

> "**WEBER AND FIELDS STAR IN WORLD RELEASES.**
> Famous Comedians Will Make Exclusive Appearance in Fifty-Two Releases—Have Begun in *Two of the Finest*."

Having made their stage debut together in 1877, they first tried other ethnic acts such as blackface and Irish before clicking as a "Dutch" act in the 1880s. They were wildly popular and opened their own theatre in 1896, producing hit shows like *Higgledy-Piggledy.* In 1904, they split up, but came back together in 1912. The Weber and Fields comedies for World were shot on the East Coast, as the company was based in Fort Lee, New Jersey. Survivors suggest that it was sort of a comedy serial where each one-reel installment followed the further misadventures of Mike and Meyer. One week they would be fighting in their grocery store, another week trying to keep their children from eloping, the next they were in jail for the damage they caused while trying to keep their children from eloping, and on and on. It's hard to say how many World shorts they actually made, but certainly not the fifty-two announced as later that year the pair traveled out West to work for Mack Sennett. Harry Aitken, who had recently combined Sennett, D. W. Griffith, and Thomas Ince to form the

Weber and Fields visit with Mabel Normand during their stint at the Mack Sennett Studio.

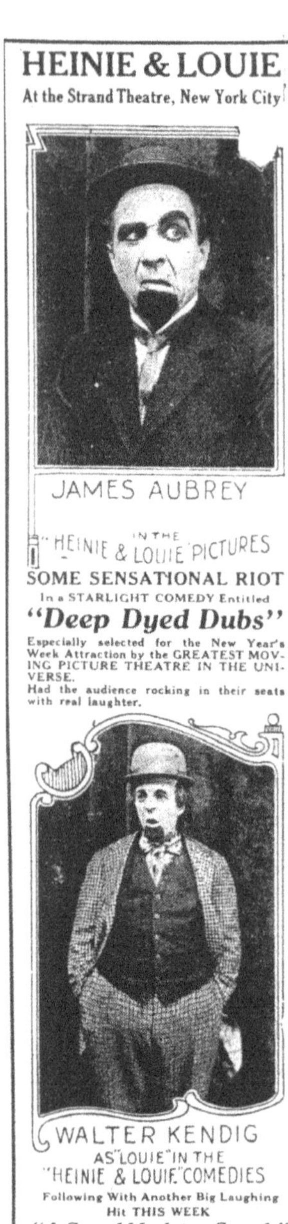

James Aubrey and Walter Kendig in an advertisement for *Deep Dyed Dubs* (1915), one of their rare surviving comedies.

Triangle Film Corporation, decided that stage stars were needed to give Triangle films class. Despite a rumored salary of $3,500 a week, Joe and Lew made only two starring shorts, *The Best of Enemies* (1915) and *The Worst of Friends* (1916). It was said the pair feared for their lives in the chaos on the Sennett lot. It seems they didn't care for filmmaking anyway and they went back to the stage, rarely appearing on film again.

Weber and Field's film sojourn was brief, but in their wake, imitators were slapped together to cash in on their popularity. A case in point were "Heinie and Louie" over at Starlight Comedies, with Jimmy Aubrey as "Heinie" and Walter Kendig as "Louie." Aubrey was a British clown and graduate of the Fred Karno Company while Kendig came from Philadelphia, where he spent time in the Lubin stock company before working in New York with William Farnum and being discovered by the Starlight people. Their one-reelers were produced by the Mittenthal Film Co. and were shot at their studio in Yonkers, New York. Described as "a Weberfieldian pair who do all manner of comical things at a seeming disregard of life and limb," Heinie and Louie did well enough to last from 1915 into the very beginning of 1917. In an odd twist, Walter Kendig appears to have been killed in an auto accident in late 1915 and was replaced by actor Elmer E. Redmond, but there was no mention of this by the makers of the films, whose response was to focus on Aubrey in publicity. From this series, Aubrey went on to support Hughie Mack at Vitagraph and there became a comedy star, continuing his screen antics for Chadwick, Joe Rock, and Weiss Brothers in the 1920s.

Another set of Weber and Fields clones, "Oscar and Conrad," were created by the Thanhouser Film Corp. for their Falstaff Comedies. Claude Cooper and Frank E. McNish played the pair in this short-lived 1916 series and if the surviving *The Guiders* (August 15, 1916) is representative, the shorts suffered from weak performances and gags, plus tons of aimless knockabout.

Finally, our last "Dutch" act is the stage team of Clarence Kolb and Max Dill. They began their career as boyhood chums in Cleveland and after working in burlesque and vaudeville, they appeared in the 1901 Broadway success *Fiddle Dee Dee*. In 1904, they appeared in a San Francisco production of the show and stayed there, becoming the West Coast version of Weber and Fields. They were very successful and helmed forty-six stage productions. A young Lon Chaney and Bobby Vernon appeared in some of their shows. In 1916, the American Film Co. launched them in a series of five-reel features like *A Peck o' Pickles* (1916), some adapted from their stage productions. They also formed the Kolb and Dill Film Co. and for the states' rights market produced the nine-reel *Glory* (1917), which starred them with former Sennett girl Juanita Hansen. After this brief film foray, they returned to the stage, but in the sound era Clarence Kolb returned and became a character actor in tons of films like *His Girl Friday* (1940) and *Adam's Rib* (1949), even playing himself in the Lon Chaney biography *Man of a Thousand Faces* (1957).

ODD MEN OUT

In 1914, there was a veritable explosion of comedy teams. That year, the Kalem Company started Lloyd Hamilton and Bud Duncan as "Ham and Bud" in their series of Ham Comedies. Hamilton came from Lubin and Frontier, Bud Duncan from Nestor, Biograph, and Apollo. They were first used as support for Ruth Roland and Marshall Neilan, but were stealing so much attention and footage that Kalem gave them their own shorts.

In more than one hundred one-reelers from late 1914 into 1917, the pair played tramps whose only distinguishing characteristic was that one was a big scuzzy bum and the other a little scuzzy bum. Rough and primitive, they were the "Burke and Hare" of silent comedy, but occasionally a keen sense of wild surrealism bubbled to the surface, which makes Ham and Bud classics like *Ham and the Sausage Factory* (1915) and *A Sauerkraut Symphony* (1916) great fun today. When the series came to an end in 1917, Hamilton moved over to Fox Sunshine Comedies and then wad-

Lloyd Hamilton and Bud Duncan in a temporarily chummy pose from 1915.

dled on to great success at Educational in the 1920s. Things didn't go as well for Bud Duncan, who spent most of the rest of his career making cheapies for independent concerns like National Film Corp., Reelcraft, and Weiss Brothers.

The Edison Film Co.'s 1914—1915 entry in the team sweepstakes was Waddy and Artie. "Waddy" was William Wadsworth, a longtime character actor in their stock company and star of their Mr. Wood B. Wedd series, and "Arty" was Arthur Housman, a fairly new recruit from the stage who went on to a long film career in which he became one of the screen's most memorable drunks. As hardly any of their adventures seem to be available or in circulation today, all we're left with is Edison publicity hyperbole:

> The 'Waddy and Arty' brand of humor is something new—something different—something that cannot be imitated, borrowed or stolen, for it belongs distinctively to the quaint 'Waddy' (Wadsworth), who is uproariously funny in his quiet humor, and 'Arty' (Housman), who can put more fun into his screen face then any comedian on the screen or stage. 'Waddy and Arty' fun is blending of the snap of the slapstick—without the insane chase—the richness of real comedy and the spice of two minds that are clever in stage lore and funniness. 'Waddy and Arty's' side-splitting surprises get a laugh in any language. They do not need sub-titles

> to explain their humor—in fact, subtitles get in their way in the speed they 'get them over' in roars of haw-haws.

The name of our next team, Pokes and Jabbs, sums up the essence of their comedy. Bobby Burns came from vaudeville and musical comedy, where he played in *The Wizard of Oz* and *Babes in Toyland*. Walter Stull also graduated from the stage, where he had been a leading man in stock and melodramatic road shows. Burns portrayed "Pokes" and Stull "Jabbs," but it's hard to tell them apart anyway in circulating titles like *Pluck and Luck* (1916) and *Play Ball* (1917).

Like Ham and Bud, their best surviving comedies are completely surreal outings, such as *Deviled Crabs* (1917). The two came together at Lubin and thrived like weeds, migrating to Reliance, Sterling, Wizard, Vim, and Jaxon in a period of about four years until Bobby Burns broke up the act in 1918. Stull wrote and directed a brief series of Finn & Hattie Comedies where he was paired with Billy Ruge and soon dropped below the radar, but Burns moved over to Cuckoo Comedies, then Sun-Lite Comedies for Reelcraft to finish the decade. He remained active for many years, first as a writer and character player in Jack White Comedies during the 1920s, then as support in Hal Roach and Columbia shorts of the sound era.

An offshoot of Pokes and Jabbs' stay at Vim during 1915-16 were the Plump and Runt shorts, which starred Oliver Hardy and Billy Ruge. The

Pokes and Jabbs' Bobby Burns (left) and Walter Stull (right) out of make-up.
Photos courtesy of Robert S. Birchard.

characters began as support to Burns and Stull, but with *A Special Delivery* (Jan. 27, 1916), they got their own one-reelers. Ruge had been half of the vaudeville team of Frobel and Ruge and appeared in films for Lubin and Wizard. At this point, Babe Hardy had been in pictures for two years, first with Lubin, then freelancing for a while in New York with companies like Edison, Wharton, and little independents. Plump and Runt made about thirty-plus shorts together, but never caught on as the characters were sometimes rivals and other times pals and never really developed a strong screen relationship. Of course, Hardy went on to better things while Ruge moved over to the Jaxon Film Co. for some Sparkle Comedies and had a very brief stint at Vitagraph. In the early 1920s, he appeared in some Funful Comedies before disappearing from films.

All of the tiniest, independent companies were getting in the team game, too. In 1916, the Emerald Motion Picture Corporation of Chicago put together Tom Keesey and Charles Huntington as a tall and short pair named Tom and Jerry, whose shorts were written and produced by Frederick J. Ireland. Emerald later lured Alice Howell and Billy West to Chicago and was one of the concerns that merged to form Reelcraft. That same year,

Officer Billy Slade about to nab Johnny Ray in *Coughing Higgins* (1917).
Photo courtesy of James Snaden and family.

vaudeville favorites Johnny and Emma Ray formed their Reserve Photoplay Co. and made a few one-reelers in Cleveland, Jacksonville, and Cliffside, New Jersey that chronicled their characters of "Casey and his wife."

Survivors such as *A Laundry Mix-Up* and especially *Muggsy in Bad* (both 1917) show that the series was low-budget, but funny. A few years later, Johnny Ray would enter more mainstream films by playing Jiggs in Al Christie's short-lived adaptation of George McManus' *Bringing Up Father.*

ON THE SENNETT LOT

Throughout the Teens, Mack Sennett reigned as the biggest name in film comedy. During the decade, he put together various combos with the most successful being the Fatty and Mabel series. Roscoe Arbuckle and Mabel Normand were already two of Sennett's most popular stars and had worked together frequently since Arbuckle's arrival on the lot in 1913. But with *Mabel and Fatty's Wash Day* (1915), the teamwork became official and led to *Fatty and Mabel's Simple Life, That Little Band of Gold* (both 1915), and more. These films were slapstick versions of the Mr. and Mrs. Sidney Drew comedies as, despite the generous helpings of knockabout, director Arbuckle still managed to include sly digs and satirical observations on marriage and male-female relationships. The last of their films together, *He Did and He Didn't* and *The Bright Lights* (both 1916), were shot on the East Coast owing to both stars' deteriorating relationship with Sennett. Fatty soon left to make Comique comedies for Joseph Schenck and Mabel went on to Sam Goldwyn features.

Sennett also combined Chester Conklin and Mack Swain for a handful of films in 1915 to take advantage of their well-known characters of "Walrus" and "Ambrose." In shorts like *Love, Speed and Thrills* and *The Battle of Ambrose and Walrus* (both 1915), Chester was usually up to no good and it was Mack who was on the receiving end. The next year, our old pal "Baldy" Belmont found his way to the Sennett studio and besides doing supporting work in shorts like *Wife and Auto Trouble* (1916), he was teamed for a number of titles with actress Ora Carew. Carew had appeared in "sister acts, single acts and in sketches" on the vaudeville stage and in various stock companies. She made her film debut for Reliance/Majestic and then joined Keystone. Their series, which included *Dollars and Sense* (1916) and *Her Circus Knight* (1917), was directed by Walter Wright and consisted of light romances, which were more situational and less dependent on physical comedy. After this group of films, Belmont went on to comedy character work for many years while Carew's career

Mabel and Roscoe in mid-spat in a scene from *Fatty and Mabel at the San Diego Exposition* (1915).

never really took off. She moved into dramatic features, but sputtered out by the late 1920s.

Sennett's other romantic team was the miniature duo of petite Gloria Swanson and little Bobby Vernon. Both had begun their careers as teenagers—Vernon had worked in West Coast theatre and made his film debut as part of the ensemble at Joker Comedies; Swanson came from Essanay's Chicago studio with her first husband Wallace Beery (a real-life comedy team if there ever was one). They were teamed on the Sennett lot in 1916 for a handful of shorts, like *The Danger Girl* and *Haystacks and Steeples* (both 1916), and their most famous title, *Teddy at the Throttle* (1917). The plots were about young lovers embroiled in some kind of misunderstanding, often caused by vamps or problems with parents that didn't approve of their match. In 1917, Bobby moved over to Christie Comedies and stayed there with great success until sound came in. According to Gloria Swanson, when Mack Sennett told her of his plans to make her the next Mabel Normand, she refused and hooked up with Cecil B. DeMille to become one of the great divas of the silent era.

Sennett's final two teams of the decade were in the traditional slapstick mode. Slim Summerville and Bobby Dunn, who were great pals off-screen, are often included in the group of "original Keystone Cops," alongside the likes of Edgar Kennedy, Charles Avery, Hank Mann, and George Jeske. While this is hard to verify, they were both at Sennett early doing bits and stunts and worked their way up to regularly featured clowns in support of Charlie Murray, Syd Chaplin, and Louise Fazenda. Previous to their movie life, Slim had hoboed around the country and appeared in small theatre companies, while Bobby had been a champion stunt and equestrian diver. Sennett teamed them in shorts like *The Winning Punch* (1916) and *Villa of the Movies* (1917). Making a natural "Mutt and Jeff" combo, the boys played opportunistic buddies not above doing dirt to each other to get ahead. Dunn soon moved to L-Ko Comedies, but then they hooked up again at Fox Sunshine Comedies in items like *Mary's Little Lobster* and *Pretty Lady* (both 1920).

In 1920, Slim began concentrating on directing and under his real first name of George helmed comedies for Fox, Joe Rock, and Universal all through the 1920s. That same year, Bobby began a starring series of Mirthquake Comedies, which were produced by Eddie Lyons and distributed by Arrow, where he has a very Chaplinesque look in a little moustache and derby. In 1924, the series ended and this time the team paired again at Universal for a year's worth of one-reelers, mostly directed by Slim. The series, which includes the very funny survivor *The Rivals* and was made up of other titles such as *My Little Brother*, *Easy Work*, and *Green Grocers*, petered out after a year. While it's documented that Slim and Bobby were paired up at Sennett, Fox, and Universal, there may have been others, illus-

Slim Somerville
and
Bobby Dunn

Mack Sennett-Keystone California

A Keystone ad for Slim Summerville and Bobby Dunn from the September 9, 1916, issue of *New York Dramatic Mirror*.

trated by this mysterious item from the October 30, 1920, Moving Picture World:

> **SUMMERVILLE IN TWO REELERS.** Slim Summerville, who appeared in Sennett comedies for five years, then in Fox comedies for a couple of years, has now become a star in his own right, and is to make a series of twelve two-reel comedies for a new organization of which Norman Manning is general manager . Bobbie Dunn, formerly a vaudeville and circus partner of Summerville's, will be chief support to the star, and Celesta Zimlick has been selected as leading lady, Joseph Bordeaux is directing. The comedies are being produced at the National Studios.

For the rest of the 1920s, both comics continued turning up in shorts and played support in features. Overall, Slim's career fared better and sound gave it a shot in the arm. After his wonderful performance in *All Quiet on the Western Front* (1930), he starred in some talking shorts for Universal, but was generally a supporting player in "A" films and a star in "B's." Often teamed with Zasu Pitts, he worked up to his death in 1946. Bobby declined to mostly bit roles, frequently at the Hal Roach Studio, where he turns up in *Me and My Pal* (1933), *Tit for Tat* (1935), and *Lucky Corner* (1936) before his death in 1937.

Sennett's other roughhouse pair of the late Teens was Ben Turpin and Charlie Lynn. First paired up in *Saucy Madeline* (1918), for a while they were rivals for the favors of Polly Moran's Sheriff Nell. But after Polly went to Fox, the boys played buddies just trying to get by as inept actors, detectives, or just plain bums. Turpin made his film debut at Essanay in 1907 after many years knocking around on the stage. Chaplin brought him to the fore by using him in *His New Job* and *A Night Out* (both 1915). In 1916, he starred in comedies for the independent Vogue Films and ended up at Sennett in 1917.

Charlie Lynn is better known as Charles "Heinie" Conklin, who came to Sennett from Joker and dropped the last name for a while so as not to be confused with Chester Conklin. "Heinie" Conklin is a comedian that's very easy to take for granted. He's always around, but is never particularly funny. His career lasted a long time, though, with bits in shorts and features up to 1958. After 1920, the boys went their separate ways, with Ben becoming one of the biggest comedy stars of the 1920s.

Roomates "Heinie" Conklin (left) and Ben Turpin (right) in the 1919 Sennett comedy *When Love is Blind*. Photo courtesy of Steve Rydzewski.

CLOWN PRINCES

Before the arrival of Laurel and Hardy, the most popular team in silent comedy was Eddie Lyons and Lee Moran. Over about six years, they made a staggering number of films together, but since very few circulate today, they've been almost completely forgotten and overlooked. Their shorts were more situational than slapstick, with the boys frequently playing buddies in hot water with their wives. Eddie Lyons looked like the boy next door while Lee Moran was goofier—tall and gangly. Often Lyons would play the straight man with Moran supplying the character comedy, as in *House Cleaning Horrors* (Sept.1, 1918), where newlyweds Eddie and Dorothy Devore hire inept handyman Lee to repaper and paint their love nest with, of course, disastrous results.

They both came from a stage background of vaudeville and musical comedy. Lyons hit the movies first in 1911 at the Biograph Studio in New York and soon joined Imp, which led to David Horsley's Nestor Company. Al Christie was in charge of Nestor's comedies and Moran debuted there in 1912. The pair first worked together in countless supporting roles and then, in 1915, they were brought together by Christie as an official team.

The next year, Christie left Universal, taking all the Nestor players with him, including Eddie and Lee, but Universal countered by offering the boys the opportunity to direct and star in their own unit. Returning to Universal, they continued under the Nestor brand and in 1918, their releases became Star Comedies. Existing examples of their written and directed shorts still have a sharp eye for the foibles of everyday life.

Eddie Lyons (left) and Lee Moran (right) were the biggest and longest-lasting comedic duo before Laurel and Hardy.

Give Her Gas (Aug.17, 1918) is a breezy little one-reeler that chronicles the misadventures that occur when Moran and his family take Eddie and his wife for a ride in their new "flivver." The comedy is unforced and entertaining and the disasters follow a logical and realistic gag progression. Perhaps the film's funniest moment is when the family dog takes the wheel and turns out to be the best driver of the bunch.

One secret of their success was that they surrounded themselves with performers such as Dorothy Devore, Gertrude Astor, Grace Marvin, and Babe London. Behind the scenes, Clyde Bruckman had one of his first film jobs on their writing staff. In 1920, they began making popular five-reel features like *Everything but the Truth* and *La La Lucille*, but in early 1921, they dissolved their partnership. No reason has been quoted for the split, so perhaps it was just time for a change. Eddie Lyons had been producing some Nestor comedies before his teaming with Moran, so after the break, he immediately moved over to the Arrow Film Corp. and produced a popular series of shorts for himself and another for Bobby Dunn. These lasted through 1924, when Eddie took on supporting roles in dramatic features such as *Declasse* (1925) and *The Lodge in the Wilderness* (1926). His career was cut short by his sudden death, which has been variously reported as due to appendicitis, a nervous breakdown, or a brain tumor, on August 30, 1926. Lee Moran remained at Universal after the split and for a while headlined in their Century Comedies before moving on to shorts for Educational, Standard, and Fox. He also made the leap to supporting roles in mid-1920s features, but his career petered out with the coming of sound and ended in 1935. He died on April 24, 1961.

THEIR OWN PRIVATE IDAHO

While there were plenty of duos and ensembles at this time, comedy trios were very rare. Harold Lloyd, Bebe Daniels, and Snub Pollard had started in Lonesome Luke Phunphilms over at Rolin Films at the very end of 1915. The three would work together until 1919, when each went off on their own. Another Teens trio was the Comique Comedies combination of Roscoe Arbuckle, Al St John, and Buster Keaton.

Of course, Arbuckle was the star, but he generously gave substantial footage to Al and Buster and their shorts together were like huge slapstick ballets as the three pals tried to top each other in stunts and falls. When Roscoe moved into features in 1920, Al and Buster each went on to their own starring series. The third threesome of the decade had Bud Duncan, on the rebound following the demise of Ham & Bud, teaming up with

Dot Farley and Kewpie Morgan in a series of Clover Comedies. Directed by Allen Curtis and distributed by the General Film Co., this low-budget group included titles such as *The Wooing of Coffee Cake Kate* and *Rip Roaring Rivals*, but only lasted through ten entries in 1918.

A unique team working behind the scenes was the writing and directing combination of Anita Loos and John Emerson. Loos was born in California in April 1889 and was a child actor on San Francisco stages: "While I was acting in Pop's stock company, fate gave me a really proper steer into a brand-new line of endeavor. Pop used to run short movies between the acts of our plays; all movies were short in those days. I adored those old silent films, knew the particular style of each company—Selig, Vitagraph, Kalem, and, best of all, Biograph, which produced more literate stories played by a more sensitive group of actors."

Having put together a story, she sent it to Biograph, where it was made by D.W. Griffith as *The New York Hat* (1912). She continued submitting stories until Griffith hired her full time in 1914. When Griffith left Biograph to join Harry Aitken's Reliance/Majestic organization, Loos went along and, among other things, wrote scripts for the Komic Comedy one-reelers with

A production shot from *His Wedding Night* (1917) shows Buster Keaton (middle left) and Al St John (middle right) getting pinched by a cop as Alice Mann, Roscoe Arbuckle, and Arthur Earle watch from the left and Joe Bordeaux peers in from the back left. Photo courtesy of Bruce Lawton.

Fay Tincher, Tod Browning, etc. When the company became Fine Arts and part of Triangle in 1915, Anita met a Broadway actor who was just arrived as part of the theatre stars acquired by Harry Aitken. John Emerson had worked for the Shuberts and Charles Frohman and had been hired to act in and direct dramas. The pair first collaborated on Douglas Fairbanks' *His Picture in the Papers* (1916) and its breezy and satiric tone was perfect for Fairbanks' tongue-in-cheek personality. After working separately for a while—Loos writing the titles for *Intolerance* (1916) and the stories for Fay Tincher's two-reelers, Emerson directing dramas like *Macbeth* (1916) with Sir Herbert Beerbohm Tree—they were finally cemented as a team for Fairbanks with *The Americano* (1916). In 1917, the pair moved with Doug over to Artcraft/Paramount for four more films, which included *In Again, Out Again* and *Wild and Wooly*. In 1918, the company gave them their own production unit and ballyhooed: "The names 'John Emerson and Anita Loos' mean a great deal to exhibitor and to motion picture patron. Their new productions will be eagerly sought, for rare indeed is the exhibitor who hasn't been asked, 'When will you show another of those John Emerson-Anita Loos pictures—the ones with the funny stunts and the gingery sub-titles?'"

During this time, they made comedies starring Shirley Mason and developed scripts for Marion Davies, Ernest Truex, and Fred Stone. In 1919, they married and began writing for Constance Talmadge, a collaboration that created a dozen comedy features and lasted to 1925. Sadly, most of these films have been lost, leaving Talmadge's career overlooked and Emerson and Loos' silent film reputation resting on their Fairbanks titles. In 1928, they adapted Anita's book *Gentlemen Prefer Blondes* into a film and in the 1930s worked at MGM on films such as *The Girl from Missouri* (1934) and *San Francisco* (1936). Emerson died in 1956 and Loos kept writing, producing a number of memoirs about her time in Hollywood right up to her death in 1981.

Another unusual pairing was the popular kiddie team of sisters Jane and Katherine Lee. After supporting Annette Kellerman in *A Daughter of the Gods* (1916) and doing a number of Fox features with Theda Bara and Stuart Holmes, the studio put them into their own features, such as *Two Little Imps* (1917) and *Swat the Spy* (1918). Some were helmed by comedy veteran Arvid E. Gillstrom and most had topical World War I themes that consisted of the moppets shaming their elders into doing their civic wartime duty

In the early 1920s, the sisters physically left films for vaudeville, but according to Moving Picture World, Fox brought them back in 1922 "in

John Emerson—Anita Loos Productions for Paramount

"Come On In!"
with Shirley Mason and Ernest Truex.
Released September 22nd, 1918.

"Gosh Darn the Kaiser!"
with Shirley Mason and Ernest Truex.
Released in November, 1918.

"When the Boys Come Home."
A Paramount-Artcraft Special.—Released in January, 1919.
with ERNEST TRUEX

1918 Paramount promotion for John Emerson and Anita Loos.

re-edited versions of some of their former successes. The pictures have been edited by Ralph Spence and cut down to two reels. The first of the series is called *A Pair of Aces*, and is made up of situations and bits of business culled from several of the original features." Both girls retired from show business by the mid-1930s.

But the oddest couple of silent comedy has to be the simian sidekicks Napoleon and Sally. Their one-reelers were made by the E. & R. Jungle Film Company, which had been formed in 1914 by J.S. Edwards and John Rounan. Napoleon had originally appeared on stages around the world with an elephant named Hip. After Hip died, the May 8, 1915, Motion Picture News announced:

> **SALLY, E. & R. STAR, RIVALS NAPOLEON IN COMEDY.** Napoleon, the chimpanzee comedy star, just returned from a successful engagement in Australia under the auspices of the

> E. & R. Jungle Film Company, has a new rival for the honors that have been his for so long.
>
> Sally is her name and she can do everything but talk. With the usual prerogative of her sex she has not admitted her age. She is about eight years old and other sources have not been so reticent.
>
> Napoleon smokes, roller skates, bicycles and does other masculine stunts. Sally keeps house, minds the baby, plays nurse, cooks and in many ways plays the lady. Unlike Napoleon, however she has never been on the stage, and training has been primarily and solely for the screen.
>
> In her latest picture her acting is so nearly human, so full of unconscious comedy that Napoleon will have to look to his laurels. The total absence of forced comedy in the parts Sally portrays for the screen makes her a fitting companion for Napoleon.

The chimps' big heyday was during 1916 when their shorts were directed by Louis W. Chaudet and they had support from Lillian Leighton and Ralph McComas in comedies like *Stung*, *Father's Baby*, and *In Dutch* (all 1916). The pair left their mark on film comedy. Their films stayed on the states' rights market for a number of years as they were rereleased by Bulls Eye/Reelcraft at the end of the decade. They spawned rivals like the orangutan and chimp Mr. and Mrs. Joe Martin at Universal, and their daughter, Snookums, got her own series appearing as Snooky the Humanzee (in male drag) in shorts distributed by Educational and Federated through the first half of the 1920s.

LAST CALL

Two final teams take us to the end of the decade—the first is the polite type and the other completely knockabout. Continuing the franchise started by Mr. and Mrs. Sidney Drew were the comedies of Carter De Haven and his wife Flora Parker. Although forgotten today, De Haven was a big film name in the Teens and Twenties who directed and wrote many of his pictures. He began his career at a very young age in vaudeville and had great success as a comedy juvenile in shows like *The Girl in the Taxi* and *George Washington Jr.* The early part of his film career was spent at Universal, where he made his debut in the 1915 feature *The College Orphan* and then starred in a series of *Timothy Dobbs, That's Me* one-reelers

Napoleon and Sally pose with human co-star Lillian Leighton circa 1916 for their series of E & R Jungle Film comedies.

about the misadventures of a soda jerk trying to break into the movies. After this, Mrs. De Haven began appearing with him and a series about a married couple's trials and tribulations developed. In 1919, they moved over to William "Smiling Billy" Parson's Capital Comedies and as Sidney Drew had recently died, De Haven helped himself to the "Mr. and Mrs." moniker. The early 1920s saw them making their shorts for Paramount and FBO in addition to a few features for First National release.

Today very few of their films are available, but a few survivors—such as *Honeymooning* (1919) and *Private-Keep Off* (1923)—plus reviews show that the comedies were witty and sophisticated, with the humor and the gags springing from the situations that Carter found himself entangled in. The list of directors and writers that collaborated with De Haven on the films include William Seiter, Charles Parrott (a.k.a. Charley Chase), Mal St Clair, Monte Brice, and Robert McGowan—some of the cleverest and most polished practitioners of silent comedy. After retiring in the mid-1920s, Carter became involved in California real estate and the De Havens eventually divorced. Their children, Gloria and Carter Jr., continued the De Haven name in films and Flora Parker passed away on September 9, 1950.

An overlooked side note of Carter De Haven's career is his role as a long-time friend and collaborator of Charlie Chaplin. Even at the peak of his own busy filmmaking, the November 16, 1918, Moving Picture World reported:

"**DE HAVEN TO ASSIST CHAPLIN.** Charles Chaplin has engaged Carter De Haven to assist him in directing a new comedy for the First National Exhibitors that was begun at the Chaplin studios the week of October 21."

He can also be seen in Kevin Brownlow and David Gill's *Unknown Chaplin* (1983) in footage of Chaplin and his crew making an impromptu film with the Prince of Denmark on the set of *Sunnyside* (1919). After his career wound down, De Haven continued working with Chaplin, receiving assistant director credit on *Modern Times* (1936) and appearing as Jack Oakie's ambassador in *The Great Dictator* (1940). De Haven died on July 7, 1977, at the ripe age of 90.

Mr. and Mrs. Carter De Haven.

The last team to be discussed in the first part of this essay, and—owing to the disappearance of their films—also the least seen, is that of Earl Montgomery and Joe Rock. From 1917 to 1920, they starred in wild, action comedy one- and two-reelers for Vitagraph, chock-full of chases and daredevil stunts. Joe Rock said, "We always finished our comedies with a shot of us running away from a cop, a schoolteacher, or a principal and then running smack into them again. If we'd run away from cops, we'd run back into cops. Then we'd break away, climb a roof, fall through a skylight, look up, see the cops and smile. We'd turn around and discover that we were behind bars in jail. The kids used to love it. Everything we did was with an eye to them. I played the young boob; Montgomery was the heavy."

Rock was born Joseph Simberg in New York in 1891. With a background in sports, athletics, and dancing, Joe reported to the Vitagraph Studio after hearing that they needed people who could do stunts. Promptly hired, he began working in the shorts that Larry Semon was directing with Hughie Mack and Jimmy Aubrey. There he met Earl Montgomery. Today, there's scant information available about Montgomery, making him something of a mystery man. He was born in California in 1894 and had done stunt work as part of the company at the American Film Co. before coming East to Vitagraph.

Montgomery and Rock can be spotted tearing up the scenery as part of the "Big V Riot Squad" in shorts like *Hash and Havoc* (1916), *Worries and Wobbles*, and *Plagues and Puppy Love* (both 1917). During this time, they formed a partnership and decided: "You do stunts. I do stunts. Let's not double for anyone else." They wrote some sample scripts, which were liked by Vitagraph head Albert E. Smith, and were on their way in one-reelers. The total unavailability of their films is a real shame, as titles like *Sneakers and Snoozers* and *Subs and Dubs* (both 1918) sound like non-stop gag fests. Joe and Monty wrote the scripts; J.A. Howe, Roy H. McCray, and Gilbert Pratt were their directors; and surviving photos and lobby cards show that "Queen of the Amazons" Blanche Payson was a regular foil for their antics. In August of 1918, all the Big V comedies became two reels and the boys continued together until mid-1920.

At this point, Vitagraph got greedy and split them, thinking that they'd have two successful series for their one. But things didn't work out as well, and although each got their own unit with talent collaborators—Chuck Reisner directed Monty, and Rock had Grover Jones—they soon moved on. Rock went on to star in comedies for Federated and Grand

Earl Montgomery (second from left) and Joe Rock (far right) are flanked by Blanche Payson (far left) and Rosa Gore (second from right) in their Vitagraph comedy *Zip and Zest* (1919).

Asher. He always handled the business for the team and now expanded into producing shorts with comics like Stan Laurel, Jimmy Aubrey, Alice Ardell, and A Ton of Fun. Monty continued on, doing a series for Carnival Comedies in addition to appearing in and writing gags for Jack White Comedies. But his career had dried up a bit by 1926 when Joe hired him to direct and he finished the 1920s piloting a number of the Ton of Fun shorts and Mickey McGuire comedies for Larry Darmour. His career wound down in the sound era and he died in 1966. Rock had moved into feature production in the late 1920s and produced features in England into the late 1930s. In retirement, Joe remained active, appearing often at Sons of the Desert events, and died in his early nineties in 1984.

Part two of this chapter will concentrate on the teams of the 1920s and will include, to name a few, the Hall Room Boys, Al Cooke and Kit Guard, Lupino Lane and Wallace Lupino, A Ton of Fun, Snub Pollard and Marvin Loback, and a couple of guys named Stan and Ollie.

Comedy Reel Every Monday: The Sennett Story

The name Mack Sennett has become the stuff of movie legend and synonymous with the frenetic anything-for-a-laugh style of silent film comedy. Over the years, a good deal of exaggeration and fantasy about Sennett has been churned out in print and spoken lore, much of it coming from Sennett himself in books such as *Father Goose* and *King of Comedy*, which has made navigating the fact from fiction in his saga a sometimes difficult feat.

He was born Michael Sinnott in Richmond, Quebec, Canada, on Jan. 17, 1880, and by the time Mack was 17, the family had moved to East Berlin, Connecticut. Burning with an ambition to sing and perform from an early age, he moved to New York around the turn of the century to seek his fortune.

He spent a few years doing small bits and appearing in the choruses of Broadway shows, plus posed as a photographer's model. Needing the money, he even swallowed his pride to work in the bottom rung of show business—the movies.

This occurred in 1908 with the American Biograph Co. One of Sennett's fellow actors in the company, D. W. Griffith, soon became the director-general of the studio and nurtured Mack, giving him occasional lead roles and using scenarios he authored. Right from the beginning, Sennett's interests and talents lay in comedy and after a few years of working closely with Griffith and Frank Powell, who headed the comedy unit, Mack was made a director in 1911. Putting together a group of players like Mabel Normand, Fred Mace, Eddie Dillon, Del Henderson, and Sennett himself, these one-reelers were situational and character-oriented. A year later, with the help of Adam Kessel and Charles O. Bauman of the New York Motion Picture Co., the Keystone Film Co. was founded with Mack as director-general.

The young Mack Sennett made ends meet by posing for photo cards when he was appearing on stage and making his first stabs at movies.

In addition to Sennett, the original core Keystone group consisted of Mabel Normand, Fred Mace, and Ford Sterling. Production began on the East Coast with shorts such as *At Coney Island* and *A Grocery Clerk's Romance* (released as a double bill on October 28, 1912) before the company settled in California in August of 1912. Henry "Pathe" Lehrman, who had worked closely with Mack at Biograph, soon joined the outfit as an actor and assistant, plus quickly began directing his own second unit. The ensemble of slapstick regulars rapidly blossomed to include Alice Davenport, Arthur Tavares, Charles Avery, Nick Cogley, Dot Farley, Edgar Kennedy, Bill Hauber, Rube Miller, Dave Anderson, Frank Opperman, Chester Conklin, Hank Mann, Minta Durfee, Al St John, and Roscoe "Fatty" Arbuckle.

Sennett liked to portray himself as a country boob or an unsophisticated ex-boilermaker. Many of his former employees played along with this myth, practically painting him as some kind of film comedy idiot savant. The truth is that for almost twenty years, Sennett was a savvy creator and producer who had his finger on the pulse of what audiences found funny (or at least his derriere, as it was said if he rocked in his rocking chair while previewing a film it was funny—if he didn't it wasn't). At Keystone, Mack took the principles of early French comedies and became the Henry Ford of silent comedy by setting up the first assembly line to mass produce Hollywood slapstick shorts. There he created the template for the genre and established most of the important comedians of the era—Charlie Chaplin, Mabel Normand, Ford Sterling, Charley Chase, Harry Langdon, etc.—almost all of whom left him for greater fame and larger salaries. Although the teens were his halcyon days, his success would continue through the 1920s. When stars would leave, he would find or create new ones.

1915 saw Mack already dubbed "The King of Comedy" and his comedian's list had swelled to include Charlie Murray, Louise Fazenda, Charles Parrott, Slim Summerville, Bobby Dunn, Frank Hayes, Harry Gribbon, Polly Moran, and Syd Chaplin. At the end of that year, he joined with D.W. Griffith and Thomas Ince as part of the Triangle Film Corporation.

Engineered by Harry Aitken as a prestige move to align three of the biggest names in Hollywood, the project was under-organized and -financed with the three principals all leaving by 1917. Sennett's exit divested him of the Keystone brand name, but he reincorporated himself as "Mack Sennett Productions" and distributed his films through Paramount, First National, and then Pathé.

A Sennett portrait not long after the formation of Keystone,

Charlie Murray (far right) looks on as Mack presents a check to Liberty Loan bigwigs circa 1918. Photo courtesy of Cole Johnson.

By this time, Sennett had taken the early beach films he had done with Mabel Normand, such as *The Diving Girl* (1911) and *The Water Nymph* (1912), and created the Mack Sennett Bathing Beauties, which became an extremely popular franchise and genre. The early 1920s saw him focusing on comedy features. His early dabbling with full-length slapstick had produced *Tillie's Punctured Romance* (1914), *My Valet* (1915), *Mickey* (1918), and *Yankee Doodle in Berlin* (1919) and now Mack created a whole slate of features that included *Down on the Farm*, *Married Life*, *Love, Honor and Behave* (all 1920), and *A Small Town Idol* (1921). Most of these features were unwieldly and erratically paced, but Mack soldiered on with Mabel Normand's *Molly O* (1921), *Suzanne* (1923), and *The Extra Girl* (1923). Other occasional features included Ben Turpin's *The Shriek of Araby* (1923), *His First Flame* (1927) with Harry Langdon, and the World War I romance *The Good-Bye Kiss* (1928).

Ben Turpin, Billy Bevan, and Ralph Graves were three of Sennett's important players of the mid-1920s and each represented a different type of Sennett comedy. Turpin's scrawny scarecrow look lent itself to spoof and parody, so a good deal of his time was spent mocking movie melodramas, especially those of Erich von Stroheim and Rudolph Valentino. Gag-

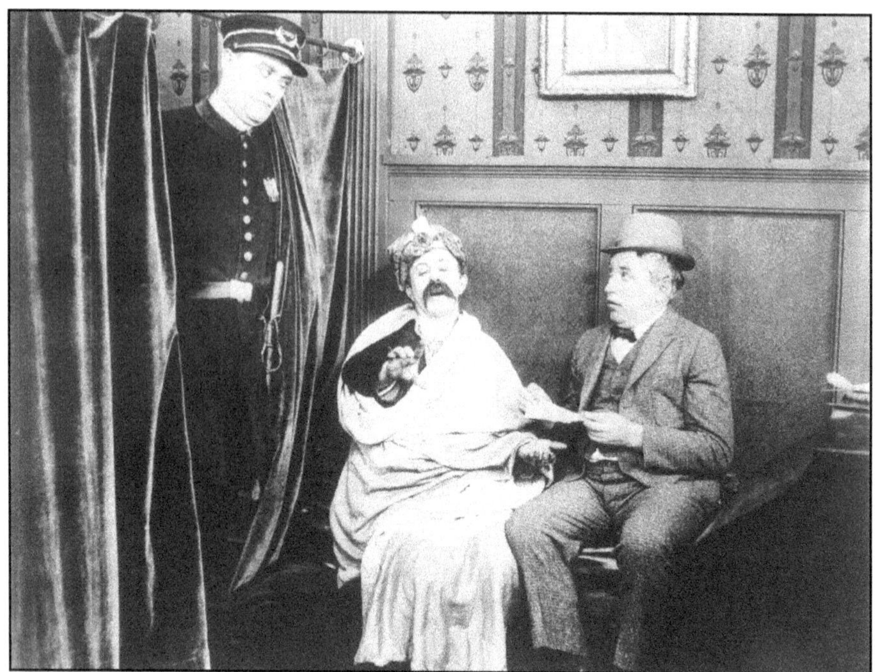

Mack with Harry Gribbon (left) and Chester Conklin (middle) in *The Country Girl*, an unreleased comedy made in 1918. Photo courtesy of Robert Arkus.

crazy, wild, and surreal shorts were the territory of Billy Bevan, who acted as a sort of walrus-mustachioed feather being blown about in a whirlwind of chaos. Finally, the films with Ralph Graves were Sennett's adaption to the more situational style of his rivals Hal Roach and Al Christie. Mack would continue this trend in the late 20s with the more domestic Smith Family, Sennett Girl, and Alice Day series.

When talking film arrived, Sennett fearlessly dove in early in 1928, but never really conquered the new medium. The one-two punch of the changeover to sound and the 1929 stock market crash dealt him a blow from which he never recovered. Struggling for a few years to maintain the studio, Mack was forced into bankruptcy in December of 1935. The last twenty-five years of his life were spent as a relic, a reminder of an earlier Hollywood, whether making cameo appearances as himself with the likes of Abbott & Costello or being honored on TV programs such as *This is Your Life*. Usually surrounded by imitation "Keystone Kops" and looking uncomfortable in a stiff gray suit, he seemed more the grumpy retired businessman than a creator of madcap comedies. By the time he passed away in 1960, most of his actual films had been forgotten, but his status as Hollywood legend was permanent.

Rediscovering Roscoe: The Careers of "Fatty" Arbuckle

A FRESH LOOK at the films of Roscoe "Fatty" Arbuckle has been long overdue. For ninety years, in the wake of the famous scandal and trials that buried his reputation in the 1920s, it's been impossible to separate the legend surrounding Arbuckle from his work as a filmmaker and comedian. Years later, when critics and film historians began reexamining silent comedy, the taint still remained, causing squeamishness about delving into his films. Routinely dismissed as "primitive," "vulgar," or "not funny in himself," until recently the films were rarely revived.

The exception to this was his shorts with Buster Keaton, but when something was found to be funny in those comedies, modern commentators usually said it had to have originated with Buster. The time has come to give the man, who for a number of years was second only to Chaplin in popularity, his due. A large number of the films survive and reveal not only an immensely likeable clown, but also an innovative comedy creator and sophisticated director.

He was born on March 24, 1887, in Smith Center, Kansas, on the Great Plains into an early life of poverty and drudgery. The family later moved to California and Roscoe, enamored of the theatre, made his debut at age eight when a replacement was needed for a touring company's local performance. After his mother's death when he was twelve, Roscoe was shunted around to various family members, but often fended for himself with multiple odd jobs—at first in hotels or restaurants and then more and more in the theatre. From singing "illustrated songs" with slides, he graduated to touring with stock companies, where "on the road" in the U.S. and Asia from 1904 to 1913, Roscoe became a well-seasoned performer and comedian.

Luke (right) and his master looking spiffy for the camera circa 1916.

His first brush with films was in 1909 for the Selig Company and later Nestor before his movie career began in earnest in April of 1913, when he joined the company of comedians at Mack Sennett's Keystone Studio. Appearing in a one-reeler almost every week, he learned film basics from Sennett and Henry "Pathe" Lehrman—two of the most important pioneers of American silent comedy. His screen persona rapidly solidified into a moon-faced, innocent, fun-loving fat boy and while perhaps never as complex a character as Chaplin or Keaton's, he became an international star. By early 1914, he was directing his own shorts and from the beginning showed an easy mastery of setting up and shooting physical action in a clean and precise manner.

Within a year, in shorts like *That Little Band of Gold* and *Fatty's Tintype Tangle* (both 1915), he was using better-developed stories that showcased his prowess as a fun-maker. Incredibly light and fast on his feet, he took tremendous falls and had a dexterity with props that was truly amazing. Appearing frequently with Mabel Normand, by 1915 they were the most popular stars on the lot and their teamwork became official, leading to a series that included *Fatty and Mabel's Married Life* and *Wished on Mabel* (both 1915).

Roscoe had become invaluable to the Sennett organization. Besides being big at the box office, shorts like *Fatty and Mabel Adrift* (1916) show him to be the most skillful director on the lot and as early as August of 1914, whenever Mack would be away on business, Roscoe would take over as director-general of the Keystone plant. In 1916, he had the opportunity to work away from the Sennett lot at Triangle's East Coast studio and there made his most mature shorts yet—*The Waiter's Ball*, *His Wife's Mistake*, and particularly *He Did and He Didn't* with its combination of

Roscoe and Corinne Parquet in the Fort Lee, New Jersey-made *The Waiter's Ball* (1916).

dramatic feature lighting, camera work, and adult situations rarely seen in a comedy short. This taste of creative freedom made him realize that to continue to develop, artistically and financially, he had to leave Sennett.

Roscoe signed with producer Joseph Schenck, who set up the Comique Film Corp. to make shorts that would be released through Paramount. Although his late Sennett films had become more sophisticated, for his initial Comique releases Roscoe returned to roughhouse on a grand scale. Having brought nephew Al St John along with him from Keystone, Roscoe added former vaudevillian Buster Keaton to the mix and with the three best tumblers in the business, many of the shorts seem like a contest to see who can top who. Once the exhilaration of freedom settled, Roscoe returned to the old finesse in shorts like *Camping Out* and *Love* (both 1919), as well as developing his gift for parody with *Moonshine* and *Out West* (both 1918).

Now wildly successful worldwide, a deal was worked out between Schenck and Paramount for Roscoe to star in features. After the first, *The Round-Up* in 1920, which was a serious western with a basically straight role for Roscoe, the features were polite drawing room comedies. Paramount decided to go for more prestige by bringing in name directors such as Joseph Henabery and James Cruise, but it's obvious that Roscoe was an active participant and that he had definite ideas about pepping up the polite comedy plots with well-placed and frequent bits of physical business.

He and his old teammate Mabel Normand were the first slapstick people to move into full-length films, but we'll never know how his career would have continued to develop as it came to a screeching halt with the events that followed Labor Day weekend 1921.

Roscoe hosted a gathering at the St. Francis Hotel in San Francisco to celebrate the completion of three features that had been shot simultaneously. During the party, a young woman named Virginia Rappe was taken violently ill and died a few days later. Arbuckle was accused of raping her and San Francisco's District Attorney, Matthew Brady, saw the case as a way to make a national name for himself. The subsequent trials were media circuses with the newspapers, which printed rumors as facts and published doctored photographs, creating a public frenzy. After two mistrials, Roscoe was completely exonerated and the final jury issued an apology saying that the case should never have come to trial at all. However, the Hollywood establishment, under pressure because of this and other scandals, made Roscoe the sacrificial lamb, officially banning him from the screen on April 8, 1922. Eight months later, Will Hays lifted the ban, but the outcry was so great that it killed any thoughts of Roscoe performing in movies.

Roscoe and Lila Lee, the frequent leading lady of his features.

Emotionally shattered, in debt, and out of the business for many months, Roscoe tentatively returned to work, helping out his former apprentices Al St John and Buster Keaton. At the time, St John was directing and starring in two reel Fox comedies and a surviving example like *All Wet* (1922) is a partial remake of *Fatty and Mabel Adrift* with many of the same camera angles, locations, and gags. *Out of Place* (1922) contains big physical comedy set pieces that exhibit the kind of staging and split-second timing that was an Arbuckle specialty. For Keaton, Arbuckle is said to have written story and gags for *The Frozen North* (1922) and others. But Roscoe needed steady work, so a group of friends that included Joe Schenck, Lou Anger, producer Jack White, and Roscoe's lawyer Gavin McNab formed Reel Comedies, Inc., a production company for shorts that Roscoe could direct anonymously for distribution by Educational Pictures. Two seasons of releases were made between 1923–1925, starring vaudeville comedians Ned Sparks, Harry Tighe, circus star Poodles Hanneford, and Al St John. The series ranged from out and out slapstick of shorts, like *No Loafing* (1923) and *Stupid but Brave* (1924), to cutting movie genre parodies such as *The Iron Mule* and *Curses* (both 1925).

Location shot during production of *The Iron Mule* (1925) with Roscoe in middle holding crop. He's flanked by Glen Cavender (sitting left), Al St John (reclining), and George Davis (sitting right of Roscoe). Lotus Thompson is left of Arbuckle, leaning on man's shoulder, Billy Franey is sitting atop carriage to the right, and Walter C. Reed is down front shading his eyes. Photo courtesy Sam Gill.

Scant attention has been given to Roscoe's directing career. His films go about their business with crisp efficiency and his camera is unerringly in just the right place to capture the physical action. A restrained approach to his material allows the slapstick to grow logically out of the situations. The use of long takes, punctuated by close-up reaction shots, gave his comics room to do their stuff and Roscoe got very natural performances from his leads and a supporting stock company that included Blanche Payson, George Davis, Glen Cavender, Doris Deane (the second Mrs. Arbuckle), Florence Lee, Johnny Sinclair, and Christine Francis. Roscoe began working directly for Educational in the fall of 1925 under the pseudonym of William Goodrich that he took from his father William Goodrich Arbuckle. To the end of 1926, he piloted ten shorts for Educational's popular stars Lloyd Hamilton, Lupino Lane, and Johnny Arthur, regaining his slapstick sea legs. His success led to offers to direct features. In 1927, he did two—Marion Davies' *The Red Mill* and *Special Delivery* with Eddie Cantor, but both turned out to be frustrating experiences for him due to producer and studio interference.

Throughout the 1920s, between directorial duties, Roscoe had been making many stage appearances and short vaudeville tours and from 1928 to 1929, he temporarily turned his back on films. The depression brought him back; after losing investments in a nightclub and real estate, Roscoe returned to Hollywood in 1930 as a writer in RKO's scenario department. Soon Educational welcomed him back to direct sound shorts with Lloyd Hamilton, Al St John, Monty Collins, and Tom Patricola and he directed a series of two-reelers for RKO. Shorts like *Bridge Wives* and *Mother's Holiday* (both 1932) show that as a director, he adapted easily to the new sound technology. He avoids the static quality of the earliest talkies with frequent and fluid camera moves and briskly paces the dialogue. It would have been interesting to see how he might have handled a feature at this time, but before that could happen, Roscoe got the call he had been waiting ten years to receive.

In February of 1932, Warner Brothers approached him with an offer to star in a short and he went on to make a total of six at the Vitaphone Studio in Brooklyn. For these films, Roscoe seemed to turn back the clock, looking

Roscoe on the street in Brooklyn on location for his Vitaphone short *Hey, Pop* (1932).

fit and hardly older than he had when his career was interrupted in 1921. He adapted easily to sound, revealing a soft mid-western voice. While the directorial chores where handled by Alf Goulding and Raymond McCarey, the reworking of large amounts of old routines and bits in the finished films show that Roscoe was very much in charge. The shorts were a success and there was talk of a starring feature, but on June 28, 1933, Roscoe Arbuckle died quietly in his sleep in New York.

Billie Ritchie: The Man from Nowhere

Working on the costumes for *The Great Dictator* (1940) was Winifred Ritchie. As a former Fred Karno performer, Winifred's expertise with trick and comedy costumes had found her a position on many Chaplin productions since the 1920s. But what few of the people working on *The Great Dictator* remembered, or were even old enough to know, was that twenty years earlier, her late husband, Billie Ritchie, was a film rival of Chaplin's and even claimed to have originated the tramp character.

If Billie Ritchie is mentioned at all today, he's lumped together with someone like Billy West as an out-and-out Chaplin imitator. This classification isn't accurate, as Billie had a long stage career before Charlie became famous and in his first film, *Love and Surgery* (October 25, 1914), Ritchie bursts on the screen full-blown and seems to be going about his comedy business as usual.

The situation was summed up well by John Montgomery in his 1954 book *Comedy Films*. Referring to Ritchie, he writes:

"In his films he wore clothes similar to those adapted by Charles Chaplin, so that some critics were quick to suggest that Chaplin was imitating Ritchie, or that Ritchie was imitating Chaplin. Certainly, Chaplin had taken over Ritchie's stage part, and learned the technique, and both comedians received the same training while with Karno. But they were not really alike."

No one has systematically examined Ritchie's films due to the difficulty in finding and screening the surviving work. But after seeing a number of his L-Ko Comedies, I was amazed to discover that not only is Ritchie different from Chaplin, but also that he deserves his own place in silent comedy history for presenting possibly the most low-down, despicable, and unlikable character ever seen on the screen.

Billie contemplates his unruly brood in *Live Wires and Love Sparks* (1916). Photo courtesy Robert Arkus.

Ritchie's early years are sketchy, but, according to his family in Europe, he was born William "Billie" Hill in Glascow in 1874. The last name, Hill, is fascinating, as Chaplin's mother's family name was Hill, and this raises the question of whether Chaplin's generosity to Billie's widow and daughter–they were also regular visitors to his mother in California–was the result of family ties. However, since Hill is a very common name in the U.K., this remains only a tantalizing possibility. Billie's parents and sisters were performers and the whole family had a stage show when he was a child. Ritchie later claimed that he first used his "tramp" make-up and attire in 1887 in an act with his sisters called *The Ritchie Trio*. He also said that he performed for Queen Victoria at Balmoral Castle while he was clowning with the Pinder and Ochs Circus in 1893. Other items refer to Ritchie being trained to stock work at the Theatre Royal in Plymouth, playing the father in *Ten Nights in a Bar-Room* at a very young age and appearing at the Drury Lane Theatre in London with Fred H. Graham in the pantomime *Cinderella* as Baron Near Broke.

A prosperous-looking young Ritchie in 1908, during the time he was touring the United States in various Gus Hill productions.

Around the turn of the century, Billie became a member of Fred Karno's pantomime company. He played a street musician in *Early Birds* and was in the original version of *Mumming Birds*. Ritchie played the part of the conjuror in the first production, in which Billie Reeves created the role of the inebriated swell. In 1905, Karno brought the sketch to America, where it became known as *A Night in the English Music Hall*, and on this first U.S. tour, Ritchie played the drunk. So Billie's statements of having originated the role of the drunk are true, at least as far as U.S.

audiences are concerned. While touring with the part on the Orpheum Circuit, he received other offers and, like many Karno-ites to follow, decided to stay in America.

In 1906, Billie began an eight-year stint under the management of the Gus Hill Company (again, no relation as far as is known), starring, producing, and touring the country in the musical revues *Around the Clock*, *The London Fire Brigade*, *A Night in Bohemia*, *A Night Out*, and *Vanity Fair*. Ritchie's wife, Winifred, was the singer and dancer Winifred Francis, who was featured prominently in these productions. Surviving reviews suggest that these revues were more or less the same and included a version of *Mumming Birds* with Billie playing the drunk, whom he called "Bill Smith, the Man from Nowhere." Their notices were very good:

> In *Around the Clock*, which was placed on the boards of the Bijou yesterday, Brooklynites will find bright farce and some rattling good music. The company is Billy Ritchie's and the hit of the performance is the reproduction of a scene in a London music hall. To make this possible a stage is shown on the stage, the sides of the real Bijou stage being made up to represent a portion of the front of the theatre, including the orchestra boxes. An orthodox music-hall production of the London type is staged, and a number of the members of the company, seated in the boxes, add to the merriment by their antics.
>
> Billy Ritchie, impersonating an intoxicated but happy Londoner, is the life of things for a few minutes, and the entire affair is simply mirth-compelling. This part of the performance is perhaps a trifle broad, but is so impregnated with fun and good humor that anything of the sort is completely lost sight of. (*Brooklyn Eagle*, November 23, 1907.)

> Billy Ritchie 'the Original Drunk' is at the head of the new *Vanity Fair* burlesque, which is at the Westminster Theatre this week. The show is lively and provides several musical hits. Billy Ritchie's characteristic impersonation of a 'drunk' is very good. He provokes a laugh every time he makes a move and the best part of it is that he does not carry out the same old way of caring for such a part. (*Providence Journal*, September 23, 1913.)

Billie on stage (left of middle on knees) during his touring days in America.

Constantly touring, even at its best in successful shows, is a difficult and strenuous life. Vaudeville and stage performers who had originally ignored the "movies" and looked down on them as a sort of bastard stepchild began to realize, during the period that Billie was on the road in America, that movies offered an easier and potentially more lucrative lifestyle. In the summer of 1914, Billie was tapped for films and probably eagerly jumped at the offer. The man who brought him to the screen and would oversee his entire film career was Henry "Pathe" Lehrman.

Although generally dismissed today as a sort of second-string Mack Sennett, Lehrman was an important pioneer of American silent comedy and one of the biggest comedy producers of the Teens. By all accounts, he was also a callous and nasty individual who was nicknamed "Suicide" by the comics who worked for him due to the cavalier way he had of putting them in physical danger. It's said that extras in the know would always pass up work on a Lehrman picture. One of the very few good things said about Lehrman is that he took young directors like Jack White and

Norman Taurog under his wing and gave them their first opportunities, although Taurog later told historian Sam Gill that much of this was due to Lehrman's laziness and willingness to have the comedy fledglings do a lot of his work. But at the same time, Taurog felt that he learned more from Lehrman than anyone else in the business.

Born in Austria in 1883, Lehrman later spun dubious accounts of a wealthy steel manufacturer father and having been a lieutenant in the Austrian army. But, according to legend, in 1909 he was working as either a streetcar conductor or movie usher in New York when he presented himself at the Biograph Studio as a director from the Pathé Frères Company of France. It was soon apparent to everyone that he had never been inside a studio before, leading D. W. Griffith to dub him "Pathé," but he was kept on and soon became Mack Sennett's right hand man—first in the comedies Sennett directed at Biograph and then in the formation of Keystone, where Lehrman was influential in creating the studio's style and maintaining the output. Two years later, he left Keystone for a brief sojourn directing Ford Sterling at Sterling Comedies. While there, Lehrman secured a deal with Universal's head Carl Laemmle and formed L-Ko

A 1916 L-KO Company shot that includes Dan Russell (left) and Bert Roach (right) sitting on the ground in front. Sitting in the first row is Charles Hochberg (second from left), Jack White (to Hochberg's right), Billy Bevan (right of White in straw hat), Lucille Hutton (to Bevan's right), director Jack Blystone (to Hutton's right), and Ritchie is in flat cap directly behind Dan Russell. Back row standing has Fatty Voss in the middle in hat and bow tie with Charles Lakin behind Ritchie's right shoulder.

(Lehrman Knock-Out) Comedies. He then raided Sennett's company, trying very hard to lure Mabel Normand away. Although unsuccessful with her, he did nab Hank Mann, Alice Howell, Rube Miller, Peggy Pearce, Eva Nelson, George Nichols, and others.

Ritchie was hired as L-Ko's star. As Chaplin fans well know, Lehrman was Charlie's first director at Keystone (*Making a Living* and *Kid Auto Races*, both released in February 1914) and their relationship was far from harmonious. Lehrman left Sennett after *Between Showers* (February 28, 1914) and not too long after, Chaplin's popularity went through the roof, which is said to have rankled Pathé. From everything that's been said and written about Lehrman, it's not much of a leap to assume that in his mind he felt that he was responsible for Chaplin's success—that he taught Charlie how to act for the camera and got him started on the road to success–and he may have even believed that he came up with the tramp character. Lehrman must have thought that if he obtained another comedian with Chaplin's background, he could "do it again" and this time, he would benefit from the success and control it. To make sure of that, Billie was signed to a personal contract with Lehrman, not L-Ko. Although Lehrman's intention may have been to create another Chaplin, and many of the externals are similar, Billie's screen character was cut from different cloth entirely.

Of the nearly sixty L-Ko's that Ritchie starred in, only around twenty are known to exist, including the initial releases *Love and Surgery* (October 25, 1914) and *Partners in Crime* (November 1, 1914). At first glance, Billie definitely seems to be aping Chaplin with the moustache, bowler hat, mismatched clothes, big shoes, and bamboo cane. And as they both were steeped in music hall traditions, there's an overlapping of gags, situations, and routines. For instance, Charlie, like Stan Laurel, often has difficulty defiantly snapping his fingers at someone. In *Partners in Crime*, Billie does, too, and his unsanitary solution is to lick his finger and thumb to create the proper snapping friction. Another stock routine appears in *A Dog's Life* (1918) when Charlie knocks out thief Albert Austin and then manipulates him like a puppet. In *Live Wires and Love Sparks* (March 19, 1916), Billie hides behind Peggy Pearce and substitutes his arms for hers so he can flirt with a rent collector and steal his money. But while Chaplin expands the basic routine and makes it something special, Billie uses it as a quick throwaway bit.

Probably the most dramatic overlap is the drunk act from *Mumming Birds*. Since both had performed the sketch to acclaim with Karno and

Louise Orth, Billie, and a friend from *Silk Hose and High Pressure* (1915).
Photo courtesy of Robert Arkus.

Billie toured America with it for almost a decade, it was inevitable that they would each put their respective versions on film. Chaplin did in *A Night in the Show* (November 20, 1915), Billie in *Silk Hose and High Pressure* (November 8, 1915).

Whether by accident or design, Ritchie and Lehrman managed to get their version into the cinemas twelve days before Charlie's. *Silk Hose* has Billie as a layabout who does nothing but cause trouble in the boarding house where he lives. In the second reel of this three-reeler, everyone from the boarding house goes to a vaudeville show. Billie, sitting in a box near the stage, ogles the dancing girls, heckles singer Eva Nelson into tears, then forces one of the actors in a Shakespearian sketch off the stage and plays the part himself. The disgruntled actor returns, gunning for Billie, who pulls out his own pistol and empties the theatre in the ensuing melee.

But while dressed like Charlie and sharing a common comedy vocabulary, Ritchie does not mimic Chaplin's mannerisms or body language. In contrast to Chaplin's famous shuffle walk, Billie's is a cocky, stiff-legged strut that breaks into an odd horse's gallop when he gets excited or provoked into action. His gestures are blunt and brusque with none of the contrasting delicacy of Chaplin's and with his rear end defiantly sticking out at the back and his jaw and chest aggressively jutting out at the front, he comes across as a living dose of spleen that's waiting to be vented. The closest the two would be is in Chaplin's *Kid Auto Races* (February 7, 1914). This prototype of Charlie has much of the same bluntness and even ends the film grimacing into the camera, but Chaplin would soon take the character in different directions.

In many ways, Ritchie's persona is closer to the character of Gussle that Syd Chaplin played for Mack Sennett in 1914 and 1915 than to Charlie. Gussle is a scoundrel and scamp like Billie, always looking for booze, ill-gotten gains, or ways to get rid of a battle-axe wife. Physically, their heights, body rhythms, and costumes are similar. Like Syd's trousers, Billie's are baggy at the waist and crotch, but tight in the legs and each man wears a frock coat buttoned high on his chest. Both use the stuck-out rear end strut and pivot-spin before falling when conked on the head. But unlike Ritchie, Syd, as a performer, has some of Charlie's playfulness and pantomimic delicacy.

Among the other Karno graduates, there are also aspects of Ritchie in the combative mojo of Jimmy Aubrey and the wild anything-for-a-laugh energy of the early Stan Laurel. But what really sets Ritchie apart from his fellow Karno veterans and other silent film comics is his toxic and completely unredeemable screen character. Many comedians before and after Billie, like Ford Sterling, Frank Daniels and W.C. Fields, played rogues and connivers, but always with a sly wink or twinkle in the eye.

In contrast, Billie's persona is a borderline psychotic who is always ready to hit on a pretty girl, steal something, or fight dirty. His hair is a mop of standing nerve ends and his face is usually scrunched into a scowl or grimace. This can even be seen in surviving photos and ads that often have Billie glaring belligerently into the camera.

It's almost as if Ritchie was channeling the unfettered id and guile of Henry Lehrman and in many ways he seems like the Andy Kaufman of the teens—pushing the envelope and almost daring the audience to detest him. It's this scorched-earth approach to his character that makes Ritchie unique and funny. He's so despicable that it's absurd. You're never sure what he's going to do, since he looks capable of anything from eye gouging to mass murder. Then, just when you think that he couldn't possibly go any lower, he does.

In keeping with his cutthroat nature, revenge fuels the plots of many of his films. *Sin on the Sabbath* (December 8, 1915) has him trying to

Not sure exactly what Billie has over his shoulder in this shot from *Scars and Stripes Forever* (1916). Photo courtesy of Robert Arkus.

poison his rival for Louise Orth's affection. In *Love and Sour Notes* (May 19, 1915), he's booted out of a local orchestra for lousy trombone playing and vows to ruin their forthcoming show. In *Cold Hearts and Hot Flames* (September 20, 1916), after he's been banished from Vin Moore's boarding house for not paying his bills, Billie dumps dynamite into the building's furnace, so the film climaxes in a slapstick orgy of flames, firemen, water hoses, mud, and bodies flying and colliding on very visible piano wires.

Of course, Billie's plotting always boomerangs and ends up exploding in his face. Ritchie thinks he set up a cinch for himself in *Billie's Water-*

loo (June 7, 1916) when he agrees to a boxing match with a stiff reverend. Turns out the minister was a champ during his seminary days and proceeds to wipe up the floor with Billie.

Billie's L-Kos were popular, but no real threat to either Chaplin or Sennett, although one of the films, *The Fatal Note* (April 7, 1915), is credited with causing a medical miracle. Corporal Robert Beck, a wounded British soldier, laughed so hard at Billie's antics that blood gushed from his ears, restoring his hearing and speech. Lehrman milked this for publicity and also pushed items naming Ritchie as "the original drunk," with Billie stating, "I first used my present make-up in my vaudeville act with my sisters in 1887," which would be two years before Charlie was born. Seen today, the surviving L-Kos are faster-paced and more cinematic than the average 1914-1916 Sennett comedies and *Silk Hose and High Pressure*, *Live Wires and Love Sparks*, and *Cold Hearts and Hot Flames* look like they were made with bigger budgets as well.

Lehrman was ousted from L-Ko by Carl Laemmle's brothers-in-law Julius and Abe Stern in autumn 1916 and he and Billie went over to the Fox Studio, where Lehrman was put in charge of Fox Sunshine Comedies.

A scan from the only known surviving print of *The House of Terrible Scandals* (1917), Billie's first film for Fox, which show him minus his regular character make-up. Photo courtesy of Eye Film Institute, Netherlands.

It's impossible to judge how much Ritchie's character or style of comedy changed with the move as very few Fox Comedies are known to survive.

One of the survivors, the first reel of their first Fox release *The House of Terrible Scandals* (March 19, 1917), stars Billie and Lehrman with Pathé wearing the comedy make-up and Ritchie being au natural, although photos from the later *Son of a Gun* (January 6, 1918) have Billie with his usual comedy look. It isn't even certain how many of the shorts Billie appeared in. What is known is that at some time in 1918 or 1919, during his stay at Fox, Billie was injured. Injuries were occupational hazards for slapstick comedians, particularly those that worked for Lehrman. Billie had been hurt a few times doing his stage act and an incident occurred at L-Ko that made the press in 1916:

> **BILLIE RITCHIE STUCK IN MUD. DIVES INTO THICK SLIME AND STICKS. HE IS RESCUED BY FELLOW PLAYERS.** It is a well-known fact that those men in the moving-picture profession, known as stunt actors, nearly always take their lives in their hands when they perform some particular daring action before the camera, but it is not expected that a high-salaried comedian will take unnecessary chances with life and limb. Recently, however, Billie Ritchie, the original, while out on location, had a narrow escape from death, being nearly suffocated when he was caught in the slimy mud in Hollenbeck Park.
>
> The scenario called for Ritchie to dive from a high elevation into the shallow water. Everything was made ready and the little comedian got the signal from the director.
>
> Without hesitancy he dove, head first, and then—he did not come to the surface. A full minute passed before the assembled players realized something was wrong.
>
> Several of the men dove into the water, and the diminutive one was brought to the surface, his eyes, ears, and mouth filled with the slimy mud. Although nearly exhausted, the little fellow insisted on finishing the scene.

It's more likely that Lehrman or one of his minions insisted on finishing the scene and although this is passed off as a "humorous and colorful" movie story, it's ominous in the light of what ultimately happened. Ritchie was seriously injured twice while with Fox. In the first accident, he sustained internal injuries in a stunt that went wrong and was laid up for a number of months. Then, when he went back to work, he was attacked by ostriches while doing a scene. Billie never really recovered, but hung on for a couple of years, working when he could.

After a falling-out with Fox, Lehrman began releasing comedies through First National and Billie is in at least three of these. The initial entry, *A Twilight Baby* (January 24, 1920), stars Lloyd Hamilton and Virginia Rappe and is about a sissified country boy who proves himself to be a man. Ritchie turns up in support as a local bootlegger and looks very different, his usual make-up and costume discarded for a walrus moustache, floppy cowboy hat, and a long dark coat. He seems thin and a little shrunken, but pops in and out of the film, participating fully in the strenuous slapstick.

But in the ensuing months, his health steadily deteriorated and in *Wet and Warmer* (December 1920), his last known appearance, Billie seems "out of it." Looking gaunt and heavily medicated, he spends a good deal of time sitting things out while the Lehrman chaos swirls around him. He died seven months later, officially of carcinoma of the stomach, on July 6, 1921, survived by Winifred and their young daughter Wyn.

Billie with Virginia Rappe and Lloyd Hamilton in the Lehrman First National Special *A Twilight Baby* (1920). Photo courtesy of Jim Kerkhoff.

Billie had entrusted to Lehrman not only his career but also his family's financial future. Lehrman had promised that Winifred and Wyn would be taken care of, but true to form, left them penniless. Fortunately, Chaplin frequently used Winifred as a seamstress on his productions, no doubt encouraged to do so by right-hand men Alf Reeves and Henry Bergman, both former Ritchie colleagues.

In a stroke of poetic justice, Billie's death signaled the downturn of Henry Lehrman's career. By 1921, his glory days as a star producer were over, brought about by his egocentric nature and continual clashes with his backers. Another factor in his slide was his extremely severe condemnation of Roscoe Arbuckle at the beginning of the latter's manslaughter trials. Hollywood knew the real story of Lehrman and Virginia Rappe; not only was Virginia said to have been pregnant with Lehrman's child and trying to get an abortion, but at the time of her death, he was in New York with a new girlfriend. In Lehrman's defense, his severe comments were a reaction to the inflammatory coverage he'd read in the newspapers, but his long involvement with Virginia may have made him someone many in the film community didn't want to deal with. He subsequently bounced around from job to job, directing shorts and programme features, eventually finding a berth as a sort of jack-of-all-trades troubleshooter at 20th Century-Fox. He died in 1946.

Thanks to Charlie's enduring popularity, Billie Ritchie's name is still bandied about as a Chaplin imitator eighty years after his death. Being misremembered seems preferable to being completely forgotten, the unhappy fate of silent comics Marcel Perez, Fred Ardath, Wanda Wiley, Eddie Nelson, Charles Puffy, and Jess Devorska. Hopefully, more of Ritchie's lost films will be recovered and make their way into circulation so that silent comedy devotees and film historians can see Billie in action and judge his work for themselves.

Alice Howell: Forgotten Slapstick Queen

ALICE HOWELL IS A NAME that pops up in writings on silent comedy, often listed with Mabel Normand, Louise Fazenda, Gale Henry, and Anita Garvin as one of the notable comediennes of the era. And that's usually it—just a mention. Alice was a popular comedy star who had a unique style that combined feminine delicacy with out and out roughhouse, but outside of some attention by historians such as Anthony Slide, Kalton C. Lahue, and Sam Gill, there's been next to nothing of anything detailed written about her.

Entering films in 1914, she quickly became so popular that she was launched into her own series for the independent market. During her peak years of 1916 to 1921, her comedies were produced expressly to showcase and exploit her talents and the characterization that she had made famous. Although time has obscured her accomplishments, her career deserves a thorough reexamination.

Alice Howell was born Alice Florence Clark on May 20, 1886, although on later legal documents, she would give her name as Alice Florence McGinnis, to an American mother and an Irish father. In 1904, she married Simon Vincent Shevlin, with her daughter Yvonne born the next year, but she and her husband soon separated and Alice began a stage career. With no previous experience, she began working and met actor Richard Smith in a 1910 DeWolf Hopper musical comedy and he became her second husband. The couple then toured the country in vaudeville (taking the name "Howell and Howell" from an act that had failed to show up for an engagement) with their own comedy and eccentric dancing act.

Their stage careers ended when Smith was diagnosed with tuberculosis and sent to California to recuperate. Not only did Alice have to

Alice waving to the camera during an early publicity shoot for Century Comedies. Photo courtesy Museum of Modern Art/Film Stills Archive.

oversee his convalescence, but also became the sole wage earner for the family. To that end, she became an extra in 1914 at Mack Sennett's Keystone Studio:

> I came to California because the health of one of the members of my family demanded it. Pictures claimed me because I had to earn a living. I've tried my best to make good. It was a pretty hard struggle for me to get along at first. When I started with the Keystone there were times when rainy weather kept my salary down to as low as six and nine dollars a week. That

wasn't very much to live on, was it? Thank goodness that period is over. (*Moving Picture Worl*d March 2, 1918)

It's rumored that Dick Smith had known Sennett in New York and that Mack had already suggested that the husband and wife should work

As the put-upon country girl in L-KO's *Dad's Dollars and Dirty Doings* (1916), Alice co-starred with Phil Dunham, Dick Smith, and Fatty Voss.

in films. Whether or not this is accurate, Alice had her own ways of getting noticed:

> It started about five years ago at the Mack Sennett studio. I was one of the mob in a police raid. Suddenly I threw myself into the thick of the fray. The other women drew back. We all had on evening gowns and the girls didn't want to spoil them. I had no scruples. I fell downstairs and literally wiped up the floor with my gown. Mack Sennett was impressed and decided to give me a chance. (*Moving Picture World*, June 26, 1920)

In no time, she had worked her way up from crowd scenes to featured parts in shorts such as *Cursed by His Beauty* and Chaplin's *Laughing Gas*. As few of the 1914 Keystones are in circulation, it's impossible to know how many she actually appeared in, but she's recently been spotted in Roscoe Arbuckle's *Lover's Luck*, which is a good example of the type of character she played at Keystone. Alice is the leader of a group of lower-class neighbors who are snooping and watching the antics of Fatty, Minta Durfee, and Frank Hayes with great relish (keeping themselves occupied in the days before television).

Becoming known as "the Keystone scrub lady," Alice starred in at least one short, *Shot in the Excitement*, where she plays the sweetheart of Al St John. When a jealous rival shows up, complications ensue and the film ends with Alice, Al, the rival, Alice's dad, and a couple of cops all being chased by flying cannonballs. This one-reeler is her earliest starring comedy and shows that her timing and soon-to-be trademark penguin-waddle walk are already in place, as is her ability to take punishment. During the course of the film, she slips down stairs, gets soaked with water, is chased by a cannonball, and has a rock bounced off her head.

In the summer of 1914, Henry "Pathé" Lehrman set up the L-Ko Komedy Co. in direct competition with Keystone, where Lehrman had been Sennett's second-in-command. Having obtained former Fred Karno comedian Billie Ritchie as his main star, Lehrman soon raided the Sennett lot and lured away Hank Mann, Peggy Pearce, George "Pop" Nichols, and Alice. For Alice, it was an opportunity for more money and screen time. She was put to use supporting Ritchie and Mann in shorts such as *Silk Hose and High Pressure* (1915) and *Their Last Haul* (1915) and playing a leading lady in one-reelers. It was during her early days with L-Ko that her screen persona solidified.

Alice slaving away for Henry Lehrman and L-Ko in *Cupid and the Scrub Lady* (1915).

The character that she developed was a slightly addled working class girl–beanery waitress, maid, charwoman–anything that fell under the term "slavey." Although she was attractive, her comic get-up emphasized the eccentric. A round Kewpie-doll face with large eyes and bee-stung lips was topped off with a mountain of frizzy hair piled high on her head that resembled smoke billowing from an active volcano. To compliment her look of someone who had just kissed an electric light socket, she wore old-fashioned plaid or checkered blouses, long print skirts, and big clod-hopper shoes. Her physical movements were as clean and precise as Keaton and Chaplin's and she could match tumbles and falls with Al St

John and Billie Ritchie. A stiff-backed penguin-waddle walk and her pile of hair became her signature trademarks.

As her popularity grew, Alice was no longer used to back up other comics and had people such as Raymond Griffith and Fatty Voss supporting her. L-Ko began touting her as "The World's Greatest Female Screen Comedian" and trumpeted in the July 7, 1916 *Moving Picture World*:

> Some of her big and recent successes include '*Pirates of the Air*' where Alice dropped from one aeroplane to another in midair. '*How Stars are Made*,' a comedy scream where this versatile young woman posed in a street parade in Los Angeles and almost busted up the procession, '*A Busted Honeymoon*,' which was a hilarious medley, even funnier than the title, and '*The Great Smash*,' a comedy built around a railroad wreck which causes convulsions of laughter wherever shown.

Alice had additional support from Phil Dunham, Billy Bevan, and Dick Smith. Smith's health seems to have improved fairly rapidly as he turns up in two late 1914 Keystones, *Gussle the Golfer* and *The Noise of Bombs*, not to mention *Tillie's Punctured Romance*. He also joined the L-Ko company in 1915 and stayed about a couple of years, eventually moving over to Vitagraph to support Jimmy Aubrey alongside Oliver Hardy.

In late 1916, "Pathe" Lehrman left L-Ko for Fox Films and it was taken over by Julius and Abe Stern with John G. Blystone as Director General. Blystone had begun his career at Universal as a property man and sometime actor in the early teens and eventually became one of their staff directors. At L-Ko, and later Century, Blystone oversaw most of Alice's films. At the very end of 1918, he left to rejoin Lehrman at Fox Sunshine Comedies and again outlasted him there, working into the early 1920s on shorts with Lupino Lane and Clyde Cook. In 1923, he made the leap to directing features with *A Friendly Husband* (1923), starring Lupino Lane, and continued with Keaton's *Our Hospitality* (1924) and the sci-fi comedy *The Last Man on Earth* (1924), not to mention ten of Tom Mix's popular light-hearted westerns. Through the 1930s, he worked steadily directing all types of features and his last two films, Laurel and Hardy's *Swiss Miss* and *Block-Heads* (both 1938), marked a return to his slapstick roots. Sadly, Blystone died of a heart attack just two weeks before *Block-Heads*' release.

Alice had become such an audience favorite that the Stern Brothers set up a separate company for her films. Originally it was to be called

Howl Comedies, so slogans like "You'll Howl at Howell" or "Every Howell a Howl" could be used. In mid-1917, the company settled on:

"**CENTURY COMEDIES ATTRACT BUYERS**. Under the trademark of Century Comedies Alice Howell will appear in a series of merrymakers personally directed by J.G. Blystone, and the first release will be "*Balloonatics*." (*Moving Picture World*, June 2, 1917)

Oddly enough, even though the Stern Brothers were the brothers-in-law of Universal head Carl Laemmle, the first year of Century Comedies were not distributed by Universal, but by the Longacre Distributing Company for the states' rights market. At this writing, only one of the independent Century's, *Neptune's Naughty Daughter* (May 1917), is known to exist.

Universal finally picked up the series at the very beginning of 1918. One of the few survivors, *Hey Doctor*! (1918), has Alice as a receptionist in a doctor's office that is seriously short on patients. To get more, she walks down the street dropping banana peels on the sidewalk. As the pedestrians begin slipping and falling, Alice distributes cards for the doctor. The second half of the film details her misadventures at a fancy soiree

Pulling the wool on one of her neighbors in the fourth Century Comedy *Her Barebacked Career* (1917). Photo courtesy of Museum of Modern Art/ Film Stills Archive.

where she is completely out of place and causes much embarrassment. Although considered "one of the screen's leading exponents of the rough-and-ready in comedy work," Alice maintained a realistic and understated pantomimic style that was based on her experiences of life and her down-to-earth personality. She told the *New Jersey Tribune* in 1917:

> The days are not so far in retrospection when I was glad to do any kind of work and I have not forgotten how it feels to stand in line waiting for a chance to do extra work. I wanted the money so badly that I offered to wear any eccentric sort of make-up or take any chance so long as there was a pay check at the end of the week.
>
> I often felt then like the down-trodden, put upon, much abused slavies that I struggle to portray humorously today. Most of my scenes are broad farce, of course, but when I get an opportunity I try to register faithfully the character of such a girl.

Alice, Phil Dunham (far left), Frank J. Coleman (derby and brush moustache), and an unknown little person tear up the scene in an unidentified L-Ko or Century Comedy. Photo courtesy of Robert Arkus.

Alice's popularity continued to build during the two and a half years she spent with Century, helped by support from veterans like Billy Armstrong, Neal Burns, Jimmy Finlayson, Eddie Barry, and Hughie Mack, but when she realized that the Stern Brothers were more interested in promoting shorts with Joe Martin the orangutan and Brownie the Wonder Dog, she left. In October of 1919, the *Moving Picture World* announced:

"**ALICE HOWELL JOINS EMERALD**. Alice Howell has been added to the list of Emerald comedy stars. This was announced yesterday by Frederick J. Ireland, president of the Emerald Motion Picture Company.

Mr. Ireland is now preparing a series of comedies especially for Miss Howell."

Emerald was based in Chicago and had just secured the talents of Chaplin imitator Billy West, who had left Bulls Eye Films to join them. President Frederick J. Ireland is an interesting figure, a former vaudeville song and dance man that was Chicago's answer to George M. Cohan who, in a surviving starring Emerald farce comedy, *When the Cat's Away* (1920), is a human dynamo–popping in and out of doors, running from room to room, etc.–and must have been one in real life, too, as he not only directed his own series and Billy West's, but alternated piloting the new Alice Howell series with Dick Smith, who also served as her main support.

After production began on the first few shorts, Emerald merged with the Bulls Eye Film Company, the Bee Hive Film Exchange, and the Interstate Film Co. of New York to form the Reelcraft Pictures Corporation. Reelcraft was organized to produce and distribute short subjects for the states' rights market and, besides handling Alice's films, also had Gale Henry, Billy West, Billy Franey, Milburn Moranti, and Texas Guinan.

Three of the Howell Reelcrafts survive. *Lunatics in Politics* (1920) is an enjoyable but routine short while *Cinderella Cinders* (1920) and *Distilled Love* (1920) are perhaps the best existing examples of Alice's work. In *Cinderella Cinders*, she plays a waitress/cook at a crummy diner who gets fired and ends up as a maid for a wealthy family. For a society party, Alice and butler Dick Smith are enlisted to pose as the Count and Countess DeBunco, who are actually crooks. Of course, everything ends in confusion with Alice saving the day. Alice is really the whole show, and is hilarious as she primps and flirts with the customers in the diner, at one point putting up a musical chart and conducting their loud soup slurpings. Other highlights include a rollicking chase where she races to get a position on foot, bicycle, and finally roller skates pulled along by a

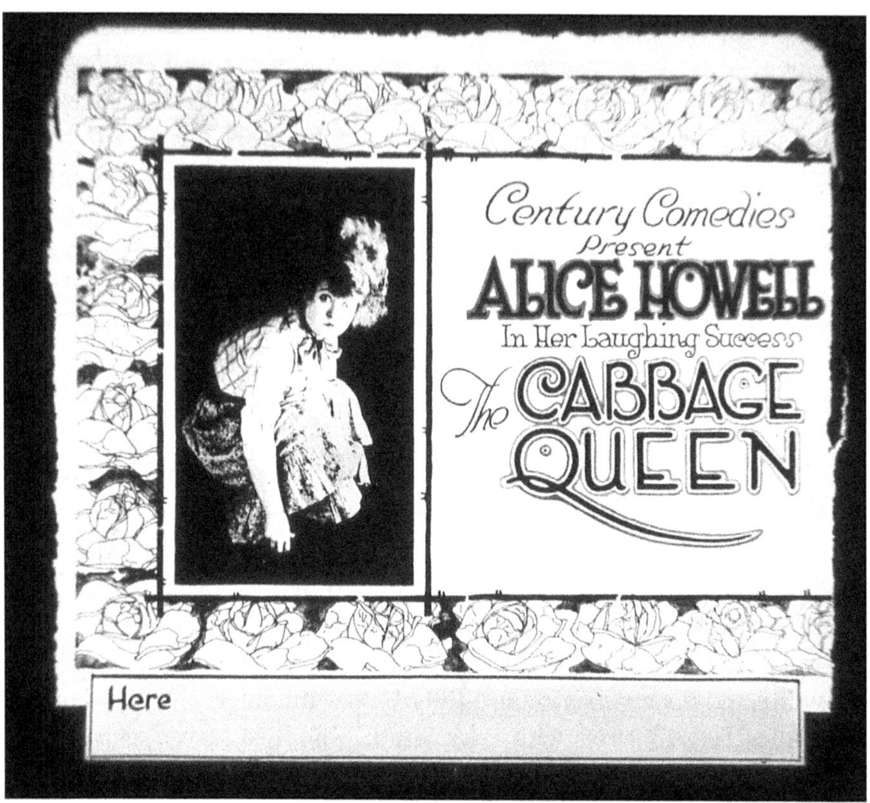

The Cabbage Queen (1918) is a World War I spoof that concerns German spies trying to get Alice's secret formula for sauerkraut.

bulldog to beat a horde of out-of-work maids from getting there first and a fruity, fancy dance exhibition with Dick Smith, where their spoofs of ballroom dancing probably date back to their vaudeville act.

The origins of *Distilled Love* are something of a mystery. Although released by Reelcraft, it appears to be an unused film from her days at L-Ko or Century due to the California locations and the participation of Oliver Hardy, Billy Bevan, Fay Holderness, and the co-direction of Vin Moore. Alice plays a farm girl who's framed as the mother of a baby by evil bootlegger Hardy. Forced to leave the farm, she goes to the big city with baby in tow and works for Hardy doing her eccentric dancing in the streets. The climax takes place at another big society party, which Alice makes a shambles of, but all ends happily with the arrival of her former farm lover Dick Smith.

Chock-full of gags, which are executed with snap and precision by the cast of comedy pros, the highlights include Alice performing the gag made famous by Mary Pickford where she wants to eat some pie but sees a placard of "Thou Shalt Not Steal" on the wall, which stops her until she sees a second that says, "The Lord Helps Those That Help Themselves." Another is when Alice arrives in the big city with the hungry baby and spots a milk truck driving by. In a great traveling shot, she runs behind the truck, opens the back door, and produces a hose, one end of which she sticks in a can of milk and the other in the baby's mouth so he can siphon down lunch as they trot along. Bits at the society party include riding from room to room on the long train of Fay Holderness' gown–even

transferring to someone else's gown–and a flirtation with a rich old goat (a white-whiskered Billy Bevan) that ends in a tit for tat slap fest. Again, Alice uses an underplayed pantomimic style and has some effective moments of pathos, especially when she's driven off the farm during a raging storm, though a bolt of lightning that just happens to strike her in the rear end brings the pathos to an abrupt end.

After six months and six shorts in Chicago, Alice and Smith moved back to California, where they made three more comedies and then appear to have severed their relationship with Reelcraft. A statement in the December 4, 1920 *Moving Picture World* announced:

> **CELEBRATED PLAYERS SECURES UNITED STATES RIGHTS TO SUNKIST COMEDIES WITH ALICE HOWELL AS STAR.** J.L. Friedman, president of Celebrated Players Film Co., has closed with George B. West, general manager of Sunkist Comedy Co., for the entire United States rights to the new series of Alice Howell comedies. These comedies have met with the highest praise. They were directed by Dick Smith and present the comedienne in roles in which she excels and unadulterated slapstick. The Sunkist Company is making a series of 52 single reel comedies. The first to be released with Miss Howell starring will be "*Boulevard Profiteers*." This will be followed by "*Who Chose Your Wife?*

George B. West was the brother of comedian Billy West and his partner in the later West Brothers Productions. Outside of a few trade magazine items and exhibitor ads boldly announcing fifty-two releases a year, little is known about this venture or how many shorts were actually made or released. The two films mentioned could have been made up from footage shot for unreleased Reelcraft titles or completely new material. In fact, the next three years of Alice's career are very clouded with only a few tantalizing scraps of information. It's recently come to light that Dick Smith directed the fabled lost Marx Brothers silent short *Humor Risk* in the spring of 1921. Shot in the New York area, it was to be the first of a series starring the Marxes, but it's thought that the finished film didn't preview well and the others were never made. A few months later, it was announced that Smith would direct a group of Pearl Sheppard comedies for Reelcraft. At that time, most of the Reelcraft product was being made by Schiller Productions at the Mittenthal Studio in Yonkers, NY. Nothing seems to have come of this series, probably due to the impending collapse of Reelcraft. Since all this was happening on the east coast, it's possible that Alice was with Smith and perhaps taking a well-earned vacation.

The next mystery item is a listing in the April 1924 *Motion Picture New Booking Guide*:

HOLLYWOOD COMEDIES. Produced by L.K.C. Productions. Distributed by Selznick Distributing Corp. Starring Alice Howell & Chester Conklin. Directed by Fred Caldwell. Length 2 reels.
Bishop of Hollywood, The Released Feb. 15,1924
Cream of Hollywood, The Released Jan. 15, 1924
Elite of Hollywood, The Released Nov. 15, 1923
Sheik of Hollywood, The Released Dec. 15, 1923

The Sheik of Hollywood is in circulation and is an extremely low-budget outing. Alice and Chester Conklin are nowhere to be seen; in their place are Gale Henry and Victor Potel. But photos have turned up from *The Elite of Hollywood* with Alice and Potel, plus an unidentified print at UCLA labeled "*Oil Well Comedy*" with Alice and Potel, which seems to be this film. It may be that Alice began the series, but left due to the shoddiness of the venture.

What's definite is that she appeared as comic relief in two features, *Love is an Awful Thing* (1922) and *Wandering Daughters* (1923), and returned to Universal in 1924 to begin her last starring series of comedies. This new series teamed her with Neely Edwards and Bert Roach, about a married couple (Neely & Alice) and their goofy butler (Roach). Alice's character was still addled and had her trademark hair and walk, but had graduated to a comfortable, middle-class status. No longer the young slavey, she takes care of the nice house while hubby works and traded in her old mismatched costume for more up-to-date attire. Similar in tone to the earlier films of Mr. & Mrs. Sidney Drew and Mr. & Mrs. Carter De Haven, the series still managed to work in generous helpings of slapstick and, at one-reel, were short and sweet.

Three entries from the series still exist, the best of which is *Under a Spell* (1925). Alice suspects Neely of sneaking a woman into the house and hires "Professor Svengoolash A.T.C.M.V." to hypnotize hubby and get to the truth. Svengoolash makes Neely think he's a monkey, but then gets knocked out. Neely escapes and his ape antics, along with Alice and butler Roach's attempts to lure him back home, provide the film's funniest moments. After Svengoolash revives and cancels his monkey spell, it's revealed that Alice's suspected other woman is actually "The Bobbed Hair Bandit," a burglar who robs houses in drag, which gets Neely off the hook for a happy ending. Director Dick Smith keeps the pace moving and the absurdities building for a very entertaining ten minutes.

Alice as support in the Owen Moore (standing) feature *Love is an Awful Thing* (1922). The little boy on Alice's lap is Walter Wilkenson.

The trio continued their misadventures until late 1925 (with Billy Bletcher and Harold Austin occasionally standing in for Neely Edwards), after which Alice slowed down the pace of her work. Her last known films are a couple of Fox Comedy shorts: the very funny *Madame Dynamite* (1926), which has Alice as a pesky mother-in-law, and *A Society Architect* (2/13/1927), one of the Van Bibber in Society two-reelers. By this time, Dick Smith had stopped acting, but continued directing Universal shorts with comics on the order of Baby Peggy, Charles Puffy, Slim Summerville, and Neely Edwards until the end of the silent days, plus still contributed as a writer into the 1930s. Not long before Alice retired, her daughter Yvonne began acting and appeared as a comedy ingénue in many shorts such as Charley Bowers' *Hop Off* (1928) and a few features. Billed as Yvonne Howell, it's plain to see from her funny performance in the surviving Glenn Tryon comedy *Flaming Flappers* (1925) that she inherited a nice bit of her mother's comic timing and screen presence. Yvonne's career was brief, as it ended in 1930 when she married Hal Roach cameraman (and soon to be famous director) George Stevens. Alice's grandchild, founder of the American Film Institute George Stevens Jr., was born in 1932.

After the changeover to sound, silent films were looked on as ancient history or curios and many former favorites who weren't currently visible in talkies were forgotten. When Dick Smith died in 1937, about ten years after Alice retired, his February 10th obituary said:

"**RICHARD SMITH**. Dick Smith, 50, comedy writer-director of silent pictures, died of pneumonia, Feb. 7, in Los Angeles. Widow survives."

This appeared in *Variety*, the main industry paper, and didn't even bother to mention who the widow was (or had been). Whether or not this kind of neglect bothered Alice isn't known, although her daughter has been quoted as saying that her career in show business didn't mean that much to her mother, that it was more "of a means to an end." George Stevens Jr. has said that he didn't really realize that his grandmother had been in films and that "she seemed to me to be a loving, red-haired grandmother businesswoman with a lively sense of humor." Having invested her earnings well in California real estate, Alice lived comfortably managing her investments and enjoying her family until her death on April 11, 1961.

Aside from the dominance of men in the field of silent comedy, the main reason for most of the neglect of Alice's work is the unavailability of her films. Although she was prolific, the bulk of her films were made for Universal and Reelcraft, both of which have terrible survival rates. A number of the Keystones where she has supporting bits are around, but out of her seventy-plus starring comedies, only about two are readily available to silent comedy fans. Her other surviving films, representing only a fraction of her output, are scattered in various distant archives and are difficult to see. The revival of interest in silent comedy began in the 1950s and, because her films weren't around, she never appeared in festivals or highlighted in a Robert Youngson compilation feature and so ended up as no more than a name in film comedy history books. But

Out of her slavey clothes, Alice poses for a more formal portrait. Photo courtesy of Museum of Modern Art/Film Stills Archive.

there have been new developments. Recently, three previously "lost" Alice Howell shorts have turned up and others have been identified. Hopefully, more will continue to resurface so that scholars and comedy fans can take a look and give Alice a chance to stand alongside the men of silent comedy and be counted.

Vitagraph Comedies: Two Forgotten Series

In the early teens, the Vitagraph studio was the bastion for clever and polite situational comedies. Today, the best-remembered and most viewed of these films are the shorts of John Bunny (with and without Flora Finch) and Mr. & Mrs. Sidney Drew. Less-remembered, though very popular in their day, are the Cutey series starring and directed by Wally Van, the Dimples shorts with Lillian Walker, and the Mr. Jack, Captain Jinks, and Kernel Nutt comedies of Broadway transplant Frank Daniels.

The general run of Vitagraph comedies are just as entertaining and benefit greatly from a stock company that includes Kate Price, Hughie Mack, Florence Turner, Charles Eldridge, Eddie Dunn, and Donald McBride, plus behind-the-camera talents such as George D. Baker, Larry Trimble, and C. Jay Williams.

Two other series–the Josie and Jarr Family comedies–have completely dropped off the film history radar due to the unavailability of the films. As with most of the studio's series, both were built around well-known and long-experienced stage performers. With the exception of Biograph, of all the New York studios, Vitagraph seems to have taken the best advantage of the handy theatrical talent pool and at the same time grasped that film acting entailed a more realistic and intimate style. That's why much of the humor in the surviving Vitagraph comedies comes from the play of emotions across John Bunny's broad face or from the little realistic details and accumulation of everyday frustrations in the Sidney Drew comedies.

THE JOSIE COMEDIES

Josie Sadler, along with Marie Dressler, Rose Melville, and Elfie Fay, was one of the best-loved stage comediennes at the beginning of the 20th Century. Small and rotund, she began her career at age nine after being discovered by impresario Tony Pastor and became famous for playing naïve immigrant girls in shows like *Prince Pro Tem* (1899), *The Silver Slipper* (1902), and her biggest success, *Peggy from Paris* (1903). Running the gamut from Dutch, Cockney, French, Swedish, and German, Sadler wrote many of her own musical specialty numbers, a few of which she recorded for Victor. During her years onstage, she worked with Weber & Fields, Eddie Foy, Fay Templeton, Sam Bernard, and Fred Mace, not to mention her future Vitagraph cohorts Sidney Drew and Harry Davenport, and even appeared in the 1912 *Ziegfeld Follies* with Leon Errol, Bert Williams, and Harry Watson, Jr.

Sadler joined the Vitagraph ensemble in 1913 and her first appearance was supporting Norma Talmadge in *Omens and Oracles* (May 5, 1913). She also turned up with Bunny, Drew, and Hughie Mack and before long, the studio began tailoring films to her stage fame. *The Coming of Gretchen* (June 17, 1913) and *The Maid from Sweden* (June 5, 1914) were about the misadventures of immigrant women and a month after the latter film, the Josie series was launched.

The Arrival of Josie (July 15, 1914) told the story of an orphaned German household drudge who chucks it all to come to America. The rest of the film details her seasickness on the boat over, confusions concerning the big city and American customs, and a budding romance with a grocery boy named Hank. Over the next three months, Josie would work as a domestic for a variety of employers, become obsessed with romance novels, have a raucous time with Hank at Coney Island, and in the last installment, get saddled with two kids from a deceased aunt.

Josie and friend sit on a real Brooklyn porch in 1914's *Josie's Legacy*.
Photo courtesy of Billy Rose Theatre Division, The New York Public Library for the Performing Arts, Astor, Lenox and Tilden Foundations.

A total of five episodes were made and besides Sadler, the other regulars involved were writer Kenneth S. Webb, director Lee Beggs, and actor Billy Quirk. Kenneth Webb had a varied career–writing numerous films and nine Broadway shows, directing feature films from 1918 to 1929–but his greatest claim to fame is the book for the Fred Astaire/Cole Porter show *Gay Divorce* and its adaptation into the movie *The Gay Divorcee* (1934). Director Lee Beggs was a stock and vaudeville veteran who had come from Solax Films and, after the Josie shorts, directed and co-starred in Billy Quirk's starring Vitagraph shorts, such as *The Egyptian Mummy* (1914) and *Billy the Bear Tamer* (1915), and continued as a supporting actor in films and on stage until his death in 1943.

Josie's goofy boyfriend Hank was played by Billy Quirk, who sadly was as forgotten during his own lifetime as he is today. One of the pioneer American screen comics, after years on stage, Quirk began appearing in Biograph films in 1909 after being taken to the studio by his friend John Cumpson. He was soon teamed in light romances with Mary Pickford and got his own Muggsy comedies. From there, he moved on to series for Solax, Pathé Frères, and Gem, where he always played the young college man or hubby and was regarded as the best of the "boy comedians." He arrived at Vitagraph in 1914 and, following the Josie shorts, he and director Lee Beggs moved on to Billy's own series, where he was supported by Constance Talmadge.

This early period–1910 to 1915–was the peak of his career. After finishing at Vitagraph, Billy had to go far afield to find work, directing and starring in some Black Diamond Comedies that were shot in Wilkes-Barre, PA, supporting Minta Durfee for a Truart series made in Providence, RI, and a Florida-based group of Sun-Lite Comedies for Reelcraft. All of these were small, states' rights units and the Reelcraft films were his last as the star.

What happened to Quirk's career? Surviving films show that he was funny—not hilarious or innovative in any way, but charming and breezy in the light leading man mode. It may be that as a "boy comedian," his age was catching up with him and he was being replaced by people like Bobby Vernon, Harry Depp, and other Al Christie leading men. Minta Durfee remembered that he was an alcoholic, which may have made him unreliable and hastened his slide. He had tried to kill himself in 1920 by jumping out of a third floor window and after the Reelcraft series, his only

Josie Sadler, Mr. Sneeze (center), and Billy Quirk (right) go native in *Josie's Coney Island Nightmare* (1914). Photo courtesy of Billy Rose Theater Division, The Library for the Performing Arts, Astor, Lenox and Tilden Foundations.

roles were a few bit parts in some independent features. After 1924, he never worked again and died at the Virginia Rest Home in Hollywood on April 20, 1926. He was fifty-three years old.

After her Josie comedies, Josie Sadler did one final film for Vitagraph, the surviving *Bunny Backslides* (October 30, 1914), a very funny short where John Bunny agrees to go to a fat farm to please his fiancée Flora Finch. While there, Bunny is continually frustrated by his inability to lose weight and meets a flirtatious fat woman (Sadler). Finally fed up with Flora and her demands, Bunny and Josie decide to be fat together and elope. Leaving Vitagraph, Sadler slowed down the pace of her working to make occasional stage appearances and only two more films, one of which was the William A. Brady feature *What Happened to Jones?* (1915), which teamed her with Fred Mace. In 1920, she retired to run the electrical business of her late husband and died in 1927. Today, she's part of the huge list of neglected silent comediennes and although her film career was short, her immigrant servant girl persona was a forerunner for ladies like Louise Fazenda, Jane Bernoudy, and Alice Howell, who would soon follow.

THE JARR FAMILY

Unlike the Josie series, the Jarr Family comedies were based on preexisting material. Author Roy McCardell was a popular humorist in the George Ade style, who wrote the first collection of Jarr Family stories in 1907 and continued to serialize their misadventures in daily newspapers for more than twelve years. According to McCardell, he grew tired of the stories, but they turned out to be his most reliable meal ticket and in 1915 made the jump to the screen. The direction of the series, as well as the leading role of the father of the Jarr clan, was given to recent stage-to-film convert Harry Davenport.

Davenport, better remembered today for his later character roles as Dr. Meade in *Gone with the Wind* (1939) and Grandpa in *Meet Me in St. Louis* (1944), was a member of an illustrious theatrical family. His father E.L. Davenport and sister Fanny Davenport were huge dramatic stage stars, but young Harry specialized in comedy. Making his debut at age five with his parents, Davenport spent most of his life on stage and some of his major successes include *The Naked Truth* (1908), *The Commuters* (1911), and *Three Wise Fools* (1918).

Married three times, his second wife was Alice Shepard, who's familiar to film comedy buffs as Alice Davenport of Keystone and Fox Sun-

Stage portrait of the young Harry Davenport. Photo Courtesy of Billy Rose Theatre Division, The New York Public Library for the Performing Arts, Astor, Lenox and Tilden Foundations.

shine comedies. It appears that their union was short-lived, but produced a daughter Dorothy (the future Mrs. Wallace Reid) and during the early days of the 20th century, Alice had him continually in court for back alimony payments. His third marriage to Phyllis Rankin made him the brother-in-law of Lionel Barrymore and Sidney Drew (who were married to Rankin's sisters) and Harry made his first Vitagraph appearances in Sidney Drew comedies, such as *Too Many Husbands* and *The Professional Scapegoat* (both1914).

Chronicling the comic trials and tribulations of a middle-class family, the series began with *The Jarr Family Discovers Harlem* (March 8, 1915), where the tribe leaves Brooklyn for new digs in upper Manhattan. Along with Davenport as head of the clan, the rest of the ensemble included Rose Tapley as the Mrs., Audrey Berry as daughter Emma, and Paul Kelly as son Willie. The Brooklyn-born Kelly had worked onstage and began at Vitagraph in 1911 when he was twelve years old, staying with the company until 1916. Despite serving twenty-five months for manslaughter in the late 1920s, Kelly spent the next forty years in films and on Broadway as a dependable character actor, best remembered for his tough-guy roles in film-noirs such as *Crossfire* (1947) and *The File on Thelma Jordan* (1950). Rose Tapley was a stage veteran and dramatic actress who had her only real sojourn in comedy with this series. After her days at Vitagraph, she became a reformer, stumping for "clean pictures" and protecting young women from the lure of the movies.

Other regular series characters included Mr. Jarr's boss, Gertrude their servant girl, assorted neighbors, and even Gus, the local bartender. Occasional guest appearances were made by Vitagraph favorites like Flora Finch, Jay Dwiggins, Julia Swayne Gordon, William Shea, and Billy Bletcher. For six months in eighteen episodes, the Jarrs moved to a new home, experienced mother-in-law trouble, went on a disastrous vacation, suffered a bout with poison ivy, had a mix-up in pets, plus even got involved with a fat lady and other circus freaks. The plots and situations were already familiar at the time and continue to be used in sitcoms to this day.

After the series finished with *Mrs. Jarr and the Society Circus* (September 6, 1915), Harry Davenport branched out as an actor working for Kalem and Rolfe Photoplays. As a director, he moved into features, the most famous of which is *Tillie Wakes Up* (1917), where Marie Dressler and Johnny Hines go on a Coney Island spree.

Around 1920, he left films to concentrate on his stage work, but returned in the 1930s and played important character roles up until his death in 1949. Author Roy McCardell continued publishing books and besides Vitagraph, he wrote scenarios for Selig, Equitable, and Reelcraft, but his most famous screen work was adapting the play *A Fool There Was* into the 1915 feature for Theda Bara. He also is credited with the dubious distinction of being the first person to use the derogatory term "kike" in print (*The Showgirl and her Friends*, 1904). McCardell died in 1961 at the age of 90.

Marie Dressler in the Harry Davenport-directed *Tillie Wakes Up* (1917).
Photo courtesy of Sam Gill.

In 1916, the comedy style at Vitagraph began to change. John Bunny had died in 1915 and the other regulars–the Drews, Wally Van, Flora Finch, etc.–all exited to greener pastures. A young newspaper cartoonist named Lawrence Semon came in as director and writer of comedies for Hughie Mack and Jimmy Aubrey. Semon brought the surreal gags and anarchistic spirit of comic strips to the studio and sophisticated comedy went out the window. By 1918, their comedy stars were Semon, Earl Montgomery & Joe Rock (class valedictorians from the Big V Riot Squad), and Jimmy Aubrey. Although now in the business of extreme slapstick, Vitagraph's earlier situational style would still be seen in the films of Mr. & Mrs. Carter De Haven, Charley Chase, Reginald Denny, and Douglas MacLean, plus the elegant features of directors such as Mal St Clair, Monta Bell, and Harry d'Arrast.

The Elongated Comedienne: Gale Henry

AT THE TOP OF ANY LIST of overlooked silent comediennes is Gale Henry, who, like contemporaries such as Alice Howell, Louse Fazenda, and Polly Moran, starred in her own popular series of comedies as well as provided sterling support for other comics. She was the daughter of Charles and Mai Henry, born in June of 1893. The 1900 US Census states that she was born in Texas and living in Los Angeles where Charles was a saloon-keeper. Gale told a slightly different version of her early days to *Picture-Play* magazine: "We lived on a Ranch–mother, Dad, and I, until I was fourteen, then we came to Los Angeles." In the 1910 Census, she's seventeen and already an actress. She began her career onstage as a member of the Temple Opera Company, tersely described by Gale as "Comic–not grand." Tall and extremely skinny with large eyes and a prominent nose, she was a dead ringer, and possibly the prototype, for Popeye's girlfriend Olive Oyl.

Her looks defined her type of roles from the very beginning and again she reported to *Picture- Play*:

> I saw an advertisement in the Los Angeles Times which called for seventy chorus girls. I answered the ad, in a little white dress which came not far below my knees, and a funny little straw hat; my mother had trimmed it with a wreath of tiny, pink cotton roses, and the outfit was not unlike the comedy costumes I later used in pictures. Think of the figure I must have cut among those more or less sophisticated girls—for I could neither sing nor dance. I went home that night—my hopes blasted! Not a word had been said about my coming back. But the next morning the postman brought me a card

Gale in character for her Model Comedies.
Photo courtesy of Jim Kerkhoff.

> which requested that I "report for rehearsal" the next day. And that day was the very happiest of my life. To think that I, Gale Henry, was a full-fledged actress—for so I considered myself. The days that followed were happy ones, too, and what do you think—that cast included Fatty Arbuckle, Louise Fazenda, and Blossom Seeley.

In 1914, she entered films at the Universal Film Company:

"I knew a girl who worked at Universal; she took me out with her one morning, and I got a job. That's all there is to it, except I remained there five years and was featured in two hundred comedies."

Joker Comedies was started by Universal in 1913 to compete with Sennett's Keystones and the shorts were one-reel knockabouts and burlesques that were cranked out at an alarming rate. Gale joined the unit that was under the direction of Allen Curtis with Max Asher as the designated star in an ensemble made up of Harry McCoy, Billy Franey, Louise Fazenda, and Bobby Vernon. McCoy left early to work for Sennett, as would Fazenda, Vernon, and scenarist Clarence Badger. Gale became part of the group in early 1914, which soon included Milburn Moranti, Lillian Peacock, and Charles "Heinie" Conklin. Director Curtis turned out a staggering number of one-reelers and finally got a break when William Beaudine took over some of the directorial duties in 1916.

Gale helps Max Asher get a leg up on his packing in *When Hiram Went to the City* (1915). Photo courtesy of Robert Arkus.

Universal also distributed Nestor and L-Ko comedies and although Gale was busy making Jokers, she occasionally turned up in other Universal releases with Universal Ike (Augustus Carney) and Universal Ike, Jr. (Bobby Feuhrer a.k.a. Bobby Ray) and appears as a harem girl in a photo with comic Carter De Haven, possibly from one of his Universal *Timothy Dobbs* comedies. In 1915, Pat Powers produced the *Lady Baffles and Detective Duck* series, a spoof of cliffhanger serials in eleven one-reel chapters. Max Asher played brilliant inventor and master of disguise Detective Duck, who was always hot on the heels of his nemesis, the mysterious crook Lady Baffles (Gale). Witty and surreal, chapter titles like *The Signal of the Three Socks* and *The Dread Society of the Sacred Sausage* tell the whole story.

Out of the huge number of Jokers that Gale appeared in, only a handful are known to survive. While photos often give the impression that they were primitive and vulgar, one of the few circulating films, *A Millionaire for a Minute*, is very well-made for 1915. Max Asher plays a country bumpkin in love with school marm Gale. Her gouty, Egyptologist uncle Billy Franey is against their marriage, but when Max gets a telegram about an inheritance, the couple decide to elope. Of course, the usual misadventures with windows and ladders ensue and a pair of crooks who have heard about the inheritance breeze into town to fleece Max. The lady crook makes a play for him and at a big party to celebrate his wealth, it's discovered that what he's inherited is Cleopatra's ring. The crooks and partygoers leave Max in disgust, but faithful Gale still wants him. When her uncle finds out that Max has Cleopatra's ring, he's more than willing to trade Gale for it to provide the happy ending.

The simple story is told in a clean and economical way by director Curtis with the slapstick growing logically out of the situations. The acting style is relatively subdued for a knockabout comedy and Gale has a very nice moment when she's sitting in her bedroom with her bags packed waiting for Max to arrive with the ladder. Sadly giving her room a final farewell look, she plants a tender little goodbye kiss on her bedpost. At the end of 1917, Gale stopped working for Joker and began appearing in Universal's other shorts series:

> **GALE HENRY IS NOW L-KO STAR.** Carrying out his purpose to strengthen the drawing power of his trade mark by adding comedy stars, President Julius Stern, of L-Ko, has arranged for a transfer of Gale Henry from Nestor Comedies,

Billy Franey (center) puts Gale in a trance for a delighted Max Asher (right) in *How Billy Got His Raise* (1915). Photo courtesy of Robert Arkus.

> a Universal brand, to head an L-Ko company directed by Archie Mayo. Mr. Stern, who is on a business trip in Hollywood, Cal., where L-Ko's come from, made the arrangements and announces an early release of Miss Henry's first comedy. *The Price She Paid* will be the title, and Hughie Mack will appear with Miss Henry as her featured supporter.

During her tenure at Universal, Gale wrote many of the stories for her comedies and developed her screen character. Like Alice Howell, she often played put-upon slavies, but her angular and unconventional looks also made her perfect as lovelorn spinsters, overbearing wives, and burlesque country girls. Her thinness gave her the appearance of a living stick-figure–all gangly arms and legs with incredibly expressive shoulders that would rise up to her ears with joy at the arrival of a new beau or plunge and almost disappear due to some embarrassment or disappointment. Her nose was a sharp beak surrounded by large eyes that seriously threatened to cross in her signature big take of surprise. She had a mouth and eyebrows that seemed to be made of elastic and a chin that dropped off suddenly into a long ostrich neck. Her hair was dark with bangs in the front and a bun in the back. On top was a wide brimmed hat, which looked like a satellite dish on her skinny body, usually garnished with a skimpy floral display. A tight, old-fashioned button-up blouse with short sleeves to accentuate her long arms, a long plaid or checkered skirt, and clunky high-top shoes finished her ensemble.

Her overall appearance had a feel of L. Frank Baum's Scarecrow of Oz, as if she were put together from odd, mismatching parts. While her

Gale puts on the dog in an unidentified Model Comedy.
Photo courtesy of Jim Kerkhoff.

performing style could be very broad, she also had a gift for small insightful gestures that could bring a moment of pathos and feeling into the knockabout. She was equally adept at being demure or projecting a world-weary cynicism. Gale's time at Nestor and L-Ko comedies was brief, as she left Universal in early 1918. The trade papers soon announced:

> **GALE HENRY FORMS COMPANY.** Gale Henry, who has just returned from a three month vacation, has organized her own producing company and will make a series of comedies such as gained fame and prestige for her during her long engagement with Universal. Miss Henry has rented a space at Diando Studios in Glendale, and under the direction of Bruno J. Becker will immediately begin on her first production. Milburn Moranti, who supported the comedienne in both her Universal and L-Ko productions has been engaged to play the principal male roles in these new comedies.

Billy Franey, Eddie Baker, Phyllis Allen, Hap Ward, and Richard Currier rounded out the regular support and Bruno J. Becker was Gale's husband. Becker had been Allen Curtis' assistant director at Joker and the couple married in 1916. As supervisor of her shorts and general manager of the new company, he appears to have been very much in charge of her career at this point. Her organization was named the Model Comedy Co. and soon had a distribution deal with the Bulls Eye Film Corporation, which had been formed in December of 1918 by Milton C. Cohen with Nat Spitzer in charge of production. Billy West was Bulls Eye's other big name and their other releases included Bulls Eye Master Comedys, the Napoleon and Sally Monkey Shines, and a comic newsreel The Weakly Indigestion.

Gale and company turned out the Models at a hectic pace–at least nineteen were released in 1919. Of the few survivors, *The Detectress* (1919) presents Gale as a detective wannabe who's investigating a Chinatown ganglord's plot to steal the plans for an invention that will enable diners to see what's in the chop suey they are eating. A non-stop chase through the Chinatown maze of trapdoors and secret panels makes up the bulk of this short, but at the end, everything turns out to be Gale's opium-induced dream and she's taken away in the "Nut Wagon."

The Slavey (1919) chronicles Gale's misadventures in work and love as the girl-of-all-trades at a cheap boarding house. Another circulating

Eddie Baker throttles Gale as Hap Ward (right of Baker) looks at a secret message and cop Milburn Moranti reaches for the sky (thug Richard Currier is to his left) in *The Detectress* (1919). Photo courtesy of Jim Kerkhoff.

Model, *Her First Flame* (1919), is set in the future of 1950, where women have taken over and men wear dresses and take care of the children. Gale is running for the office of fire chief and after she wins, loser Phyllis Allen kidnaps Gale's boyfriend, a frilly Milburn Moranti. When Milburn spurns her advances, Phyllis ties him up in a burning house, but Gale saves the day in a frantic last-minute rescue.

For this series, Gale was billed as "The Elongated Comedienne," a very apt description of her appearance as a stick figure brought to life. Although the Models were well-received and their popularity even led to a comic strip featuring Gale, it appears the relationship between Bulls Eye and Gale's company was not smooth. Perhaps due to the grinding production pace or monotony from the sameness of the material, items began to appear about Gale's desire to make a feature "to be put on simply as a test picture; to show what Miss Henry can accomplish in five-reelers and to comply with the wishes of the exhibitors. If the first one is a success, it is possible the comedienne may leave the two-reel class altogether. The story Miss Henry is to make is already prepared, and is a straight human comedy, with thrills, and here and there a touch of pathos." Then in February of 1920, the Moving Picture World announced:

> **COMEDIENNE GALE HENRY IS NO LONGER WITH BULLS EYE.** The Model Comedy Company announces that Gale Henry, comedienne and head of the company, severed connections with the Bulls Eye Film Corporation which has been distributing her releases, and has signed a contract with a prominent distribution company. She will produce only six two-reelers a year, instead of twenty-four a year as heretofore.

A month later, Bulls Eye became part of the merger that formed the Reelcraft Pictures Corp. and although Gale was not making any new comedies for them, Reelcraft continued to distribute her Model shorts on a states' rights basis all through 1920. The period from 1920 to 1922 was an important transition in Gale's career. It appears that she and Bruno J. Becker divorced and that she took some time to examine how she wanted to continue in films. Although many statements were released about her

Director Eddie Cline (lower left) has a less than hypnotic effect on Gale, Victor Potel (standing left), Tully Marshall (right of Gale), and Viola Dana (leaning on camera) on the set of *Along Came Ruth* (1924).

future plans–starring in features or even a new series of twelve shorts for the Special Pictures Corporation–she appears to have decided to work at a more relaxed pace and became an ace supporting player. Her popularity with viewers and dead on comic timing were valuable assets, which put her in demand for features all through the 1920s.The first was *The Hunch* (1921) and she appeared in a total of eighteen. Most memorable were *Open All Night* (1924), where she was teamed with Raymond Griffith, and *Stranded* (1927). In *Stranded*, she gives an excellent performance as a cynical, well-seasoned Hollywood bit-player who takes a young Shirley Mason under her wing and teaches her the ropes of working at the studios. In all of Gale's work in features, she has the air of a no-nonsense veteran who's taking advantage of every second of her screen time to give the audience maximum entertainment.

At the same time, she was making frequent guest appearances in other people's shorts. The costumes and hairstyles may have been fancier, but it was the same old "two-reel Gale" willing to do anything for a laugh. Among others, she worked at Christie with Neal Burns and Jack Duffy and was a human exclamation point in contrast to "Fatty" Alex-

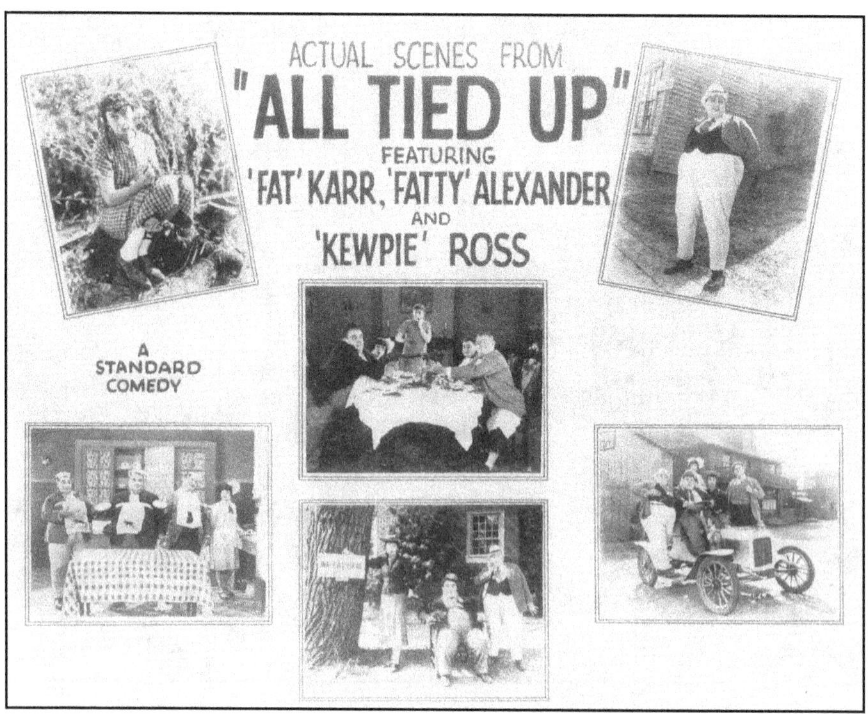

Gale played the landlady to the zeppelin-sized Ton of Fun in their Standard Comedy *All Tied Up* (1925). Photo courtesy of Cole Johnson.

ander, "Fat" Karr, and "Kewpie" Ross's balloon shapes in the Joe Rock produced A Ton of Fun comedies, but her moments of glory came with Charley Chase.

After acting or directing as Charles Parrott for practically every comedy unit in Hollywood, Chase began his starring series for Hal Roach in 1924. Soon, he was teamed with Leo McCarey as director and together they made some of the most sophisticated farces ever put on the screen. Chase had been a director at Bulls Eye and knew that Gale was a perfect foil for him. Out of her many appearances with him, two particularly stand out. In *His Wooden Wedding* (1925), Charley has called off his wedding because his best man has convinced him that the bride has a wooden leg. The best man is after the diamond ring that Charley has given her and later, on a boat cruise, Charley learns the truth and drops the ring down fellow passenger Gale's back to hide it. But Charley has trouble getting it back as Gale is a flirty spinster who thinks that his attempts to retrieve the ring are amorous advances. Finally, Charley takes her to the ship's ballroom, where he goads her into wilder and wilder dances, which causes her make-up, watch, garter belt, and ultimately the ring to fall out on the dance floor.

Charley Chase poses for shutterbug Gale in 1927's *A One Mama Man*.
Photo courtesy of Cole Johnson.

A One Mama Man (1927) has Charley as a European count arriving in America, who, through a series of comedy complications, ends up being hired to impersonate himself at a society party. Gale, who had been a passenger with Charley on his voyage to America and knows that he really is the count, shows up at the party, where he has to keep her from revealing the truth. Luckily, Gale has an affliction, or as a character explains via title card, "Miss Glutz was in a street-car accident–And the sound of a bell always shocks her into a trance!" Of course, Gale's version of a trance has her suddenly freezing on a tilt like the leaning tower of Pisa with her eyes crossed. In a wonderful scene on the dance floor, Charley must repeatedly find new bells to ring to keep Gale from revealing his true identity. Eventually, everyone is happy when they find out who he really is, which leaves Gale to say, "I've been trying to tell you. But there's too many damn bells around this place." Comedy fans are usually familiar with Gale from these appearances as the Chase films are popular and frequently screened today.

When sound took over the film industry, Gale seemed to dive right in, appearing in two features, *The Love Doctor* (1929) and *Darkened Rooms* (1929), plus Charley Chase's first talkie *The Big Squawk* (1929). Her voice was fine and well-suited to her established character, but outside of an occasional role with Chase, she retired from the screen, most likely because she began a new screen profession. After divorcing Bruno J. Becker in the early 1920s, Gale married Henry East, a Hollywood prop man, in 1925. In those days, part of a prop man's duties was to supply dogs if they were needed for a scene. Gale and Henry had adopted a little part bulldog/part terrier named Buddy, who proved to be a film natural. Soon, he was appearing in tons of features and shorts, including many on the Roach lot with pal Charley Chase, such as *What Price Goofy?* (1925), *Mighty Like a Moose* (1926), and *Dog Shy* (1926). Buddy got the couple started in the dog training business, but another dog, Skippy, really put them on the map when he became famous as "Asta" in the Thin Man series, not to mention other big pictures such as *The Awful Truth* (1937) and *Bringing Up Baby* (1938). Eventually, the Easts set up the East Kennels on two acres outside Hollywood and supplied dogs for movies and TV for many years.

Gale's last known appearance is in Charley Chase's 1933 *Luncheon at Twelve* and from there, she literally seems to have "gone to the dogs." Hardly the lovelorn spinster that she often played in films, she had a third marriage to Frederick Ernie Near, a dog trainer nineteen years her junior, and continued to run the dog kennel with ex-husband East. When she died of pneumonia on June 6, 1972, her acting career was sadly over-

Gale, Evelyn Brent, and Neil Hamilton in the early sound feature *Darkened Rooms* (1929). Photo courtesy of Cole Johnson.

looked. Mostly remembered today for her shorts with Chase, it's hoped that more of her Joker and Model Comedies are recovered so that she'll have the opportunity to move from the forgotten category and take her rightful place among the great screen clowns.

Tweedy's Tangled Tale

In the history of silent film comedy, there are many "unknown soldiers"–i.e. once-loved performers, respected directors and producers, invaluable gag writers, etc.–who for whatever reasons have slipped through the cracks into total obscurity. Comedian/animator Charley Bowers is an example of someone who has only recently been rescued from this group, while Stern Brothers comedienne Wanda Wiley and the Danish comedy team of Carl Schenstrom and Harald Madsen (Pat and Patachon) are still neglected. Another whose career is in dire need of re-examination is Marcel Perez.

Marcel Perez presents a selection of the characters that he plays in his 1916 Eagle Comedy *A Busy Night*. Photo courtesy of James Snaden and family.

Perez was one of the earliest European screen clowns and became popular around the world. He came to America in 1915 and worked over here as a comedian, director, and writer until 1927.

Along with Max Linder, he was one of the few direct links between European and American silent comedy. Unforeseeable events brought an abrupt end to his performing career and shortened his life. Today, despite his prolific output and some surviving films, another twist of fate has caused him to be unjustly forgotten.

He was born Manuel Fernandez Perez in Madrid in 1884. He spent most of his youth in Paris and grew up in the theatre, clowning in circuses and music halls. According to a 1916 *Motion Picture News Studio Directory* entry, he was five feet tall, weighed 125 pounds, and started his film career at age 15. That would put his debut in 1900 and while perhaps exaggerated, he did appear in films for Pathé, Eclipse, and Éclair in the early 1900s. Titles and information on these early shorts is practically non-existent, but in 1916, when he was filming *The Near-Sighted Auto Pedist* for Eagle Films, publicity said it was a remake of *The Near-Sighted Cyclist*, a short he made for Eclipse, which was so popular that "his comedies in Europe when he was with the old Eclipse company, sold more prints than Chaplin or any other comedian in the business. Think of selling 950 copies of one picture. That's what they did on the other side with Tweedledum's *Near-Sighted Cyclist*."

Both the Museum of Modern Art and the BFI have copies of the film as *The Short-Sighted Cyclist* (1907) and it's definitely Perez as the bike messenger who loses his glasses and runs into workmen, horse carts, shop displays, and anything else in his path before finally driving off a bridge into the river. Thanks no doubt to its popularity and number of prints sold, it's considered to be one of the earliest surviving Eclipse films. Another survivor from his early days in France is the 1910 Gaumont film *La Police l'an 2000* (*Police in the Year 2000*), about a future police force who travel in a dirigible capturing wrongdoers with long hooks. Perez portrays an apprehended safecracker and spends most of his screen time trying to grab the camera's attention.

At this time, European comedy films were booming and had progressed from the early little one-joke jests or funny incident films to stories where the comedy came from the performance and character of the main actor. Andre Deed may have been the first star, but he was soon followed by Max Linder, Charles Prince, Ferdinando Guillame, and many others. These original screen clowns were anarchic creatures that lived to

Perez during his days as Robinet for the Ambrosio Company.

turn bourgeois society upside-down and practically bounced from scene to scene like rubber balls. Aside from Linder, who had developed his own elegant style, they were pure buffoons with nicknames such as Crettinetti and Foolshead to prove it.

In 1910, Perez joined their ranks as Robinet in a series of one-reelers for the Ambrosio Company of Italy. Starring and directing under the name of Marcel Fabre, the series was a big hit and in 1911, actress Nilde Barracchi joined him as his love interest Robinette in addition to marrying him off-screen. Many of the Robinet films survive and show that Perez had much in common with his fellow Euro-clowns. Like them, he was a small man with a large nose, used the same extravagant gestures and expressions, and shared their sense of surrealism. In *Robinet Boxeur* (1913), he challenges a boxing champ to a match and, after training, becomes a boxing fool. He knocks his punching bag into orbit and when taking a poke at a photo of his opponent, his fist goes through the wall and lambasts his neighbor, who is shaving in the next flat. Drunk with power, he then runs amok in the streets and makes fat men explode, in-

Nilde Baracchi as Robinette.

nocent pedestrians backflip down the sidewalk, and trolleys fly in reverse with the power of his mighty punch.

Many of the surviving comedies center around Robinet's single-minded obsessions, which lead to absurd extremes. In *Robinet inamorato di una chanteuse* (*Robinet in Love with a Cabaret Singer*) (1914) his passion for the titled singer causes him to disrupt the entire show and even stalk her at home. *Robinet Aviatore* (1911) sees him build his own plane and fly it with disastrous results.

Mistaken obsession is the whole theme of *Robinet e geloso* (*Robinet is Jealous*) (1914) where his suspicion that Robinette is cheating on him causes him to follow her to a building to catch her in the act. Unfortunately for him, he keeps bursting into the wrong apartments and is continually beaten and pummeled until he finds that his wife had only commissioned an artist to sculpt a bust of him. Sexual politics also play an active role in the films, such as *Madamigella Robinet* (1912), where to escape being caught by his lover's husband, he dresses in her clothes and poses as a visiting friend. After making his escape, he has to walk home in drag and as a penance, he's chased after by the majority of the older men in town. *Robinet troppo amato da sua moglie* (*Robinet is Too Much Loved by His Wife*) (1912) has his wife driving him crazy with her devoted attentions. Trying to escape her fussing, he meets a cute girl in the park and manages to lock wifey in a closet so he can spend the afternoon with his new sweetie.

In addition to the Robinet comedies, in 1914, Perez embarked on a serialized adaptation of *Le Avventure Straordinarissme di Saturnino Farandola* (*The Extraordinary Adventure of Saturnino Farandola*), a book by Ferdinand Robida that was a parody of the Jules Verne type of adventure epics. Originally told in four episodes, Perez tones down his Robinet persona to play the young hero who (despite being raised by monkeys on a tropical island) is valiant and ever-resourceful in all kinds of fantastic scrapes. The locations include the bottom of the ocean, a mad scientist's laboratory, ancient Asia, an America with hostile Indians, and war dirigibles in the sky. Existing today only in a seventy-eight-minute condensation, there are continuity problems and a bit too much action crammed together, but it's a superb and breathtakingly beautiful film where director Perez keeps his tongue firmly in his cheek. While the scope of the production and sets match many of the epic German films of the teens and '20s, *Farandola* always remains charming and funny.

Perez can even be seen shooting a scene from it in the 1913 Ambrosio film *Cenerentola* (*Cinderella*), which is set at the studio and features

many of their regular staff in the background. But by far, Perez's best-known film from this period is *Amor Pedestre* (1914) (*Love Afoot*), which showcases his sophistication and ingenuity as a director with a clever version of a love triangle soap opera that is performed entirely by the actor's feet. Perez/Fabre became known around the world and is still remembered today in Europe for this series. In America and England, he was called Tweedledum and around one hundred and fifty-seven entries were produced from 1910 to 1915 when Perez embarked to the United States.

Trade journal items state that he left Europe due to the outbreak of World War I. Although records exist of an earlier Perez trip to Mexico and Arizona in 1910, it's not known whether he had specific offers here in 1915 or just took a chance and came. The first American credit that I've located for Perez is as co-director with Allen Curtis on *A Day at Midland Beach*, an October 30, 1915 Universal Joker one-reeler. It also appears that he starred in the film as well, since trade journal descriptions refer to the main character as Tweedledum. His connection with Joker must have been very brief, for in January of 1916, it was announced:

"**BUNGLES IN VIM COMEDY**. Commencing Thursday, February 27, Vim comedies will supersede MinA Comedies on the General Program. Bungles, the leading and most popular comedian in Europe, was forced on account of the war to cancel his contracts in Europe, and judging from his work in Vim comedies (the first of which will be *Bungles Rainy Day*, released on the General program February 10), he promises to soon become as famous and as great a success in this country as he has been abroad—second to none. He plays the leading parts in all his comedies, directs them, and writes his own scenarios. He has made a long contract to appear in Vim comedies." (*Moving Picture World* , January 15, 1916)

Bungles is, of course, "Fernadea Perez, a world famous comedian, recently from Italy, formerly known as 'Tweedledum,' the world famous funmaker," but the long contract turned into only four shorts: *Bungles Rainy Day*, *Bungles Enforces the Law*, *Bungle's Elopement*, and *Bungles Lands A Job*. Vim was formed by Louis Burstein, who later helped form King Bee, in the fall of 1915 and turned out one-reelers at an alarming rate. Mostly known today because of the presence of a young Oliver Hardy in the company, Vim also featured Walter Stull and Bobby Burns as Pokes and Jabbs, the more refined comedies of Harry Myers and Rosemary Theby,

As Bungles for Vim, Perez adopted the Keystone style of facial hair, clearly visible in this rare image from *Bungles Rainy Day* (1916). Photo courtesy of Steve Rydzewski.

Hardy and Billy Ruge as Plump and Runt, and a player roster that also included Raymond McKee, Kate Price, Billy Bletcher, Ethel Burton, and Helen Gilmore.

Pretty blonde Elsie MacLeod was Perez's leading lady with Oliver Hardy in support. None of the Bungles shorts are known to exist, but contemporary reviews were very favorable. Photographs show Perez looking very different than he did as Robinet with a big, bushy moustache and eyebrows. Later items on Perez state that he was very aware of the differences between American and European comedy tastes and spent a great deal of time studying American comedies. At the time of his arrival in the U.S. and employment at Vim, Mack Sennett's Keystone Comedies were the rage and the standard to which other slapstick was compared. It's possible that Bungles' sprouting of facial hair was prompted by the fact that almost all of Sennett's popular clowns wore huge moustaches, goatees, etc.

After the four shorts, Perez moved on. Although fluent in Spanish, Italian, and French, he didn't speak any English on arrival here and later said that he had to direct initially with the help of an interpreter, although he felt much of what he intended was lost in translation. Perhaps the language complications soured his relationship with the company. The Vim

Jacksonville, Florida's Eagle Film Studio in 1916. It later became the Norman Studios and is still standing today. Photo courtesy of James Snaden and family.

films were made in Jacksonville, Florida, which was a beehive of film activity in the teens. Besides Vim, there was Lubin, Jaxon, Gaumont, Klever Komedies, King Bee, and Josh Binney Comedies. All were based or had production companies there.

After leaving Vim, Perez resurfaced three months later in a new series for another Jacksonville concern, the Eagle Film Company, under the supervision of William J. Dunn. Eagle had been formed in Chicago and released through the Unity Sales Corporation on a states' rights basis, which meant that instead of being released on one date nationwide, the films' distribution rights were broken up into different territories and sold individually. For instance, the Merit Film Corp. might start showing a short on Feb. 15 in Northern New Jersey while the Liberty Film Renting Co. might buy the rights for the same short a little later and not start showing it in the Pittsburgh area until June 15. In addition, a states' rights company would sell a series of ten or twelve shorts for the year and usually make half right away. Then they'd complete the rest after a sufficient number of territories had been sold. All of Perez's future starring work would be in states' rights series, which often makes it difficult to pinpoint when an individual comedy was actually first released.

For Eagle, Perez used the name under which he had previously been known in the U.S., Tweedledum, and got rid of the facial hair. Returning to his basic Robinet character, he's a bungler who's always in trouble, but is wily and clever enough to come up with incredible schemes to get himself off the hook. In *Lend Me Your Wife* (1916), he's broke and faces the prospect of marrying his landlady Louise Carver (a fate worse than death) to keep from being evicted. Getting a telegram that says his rich uncle is going to visit and bring him a large chunk of money if he is married, Tweedy makes a deal with a buddy to borrow his wife. The buddy comes along to play their servant, but gets upset with the way the uncle treats him and the way that Tweedy gets too friendly with his wife. Finally, uncle catches the wife and servant together in a compromising situation and the jig is up.

But Tweedy manages to find his own partner before uncle leaves. Perez's wife and old partner from Italy, Nilde Barrachi (renamed Babette Perez), is his co-star in the series as Tweedledee and the stock company includes talented comic character actors on the order of Louise Carver, Tom Murray, Rex Adams, and Billy Slade. Husband and wife Murray and Carver would eventually move to California and become silent comedy regulars.

Besides *Lend Me Your Wife*, at least two other titles survive from the total eleven Eagles he made. *Some Hero* (1916) is a hilarious spoof of seri-

Perez slugs Billy Slade as Louise Carver (left), Rex Adams (below), and Babette Perez stand by in *Torpedoed by Cupid* (1916). Photo courtesy of James Snaden and family.

al cliffhangers that has Babette kidnapped and tortured by a gang of thugs with Tweedy in hot pursuit to save her. Full of wonderful cartoon gags, at one point when Babette is tied up in a basement that's filling up with water, Tweedy drinks all the water and then sprays it out of his mouth like a fire hose to douse the crooks senseless. *A Busy Night* (1916) is a tour-de-force which starts out with Tweedy getting inebriated while out on the town. When he goes home and sleeps it off, he has a nightmare, which is a love triangle melodrama where he plays all the different roles–so he not only makes love to himself, but ends up chasing himself from room to room as lover and irate husband. The special effects are wonderfully realized and are seamless, without a visual hitch or an abrupt change in the lighting when the camera had to have been stopped and then re-started. It's a huge leap from the primitive effects of only three years earlier in *Robinet Boxeur* and looks good even by today's standards.

From the amount of coverage and good reviews in exhibitor magazines, it seems that this series was well-received and popular, but at the end of 1916, Eagle went into bankruptcy. It appears that, for a while, Perez remained in Jacksonville making films, but information on this period is very scant. According to trade magazine items, Perez joined comedian Harry Myers in forming Encore Pictures in January of 1917 and appeared at the Jacksonville Screen Club Ball on February 13, 1917, along with Oliver Hardy and Victor Moore.

The autobiography of the wife of one of his Eagle Films supporting players, Billy Slade, states that Slade was hired again by Perez and he and his family returned to Jacksonville for the series. One of these films may be the Tweedledum comedy entitled *Two of a Kind*, which is listed as a Jockey Comedy and distributed by Unicorn. A distribution corporation formed in the spring of 1916 under the direction of Ike Schlank, Unicorn specialized in "one and two reel subjects, dramas, comedies and westerns, intended primarily to be used by exhibitors to balance feature programs." Unicorn released a few of Chaplin imitator Billy West's early comedies and lasted in the business for about a year. The supporting cast of *Two of a Kind* is made up of Babette Perez, Tom Murray, and Rex Adams, so it appears that Perez may have been able to reassemble some of his Eagle crew after the company's collapse. Hopefully, more items will surface and give the full story.

In 1918 and 1919, Perez starred in a two-year series of Jester Comedies produced by William Steiner and shot in Cliffside, New Jersey with a brief foray to San Antonio, Texas. Steiner, known as "Big Bill," was a longtime independent producer and said in a 1918 *Moving Picture World* interview:

In *The Near-Sighted Auto Pedist* (1916) Perez is in the lead with Billy Slade close behind in the checkered cap on the right. Photo courtesy James Snaden and family.

> Here I have been manufacturing film of every description but comedies for the past twenty-three years. Up to a few months ago if you mentioned the word 'comedy' I felt as if I wanted to fight, but now it is different. The work I find very interesting and to my liking. With Twede-Dan as my comedian I have a 'find.' Not only is he an unusual comedian with a style that is original and all his own, but he possesses a dramatic touch that is not often found in a man doing his class of work.

Steiner released the shorts on a states' rights basis and used what he dubbed the "show you" policy, which was constant screenings of completed comedies for exhibitors to view before they bought the series. Perez and Steiner also altered his screen character's name:

> **TWEDE-DAN IS TWEEDLEDUM.** William "Big Bill" Steiner says the jig is up—he has been caught with the goods—and confesses that Twede-Dan, appearing in Jester Comedies, is none other than Tweedledum of European fame, prominent in the comedy field several years ago appearing in pictures released under Pathé, Eclipse, Eclaire and Ambrosia brands.

Nilde ducks in the nick of time as Twede-Dan comes flying along on a shell in the first Jester Comedy, *The Recruit* (1918). Photo courtesy of Sam Gill.

> Twede-Dan, as he is now known to the American movie-goer, has now been in this country for nearly two years, and has spent the greater part of that time studying the American methods of making pictures and developing a new line of comedy, as shown in the first three Jester releases, "The Recruit," "His Golden Romance" and "All Fur Her." Today we see Tweedledum, alias Twede-Dan, doing things the American way. It was hard at first, but now he is presented as a real American type of actor with a distinctive line of comedy. (*Moving Picture World*, April 13, 1918)

Babette returned as his leading lady, though rechristened Nilde Babette for this series, and for some reason it was decided to tell the press that she had just arrived in America despite the fact that her entry as Nilde Barrachi in the April 12, 1916 *Motion Picture News Studio Directory* has her working with the Eagle Film Co. The April 16, 1918 *Moving Picture World* reported:

> Nilde Babette, appearing as a leading comedienne opposite Twede-Dan in Jester comedies, while a newcomer in America is not new in the film art, as she has appeared in many pictures made in France and Italy, and also acted on the stage in Paris. Miss Babette has only been in this country for a few months, but is fast becoming Americanized, and what little she has seen of America thus far she proclaims as most charming. She has seen a great deal of the war in Europe, and has several brothers in the French army and a number of sisters with the French Red Cross.

The series began in February and in March, Tommy Regan, who had been assistant director with Pathe, Mittenthal, Pokes & Jabbs, and the World Film Company, was engaged as the company's assistant director. In June, William A. Seiter came in to direct the series. Seiter, well-remembered today for his silent comedies with Reginald Denny and Laura LaPlante and many talking films, came to Jester from directing Chaplin imitator Ray Hughes for Pyramid Comedies and would soon move on to direct Mr. & Mrs. Carter De Haven for producer William "Smiling Billy" Parsons at Capitol Comedies. Perez and Seiter would work together again at Universal in 1927. Reviews for the comedies were very good and Stein-

A beautiful shot of Nilde Baracchi (a.k.a. Babette Perez, a.k.a. Nilde Babette, etc. etc.) in a lobby card for 1918's *The Fly Ball*. Photo courtesy of Sam Gill.

er appears to have had great success in selling the series, so much so that in October, he announced that he was adding Jimmy Aubrey and Pearl Sheppard in a new group of comedies. A lobby card has turned up with Jimmy Aubrey in a Jester Comedy entitled *The Fatal Flower*, but it seems that these additions were short-lived and by 1919, it was only Twede-Dan again.

Out of the twenty-five Jester Comedies produced only five are known to exist today. The only two from the first season are the Museum of Modern Art's chunk of *Oh, What a Day* (1918), which chronicles Tweedy and Babette's problems when their car breaks down on the way to a seaside park. When they find they're out of gas, Tweedy uses booze for fuel. The other survivor is the second reel of *Camouflage* (1918) at the Library of Congress, in which Tweedy thinks Babette is a German spy and trails her all over town to a meeting with the Kaiser, which turns out to be a movie being shot. By the second year of the series in 1919, Steiner is calling his production company Territorial Sales Corporation and, while still doing the Jesters, is expanding into features and two-reel westerns. There's much less publicity and reviews for the Twede-Dan's as if Steiner was letting the series run on its own steam while he actively promoted new projects.

There were also changes in the personnel of the shorts. Babette is gone and appears to have returned to Europe. Taking her place as leading lady was the twenty-two-year-old Ithaca, New York girl Esther Elmendorf. Renamed Dorothy Earle, she became Perez's co-star for the remainder of his comedy shorts and married him in real life. An important addition to his supporting stock company was the gigantic, 342-pound Belgian Jean Pierre Pierard. The bald-domed Pierard was not only a former circus performer and wrestler (where he was billed as La Collosse or Pierre Collosse), but also, like Perez, a veteran of early European films for Pathé and Eclipse. It's unknown if he and Perez had known each other in Europe, but La Collosse would remain as Perez's Mack Swain through his Reelcraft shorts. As his large size and shiny head made him a perfect comedy heavy, he also worked for other east coast-based companies such as Vitagraph, Gaumont, Pyramid, and even features on the order of *Manhandled* (1924) with Gloria Swanson. His last known appearance is in the Charley Bowers short *Many A Slip* (1926).

Perez has the opportunity to create havoc behind the scenes at the Jester Studio in the surviving *You're Next* (1919) with Pierre Collasse (left) and Dorothy Earle. Photo courtesy of Cole Johnson.

Three shorts from the second year of Jesters survive. The Library of Congress has *The Tenderfoot* (1919), where Tweedy is out west and in love with a pretty cowgirl. Wildcat Winnie, the unattractive saloon owner, wants him for herself and ties him up in a shed next to a lit keg of dynamite so he has to choose between her or death. This is one of the comedies that had been shot when the company went on a location trip to San Antonio, Texas, in the fall of 1918, when producer William Steiner rented the facilities of Sunset Pictures, and seems to be one of Babette's last appearances. Other shorts made during the Texas trip include *A Mexican Mix-up* (1919) and *The Wisest Fool* (1919). Two other surviving Jesters were made back in New Jersey and are some of the best examples of his American work. *Can You Beat It* (1919) was recently restored by George Eastman House and has Tweedy engaged to fat rich girl Angelica. After trying to put up with her large and annoying family for the sake of the money, he ends up with Angelica's cute maid Ninette.

You're Next (1919) has Perez thrown out of his flat and taking up residence with all his furniture in the street. When cops come and tell

Perez and Flo Bailey on the glass slide for *Can You Beat It?* (1919), a Jester Comedy recently preserved by George Eastman House. Photo courtesy of Ben Model.

him to move, they take pity on him and let him set up housekeeping in the jail. After throwing a wild party there, he's back on the street where he meets Dorothy, herself a victim of lack of rent money. When Dorothy gets hired to act in a movie, Tweedy comes along as general studio gopher and, of course, causes all sorts of problems during shooting. The second reel of this short is set in the Jester Studio and gives a wonderful behind the scenes tour.

The Twede-Dan series ended at the end of 1919, although the finished shorts continued to be distributed into 1920. Instead of jumping to a new series of shorts, Perez embarked on something new–directing features. Although he would seem a natural to direct slapstick features, in 1920, there weren't any. Mabel Normand and Roscoe Arbuckle were the only comics who had jumped from shorts to features and these were polite, situational comedies with a few sight gags used as occasional seasoning. Instead, Perez directed two society dramas that William Steiner was involved in producing for the independent market. *The Way of Women* (1920) and *Luxury* (1921) both starred Rubye de Remer, a former Ziegfeld beauty who had recently entered films. It was during this period that he settled on the name Marcel Perez. He may have thought it sounded a

Dorothy Earle and Perez have picked up an unwanted rider in *Vacation* (1921). Photo courtesy of Cole Johnson.

little fancier for the features and he kept it for the rest of his career. Another event that happened at this time was the birth of a son, Marcel Jr., to him and Dorothy.

As a performer, he was off the screen for almost a year and a half, but on April 9, 1921, the *Moving Picture World* announced:

> **TWEEDY DAN WITH REELCRAFT FILMS.** Tweedy Dan, known on both sides of the Atlantic as a comedian, is to be the star of a new series of two-reel comedies to be distributed by Reelcraft Pictures Corporation. The organization for the series has been completed and the first picture is now being made at the Mittenthal studio in Yonkers.Tweedy Dan was one of the first actors to appear before the camera. He was with Pathé for five years then with Éclair, and later with Ambrosia in Italy, where he was the featured comedian in a series of one-reel comedies distributed throughout the world, and which proved to be very popular. He became director-general of that company and later came to the United States and was featured in a series of Jester Comedies for William Steiner. His efforts have been recently confined to directing, having produced a series of features under the name of Marcel Perez.

Reelcraft was a distribution company that specialized in comedy shorts. It was formed in 1920 when the Bulls Eye Film Co., the Emerald Motion Picture Co., and Bee Hive Film Exchange merged. The president was R.C. Cropper and the company released the films of popular comics such as Alice Howell, Billy West, Gale Henry, and Milburn Moranti. They also handled people completely forgotten today, like William & Gordon Dooley, Frederic J. Ireland, and Billy B. Van, in addition to picking up stray shorts, such as Stan Laurel's *The Lucky Dog* (1921), for distribution.

Twede-Dan was soon shortened to Tweedy and the series was named Mirth Comedies. Perez joined Reelcraft during its last days. The bigger names were gone and most of the product was being made by Schiller Productions. Morris and Julius Schiller produced Perez's Mirth Comedies, plus Aladdin Comedies starring Bud Duncan and Sun-Lite Comedies with Billy Quirk (and a young Jobyna Ralston). Although the Sun-Lites were mostly shot in Florida, the Schiller's base was in Yonkers, NY, and the Mirths and Aladdins were shot there at the old Mittenthal Studio.

Rejoined by Dorothy and Pierre Collasse as support, only a couple of the Mirth comedies are known to exist today. The Library of Congress has a copy of *Sweet Daddy* (1921), which is one of his best surviving films. Tweedy is a henpecked husband whose militant suffragette wife keeps him chained by the neck to the kitchen wall doing dishes. When he tries to stand up for himself, she shoves him out the window and there are hilarious shots of him hanging by his neck out the window three stories up in the air. The wife finally hauls him back in and sends him on an errand to the grocery. On the way, he passes billboards for a musical show and in a charming scene, he imagines that the girl in the photo comes to life, so he flirts with her and gives her a kiss. Continuing on his way, he comes across the real girl from the poster being accosted by a couple of thugs and he helps to rescue her. Smitten, he goes to see her show and afterward, they go to a restaurant together. Tweedy is having a great time eating spaghetti with his sweetie when his wife comes in with two of her suffragette friends and sits at an adjoining table. Tweedy's in a panic but gets a plan. He sends Dorothy out and when she comes back, she's dressed as a nurse and begins wrapping Tweedy in bandages. His alibi is that he's been in an accident. At first, it works as his wife frantically sends for a

Tweedy plays a plumber's helper in his Reelcraft Comedy *Pinched* (1921) with support from Pierre Collasse (left), Dorothy Earle, and Billy Moran (right).

doctor, but soon she catches on and everything hits the fan, which results in a marvelous chase. Tweedy, whose lower half has been wrapped up like a mummy, literally hops through the entire chase, in and out of rooms, up and down stairs, etc. Although it's hard to describe and really needs to be seen, it's quite a feat of acrobatics and is very clever and riotously funny. Finally, Tweedy gets cornered by his wife and the doctor, who grab ends of the bandages to unwrap him. This spins him like a top and at the fade-out, he's been screwed completely into the ground.

The first reel of *Weekend* (1921) also survives and chronicles Tweedy's misadventures when he and Dorothy get invited to a weekend in the country. Besides missing the excursion boat, when Tweedy gets pulled into the water while fishing and crashes over a waterfall, all he has to show for a catch is an old boot. These films show that Perez has continued to refine his comic persona. In *Sweet Daddy*, there's a touch of pathos and wistfulness in his mistreatment by his wife and a lot of charm in the scene where he imagines that the girl on the poster has come to life. At least fifteen Mirth Comedies were made; in addition, Perez directed a number of the Aladdin Comedies, such as *Fireworks*, *Blowing Bubbles*, and *Shot* (all 1921), that featured Billy Moran and Dorothy Earle. Reelcraft ceased production in late fall in 1921. Looking through exhibitor magazines of the time, there's progressively less and less items on the Reelcraft product, then after November, nothing. Finally, an item in the June 17, 1922 *Moving Picture World* reports:

> **BANKRUPTCY INVOLVES REELCRAFT**. New York—An involuntary petition in bankruptcy was filed here on Wednesday June 7, against Reelcraft Picture Corporation, a producing and distribution company with offices at 220 West 42nd Street, on the complaint of three creditors. Nothing in the petition filed disclosed the identity of those connected with the corporation in an official or other capacity, but the complaint alleges the liabilities are $150,000 and the assets $50,000. Judge John C. Knox appointed Max Cedarbaum receiver for the concern with a bond of $2,500.

This was followed on October 28, 1922, with:

> **EXPORT—IMPORT BUYS REELCRAFT**. Export & Import Film Company, Inc., this week announced that it had purchased from the receivers of the Reelcraft Pictures Cor-

> poration all rights, title and interest in negatives in the possession of the latter firm. These negatives embrace 160 in number, including one and two-reel subjects with Billy West, Texas Guinan, Billy Franey, Matty Roubert, George Clarke, and Milburn Moranti comedies.

With Reelcraft out of commission, Perez turns up in the spring of 1922 working for producer F.M. Sanford to direct a series of eight western features starring Pete Morrison and a new group of twelve Tweedy comedies. Unfortunately, neither series was completed. Director Robert Florey, who had arrived in Hollywood in the early 1920s and sent articles about it back to European film journals, said in his 1948 memoir, *Hollywood d'hier et ajjourd'hui*, that Perez had an accident during the making of one of his comedies. While shooting a scene, he fell on an upturned rake. The teeth of the rake sank into his leg and penetrated the bone, resulting in the leg having to be amputated. No press or news items have yet to surface (Perez and company may have kept it quiet), but the accident seems to have occurred at the very end of 1922 or the beginning of 1923. The last item I've found about Perez before a long break in any information is in the November 11, 1922 *Moving Picture World*, which says that he had just

Lobby card for Perez's last starring comedy *Friday 13th* (1923).

finished a new Pete Morrison western. He had completed a total of three Morrison westerns and six Tweedy comedies for Sanford. Some of these titles were in distribution in 1923 while he was recovering. Robert Florey said that the accident impaired his health for the rest of his life.

How he dealt with the blow mentally is anybody's guess, but the evidence suggests that he was eager to get back to work. After an absence of two years, he was back in harness again in the fall of 1925 directing two-reelers for producer Joe Rock.

Rock, born Joseph Simberg, started his career as a member of Vitagraph's "Big V Riot Squad." The squad also included Earle Montgomery, Joe Basil, and Pietro Aramando (a.k.a. Pete Gordon) and its function was to make screen life difficult for Larry Semon, Jimmy Aubrey, and Hughie Mack. Around 1918, Simberg, now redubbed Rock, was teamed with Earle Montgomery in a popular series of stunt comedies. After they separated, Joe produced his own starring shorts for the independent market and a couple of years later more or less retired as a performer to produce series with other comics like Stan Laurel and Jimmy Aubrey. By mid-1925, Rock was concentrating on two series–Standard Comedies, also known as Fat Men Comedies, starring heavyweights Frank "Fatty" Alexander, Hilliard "Fatt" Karr, and William "Kewpie" Ross, and Blue Ribbon Comedies with Alice Ardell, who was billed as "Joe Rock's latest find" and "a young Parisian girl who it is prophesied will be one of the screen sensations of the year."

Perez began directing the Ardell series with its third comedy *Hold Tight* (1925). A gimmick for this series was having a different male comedian play opposite Ardell in each short. So Chester Conklin, Lee Moran, Slim Summerville, Neely Edwards, and Joe Rock himself took turns appearing as well as supplying most of the laughs. Ardell was pretty, athletic, and had a pleasing personality–but wasn't funny. The shorts are funny due to the talents of people like Perez behind the camera and her leading men and supporting comics on screen. Historian Sam Gill opines that Perez may have been brought in to direct the bulk of these comedies because Ardell only spoke French and Perez was fluent in it. Publicity items for the films usually noted that "Tweedy, who is handling the megaphone, was once a comedian" or "This production was directed by Marcel Perez, himself a well-known comedian and better known to film fans as 'Tweedy.'" Surviving entries, such as *Hold Tight* (1925) and *A Peaceful Riot* (1925), show a strong directorial hand. The shorts clip along at a nice pace and there are many large physical comedy set pieces which are directed with snap and precision.

Alice Ardell and Joe Rock in the Perez-directed *Hold Tight* (1925).

It's definite that Perez directed five of the Ardell's and one of the Fat Men Comedies, *The Vulgar Yachtsmen* (1926), but directorial credits are hard to establish on many of the Rock shorts, so it's probable that he worked on more. It's also been reported that he directed some of Rock's 1925 Jimmy Aubrey series. Besides the shorts, he resumed working on independent features, mostly low-budget westerns, such as *Pioneers of the West* (1925) with Dorothy as the female lead and *Lash of the Law* (1926), where he took a final acting role as the heroine's crippled brother. Perez continued to work on the Rock comedies until late 1926 and then entered the last phase of his career. A *Moving Picture World* article from February 5, 1927, lists him in the stable of writers at work on Reginald Denny features and other comedies at Universal.

Despite the frustrating lack of an obituary, it appears that Marcel Perez died at the very end of 1927 or the beginning of 1928. His last known credit was as director on a Universal Charles Puffy one-reeler, *His in Laws*, which was released on March 12, 1928, but had been copyrighted earlier on October 19, 1927. For a description, we have to go back to Robert Florey's memoir. Florey said that he had gone to a hospital to visit actress

Renee Adoree, who was undergoing some kind of abdominal surgery. At the hospital, he found out that Perez was there and had been for six weeks. He was near death and the doctors had kept the seriousness of his condition from him. They talked at length about Charles Prince, Max Linder, Andre Deed, and other friends from Pathé. Florey said Perez died ten days later, alone and ignored.

He wasn't completely ignored, as he had Dorothy and eight year-old Marcel, Jr. By 1930, the two were living in Manhattan, where Dorothy was working as a hotel hostess and living with her mother and aunt. In 1936, she remarried and passed away in 1958 in Los Angeles. Marcel, Jr. died in 1996 at age seventy-five.

But alone and ignored is a good description of how Perez has been treated by posterity. Much of this is due to his constantly changing name and the name of his screen persona as he made his gypsy-like way through the history of early screen comedy. Many film histories refer to Marcel Fabre and his character of Robinet, but few realize that he continued in America as Marcel Perez, Fernandez Perez, or Marcel F. Perez and that the characters of Bungles, Tweedledum, Tweede Dan, and Tweedy were all

Perez and Nilde Baracchi (left) have their version of dinner in an unidentified Jester Comedy. Photo courtesy Cole Johnson.

the same comic. While some of these changes may have been due to legal ownership rights as he moved from company to company, much of this seems to have been a legacy from his early European days.

But the main reason for his neglect is the unavailability of his films. A few of the comedies that he directed for Joe Rock get around and a number of his Italian films have started circulating online, but none of his starring American comedies are readily available to silent comedy fans. Without access to a major archive, that work is impossible to see. Although his output here was prolific, it was done for very small independent companies with dismal survival rates. Over the past few years, a number of the films have turned up and hopefully more will join them and make their way into the hands of comedy fans so they can experience and enjoy his work and unique talents.

Charles Parrott: Comedy's Best-Kept Secret

OVER THE LAST DECADE, Charley Chase has begun to get some of the overdue accolades that he deserves as one of the top onscreen comics, but what about writer, director, songwriter, and comedy supervisor Charles Parrott? For almost a decade, from 1916 to 1924, Charley worked exclusively as a behind-the-scenes comedy creator, spending time at almost every comedy unit that existed at that time and rubbing elbows with practically everyone in the business. Although this period is routinely overlooked, it laid the foundation for the success of the rest of his career.

After years in vaudeville, where he specialized in comic monologues and songs, Charley made his film debut in 1914 with a brief stay at Nestor Films and then soon settled in at the premiere laugh factory of the day–Mack Sennett's Keystone studio. Because his youthful and dapper appearance limited his onscreen roles in the exaggerated Keystone universe, he also began contributing gags and stories in addition to becoming an assistant director. By 1916, he was a full-fledged comedy director helming shorts, such as *A Dash of Courage* (1916), on his own and at this time, he left Sennett to become a veritable silent comedy bee–flying from studio flower to studio flower.

The first place he lit was the newly-formed Foxfilm Comedies unit at the Fox Film Corporation. At the very end of 1916, studio founder William Fox announced his bid to go into competition with comedy outfits such as Keystone and L-Ko and gathered together a staff that included Charley, Walter C. Reed, Harry Edwards, and cowboy Tom Mix as directors, plus performers on the order of Hank Mann, Charles Arling, Frank "Fatty" Alexander, and Caroline Rankin. Charley was initially teamed with fellow Keystone veteran Hank Mann for five shorts, such as *There's*

Au Natural shots of Hank Mann and Charley from the 1916 *Motion Picture Studio Directory and Trade Annual.* Photo courtesy of Steve Rydzewski.

Many A Fool and *His Ticklish Job* (both 1917), and piloted "Heinie" Conklin through three misadventures as well.

The Foxfilm series only lasted for nine months before making way for Henry "Pathé"Lehrman and his Fox Sunshine Comedies. Sadly, only one of Charley's entries in the group is known to exist today, which is a good illustration of why his directorial work is neglected–most of it is lost and unavailable, with the few survivors residing in film archives or the hands of private collectors, making them tricky for the average public to see.

Charley soon resurfaced at King Bee Comedies, which was set up in 1917 by Louis Burstein, Nat Spitzer, and Louis Hiller to showcase the talents of Billy West, the most famous of the Charlie Chaplin imitators. West had spent ten years in vaudeville, where he eventually developed an act called *Is He Charlie Chaplin?*, which featured his version of the Little Tramp. Recruited for films, West made early shorts such as *His Married Life* and *Bombs and Boarders* (both 1916) before headlining at King Bee. With a company that included director Arvid E. Gillstrom and supporting character heavy Oliver Hardy, twenty shorts were made in Florida, New York, New Jersey, and finally Hollywood. In early 1918, Gillstrom left to direct Fox features with Jane and Katherine Lee and Charley was tapped to take over.

Survivors such as *Bright and Early* and *Playmates* (both 1918) show Charley using a fast and furious, anything-for-a-laugh style for the West

Glass slide image of Hank Mann for *There's Many A Fool* (1917).
Photo courtesy of Cole Johnson.

comedies. *Playmates* is notable for its opening, where West, Oliver Hardy, and Myrtle Lind play children on oversized sets that predate Laurel and Hardy's *Brats* (1930), and for Parrott's cameo as a haggard and hallucinating drug addict. Although busy as a director, Charley must have been itching to get in front of the camera again since he almost always turns up in attention-grabbing small bits.

When Billy West had a bout with influenza in the summer of 1918, King Bee folded, so Charley and Oliver Hardy went over to the L-Ko unit to work on a handful of comedies, such as *Business Before Honesty* and *Painless Love* (both 1918), that starred the likes of Harry Gribbon and ex-Fred Karno performer Billy Armstrong. The raging flu epidemic led to a general shutdown of studios in October of 1918 and by the time L-Ko reopened, Charley had another engagement, although the films he made for the company would be sporadically released into 1919.

At the end of 1918, the bulk of the King Bee crew reassembled under the aegis of the Bulls Eye Film Corporation, but their first release, *He's in Again* (1918), appears to have been a leftover from the King Bee days due

Carmen Phillips regards Charley doing a cameo role in the 1917 Fox Comedy *There's Many A Fool*. Photo courtesy of Cole Johnson.

to the presence of Oliver Hardy. Penniless Billy makes numerous attempts to get a drink in a beer garden that's more than a little reminiscent of the one in Chaplin's *A Dog's Life* (1918).

Forced to work out his tab by being a waiter, Billy also fills in for a boxer and dons drag to replace a missing cootchie dancer. Director Parrott keeps the action moving to cover the lack of a real plot here, plus surfaces as the dive's drunken and manic piano player. The first actual short made for Bulls Eye is *A Rolling Stone* (1919), where Billy gets mistaken for Bolshevik leader Leo White and takes his place in jail. The film's funniest scenes depict prison life, such as a visitor's day where the convicts each do a little "specialty number" to entertain their guests. Stanton Heck had replaced Oliver Hardy as the company's chief heavy, but Babe's comic touch is missed as Stanton was big and burly, but not at all funny.

Ship Ahoy (1919) sees Billy living in an extremely seedy seaport boarding house where knife-throwing stage acts practice in the halls and tough jewel thief Stanton Heck kidnaps house slavey Ethlyn Gibson. The most interesting directorial touch is when Billy comes to Ethlyn's rescue in a four-roomed waterfront dive that's a cutaway set which shows all four rooms and the hallways as the characters run from room to room and floor to floor. Probably the apogee and best-known example of this gag appears in Buster Keaton's *The High Sign* (1921), but a version also turns up in Larry Semon's *The Star Boarder* (1919) and all of the above were predated by Fox Sunshine Comedies, where there was a standing set on the backlot used in shorts such as *A Neighbor's Keyhole* (1918).

After a couple more shorts, star West left Bulls Eye and went to the Emerald Motion Picture Company in Chicago. Since Bulls Eye had contracts with distributors and exhibitors to supply Billy West comedies, Charley kept cranking them out, but with second banana Harry Mann standing-in in the little tramp get-up doing his imitation of West's imitation of Chaplin. Mann's imitation was pretty limited and he mostly stood around in the costume, so almost all of the comedy heavy lifting was done by players such as Jimmie Adams, Charles Dorety, Mack Swain, and Monty Banks.

Although weak on the Chaplin imitation, shorts such as *The Flirts, Her First False Hare, Don't Park Here* and *Her Nitro Night* (all 1919) are all solidly crafted comedies that benefit from the talented casts, a zippy pace, and wall-to-wall gags.

1920 was a busy year for Charley with stints at Arrow, Paramount, and Jack White Comedies. His old teammate Hank Mann had recently em-

Harry Mann does his ersatz Billy West with Leo White (left), Beatrice Lovejoy, and burly Stanton Heck (right) in an unidentified Bulls Eye Comedy. Photo Courtesy of Sam Gill.

barked on a series produced by Morris Schlank for distribution through the Arrow Film Corp. and when Hank made the leap from one reel to two, Charley was brought in as part of the unit. According to an item in the *Exhibitors Herald*, the outfit had two working companies, each with its own director, so that when one comedy was completed, Mann would step into a picture that was ready to go with a second director while the first director would cut and edit the just-finished production. This way, they were able to turn out twenty-six two-reelers that year, using a roster of directors that also included Alfred Santell, Herman C. Raymaker, and Tom Gibson. Specific director credits are not available for the individual shorts, but thanks to on-the-set photos that appeared in trade magazines and Charley's penchant for appearing in cameos, two titles have definitely been established as Charley's work. In *Way Out West* (1920), Hank is a tenderfoot in trouble with outlaw Vernon Dent and Charley's baby

Carter De Haven in a scan from the only known surviving print of the Parrott-directed *Hoodooed* (1920). Photo courtesy of Eye Film Institute, Netherlands.

brother James has a major role as the corrupt town sheriff. The other confirmed Parrott title, *When Spirits Move* (1920), concerns Hank thinking he's died and gone to the other place when he sees Vernon Dent and his pals dressed as devils for a masquerade party. This time, Charley outdoes himself in the cameo department, showing up in five different bits as everything from an Italian laborer to a minion of the devil.

From the out-and-out slapstick of this series, Charley moved to the more situational and sophisticated comedy of Mr. and Mrs. Carter De Haven. De Haven had come from the stage and began working in films for Universal. By the late Teens, he and his wife Flora Parker were appearing in their own series for Capitol Comedies before going to Paramount for this series. Although the guiding hand for his shorts, De Haven worked with talented collaborators on the order of Parrott, William Seiter, and Mal St Clair and seems to have made an impression on Parrott that carried over into his later Charley Chase silents. Unfortunately, at the moment, none of the five Parrott-directed De Haven films are available for appraisal.

Finally, Charley rounded out the year with a very brief sojourn at the fledgling Jack White company, where he helmed the Lloyd Hamilton two-reelers *April Fool* (1920) and *Moonshine* (1921). The latter short is a spoof

In *Married to Order* (1920), Babe Hardy and Charley square off as Rosemary Theby tries to effect a peace. Photo courtesy Sam Gill.

of the Hatfield-McCoy type of feud, this time with dueling bootlegger families. The film opens with a race between a doctor in a horse cart and a stork with a baby to see who gets to the cabin first. The infant grows up to be persnickety Lloyd Hamilton, the scion of a family of moonshiners, who waddles his way through the short with his usual aplomb. Although very simpatico, with Charley even later saying that when acting a scene in one of his own comedies, he would say often to himself, "How would Ham play this?," Hamilton and Chase never worked together again.

An addendum to Charley's prolific output of 1920 was the release of *Married to Order*, a King Bee comedy shot in 1918 but picked up and released by Reelcraft two years later. Even more unusual is the fact that Charley stood in for ailing star Billy West and the result is a blueprint for his "Jimmie Jump" comedies to come. Charley's in love with Rosemary Theby, but her stuffy (and nearsighted) father Oliver Hardy can't stand him.

The film details the young couple's misadventures tricking myopic dad and shows that Charley's onscreen chemistry with Oliver Hardy, at its peak in shorts such as *Be Your Age* (1926) and *Fluttering Hearts* (1927), was there from the beginning.

In 1921, Charley stopped freelancing and took up residence at the Hal Roach Studio. Always having excellent radar, Roach must have been well aware of Charley's expertise and track record, plus his brother James had been on the payroll since 1917. Put in charge of the anything-for-a-laugh Snub Pollard series, Charley made good use of his well-developed sense of the absurd and the films took a decided upswing. *The Dumb Bell* (1922) is a good example that spoofs film production, studio bosses, and the temperamental Eric von Stroheim type of directors.

Impressed with his taste and creativity, Roach soon made Charley director-general of the entire studio, where he oversaw all comedy production (except the Harold Lloyd films). As supervisor, one of his most important assignments was the creation of Our Gang. Roach had the idea and gave it to Charley to develop, who put together a top-notch unit that included H.M. Walker, Tom McNamara, and most importantly, a writer he had worked with on the De Haven comedies–Robert F. McGowan. Over the years, Charley would bring a number of colleagues into the Roach studio family, such as Oliver Hardy, Mae Busch, Del Henderson, and his old vaudeville partner Harry Bernard.

When Harold Lloyd left the Roach organization in 1923 to set up his own company, Roach was looking for a new series and decided to give his director-general a shot. Redubbed Charley Chase, he took the

Snub Pollard and friends in the 1922 Parrott-directed Hal Roach two-reeler, *The Old Sea Dog*. Photo courtesy of Jim Kerkhoff.

style that Roach and Lloyd had started–recognizable people in outlandish situations–and built upon it, taking the wild slapstick and sight gags from his Sennett and Snub Pollard films and combining it with the situational comedy and polish of the Carter De Haven films. With this starring series, Charley's performing moved to the forefront, but he never really stopped directing. Like Stan Laurel on the Laurel & Hardy comedies, Charley was the "official unofficial" guiding hand of his starring shorts. In the sound era, he would eventually take credit on his films as Charles Parrott, plus helm occasional one-shot items, such as *The Bargain of the Century* (1933) and *Music in your Hair* (1934).

After his move to the Columbia shorts department in 1937, Charley continued to share his comedic guiding hand. In addition to his starring duties, he directed five Three Stooges shorts, a few with Andy Clyde, and others with Smith & Dale, Johnny Arthur, Tom Kennedy, and Walter Catlett.

With the Stooges, Charley was able to inject a little more charm and innocence to their knockabout and in *Violent is the Word for Curly* (1938) even gave them one of his signature musical numbers, the delightful "*Swingin' the Alphabet*." Always ready to rework tried and true material, *Halfway to Hollywood* (1938) is a remake of his 1929 *Off to Buffalo* about a family's

Portrait of Charley not long after he resumed his performing career as Charley Chase.

doomed attempt to make an elaborate home movie, and his starring short *Teacher's Pest* (1939) is a redo of Snub Pollard's *Teaching the Teacher*, which Charley piloted in 1921. Sadly his early death in 1940 brought a premature end to the career of one of the great renaissance men of film comedy. Hopefully more of his directorial efforts will resurface and spur greater interest and examination of his creativity behind the camera.

Some Job: The Film Career of Fay Tincher

THE STARRING PERFORMERS of silent comedy labored hard to develop distinctive comedy characters that they could play from film to film, which made them instantly recognizable and identifiable to their audiences. While some were able to easily transfer characters that they had already created on stage, others, like Harold Lloyd and Stan Laurel, spent years and many one- and two-reelers crystallizing their screen iconography. After creating and honing a successful cinema personality, most comics would hang on to it for years until either advanced age or career attrition set in.

An exception to this slapstick maxim was comedienne Fay Tincher, who had three different comic personas–Ethel the stenographer, cowgirl Rowdy Ann, and Min Gump–during a film career that lasted less than twenty years. Although she found popular film success very quickly, Fay's desire to move out of the short comedy niche may have stymied the trajectory of her career and kept her from reaching her full comic potential.

She was born in Topeka, Kansas on April 17, 1884, to George W. Tincher and Mary Elizabeth Hartley Tincher. The Tinchers were an affluent family and Fay, the oldest of four daughters, began elocution lessons and appearing in amateur theatricals at an early age. After graduating from Topeka High School, she traveled to Chicago and attended the Ziegfeld Musical College. Following her stay there, she entered show business as a chorus girl in vaudeville and musical comedies in New York and on tour. In 1905, she appeared as a "Sing-Song Girl" in *The Sho-Gun* and soon joined Joe Weber's company where she stayed for a number of years working in shows such as *Dream City*, *Hip! Hip! Hooray!*, and *Twiddle Twaddle*.

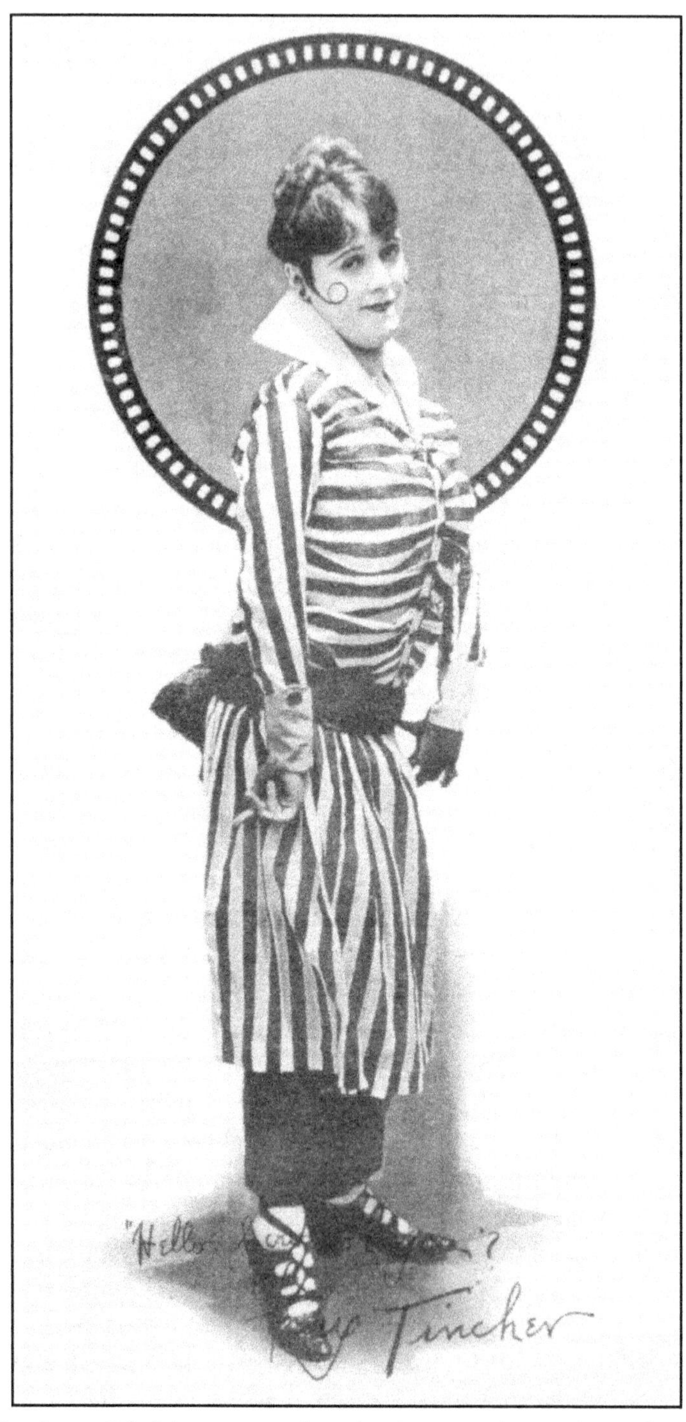

Fay Tincher as Ethel the stenographer, the character that made her famous in the Bill the Office Boy Comedies.

She got a lot of publicity in 1908 due to an odd incident where she went through a joke wedding with performer Ned Buckley on a dare, which may have been conducted by an actual civil servant and therefore legal. Many newspapers covered the story and quoted an upset Fay:

> Miss Fay Tincher, or Mrs. Edward Buckley, of *The Merry Go Round* company, does not know whether she is married or not. The young woman went with the company to Boston on the 5 o'clock boat yesterday. She was booked as Miss Tincher, but she said tearfully she feared she married Ned Buckley on a dare last week.
>
> "Not that Ned would not make desirable husband for any girl who wished to marry," said Fay. "He's a good fellow, a graduate of Yale, I'm told. He lives at Bridgeport, has a country home at Fairfield, no end of money and spends it generously. But I do not want to marry him nor any man."

1906 portrait of Fay as a chorus girl.

Fay also said that she told her lawyer Nathan G. Goldberger, "for gracious sake to learn if I am married, and if I am to get me a divorce right away." Mr. Goldberger admitted that he was confused on the issue, but sadly, the newspapers didn't seem to bother to cover the outcome.

Perhaps to recover from this experience, she went for an extended stay in Europe and the British Isles, but on her return, she was back onstage in the vaudeville sketch *The Dance Dream* and during the next few years, appeared with Joe Weber, Lew Fields, William Collier, Lillian Russell, and Fay Templeton in the shows *Weber & Fields Jubilee, Hokey-Pokey*, and *Bunty Pulls the Strings*.

Her film debut occurred on the east coast and the accepted version is that she was discovered by D.W. Griffith with her first film, his feature *The Battle of the Sexes* (1914). She had actually begun in 1913 in a few American Éclair shorts that were shot in New Jersey and distributed by Universal. Of course, the Griffith story sounded better, so Fay stuck with that and passed it along to interviewers. Griffith had just left the Biograph Studio and was now working for Harry Aitken's Reliance/Majestic organization, where he was directing inexpensive four- or five-reel features while he planned a "super production" that eventually became *The Birth of a Nation* (1915). *The Battle of the Sexes* was his first for Aitken and Fay was cast as Cleo, a vamp who lures a middle-aged man away from his family (this role was played by Phyllis Haver in Griffith's own 1928 remake). Although reportedly referred to as a "pot-boiler" by the director, *Sexes* made money and Fay joined the Reliance company, having small bits in Griffith's next two features, *Home Sweet Home* and *The Escape* (both 1914), plus appearing in one-reel dramas like *Too Proud to Beg* (January 31, 1914). In January of 1914, the company moved to California and soon:

"It was after I came west with the company that I started the black and white color scheme. I was the telephone girl in the Ethel and Bill series. Mr. Griffith said I looked like Mabel Normand and could do the broad comedy."

Fay became part of a Griffith-supervised unit making one-reel shorts under the brand name Komic Comedies. Like his features, these shorts were distributed by Mutual. The Komics were directed by Edward Dillon, who was also part of the regular acting ensemble along with Tod Browning, Max Davidson, Tammany Young, Elmer Booth, Joseph "Baldy" Belmont, and Chester Whithey. A later addition to the group was fourteen-year-old Bobby Feuhrer. Feuhrer, previously "Universal Ike Jr.," later changed his name to Bobby Ray and is best known for his starring comedies for Arrow and Rayart. Many of the Komic scripts were written by Anita Loos and the company maintained a hectic output of one release a week.

A few months after the unit was up and running, they acquired the screen rights to the *Bill the Office Boy* stories by Paul West. The Bill comedies were an instant success and appeared every other week on the Komic schedule. Tammany Young, later W.C. Field's flunky in *The Old Fashioned Way* and *It's A Gift* (both 1934), played Bill, the street-wise office boy with a knack for fouling up his co-workers plans. Fay co-starred as Ethel the office stenographer and became wildly popular.

The character was a gum-chewing, no nonsense working girl that was always scheming how to get more money from her boss or find a rich millionaire to marry. What immediately grabbed the audience's attention was the character's eccentric style of dress. Fay said, "My part wasn't very big and I wanted to make it stand out." Ethel was outfitted completely in black and white with loud garish stripes that made her look like a human zebra. Claiming that she designed all of Ethel's dresses herself, Fay said that she took her inspiration from Griffith's statement, "She's just a plain black and white type, always photographs as you see her," and ran with it. The addition of large spit curls and the continual gum-chewing got Fay

Fay, "Fatty" Crane (center) and Tammany Young (right) in the 1914 Bill the Office Boy Comedy *Bill Goes into Business for Himself.* Photo courtesy of Billy Rose Theatre Division, The Library for the Performing Arts, Astor, Lenox and Tilden Foundations.

the attention she desired. A typical 1914 review from the *Chicago Herald* reported:

"Miss Tincher's burlesquing of the young women who take dictation as a means of livelihood has probably stirred considerable feminine indignation, but it must be admitted that she has a genuine talent as a photoplay funmaker, and may probably be considered the dominant attraction in the *Famous Bill Series*."

Today only a handful of the shorts are known to exist. The funny *Ethel's Roof Party* (November 8, 1915) seems pretty representative of the series and has Ethel inviting her rich fiancée and his swanky friends to an open-air lunch on the office building's roof. Having been told that he's not invited under any circumstances, Bill gets his revenge by locking the only door and trapping Ethel and her guests on the roof. After much panic and a rescue by the fire department, Ethel's put-on airs are deflated and she finds out that not only is her rich beau ("Baldy" Belmont) a coward, but that he wears a toupee to boot!

In addition to the Bill series and one-shot Komics, the studio occasionally starred Fay in two-reel "specials." *The Love Pirate* (January 30, 1915), a drama about a selfish woman who allows men to ruin themselves for her,

Elmer Booth gives Fay a hug in the Komic Comedy *Where Breezes Blow* (1915). Photo courtesy of Robert S. Birchard.

garnered good reviews for Fay and gave her the opportunity to work with Raoul Walsh and Elmer Clifton. *Music Hath Charms* (February 14, 1915) teamed her with former "Alkali Ike" Augustus Carney in a comedy about rival musicians fighting over a girl. By this time, Carney's stardom had waned and he'd already left Essanay and Universal with a reputation for being "difficult." Sadly, this short was just a brief stop on his road to obscurity.

The Bill series came to an end in May of 1915. She continued starring in Komics and had become so well-known that her screen characters were now usually just named Fay. Her last Komic was *Over and Back* (September 5, 1915). At some point, Reliance/Majestic became known as the Fine Arts Company and the physical studio itself was a ragtag collection of open-air stages and wooden sheds (later an early home of Jack White Comedies) located at 4500 Sunset Boulevard in Hollywood.

In 1916, Harry Aitken merged Griffith's Fine Arts Studio with Mack Sennett's Keystone and the companies of Thomas Ince, forming the Triangle Film Corporation. The creation of Triangle was really for strength in distribution as the studios remained separate and maintained their own production schedules. Another of Aitken's schemes was the bringing of established stage stars to Hollywood to "legitimize," and hopefully give class to, the Triangle product. From the many theatre people that Aitken tapped, Mack Sennett ended up with Raymond Hitchcock, William Collier, and Weber & Fields and Griffith got Sir Herbert Beerbohn Tree, Douglas Fairbanks, and DeWolf Hopper.

DeWolf Hopper had been a star since 1890 and was not only one of the most popular and busiest comic-opera comedians of his day, but also famous for his recitation of "*Casey at the Bat*." When the immensely tall Hopper arrived in Hollywood, petite (5'2") Fay was chosen to be his comic foil and supported him in three features–*Don Quixote*, *Sunshine Dad*, and *Mr. Goode, the Samaritan* (all 1916). These features gathered quite a bit of publicity, favorable reviews, and good notices for Fay:

"Fay Tincher as Dulcinea will surprise her most ardent admirers. She plays with real humor and she is responsive for no small amount of the comedy" (*Hartford Daily Currant*, March 10, 1916).

"For Dulcinea herself, I have nothing but praise; Fay Tincher's performance is little short of wonderful. All things considered, she surpasses Hopper. A young woman who can do this sort of thing deserves stardom" (*Photoplay*, March 1916).

But Hopper himself didn't click with movie audiences and after a couple of other pictures, he returned to the stage. His lasting contribution

Eddie Dillon (center) and Fay are up to something in *Mr. Goode, the Samaritan* (1916), one of DeWolf Hopper's starring features for Fine Arts/Triangle.

to Hollywood was his then wife Hedda Hopper, who stayed on as a bit actress and eventually became the infamous gossip queen of the 1930s, '40s, and '50s.

After her association with Hopper, Fay was then put into her own starring series of shorts. The May 20, 1916 *Motion Picture News* announced that Triangle was going to start producing two-reel subjects and then describes the two inaugural efforts, the first being Doug Fairbanks in *The Mystery of the Leaping Fish* (1916) and:

"The second two-reel subject is that which will star Fay Tincher. She will be remembered as having characterized the stenographer in the one-reel Komic brand made at this studio, and will have the support of Max Davidson, Jack Cosgrove, and Edward Dillon, who will also direct the production. Miss Tincher plays the part of an unusually fresh sales girl."

Edward (Eddie) Dillon, while almost completely forgotten today, was an important player in Tincher's career as the director of the films that made her famous. Dillon's early years were spent as a jockey, after which he became a comedy juvenile and worked on stage with Otis Skinner, Dustin Farnum, and Rose Melville (in her monster comedy hit *Sis*

Hopkins). He made his film debut for Bison, then arrived at Biograph in 1908 and appeared in all types of films directed by Griffith and the other staff directors. As time went on, he gravitated to their comedy films and became a stock member in the films directed by Mack Sennett and Del Henderson. When Sennett left to start Keystone, Biograph gave Dillon his own comedy unit and he directed many shorts that starred Charlie Murray, such as *A Barber Cure* and *In the Hands of the Black Hand* (both 1913). Eventually, D.W. Griffith broke with Biograph and took most of the company, including Dillon, with him to Reliance/Majestic. During his time with Reliance/Majestic and later Fine Arts, Eddie continued acting and directed the Komic shorts, plus Fay's films with DeWolf Hopper and other features starring Bessie Love. Later, after his association with Griffith, his work became more routine and by the early 1920s, his films were

Edward (Eddie) Dillon in a Biograph Studios publicity portrait.

basically programmers with minor stars like George Walsh and Elaine Hammerstein. His last feature was *The Dice Woman* in 1927, but he continued to turn up in character roles. In early talkies, he appeared in quite a few Hal Roach comedies, like *Looser Than Loose* (1930) and *Young Ironsides* (1932), which, in a way, brought his career full circle before his death from a heart attack in 1933.

Dillon was put in charge of Fay's Triangle Komedy series and while many of her former Komic compatriots were no longer available–Tod Browning and Chester Whithey had moved on to writing and directing, Elmer Booth had been killed in an auto accident–Max Davidson was still on hand for regular support and Anita Loos supplied most of the scripts. Only a chunk of the first one, *The Two O'Clock Train* (May 28, 1916), is known to exist at the moment and has Fay portraying a brash shop girl, while trade magazine descriptions suggest that the overall series provided a wide range of characters for her–a lady drummer, a country maid with ambitions to be a big city vampire, and a headstrong socialite. The unifying link in these roles was Fay's no-nonsense demeanor and feistiness, which were in comic contrast to her tiny stature. A good illustration of this is a poem contributed by a fan, Mary E. Rouse of Chicago, to the December 19, 1916 issue of *Motion Picture Magazine*:

> When she's on the screen it's a cinch her
> Smile will compel you to clinch her,
> She's huggable, quite
> But look out for her right,
> She's there with the punch is Fay Tincher.

Surviving footage, clippings, and photos show that while Fay got rid of Ethel's spit curls and gum-chewing, she kept the black and white costume motif as her trademark. She toned it down a bit, using less garish stripes and more solids, say a black top and skirt adorned with a white collar and bow with striped stockings and black shoes as the final touch or a black and white striped dress with a black bow and belt. Even disguised as a man in the crook comedy *Skirts*, Fay kept it up by using a black and white checkered cap, etc.

Because Fay's Triangle Komedys were lumped together with the Keystones on the Triangle release schedule, it's led to some modern confusion that Mack Sennett may have been involved in their production, but all of her shorts were produced and made by Fine Arts. The series seems

A behind the scenes shot at the Fine Arts Studio of Fay in male attire for her comedy *Skirts* (1916). Photo courtesy of Billy Rose Theatre Division, The New York Public Library for the Performing Arts, Astor, Lenox and Tilden Foundations.

to have come to an end by December of 1916, when it was announced that Anita Loos would be writing the titles for the upcoming Douglas Fairbanks films. Years later, in her 1977 book *Cast of Thousands*, Loos reminisced about Fay with a little statement that not only casts aspersions on her acting talent, but also drops a personal bombshell:

> The heroines of many of my half-reel farces were played by Fay Tincher, who has been long forgotten. Ideal for those rowdy scripts, Fay required no acting ability. Let's say she had the pert allure of a "Patsy" and could be a provocative target for slapstick. Fay was anything but a sex symbol, and—in those days before lesbians came out of the closet—her fans never dreamed that their rambunctious little idol harbored a preference for g-i-r-ls!"

Many of the statements that Loos made late in life have to be taken with a grain of salt (sometimes the size of a salt block), as she was prone to taking potshots at colleagues who were no longer around to defend themselves. There is a hint of corroborating evidence in the 1920 US Census, where Fay's living with Maie B. Havey, who's listed as her "partner." Havey was a screenwriter involved in Fay's company for World Pictures, where she's credited for the scenario of *Oh, Susie, Behave* (1918), so the use of the term most likely refers to business partner and not "significant other." The US City Directories for Los Angeles show that the pair lived together for at least four years (1918—1921), but whether these prove Loos' statement was really true or not is anybody's guess and I'm sure Fay would agree that it's none of our business anyway.

Actually, very little is known about Fay's private life except that she was single (or possibly divorced, depending on the outcome of the 1908 incident with Ned Buckley). She appears to have been very athletic, as numerous items have surfaced about her spending all her spare time at beaches and winning local swimming and diving competitions. *The Buffalo Times* added:

"She is an ardent 'fight fan." In California, where the Komic-Mutual studios are located, women attend fights as they do in Paris and London, and she also enjoys baseball and aeroplaning."

She seems to have had a bit of an issue concerning her age. Although she looked young, Fay was born in 1884 and was already twenty-nine when she entered films in 1913 after her years on stage. Later, in a 1918 article, she gives her age as twenty-three (try thirty-four) and the 1920 U.S. Census gives her estimated age and birthdate (estimated from info supplied by Fay, of course) as twenty-nine and 1890. While it's normal for actresses and actors to shave a couple of years off their ages, Fay was routinely pulling a sleight of hand with practically a decade.

Triangle had been rife with problems, organizational and financial, almost since its creation. The three producers decided to withdraw and Griffith bailed first on March 11, 1917. He immediately signed a contract with Adolph Zukor at Artcraft Pictures and went on his way. This also marked the end of Fay's association with Griffith. Fay was the wrong physical type and too old to be one of his heroines and, although he was instrumental in getting her film career started, once Griffith decided that her true talents lay in comedy, he lost interest in her. Never caring about comedy, he had more or less done the same thing with Mack Sennett, Mabel Normand, Max Davidson, and Douglas Fairbanks–and was happy to let them develop elsewhere.

Photo courtesy of Robert Costello.

There's also more than a hint of dissatisfaction on Fay's part. After the three DeWolf Hopper features, Triangle talked of a dramatic feature where:

"Fay Tincher takes the part of an artist's model, who is the victim of drugs. The play is laid in a modern atmosphere and deals prominently with an artist, which part is taken by Tully Marshall."

When this ended up being made as *The Devil's Needle* (1916) with Norma Talmadge playing the artist's model, Fay clearly didn't relish returning to the two-reel ranks and there's an underlying tone of frustration about the development of her career in this statement to *Theatre Magazine*:

> I started out in life—screen life, of course, as a vampire. I played a heavy role in "Battle of the Sexes," and then, after that, I started playing comedy roles. In "Don Quixote" I was featured with DeWolf Hopper, and later in other Fine Arts productions, "Sunshine Dad" and "Mr. Good." I hoped to again play "heavies" or even genre leads, but my reputation as a comedienne always caught up with me and forced me to play in two-reel funnycisms.

At any rate, she went out on her own and resurfaced more than a year later in 1918 with the announcement of:

"**FASCINATING FAY TINCHER COMEDIES**. Fay Tincher, comedienne, and for a year and a half the head of her own company, is the latest addition to the World Film Corporation staff, according to the official announcement from World Film Offices."

World Film began as an importer of foreign-made features that in 1914 was bought by a group that included Lewis Selznick of Equitable Pictures, William A. Brady of Shubert Pictures, and Jules Brulator's Peerless Pictures. World became the releasing umbrella for all their films with production centered in Fort Lee, New Jersey and a talent roster made up of Clara KimballYoung, Alice Brady, Marie Dressler, Lew Fields, director Maurice Tourneur, and writer Frances Marion. Selznick later bought out World in 1919 and absorbed it into his own company.

Fay set to work in early 1918 making shorts under the direction of Al Santell. Although never making it to the top ranks, Alfred Santell (1895—1981) had a long and varied film career. He began as a scenario writer at Keystone, then switched to American, where he began directing Kolb and Dill in 1916. Before working with Fay, he directed at Kalem and afterward moved on to Smiling Billy Parson's Capital Comedies, Universal, and the

Fay's first release for her own company, *Main 1-2-3* (1918), saw her continuing to play the poor working girl.

Hallroom Boys. In the 1920s, he graduated to features, making dramas as well as comedies, and while most of his pictures were lower budget items, Santell continued working into the mid-1940s. In an unpublished 1970s interview, Santell had this to say about the creation of this series:

"I also tried to start a series with a girl named Fay Tincher who was a former D.W. Griffith comedienne and a man, a very wealthy man, M.D. Smith, who at the time owned practically all of the tug boats around Virginia, Norfolk, and so forth, and he fell for Fay Tincher in a romantic way and financed a picture."

Fay's first two World comedies, *Main 1-2-3* and *Some Job*, were shot on the East Coast and then the unit moved to California. World leased the Willis and Inglis Studio on Fleming Street, which had previously been Kalem's Hollywood studio, and the rest of the series was made where Santell had directed Lloyd Hamilton and Bud Duncan in Ham and Bud comedies just a couple of years before. Today, the site is the KCET television studio. Fay maintained her two-toned color scheme and while it's uncertain exactly how many comedies she made for World, as none are known to exist and I've only found material on three, surviving reviews give a hint of their style and reception:

> *Main 1-2-3* signalizes the return of Fay Tincher to the silver-sheet after a too-long absence. We have to thank World for giving back to us a really original comedienne. True, in her absence from our midst Fay of the stripes has somewhat gained weight; in fact, the more we see of pictures the more we realize that, if food is scarce in some places, it most assuredly is not where the heroines of the silent drama abide. However, Fay has also gained weight in our opinion, for her production of "*Main 1-2-3*." It is the first time in our knowledge that the comedy of the crossed wires has been screened, and it is admirably done. The main idea, also, that of the little waif who has no home and gets a job in a furniture store so that she may live in the completely furnished flat in the window, is deliciously original. It is all good stuff, and we wish to extend to Fay a right royal welcome of approval." (*Motion Picture*, September, 1918)

> On July 22 Fay Tincher will be seen in *Oh, Susie, Behave*. In the latter attraction Miss Tincher is seen in the role of Susie Snipp, who works for five dollars a day as an errand girl in a modish little hat shop. She has but one ambition, to become a saleslady, and her efforts in this direction are said to furnish Miss Tincher with ample opportunity to display her abilities as a comedienne. (*Motion Picture News*, July 6, 1918)

> *Some Job* in which Fay Tincher appears in the leading role, far surpasses her first comedy released by World Film. She plays the part of a waitress in a small-town hotel who discovers a very nice captain in a nearby camp on which to shower her affections. Incidentally she succeeds in rounding up some Ger-

> man spies. The humor introduced is both the polite variety which introduces funny situations and of the gag variety in which Miss Tincher exercises her fine art of being tough. The better part of the picture is clever in both respects. A particularly funny touch is scored when the captain after fleeing mess because of more beans, gets a dish of them planted in front of him when he sits down at the hotel table. There are touches that equal this, throughout the two reels, another when the captain gives the order "column right" and then, forgetting the men for the girl, comes to find them marching out in the ocean. The spy stuff is done seriously and Miss Tincher also does a dramatic scene when she bids the captain goodbye." (*Motion Picture News*, June 29, 1918)

But despite these and other warm welcomes back in the press–"Fay Tincher is a capable young miss who does all things on the screen with neatness and dispatch, from catching a burglar to darning her stockings. Fay was among the early movie comedians and after a protracted absence she returns in comedies that are being well received."–her stay with World was brief. Al Santell remembered:

> Well, I knew that this thing was not going to work out. As a matter of fact the deal had been set up by my agents and I told them in all honesty that I did not think that Fay Tincher at her age and her sort of ancient style which she used would go in modern comedies. So I advised him not to make the picture and he said well, I'll take your advice only I want to make the picture. I promised Fay that I would make it, so if you don't make it somebody else will, so you might as well make the money. Well, I said, all right Mr. Smith, you want me to make it I'll make it but remember I'm telling you I think it's a lost cause. Well, it turned out to be a lost cause—he never did get a release for a series of pictures, no one went for the first picture.

Although not entirely accurate, as at least three shorts were made and were distributed by World, it may be that exhibitors were looking for more "modern" comedies than Fay was offering.

In addition, surviving articles and comments by Fay suggest that she may have agreed to appear in the shorts with the understanding that they

Fay Tincher

would lead to starring features and it appears that when this didn't happen, Fay moved on. Comedy shorts, while loved by audiences, were treated as poor stepchildren by the industry and if a performer wanted to be taken seriously, they had to aspire to features. Another possible factor in the curtailing of this series may have been the deadly influenza epidemic that was sweeping the country in the fall of 1918, which temporarily shut down many studios and cinemas and took the life of Mack Sennett comedian Wayland Trask.

World had publicized Fay as "the pocket-sized comedienne" and stated that she was in charge of her unit:

"Miss Tincher writes her own stories (in self defense, as she puts it), chooses her own cast and directs her own pictures."

While some of this may be studio hype, she did receive script credit on *Main 1-2-3* and had definite ideas on the type of comedy that she wanted to perform. These are expressed, along with her attitude regarding shorts, in an interview with Grace Lee Mack for the *Photo-Play Journal*, where she recoiled after being asked if her World comedies will be of the "custard pie variety" and says:

> I shall strive to them—the laughs I mean, legitimately or not at all. Of course comedy drama is my aim, that is about what my first two pictures are—two-reel comedies with a little drama, a laugh followed by a tear perhaps, and capped with a laugh. If I can make the people at home and the boys from over there a little happier because of my comedies, I shall be satisfied. Later, I expect to do five reel comedy dramas, that is if we can find the right kind of stories, but believe me, it is some job.

She next turns up in March of 1919 in the Rupert Julian directed *The Fire Flingers* for Universal. Hopefully, she was more satisfied with this, as it was a seven-reel dramatic feature. Fay played a stenographer set to run off with her cheating boss and basically seems to have reprised her role from *Battle of the Sexes*. At the time, she offered her views of movie sirens to the *Chicago Tribune*:

"It's my opinion the Bara-like vamp has never existed any place but in the cinema. The saucy vamp is the only real kind. What man is fooled by a dead white skin, grotesque lips, and a posed grace that is anything but attractive. It is a vamp with a sense of humor who can really hold a man."

Not long after *The Fire Flingers* hit the theatres, the press announced:

"Fay Tincher, she of the black and white stripes and spit curls of the once famous Griffith comedies, is with us again but minus the stripes and curls. She is Al Christie's new star and the veteran comedy producer is directing her personally. Miss Tincher's vehicles will be two reels much similar to those that made her famous in the old days."

Today, Al Christie, like fellow producer Jack White, is overshadowed by the legends of Mack Sennett and Hal Roach, but Christie was one of the founding fathers of film comedy. Born in London, Ontario in 1879, he began his career as a stage manager of his hometown London Opera House and later stage-managed for various companies, which eventually brought him to New York. In 1909, he became a director of David Horsley's Nestor Film Company and had his first success in the east with a live-action *Mutt and Jeff* series. Nestor and Christie moved to Hollywood (corner of Sunset and Gower) in 1911, where they made one-reelers that were distributed by Universal. Eddie Lyons and Lee Moran soon became a popular team under Al's direction, but in 1916, he severed his connection

Fay ready to put Laura LaPlante (left of Fay) and the other girls through their paces in the 1919 Christie Comedy *Wild and Western*. Photo courtesy of Cole Johnson.

to Universal and, with his brother Charles, produced comedies under his own name for the independent market, plus Strand Comedies for Mutual. In the 1920s, he distributed his films first through Educational, then Paramount and his stars, like Bobby Vernon, Dorothy Devore, Neal Burns, and Jimmie Adams, were some of the most popular of the day.

When Fay signed with Christie in 1919, the arrangement was beneficial for both of them. Christie was able to use Fay's proven popularity to mount a move from one-reelers to "two reel specials." And for Fay, as Christie himself directed her initial films, she got personal attention and a big build-up from one of the biggest comedy producers of the silent era. After her first Christie short, *Sally's Blighted Career* (April 24, 1919), a new persona was devised for Fay and, perhaps due to the success of Polly Moran as Sheriff Nell, it was that of a wild and western cowgirl with shorts like *Dangerous Nan McGrew*, *Wild and Western*, and *Go West Young Woman* (all 1919) built around it.

Rowdy Ann (May 25, 1919) is today the most accessible of Fay's comedies and is a little gem about a quick-drawing western tomboy who's sent east to a finishing school by her rancher father "for to larn to be a lady." Of

Patricia Palmer, Katherine Lewis, and Marguerite Payne make Fay less than welcome in *Rowdy Ann* (1919). Photo courtesy of Cole Johnson.

course, this rough-and-ready girl gives everyone at her girl's school a run for their money, but after Ann prevents one of her roommates from marrying a crook, she's a hero. Playing this character to the hilt, Fay strides around completely cock-sure, sizing everyone up while she stands with her legs apart and hands on hips. Her small size is in comic contrast to the character's bravado and tenacity and outfitted in a checkered flannel shirt, cowboy hat, boots, chaps, and oversized gun belt, she looks much like a little kid playing cowboy. Christie was fond of using cross-dressing as a comic device, producing two versions of *Charley's Aunt*, and where this produces funny scenes, such as Ann putting on the flowing gown that she's required to wear for her classical dancing class, but adding her cowboy hat, boots, and gun belt to it, the juxtapositions also challenge conventional notions of femininity.

Fay got quite a physical workout in this role, galloping on horses, throwing lassos and many punches. She even takes a few knocks in a boxing match with ranch hand Al Haynes early in the film. Christie had a reputation for producing more sophisticated and polite comedies than the usual run of slapstick shorts, but at the time Fay joined him, he was adding more physical comedy while trying to retain the better developed story elements. Fay's sojourn with Christie turned out to be another brief stay–about nine months. A 1919 *Photoplay* article, titled *Is Polite Comedy Polite? Asks Fay Tincher*, gives us a good explanation why. The beginning of the piece presents Fay's initial excitement of working for Christie:

"I'm tickled to death! I'm going back into comedy—society comedies, too, if you please. You know Christie Comedies, don't you? They're nice refined little human dramas. They don't throw pies, they don't get you all mussed up, you know, real high-class stuff. These are going to be my special two-reel comedies."

But the rest of the article chronicles how these expectations are flattened as she amasses bumps and bruises doing the stunts for these "polite" comedies. While the story presents all these events with a "humorous" tone, it appears that Fay didn't find the experience funny and became disenchanted with the series.

In 1920, she had stopped making the western comedies and only appeared in three more shorts for Christie–*A Seaside Siren*, *Striking Models*, and *Dining Room, Kitchen and Sink*. Despite this fact, she still shows up prominently in Christie publicity ads into mid-1921 and went on a personal appearance tour with one of the earlier shorts, where she "delivered a monologue in which she told of her studio experiences and the manner

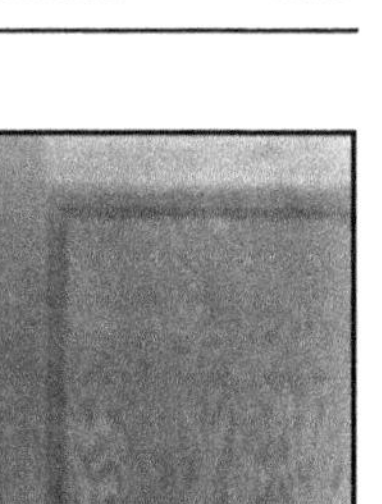

Donald Keith, Eddie Barry, and Fay in *Dining Room, Kitchen and Sink* (1920).

in which Christie comedies are made." This gives the impression that a deal was worked out where Fay finished out her contract by drumming up publicity for the Christie product.

After this, Fay didn't return to the screen until 1923 and had been off camera for two years. By the early 1920s, tastes had changed. The heyday of the female slapstick clowns had been in the Teens, when Fay, Alice Howell, Louise Fazenda, Gale Henry, Polly Moran, etc., all emerged and had their own starring series. In the early 1920s, the mode had changed to leading ladies (Dorothy Devore, Alice Day, Wanda Wiley) who could perform physical comedy and all the more eccentric women had to find new venues–Louise Fazenda, Gale Henry, and Polly Moran migrated to character roles in features, Alice Howell retired and Fay found refuge at Universal. On November 24, 1922, the *Toledo Blade* reported:

"Fay Tincher, 'the striped girl,' who has been in retirement for the last few years, has been engaged to support Lewis Sargent in some of his Messenger Boy stories, under the direction of Scott Darling."

Although she's not known to have actually appeared in any of the Sargent comedies, she must have been negotiating with Universal, as the

Moving Picture World announced on May 12, 1923:

> **FAY TINCHER AND JOE MURPHY IN GUMP COMEDIES.** Andy Gump, the famous cartoon character of comic strips in newspapers throughout the whole country, and known to millions, is to be a movie hero. He is not going to be an "animated cartoon," but a real, honest-to-goodness comedy character. Carl Laemmle found Andy's double in the person of Joe Murphy. Min, played by Fay Tincher, Chester, Uncle Bim, Widow Zander and all the cast of the laughing group have also been found in real life and will be seen in these comedies.

Based on the enormously popular strip by Sidney Smith, which had premiered in 1917, the series was produced by Samuel Van Ronkel, who had a five-year contract with cartoonist Smith, and was distributed by Universal. The Gumps followed the misadventures of a middle-class family with head of the house Andy a pompous bungler whose cry of "Oh Min!" when in trouble became a 1920s catchphrase. Fay's part of Min was described by Sidney Smith as "really the brains of the family. Gentle, loving and enduring, with a strong mother's instinct but a terror when aroused." Rounding out the regular cast was their little son Chester, a freckle-faced imp whose main pleasure in life seemed to be helping his father get into hot water.

Most of the characters in the strip had been drawn in a fairly realistic style and could be easily cast, but star Andy was pure cartoon. Incredibly tall and skinny with a big bald dome, jug-handle ears and beady eyes, Andy's most outstanding feature was his total absence of a chin. A giant push broom moustache led directly to his long, skinny pencil neck. The producers accomplished the nearly impossible task of finding a living person who looked like Andy Gump when they cast Joe Murphy. An ex-vaudevillian who is said to have been an original Happy Hooligan and performed in a *Mutt and Jeff* act on stage with Bobby Vernon, Murphy (1877—1961) entered films in the mid-teens. He said it was Vernon who got him started, and he played supporting bits at practically every comedy shorts unit in Hollywood–L-Ko, Keystone, Triangle, Fox, National, Reelcraft, and Educational. Genuinely funny, his extreme height and goofy looks always made him stand out and The Gumps elevated him to short subject stardom. But his reign was brief and with the end of the series, he returned to the supporting ranks. He continued to pop up in sound shorts, most notably as a peasant with the Three Stooges in *You Nazty Spy* (1940).

The Gumps was a big success, so much so that Abe and Julius Stern, who supplied the bulk of Universal's comedy shorts and had been specializing in animal comedies, jumped on the comic strip bandwagon and soon brought Buster Brown, The Newlyweds and their Baby, Mike and Ike, and Let George Do It to the screen.

While settling down to a regular production schedule on The Gumps, Fay also turned up in other Universal product in 1924. She made three appearances in the fourth series of *The Leather Pushers* boxing shorts–*That Kid from Madrid*, *A Tough Tenderfoot*, and *Swing Bad the Sailor*. Billy Sullivan had replaced original star Reginald Denny, who had moved on to features, and Fay was part of the supporting ensemble that also included Esther Ralston, Josephine Hill, Ruth Dwyer, Eddie Gribbon, and Edgar Kennedy. In addition, she had a small role in *Excitement*, a feature comedy starring Laura LaPlante as a thrill-seeking wife whose husband teaches her a lesson. The film was full of comedy regulars such as Bert Roach, Margaret Cullington, Rolfe Sedan, Lon Poff, and Fay was last billed as "Mammy."

After these 1924 appearances, Fay's career was swallowed up and swamped by The Gumps. The series lasted a total of five years and while some top-notch veteran comedy directors like Norman Taurog, Erle C. Kenton, Robert Kerr, and Vin Moore helmed entries, the bulk of the shorts were directed by Francis Corby, a cameraman who became an uninspired director and later returned to being a cameraman. As a rule, the post-1926 Universal comedy shorts are a pretty sorry lot, short on imagination and gags while cranked out on an assembly line schedule with a tight budget. In 1927, the role of Chester was taken over by Billy Butts and at some point in 1925, around the time of *Andy Takes a Flyer* (December 7, 1925), it appears that Slim Summerville briefly replaced Joe Murphy as Andy. Photos exist of Slim in the role and whether this was due to illness or Murphy renegotiating his contract is unknown.

The handful of Gump comedies that circulate today show that, although co-starred in billing and publicity, Fay actually took a back seat to Joe Murphy in the series, with the lion's share of footage going to Andy's slapstick trials and tribulations. Min's character was supportive, long-suffering, and unfortunately very bland. Quite a step down from Rowdy Ann and leaves no doubt that Fay's exit from Christie was a big error.

Fay and Joe Murphy in character as Min and Andy Gump.
Photo courtesy of Cole Johnson.

When The Gumps came to an end in 1928, Fay's career did, too. The arrival of sound and her typecasting as Min Gump are often suggested as possible reasons for her screen disappearance. But given her stage background and musical experience, talking films shouldn't have been a hurdle. Another possibility is offered by historian Sam Gill, who reports that there are rumors that, because of her sexual preference, Fay may have been on a fabled Will Hays blacklist that was created in the wake of the Arbuckle and William Desmond Taylor scandals.

In his book *The Day the Laughter Stopped*, author David Yallop gives a description of this list:

"In the summer of 1922 the Hays Office prepared a list of nearly two hundred people who were to be eased out of the business because they represented risks to filmdom's image—not because of their politics, because of habits like drug use, which contributed to the image of Hollywood as sin city."

Yallop claims that he saw an actual copy of said list, but Sam Gill offers that, while there may have been an informal list, he's never seen or heard of a real document turning up in all the years he's spent researching silent comedy and working at the Academy's Margaret Herrick Library. Although it is true that Fay left Christie's employ in a bit of a mysterious manner and afterward never worked anywhere but Universal, without an actual copy of the list as a "smoking gun," this is all conjecture. It may have simply have been that Fay had finally had enough of "two-reel funnycisms" and called it quits.

After the demise of The Gumps, Fay left the Hollywood area. She returned briefly when her sister died in 1932 and as the informant on the death certificate, is listed as living in Chicago. Between this point and her death, virtually nothing is known. Researcher Billy H. Doyle searched for many years for information about Fay or her whereabouts and finally in 1991 found, through Social Security records, that she died in Brooklyn, New York on October 11, 1983. She was an amazing ninety-nine years old, had never married, and her final resting place is an unmarked grave at Silver Mount Cemetery on Staten Island in New York City.

Documentation and interest in Fay's career has followed much the same path of neglect as the second half of her life. If anyone looks hard, they'll find scattered references to The Gumps, Ethel and her black and white color scheme, or the Christie cowgirl, but with 99% of her work unavailable and lost, it's understandable that she's become a distant name in film history books. Happily, Fay's reputation got a shot in the arm in 1998 with the inclusion of *Rowdy Ann* in Kino's Slapstick Encyclopedia collection. Silent comedy fans were finally able to see this feisty little comedienne in action and it's hoped that more of her films will turn up and circulate so that she can shake off the dust from the years of neglect and be counted with the other comedy greats.

Al St. John: The Silent Solo Shorts

As one of the most prolific but underrated comedians of the silent era, Al St John is chiefly remembered for the country goof character that he played in support of his uncle Roscoe "Fatty" Arbuckle, but in his overlooked solo films, Al showed much more skill and versatility than he's been given credit for.

The son of Arbuckle's older sister Nora, Al was born on September 10, 1893. Roscoe was six years older and is supposed to have lived with Nora and her husband Walter St John when Al was little. Over the years, two versions of Al's background have emerged in biographical pieces on him–one had his father hating the stage and insisting that his son have nothing to do with show business and the other version has Nora and Walter as vaudevillians with the young Al joining the act, dancing and performing trick bicycle stunts. US Census information shows that the elder St John was a farm laborer and house builder, never a stage professional, so young Al most likely entered the entertainment world through his Uncle Roscoe. In the 1910 Census, the seventeen-year-old Al is listed as an actor and in April 1916, he told a *Picture-Play* reporter:

"I've been doing this kind of stunt all my life. First I was a minstrel man, then a trick bicycle rider, then a clown, then in a musical show with Roscoe, and for the past two years I have played under his direction at Keystone. He's my uncle, you know"

What is definite is that Al shows up at Keystone practically the split second after Roscoe. From 1913 to 1916, Al was primarily part of the ensemble at Mack Sennett's Keystone studio and engaged as the villain/ rival in the shorts of his uncle Roscoe. His roles in the regular Keystone output were chiefly smaller fare, such as bellboys, waiters, scared negroes (in blackface), and of course, bumbling cops. He even enjoyed an occa-

Al displays some wire walking skills in his Warner Brothers Comedy *Cleaning Up* (1920). Photo courtesy of Sam Gill.

sional juvenile lead, as in *Shot in the Excitement* (1914) opposite Alice Howell. Bigger roles were given to him in Arbuckle's films and the signature character that developed was something like an evil gremlin's country cousin. Al became the ultimate dumb (and dangerous) hick outfitted in checkered pants, long slapshoes, suspenders, and plaid shirts all topped off with a brimless pillbox hat. Long and lean, he was the perfect physical counterpoint to the rotund Arbuckle and bounced through the films on legs like spring coils that could shoot him straight up in the air. Sometimes his nose would be red, other times he had large freckles, and often he had missing teeth, but Al's character was always ready to take offense and bloodthirsty in his revenge.

One of the most impressive elements in Al's bag of tricks was his talent as a bicycle rider. With an ease and control that's quite amazing, he effortlessly seemed to be able to get a bike to do whatever he wanted it to do. In many of his future starring comedies, such as *Special Delivery* (1922) and *Red Pepper* (1925), Al's bike is material for a lot of surreal gags–i.e. when he whistles for it, it pops and wheels over to him, etc.–and is practi-

Horace Haine bosses Al around in his first solo comedy, *The Moonshiners* (1916). Photo courtesy of Sam Gill.

cally one of the characters in the film. So well-known was his riding expertise that in the mid-1920s, he did a newsreel segment demonstrating his tricks. This chunk survives today as *A Little Cycling before Breakfast with Al St John* and gives a charming look at his skills as well as a glimpse of his off-screen personality.

Al became Roscoe's right hand man and assisted him in the direction of the films. Near the end of his stay at the Sennett studio, Arbuckle spent a few months on the East Coast making comedies such as *He Did and He Didn't* and *The Waiter's Ball* (both 1916). During this period, Al got his

Alice Lake and Al in a rare subdued moment from *The Grab Bag Bride* (1917). Photo courtesy of Museum of Modern Art/ Film Stills Archive.

first solo film in the Arbuckle-directed *The Moonshiners* (1916), which paired him with Alice Lake in a story about mountain bootleggers. In 1917, Arbuckle left Sennett for his own Comique Company and Al naturally came along to continue his dual functions in front of and behind the camera. As there was a delay before Roscoe started production in New York, Al had his first starring series in four Triangle Keystones. Many of Arbuckle's regular crew, such as director Ferris Hartman and cameraman Elgin Lessley, worked on these shorts and the one circulating example, *A Grab Bag Bride* (1917), is a fast-moving and funny one-reeler with its tongue firmly in its cheek as villainous Al tries to kidnap the girl of his dreams. Although brief, this series was an important lab experiment for Al's solo work to come.

Arbuckle's first Comique film, *The Butcher Boy* (1917), got underway in the spring of 1917 and by the end of that year, the company moved to California. Al continued to play Roscoe's main nemesis in his usual manner, but got the chance to play a slick crook in *Oh, Doctor!* (1917) and a western desperado in *Out West* (1918). Vaudeville performer Buster Keaton had been added to the ensemble and while this gave he and Al the opportunity to do incredible neck-breaking stunts and tumbling together, it also lessened Al's importance in the films a bit. By the time of *Backstage* and *The Hayseed* (both 1919), Arbuckle and Keaton are working together as a tight unit, whereas Al's character and plot function seems like a throwback to the Keystone days.

At the end of 1919, Arbuckle finished his Comique contract and was about to move into features for Paramount. Producer Joseph Schenck turned the Comique organization over to Buster Keaton, who began making shorts. Like Roscoe, Al got a deal with Paramount for his own starring shorts. Announced in August of 1919, the comedies were produced by Jack and Sam Warner and distributed through Paramount. *Speed* (December 14, 1919) was the debut entry and featured Al as a bicycle mes-

Cliff Bowes and Al double up on their way to a job in *Trouble* (1920), better known today as *The Paper Hangers*. Photo courtesy of Jim Kerkhoff.

senger boy who accidentally comes into the possession of a stolen pearl necklace. Eight comedies were promised, but after a couple, Paramount was no longer in the picture with the Warner Brothers distributing the series on a states' rights basis. Although Ferris Hartman's, Frank C. Griffin's, Herman Raymaker's, and Melville Brown's names turn up as collaborating directors, little is known about these films as almost all of them are lost. What is available to be seen are chunks of *Ship Ahoy*, *The Window Trimmer*, and *The Aero-Nut* (all 1920), the latter surviving in Robert Youngson's compilation feature *Days of Thrills and Laughter* (1961) that has Al hanging from a horizontal flagpole, plus the complete short *The Paper Hangers* (1920).

As the title suggests, *The Paper Hangers* has a lot of knockabout action with paste and paper, plus the typical strengths and weaknesses of this kind of independent series. Al makes a clever entrance–he's seen having breakfast and as the camera moves back, it's revealed that he's on his bike helping himself to food from a moving lunch wagon. Another highlight has Al maneuvering his bike through real traffic while burdened down with a ladder, tons of buckets, brushes, and paper rolls, topped off by boss Cliff Bowes riding on his shoulders. On the minus side, the budget looks pretty tight and there are some ragtag stop-action animation gags with a vacuum that sucks the hair off a pampered dog and cleans out a cop's pockets. Lobby cards have turned up that show that *The Paper Hangers* was originally released as *Trouble*. Trade magazine items, stills, and lobby cards also suggest that *Ship Ahoy* and *Fired Again* may be the same film, which leads one to wonder if Warner Brothers were doing some kind of double-dipping–re-titling the shorts to make exhibitors and audiences think they were supplying new films.

At any rate, in 1921, Al left the independent field and returned to a major studio. Studio boss William Fox had made his first foray into comedy shorts production in 1917 with a series of Foxfilm Comedies and soon joined with producer Henry "Pathé" Lehrman to turn out Fox Sunshine Comedies. Al's first few comedies for the studio were made under the Sunshine banner, but by the end of the year, he was given his own series. Fox put a lot of money into their comedies and filled them with talented people in front of and behind the camera. Sadly, few of these have survived–the handful that have are tantalizing glimpses of an elaborate, surreally wild and crazy style. Out of the thirty comedies Al made during his four years with the studio (1921–1924), only four are currently known to exist. In *The Studio Rube* and *Special Delivery* (both 1922), Al plays a bicycle delivery boy and turns up as the country boob in *All Wet* and *Out of Place* (both 1922), which shows that his well-established character and costume was maintained.

What's strikingly different is his performance style. Never exactly subtle, Al wasn't above grimacing, spitting, or crossing his eyes during his days playing Arbuckle's foe. His work in these Fox comedies is the opposite–extremely spare and subtle with a new comic seriousness. "Keatonesque" is the adjective that comes to mind and it's possible that Al "borrowed" some aspects of his former colleague's attitude and style. Another possible influence on this series may have been Arbuckle himself. Due to his famous Labor Day Party scandal and murder trials, Roscoe had been out of films, but it's rumored that to keep himself busy, he worked behind the scenes with his apprentices Keaton and St John. In fact, starting in 1922, not long after the last Arbuckle trial, Al began to take regular directorial credit on the shorts, a perfect situation for Roscoe's involvement.

Two of Al's surviving shorts in particular seem to bear Roscoe's fingerprints. *Out of Place* features Hilliard Karr as a "Fatty" surrogate, who

Al and his trusty bike try to rescue Norma Contero in the Fox Comedy *Small Town Stuff* (1921). Photo courtesy of Sam Gill.

dresses just like him, engages in signature knockabout with Al, and reenacts gags from Arbuckle's early Keystone comedy *Passions, He Had Three* (1913). Also in the short are a couple of big physical comedy set pieces that are directed with the kind of crisp staging and split-second timing that was an Arbuckle specialty. The first reel of *All Wet* is a total remake of *Fatty and Mabel Adrift* (1915), using many of the same locations and even same camera angles.

All in all, Al's sojourn at Fox resulted in a series of successful and popular comedies, but the opportunity to really work with Arbuckle again led him to move to a new organization. Reel Comedies, Inc. was formed by Arbuckle friends such as Joseph Schenck, Lou Anger, producer Jack White, E.W. Hammons, and trial lawyer Gavin McNab as a production company for shorts that Roscoe would direct anonymously. The work gave him the focus he needed for his personal life and income to get out from under his legal debts. Given the brand name Tuxedo Comedies, they were made under the auspices of Jack White Comedies and distributed by Educational Pictures. Production began in February of 1923 and the first series of six comedies starred vaudeville comics Ned Sparks, Harry Tighe,

Doris Deane and Al surrounded by George Davis (back center) and his police force in *Never Again* (1924). Photo courtesy of Sam Gill.

and Poodles Hanneford. In mid-1924, Al joined the company (probably having waited for the end of his Fox contract) as the star of their next group of Tuxedos. Directorial credits were given to either Al or writer Grover Jones.

With this series, the last remnants of Al's country boob character were gotten rid of. He was now the clean-cut (but still bumbling) man-about-town or young hubby. *His First Car* (July 27, 1924) was an excellent kick-off. A simple story of a family's new car and subsequent camping trip, Roscoe took a restrained and low-keyed approach so that the slapstick grows logically out of the situations with the actors giving very natural performances. *Stupid but Brave* (October 26, 1924) has the same qualities with the addition of some wild sight gags, in particular a sequence where Al gets a haircut and shave from burly barber Kewpie Morgan, who literally twists Al's head backwards for better cutting access. Al's co-star in *Dynamite Doggie* (March 22, 1925) is Pete the pup, famous for his Our Gang appearances, who first hates Al, but then falls in love with him and won't leave his side. The problem is that Pete has swallowed a time bomb that's set to go off, so Al spends most of the film working hard to avoid the canine companionship. In addition to Pete, other crack comedy regulars that surrounded Al in these shorts included George Davis, Blanche Payson, Doris Deane (Mrs. Arbuckle), Glen Cavender, and Johnny Sinclair.

The last two films of the series, *The Iron Mule* (April 12, 1925) and *Curses* (May 21, 1925), are perfect movie genre parodies. The first spoofs the early days of the railroads (using the train from Keaton's 1923 *Our Hospitality*) and has Al as the stalwart and woodenheaded train engineer. The latter short presents Al as "Buttonshoe Bill," the ultimate despicable villain (who actually has two left feet) in a takeoff on western serial cliff-hangers. Both shorts roast movie conventions and implausibilities to a crisp and are two of the wittiest and cleverest comedies of the 1920s.

It's always been assumed that the Reel Comedy series finished here. At this point, Al and Roscoe did move on to Jack White Comedies and work separately, but there's evidence that a few other Reel Comedies may have been made and released in the next few months through a different company.

Samuel Bischoff was a small, independent producer who would later work his way up from outfits like Mascot and Tiffany to Warner Brothers and Columbia. He was just getting started in the fall of 1925 when he launched three series of two-reel comedies—*Classics in Slang*, which were based on stories by H.C. Witwer, Gold Medal Comedies, and Biff Thrill

Although credited to Grover Jones, *Dynamite Doggie* (1925) was directed by Roscoe Arbuckle with Al's co-star the soon to be well-known Pete the pup.

Comedies. The shorts were made by various independent units, such as Ernest Van Pelt, and distributed by Bischoff. Four comedies with Al came out under the Biff Thrill Comedies umbrella–*The Live Agent* (August 10, 1925), *Service* (December 10, 1925), *Rain and Shines* (January 1926), and *His Taking Ways* (February 2, 1926). The ones known to exist today are the first and last: *The Live Agent* and *His Taking Ways*.

The Live Agent suggests a strong connection to the Reel Comedies series. As in *Dynamite Doggie*, *The Iron Mule*, and *Curses*, the direction is credited to Grover Jones and the leading lady is Bartine Burkett, the heroine from *Curses*. Most importantly, the film itself has some signature Arbuckle gags and directorial touches. Al is the suitor for the hand of Bartine, whose insurance company-owning father won't even consider him for his daughter unless he brings in a record number of new insurance policies. With single-minded determination, Al practically kills himself in the pursuit of this goal and in the end marries Bartine. *His Taking Ways*, on the other hand, really doesn't have any Arbuckle earmarks, but is quite a funny comedy with Al as a deaf burglar. The original titles credit the production to Trem Carr, who later became a prolific producer of low-budget westerns.

Another interesting aspect of the Biff Comedies is the participation of Johnny Sinclair, a very overlooked performer who was a friend of Al's and spent a number of years working for him. Having started with bits in the Fox Comedies, he got larger roles in Al's Tuxedo Comedies, such as *Lovemania* (1924) and *Curses*, and while he continued to support Al in the Biff Comedies, he starred in his own shorts, such as *Hollywouldn't* and *The Starvation Hunters* (both 1925). He seemed to be on the rise, getting comic relief roles in features on the order of *The Goat Getter* (1925) and *Rapid Fire Romance* (1926), working as support for Lloyd Hamilton, and even doing his own starring Jack White Cameo Comedy *High Spirits* (1927).

But in early 1927, he was involved with Lloyd Hamilton in a barroom brawl that resulted in the death of small-time boxer Eddie Diggins. As a result, Hamilton spent a year banned from the screen and it seems to have also put the kibosh on Sinclair's rise in the industry. After being relegated

Character study of Johnny Sinclair for his starring series of Biff Comedies.

to very small bits and stunt work, he saved W.C. Fields' life in October of 1927 after an on-the-set accident during the making of *Two Flaming Youths* (1927). From here, he spent the next eight years working for Fields as a gagman and stunt double (also getting a memorable shave from W.C. in 1933's *The Barber Shop*), and after *Poppy* (1936), he did uncredited bits until his death in 1945.

When the Biff shorts were released, Al's involvement in this series seems to have been downplayed–there's a surviving glass slide that doesn't even identify him or include his name. He had just signed with Jack White Comedies and it almost seems that a deal was reached for these Biffs to be released as long as Al's participation wasn't publicized. This is definitely an area for more research and it's hoped that more info and the other two films themselves turn up so it can be established if titles such as *The Live Agent* should be added to the Arbuckle filmography.

Al's first Biff Comedy, *The Live Agent* (1925), co-starred Bartine Burkett and somehow managed to leave both their names out of most of the publicity. Photo courtesy of Mark Johnson.

Having signed with Jack White Comedies in early 1925, Al's initial White comedies came out concurrently with his last Reel Comedies and the four Biff releases. He had also done a one-shot for the Hal Roach studio, a lost oddity entitled *A Punch in the Nose* (January 3, 1926), which was top heavy with a number of performers who never appeared before or after in a Roach comedy—Al, Lige Conley, Dot Farley, and Kewpie Morgan. Jack White was the boy wonder of silent comedy and today is its forgotten mogul. He began his career as an office boy at Keystone in 1912, where he was frequently used in kids' roles and can be seen smearing a pie in Arbuckle's face in *Fatty Joins the Force* (1913). He also plays the older nephew in *His Sister's Kids* (1913). Fired by Sennett for inadvertently delivering a rival job offer to Ford Sterling, White spent the next few years working for Henry "Pathé" Lehrman, learning editing at L-Ko and directing Fox Sunshine Comedies by age nineteen. At Fox, he formed a partnership with comic Lloyd Hamilton and became a full-fledged producer at age twenty-one in 1920 when they began distributing their shorts through Educational Pictures.

By 1925, White's comedy stars were Lupino Lane and Lige Conley and soon included Big Boy, Johnny Arthur, Dorothy Devore, and Monty Collins. Al began his misadventures for the company with *Red Pepper* (April 5, 1925) and the series covered the usual gamut of silent comedy situations—high and dizzy thrill sequences (*Hold Your Hat* '26, *High Spots* '27, *Call Your Shots* '28), marital mix-ups (*High Sea Blues* '27, *No Cheating* '27), wild animals on the loose (*Live Cowards* '26, *Pink Elephants* "26), not to mention wrestling matches and auto races (*Roped In* '27, *Racing Mad* '28). Of course, ways were found to work in Al's bicycle skills. The whole opening of *Red Pepper* details his morning pedaling to work and during a chase in *High Spots* (1927), his bike gets crunched and starts to disintegrate, leaving him on a unicycle.

With the second short, *Fares, Please!* (May 10, 1925), Stephen Roberts became the director in residence for the series, helming eighteen of the total twenty. Roberts was an ex-Marine who had been working as a gagman for Norman Taurog and started directing one-reel Cameo Comedies for Jack White in 1924. Although focused on Al's series, he continued to helm occasional shorts with the likes of Lige Conley, Phil Dunham, George Davis, and Monty Collins. In the early sound era, he was still working for Jack White, but soon moved over to shorts for Universal. His first feature was 1932's *The Sky Bride* and he directed twelve before his death from a heart attack in 1936. *The Ex-Mrs. Bradford* (1936) was

Otto Fries keeps Al's upcoming fall to himself in *Fares Please!* (1925).
Photo courtesy of Sam Gill.

his last picture and in a nice touch, Al turns up in a funny and uncredited cameo appearance.

Four leading ladies were paired with Al for the bulk of this series, all of whom are overlooked comedy heroines of the late 1920s. The two most frequently on hand were Lucille Hutton and Estelle Bradley. Lucille Hutton was already a longtime comedy shorts veteran when she began working with Al in *High Sea Blues* (January 2, 1927), having made her film debut in 1916 L-Ko Comedies at age eighteen. Before that, she had appeared on stage with the Morosco Stock Co. and after two years with L-Ko, she moved on to Christie and Universal comedies, plus a number of mid-1920s features, such as *East Side–West Side* (1923) and *Dick Turpin* (1925), before landing at Jack White Comedies. In the early days of sound, she continued in shorts for White and Universal, but retired in 1931. Most of blonde Estelle Bradley's career was spent with Jack White Comedies, where she made her debut opposite Lige Conley in 1925. This beauty contest winner and former Miss Atlanta also appeared with Lloyd Hamilton, Phil Dunham, and Monty Collins and married director Charles Lamont in 1925. She also retired in 1931 after a few sound appearances.

Two other Jack White ladies supported Al. Zelma O'Neal was a well-known stage comedienne and singer who spent about a year and a half working for the White unit and later made sporadic film appearances in the 1930s. After working with Al in 1926, she returned to Broadway for two of her biggest shows–*Good News* (1927), where she introduced "*The Varsity Drag*," and *Follow Thru* (1929), in which she sang "*Button Up Your Overcoat*." Virginia Vance was a pretty blonde who had been teamed with comedian Cliff Bowes in over fifty-one reel Cameo Comedies for Jack White. In 1925, she graduated to two-reelers, where she supported Al, Lupino Lane, Lloyd Hamilton, and Johnny Arthur. After changing allegiance and appearing in Mack Sennett's late 1920s *Dan the Taxi Man* series opposite Jack Cooper, she married actor Bryant Washburn and left the screen in 1929. In addition to these aforementioned leading ladies, Al had top-notch support in this series from regular character comics on the order of Otto Fries, Babe London, Phil Dunham, Blanche Payson, Glen Cavender, Spencer Bell, Clem Beauchamp, Eva Thatcher, Al Thompson, and Jack Lloyd.

Besides his Jack White shorts, Al had been making occasional supporting performances in serious silent features such as *Casey Jones* (1927)

Lucille Hutton catches Al with somebody's stocking in 1927's *No Cheating*. Photo courtesy of Sam Gill.

and *Painted Post* (1928). When the film industry changed over to sound, Al's career wasn't affected that dramatically at first. He continued starring in short comedies, many for Educational and some directed by Arbuckle, like *That's My Meat* (1931) and *Bridge Wives* (1932), and even memorably revived his hick character to co-star with Roscoe in the one of the latter's comeback Vitaphone shorts *Buzzin' Around* (1933). Arbuckle died suddenly of a heart attack in June of 1933 and after that, Al begins turning up predominantly in lower-budget westerns, soon developing a new screen persona. Repackaging himself with a beard and without his teeth, Al became the comic sidekick "Fuzzy Q. Jones." Having traded his bicycle in for a horse, for the next twenty years he supported screen cowboys like Buster Crabbe, Fred Scott, Don "Red" Barry, and Lash LaRue, providing the much-needed comic relief with his old routines and falls. Popular with kids around the world, the films were later cut down for European television into "Fuzzy" two-reelers with titles like *Fuzzy der Meister Cowboy*.

In 1952, unhappy with how cheap the oaters were getting, Al retired from films, but continued making personal appearances as "Fuzzy" with rodeos, circuses, and wild west shows. While waiting backstage to go on

Some hat business performed by Al and Bobby Burns in *Who Hit Me?* (1926). Photo courtesy Sam Gill.

for one of these shows, Al suffered a massive heart attack and died on January 21, 1963. Since his death, there's been a resurgence of interest in Arbuckle's films from which Al's reputation has benefited, but due to loss and unavailability, his own work is still neglected. It's hoped that more of his solo comedies make their way into the hands of comedy fans so that the wider scope of his talents can be appreciated, not just his work as Roscoe's "second banana."

"I'm Glad Now That I'm Homely": The Downs and Ups of Marie Dressler

IN THE TEENS AND TWENTIES, there was a small group of ladies who ventured into the "men's terrain" of roughhouse film comedy and developed comic characters that weren't tied to romantic plots. Taking bumps and bruises like the guys, these women starred in comedies which were produced to showcase and exploit their talents and the characterizations that they had made famous. Mabel Normand was the first, but others soon followed quickly at her heels. After Mabel, the next starring physical comedienne to make a big impact on the screen came from the stage.

"Big" is a good description for everything about Marie Dressler, from her size to her style of clowning. Adjectives such as "mammoth," "buxom," "unwieldy," "portly," "ample," and "roly-poly" were routinely used to describe her, but she was equally big-hearted and devoted much time to public causes that involved personal sacrifice and created setbacks in her career. She was born Leila Marie Koerber on November 9, 1869, in Coburg, Canada.

> The sad truth is I was born without looks or anything else in my favor. My mother said that I was the worst looking thing she ever saw. I grew into girlhood with the graceful abandon of a colt, and for years my hands and feet were always in my way. I never went to school. What little I learned my mother taught me. My father never stayed in one place long enough for me to be sent to a school. He was a musician and his temperament kept him on the jump. I was not even taught music—shoemaker's children never wear shoes, you know. Father did give about ten one-minute lessons, but that didn't help me much. Patience was not his shining virtue.

Officer William McCall ordering Marie to move along in *Fired* (1917), her second independently self-produced comedy. Photo courtesy of Sam Gill.

Augustus Koerber was also a veteran of the Crimean War who treated his family like the enemy. Marie said it was seeing her mother slave and drudge that inspired her to make something of herself. Having caught the acting bug at age five after a public performance as Cupid (where she, of course, fell off her pedestal), Marie left home at fourteen to begin her career.

With her sister Bonita in tow, Marie passed as eighteen and got a job with the Emma Nevada Stock Company. This was in 1883 and the next ten years were spent learning her trade and working up the hard way–through stock and light opera troupes. Going from company to company, doing everything from chorus bits to large roles while touring all over the United States would have defeated a lesser person, but not Marie:

"Things seemed pretty hopeless when I was a kid, but when I started out in the world I said 'I'll make you know I'm here!' And what I went through taught me something—I'll tell you, you've got to have a handicap before you can be a success."

She made her first New York appearance in 1892 with the show *The Robber of the Rhine*, starring Maurice Barrymore (father of Ethel, Lionel, and John). Although she originally intended to be a serious performer:

"I did not want to be a farceur or a romping acrobatic comedian. But soubrettes, I knew, were all small women, and prima donnas had to be beautiful, or were supposed to be so."

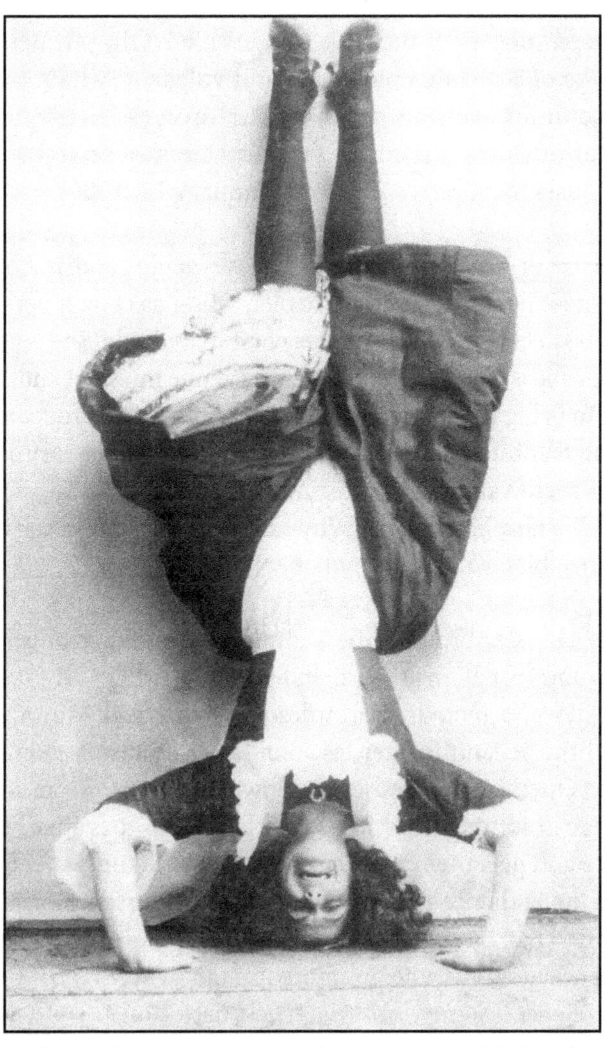

Stage photo of Marie circa 1910. Photo courtesy of Cole Johnson.

After encouragement from Barrymore and comic Eddie Foy, Marie accepted comedy as her lot in theatrical life. After all her years of struggle, she had arrived and by 1896 had her first starring hit with the show *The Lady Slavey*. Other appearances included *Hotel Topsy Turvy*, and *King Highball*, in addition to *Higgledy-Piggledy* and *Twiddle Twaddle* opposite Joe Weber. Singing, mugging, and even falling over furniture–Marie became the toast of the theatrical world and remained so for the next twenty years:

> Marie Dressler—ponderous, elephantic Marie—is the star and will close her second week at this theatre after a pronounced success in the new skit, entitled 'Oh, Mr. Belasco!' Outside of a certain coarseness and vulgarity, which the audience didn't seem to mind, Miss Dressler's burlesquing of the various mannerisms of famous actresses brought down the house. (*New Jersey Telegram*, January 12, 1907)

> To the list of American artists who have 'made good' in London must now be added Marie Dressler, who has shown herself to be a 200 lb entertainer of the very first magnitude. She is a wonder, for she is able to set you laughing at one moment and, at the next, to bring the hard lump of pathos into your throat and the fat, salt tear into your eye. When the world seems weary and all things seem vain and unsatisfying, hear Marie Dressler sing 'A Great Big Girl Like Me' or 'Why Adam Sinned' and you'll forget your troubles. (*London Opinion*, November 9, 1907)

> Marie Dressler brought the show to a screaming finish with songs and recitations that included 'A Great Big Girl Like Me,' 'The Glove,' a melodrama burlesque with equally funny incidental music, and for her last number 'The Prima Donnas of Grand Opera.' Miss Dressler is a clown, but she is also an actress, so there is nothing futile in her methods. She goes after her audience and gets them and the more tomfool stunts she did the more the audience proved that it could be just as foolish as it looked to her. In other words, it was a reciprocity of foolishness and it is a question who got more fun out of it, Miss Dressler or the audience. (*Springfield Union*, February 20, 1913)

Everything she did was news–injuries in the line of slapstick duty, opinions on things from weight loss to politics, and a bout with typhoid that almost killed her in 1902. Her popularity was so intense that it was too much for at least one critic at the *New York Standard*:

> I wish some way might be found to relieve us, if only for a brief season, of the constant intrusion into our daily lives of Marie Dressler. For weeks and months Marie Dressler has been the dominant personality in this community, and while no one

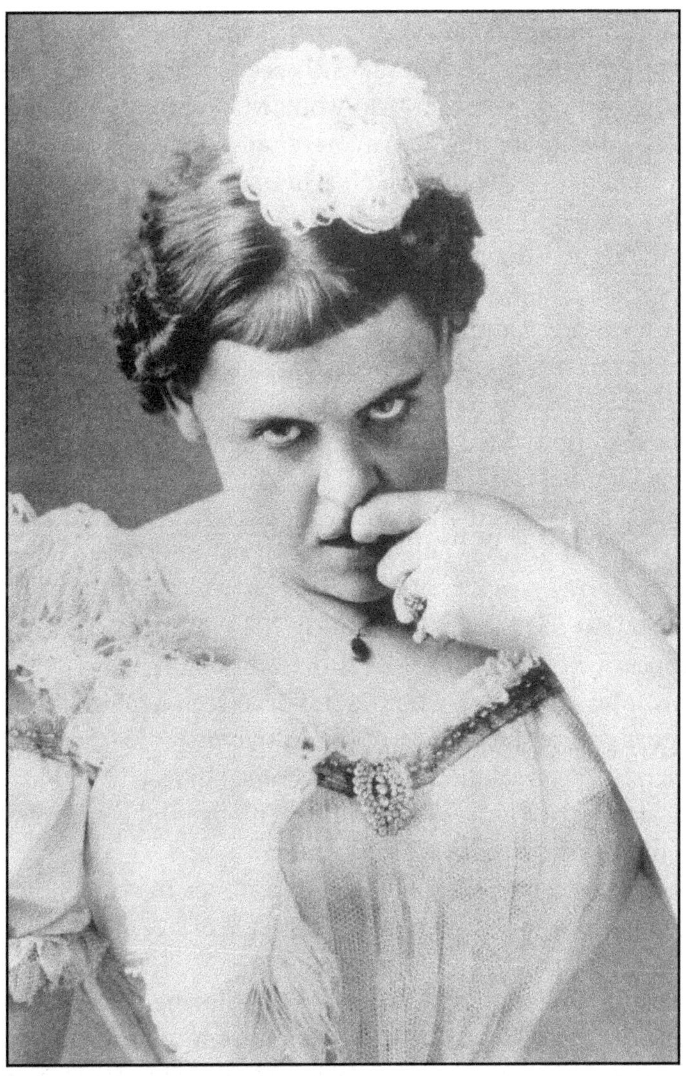

Photo courtesy of Cole Johnson.

> could surpass me in appreciation of Miss Dressler's charms and attainments, still I have grown somewhat weary of the universal pervasiveness, as it were, of the young woman.

Also in the news were Marie's periodic bankruptcies, plus a steady flow of other financial and business squabbles. Sadly, Marie had a weak grip on the business aspects of her profession, a situation that was exacerbated when she hooked up with James H. Dalton. Marie had a short-lived marriage in the mid-1890s to a man named George Hopper (rumors of a daughter who died in infancy appear to be unfounded). In 1907, she met James Dalton, who became her manager. They eventually lived together as man and wife and presented themselves as such to the press, although Dalton had a wife in Chicago who wouldn't give him a divorce. Dalton turned out to be a poor business manager and over the years was a drain on Marie's finances as he involved her in many lawsuits and even phony stock schemes.

Marie reached the peak of her stage career in 1910 with the show *Tillie's Nightmare*. In it, she played Tillie Blobbs, a boarding house drudge who's promised an evening off to attend a traveling show. At the last minute, Tillie has to stay home and work, but falls asleep and dreams up her own musical comedy extravaganza. The show was a huge hit, touring for many years, and provided Marie with her signature song, "*Heaven Will Protect the Working Girl*."

While she continued with other stage productions and made cylinder recordings for Edison, Tillie became Marie's entrée into the movies:

> **MISS DRESSLER TO PLAY FARCES FOR 'MOVIES.'** Will Appear with Members of Keystone Stock Company
> Miss Marie Dressler, who has not been seen here in musical comedy since she played in '*Tillie's Nightmare*,' will appear in a series of Mutual motion picture comedies, each of which is to be three or four reels in length. With her will be members of the Keystone Stock Company.
> These photo-farces are being staged under the direction of Mr. Mack Sennett. (*New Jersey Herald*, April 27, 1914)

According to legend, many years before during the national tour of *The Lady Slavey*, a woman named Mrs. Sinnott and her strapping son Michael presented themselves to Marie in Massachusetts. Armed with a letter of introduction from future president Calvin Coolidge, who at the time was a lawyer and big Republican in the area, they told Marie that Michael wanted to go on the stage and asked her advice as to how he should go about it. Marie generously wrote the boy a note to give to impresario David Belasco and Michael was soon in New York warbling away in the chorus of Broadway shows. Along the way, he changed his name to Mack Sennett, entered films in 1908, became a director of comedies for the Biograph Company, and opened his own Keystone Studio in 1912. As with many items in the Sennett legend, it makes a great story, but is hard to verify as true.

It is known that in early 1914, Marie was involved in a battle with producer Gilbert M. Anderson (a.k.a. "Broncho Billy" Anderson of Essanay fame) concerning a production of *The Merry Gambol* at his Gaiety Theatre in San Francisco. The upshot was the show went on without Marie and finding herself out in California in an in-between state with no new shows on the horizon, she may have decided that she had nothing to lose by giving movies a try. What is definite is that in early 1914, Sennett hired Marie for a series of comedies and used *Tillie's Nightmare* as the starting point.

Tillie's Punctured Romance was released in six reels on November 14, 1914, and broke ground as one of the first slapstick features. In the picture, Tillie is an innocent, not to mention large and boisterous, country girl who falls for traveling conman Charlie Chaplin. Charlie gets Tillie to purloin her father's bankroll and run off to the big city with him. There he takes her money and abandons her, but when he finds that her rich uncle has died, leaving her the only heir, he quickly returns and marries her. The newlyweds throw a huge party to launch themselves into society, but the not-so-dead uncle returns and kicks everyone out of the house. A huge fracas ensues with the Keystone Cops on a seaside pier, where Tillie and the cops are repeatedly dunked in the surf until Tillie decides that Charlie is no good and will have nothing further to do with him.

Marie literally burst upon the screen in her first appearance. As coy as a baby rhino, she gallumps through the film and towers over Chaplin, looking like she's going to permanently flatten him during their physical business together, which includes love play that's kicking and beaning each other with bricks. With her dark-circled eyes and bulldog face, Marie is grotesque in farm girl pigtails and circus big top-tent dresses. Marie had personally designed her outfits for the stage production and it appears that she also did so for the film. Despite the grotesqueness,

Marie as the star of the first full-length slapstick comedy *Tillie's Punctured Romance* (1914). Photo courtesy of Sam Gill.

Marie's warmth still comes through and the film was a huge success and triumph for her.

Although hired for a series of comedies, with *Tillie* shot under the working title of *Dressler No 1*, it turned out to be the only Sennett film that Marie appeared in. The reason why is explained by this item from the July 4, 1914 *Moving Picture World*:

> Marie Dressler, who some time ago signed with the Keystone, has cancelled all contracts for one year on account of an accident. Miss Dressler was in a comedy picture on the Venice Pier, and while standing near the unfenced edge of the structure an automobile backed into her, knocking her off. She fell into the sea below, tearing her hand painfully, and suffering several other injuries.

This appears to have happened while shooting *Tillie's* big climax and the fact that Marie cancelled her contract may have led Sennett to get his money's worth by making *Tillie* a feature instead of the three- or four-reeler originally announced.

It seems this wasn't the only "injury" Marie suffered due to working with Sennett. According to Marie, Sennett and his Keystone backers had agreed to let Jim Dalton handle the release and exploitation of the picture, but when the time came, turned *Tillie* over to the Alco Film Corporation for states' rights release. Dalton and Dressler battled Keystone for more than a year in court, eventually winning $50,000 and the rights to the film, which Marie rereleased in the early 1920s.

In spite of the accident and lawsuit, Marie was sold on the movies and told *The Dramatic News*:

> What do I think of motion pictures? Don't get me started on a question like that,' exclaimed Marie Dressler in Philadelphia, 'or I will never know when to stop. I'm mad about the 'movies' from every point of view. I love to go to them. I've only been in one picture so far, 'Tillie's Punctured Romance,' but hereafter I am going to devote my time for five months of the year to them, from May to October. Last summer out in California I worked for three months in a motion picture studio just to perfect myself in all the various departments of the business, and now I flatter myself that I know the technical side of the business from the ground up. When I finish my tour in 'A Mix Up' in May I'm going to start at work in earnest in this new field.

A week later, on April 14, 1915, *The Dramatic Mirror* announced:

> **LUBIN SIGNS DRESSLER.** Comedienne Will Be Starred In Series Of Specially Written Comedies
>
> Marie Dressler has signed a contract with the Lubin Company and is to be starred in a number of featured comedies written especially for her.
>
> Miss Dressler will be seen only in five-reel comedies and she will make three of these each year. Elaborate preparations are being made for the first of these big reelers. The comedienne will arrive at the studio in Philadelphia the first of June, the close of her present theatrical season, and the work of producing the first feature comedy will begin then.

Lubin's hyperactive exhibitor ad for Marie's *Tillie's Tomato Surprise* (1915).

> For her supporting company Ira M. Lowry, general manager of the Lubin company, is selecting the most expensive list of players that has ever been used in a Lubin production.

The "number of featured comedies" mentioned again only turned into one–*Tillie's Tomato Surprise*. Lubin billed Marie as "the moon, sun and star in the firmament of comediennes" and promised "two hours of howls, yells, screams, guffaws, laughs, chuckles, and roars." The surviving footage elicits mostly head-scratching today and is practically as strenuous as the ad campaign. Around thirteen minutes exists at the Library of Congress and is very odd, with Marie doing a lot of heavy mugging in a strange plot about her nutty inventor friend "The Flying Scotsman," who flies around on a pair of homemade wings.

After this feature, Marie severed ties with Lubin and according to the August 16, 1916 *Motion Picture News*:

"William A. Brady acting for the World Film Corporation has signed to appear exclusively in features supervised by himself, Marie Dressler, the famous 'Tillie' of filmdom."

Tillie Wakes Up came out in January of 1917 and this five-reel World release is probably the best of Marie's surviving early work. In it, she plays a neglected wife whose callous husband has only married her for convenience and treats her brusquely. A newspaper advice column gives her the idea to make him jealous so he'll appreciate her and she hooks up with a neighbor's henpecked husband for a spree at Coney Island. Although she gives a more subdued performance than usual, much of the film is just an excuse to turn Marie loose on the Ferris wheel, Steeplechase, and all the slides and revolving platforms in Luna Park. She even gets nauseous on the same Witching Waves ride that Buster Keaton and Al St John battle on in Roscoe Arbuckle's *Coney Island* (1917). In addition to the Coney locations, the film was shot at World's studio in Fort Lee, New Jersey.

The climactic sequence has Marie and Johnny Hines driving their car into the surf and was the occasion for Marie's second accident while filming a water scene. The car was mounted on a raft and towed out fairly far from shore. During shooting, it began sinking and tipped, spilling Marie and Hines into the water. Marie said that the auto body hit her on the head and pinned her underwater briefly. When she came up: "Somebody in a motor boat flung a rope to me and I caught the end of it in my bare hands. I was pulled through the waves to the beach. My hands are pretty sore, and I feel as if I'd been hammered all over." Her subsequent advice to aspiring film actresses was: "Stay away from the movie business unless you can swim."

This third and final *Tillie* title had the participation of a number of overlooked silent comedy veterans. Marie's co-star Johnny Hines began his career on stage as a child, where he found success supporting Madge Kennedy and working for George M. Cohan. The east coast film industry beckoned and Hines became part of the company at World Pictures, working frequently with director Maurice Tourneur in films like *The Cub* (1915) and *A Girl's Folly* (1917). In 1920, he was starred in a series of

Torchy two-reelers based on the popular stories of Sewell Ford about a newspaper office boy.

Produced by C.C. Burr of Mastodon Films, the Torchies were a big hit and in 1921, Burr began moving Johnny into features with *Burn 'Em Up Barnes.* Over the years, Hines has been grouped with Douglas MacLean and Reginald Denny and designated as a polite "demi-clown," but surviving comedies such as *Conductor 1492* (1924) and *The Live Wire* (1925) show a breezy pace and quality of gags not far below the features of Harold Lloyd. Sound ended Hines' starring days and he spent the 1930s in shorts and sporadic supporting roles in features. His last appearance was the 1941 Pete Smith short *How to Hold Your Husband—Back.*

Portrait of Johnny Hines, Marie's partner in crime in *Tillie Wakes Up* (1917).

Director Harry Davenport also had a long stage career (plus a brief, early marriage to Keystone regular Alice Davenport) and made his film debut at Vitagraph in 1914, appearing in the films of his brother-in-law Sidney Drew. The next year, he was starring in and directing Vitagraph's series of Jarr Family comedies and soon moved on to helming features. In the 1920s, he left films and concentrated on stage work, but returned in the 1930s as a popular character actor, remembered today as Dr. Meade in *Gone with the Wind* (1939) and Grandpa in *Meet Me in St. Louis* (1944).

The story was by Mark Swan with Frances Marion fleshing out the scenario. Swan was a well-known writer of Broadway farces, the most popular of which, *Parlor, Bedroom and Bath*, was later adapted for Buster Keaton. Through the Teens, he wrote comedy stories for a few features in addition to shorts for Edison, Vitagraph, Weber & Fields, and Lubin comedies for Billie Reeves. Frances Marion had started her writing career as a reporter and originally met Marie in 1911 when she interviewed her during the San Francisco run of *Tillie's Nightmare*. The two became very close and during their twenty-three-year friendship, Marion became one of the most important female writers in early Hollywood, working with Mary Pickford and at MGM. *Tillie Wakes Up* is the first film to take advantage of the dramatic talent behind Marie's clowning and it seems very likely that this came from Frances Marion, as it's a hallmark of the scripts, such as *Min and Bill*, that she wrote for Marie in the 1930s.

Flushed with success, Marie and Dalton formed the Marie Dressler Motion Picture Company, a two million dollar corporation, to produce their own two-reelers and features, but with their usual business acumen, they spent the next couple of years bouncing the films around from distributor to distributor. Mutual was announced first, but never materialized, and out of a slew of titles predicted, only four shorts came out–*The Scrub Lady* (1917) for Goldwyn Pictures and *Fired* (1917), *The Agonies of Agnes* (1918), and *The Cross Red Nurse* (1918) through a combo of Goldwyn and World. It's hard to judge this series, as only the second reel of *The Scrub Lady* is known to exist today and is a fast and furious melee of Marie modeling various funny costumes and then engaging in wartime intrigue. Em Gee Film Library used to offer it under the title *The Love Riot* and described it as "a wild one." At any rate, *The Scrub Lady* was shot in Fort Lee, then it appears that Marie moved to California for *Fired* and possibly the final two and may have directed these last three shorts herself from scenarios by Frances Marion.

From the looks of her box of dynamite, Marie may have hired the person who did the labeling on Larry Semon's comedies for *The Scrub Lady* (1917), the first short for her own company. Photo courtesy of Sam Gill.

Some of the erraticness in the production and release of these shorts can be attributed to Marie's devotion to America's participation in World War I. In *The Scrub Lady*, she battled spies in a munitions factory and she decided to do what she could in real life, too. As a German descendent, she wanted to set an example for other German-Americans to "get behind Uncle Sam in this war." Beginning in 1917, she entertained troops and the next year threw herself one hundred percent into the selling of government bonds, tirelessly touring the country along with Charlie Chaplin, Mary Pickford, and Douglas Fairbanks as part of the Liberty Loan Drive. Marie later said that she made one hundred and forty-nine speeches during one twenty-nine-day bond tour.

Practically as soon as the war ended, Marie was off on another crusade. In 1919, when the stage actor's union Actors' Equity Association was new, the chorus performers for shows decided that they wanted the same kind of protection and formed the Chorus Equity Association. Having worked herself up the hard way from the chorus, Marie became president and figurehead for the Chorus Girls' Union. Although she eventually resigned, as she felt she was out of touch with the union's affairs due to being out on tour, her time spent on behalf of the chorus members took energy away from her own career.

The first half of the 1920s was probably the low point of Marie's career and life. The wartime and Equity activities had taken focus away from her career and when she returned to it full-time, she had begun to be regarded as a relic from a different era and mostly did revivals of her previous hits or took part in "old timers' shows." Her stance with the chorus girl had made her unpopular with a number of producers and, ironically enough, she had her own problems with Actors' Equity in connection with a tour of *Tillie's Nightmare*. On top of it all, she was left devastated when Jim Dalton died at the end of 1921.

Dressler surrounded by John Rand (on left in top hat), James T. Kelly (reclining on the right), and William McCall (right as cop) in her independent comedy *Fired* (1917). Photo courtesy of Sam Gill.

During this period, Marie got by as best she could. Things got so bad that in 1924 she was given a deal on a small servant's room at New York's Ritz-Carleton Hotel in exchange for hostessing at the hotel's restaurant. After almost ten years off the screen, she had her first film work in the summer of 1926, when she shot footage for a series of *Travelaffs* shorts in Europe. These were to be produced and directed by Harry Reichenbach and while information is very scarce, they seem to have been designed to be humorous travelogues similar to the group that Will Rogers made for Clancy-Pathé, which had him appearing in the world's capitals and making pithy wisecracks via title cards. Things did not go well for Marie's version and the series never materialized.

At this point, Marie's screen career would really begin again thanks to Allan Dwan and Frances Marion. The story goes that Dwan was getting ready to shoot *The Joy Girl* (1927), a feature he was directing for Fox, when he spotted Marie in the Ritz-Carleton's restaurant and offered her a supporting role. Around the same time, her friend Frances Marion heard about her lean times. Marion, now a prolific script writer for MGM, came up with *The Callahans and the Murphys* (based on the book by Kathleen

A touching domestic scene from *The Callahans and the Murphys* (1927) between Marie and Eddie Gribbon.

Norris) and pitched the project and Marie to production head Irving Thalberg. The role of feuding Irish housewife was tailor-made for Marie and was the first of her teamings with another comedy matron, Polly Moran. Like herself, Polly had been a stage headliner and a veteran practitioner of low comedy. She also made her film debut for Mack Sennett and for a number of years was one of his resident zanies before she moved on to Fox Sunshine and Carnival Comedies. In the mid-1920s, Polly settled in as comic relief at MGM, playing a succession of landladies, maids, and frumps in dramatic pictures starring Lillian Gish, Lon Chaney, and Greta Garbo.

At the time, ethnic comedies were big box office in Hollywood. The trend began on Broadway with the huge hit *Abie's Irish Rose* and the film industry jumped on the bandwagon with their own versions, such as *The Cohens and the Kellys* and *Kosher Kitty Kelly* (both 1926). Since the genre had been so lucrative, MGM expected that they would tap into it with *The Callahans and the Murphys* (1927), as it played well to preview audiences, but when it was released, Irish-American groups protested, citing Marie and Polly's battling and boozing, and the film was withdrawn from circulation. Although not the hit that the studio had hoped for, it did jump-start Marie's career again and she continued in other character parts for MGM, such as Marion Davies' overbearing mother in *The Patsy* (1928). She also branched out to other studios, like First National and RKO.

Sound was now revolutionizing the industry, but after spending almost forty years as a star of the speaking stage, Marie had no problem adapting her comedy style to talking films and like W.C. Fields and Will Rogers, the new technology made her film persona complete. She and Polly Moran really cemented their screen partnership in the Al Christie-produced talkie short *Dangerous Females* (1929) and Marie was used to good advantage in comedy novelty numbers in *Hollywood Revue of 1929*. What suddenly elevated Marie from being a utility character player on MGM's roster to one of their biggest stars was her role in 1930's *Anna Christie*. Again, Frances Marion had created the role with her in mind and went to bat to make sure Marie played it.

As Marthy, an old waterfront hag, Marie refurbished many of her old stock bits—hiccupping, drunkenly walking down a gangplank, business with a swinging bar door–while really inhabiting the character and conveying a tremendous fallen dignity. Giving the film much-needed humor and pep, Marie worked well with Greta Garbo and made a huge impression with only a couple of scenes. The film had been eagerly awaited as Garbo's first talkie and was a huge success for both Garbo and Dressler.

Polly Moran and Marie in their first teaming in sound 1929's *Dangerous Females*. Photo courtesy of Sam Gill.

The second wind that was given to Marie's career by *Anna Christie* was clinched later in 1930 by the films *Caught Short* and *Min and Bill*. Together, they illustrate the two polar ends of her resurrected career. *Caught Short* was a low-comedy escapade with Polly Moran, short on subtlety and budget, but big at the box office. Helmed by silent comedy veteran and former Chaplin collaborator Charles F. Reisner, the success of this one paved the way for Reisner to continue with the girls for *Reducing*, and *Politics* (both 1931) Audiences loved the old girls together and the simple plots that revolved around long-suffering Marie drawn into some kind of hot water by scatterbrained Polly were always punctuated by plentiful knockabout action.

Min and Bill, on the other hand, established the dramatic vehicles where a self-sacrificing Marie bravely faced heartbreak and disappointments. Sometimes leavened with physical comedy, as in *Min and Bill* and *Tugboat Annie* (1933), or played fairly straight, like *Emma* (1932) and *Christopher Bean* (1933), these dramatic roles gave a new legitimacy to an old comedy warhorse, made official when she won the 1930/31 Oscar for Best Actress for *Min and Bill*.

Marie and Polly watch with disdain as director Charles Reisner (right) mugs for visitors Marion Davies and a friend (center) on the set of *Caught Short* (1930). Photo courtesy of Sam Gill.

By 1932, Marie was at the very top of the Hollywood heap, one of its most popular and successful stars. This triumphant comeback must have given her great satisfaction, but sadly, she wasn't able to enjoy it for very long. Almost as soon as she won the Academy Award, her health began to deteriorate dramatically. In 1931 and 32, she had surgeries to remove malignant tumors, but the cancer had spread and by late 1932, there was really nothing more that could be done. She stoically kept on working as long as she could, only shooting a few hours a day. Her last few pictures were made this way and in *Tugboat Annie* in particular, the strain shows on her face. Strangely, she seems rejuvenated in *Dinner at Eight* (1933), turning in a wonderful performance. Perhaps her best-loved and -remembered moment comes at the very end of the film, when Jean Harlow tells her that she was reading a book the other day. Marie's gargantuan take, physically reeling as if a truck has just smacked into the side of the building or the earth has suddenly shifted in its orbit, has to be seen to be believed. It is a fitting finale and farewell to her long career in comedy.

By early 1933, she could no longer work and her last film, *Christopher Bean*, was released on November 17 of that year. MGM, probably still reeling after the 1930 death of their mega-star Lon Chaney, seemed to be in denial about Marie's health and continued churning out publicity items about upcoming films and roles for her. She lingered for months and during her last weeks, the newspapers printed daily bulletins about the status of her health. The end came on July 28, 1934. Audiences responded as if they had lost a beloved member of their own family and even her old teammate Polly Moran, who enjoyed playing the madcap her whole life, made a serious exception at Marie's funeral. Betty Lee in *Marie Dressler: The Unlikeliest Star* describes Polly's trip to Dressler's mausoleum with Marie's close friend Claire Dubrey:

> Dubrey walked to the crypt with Polly Moran and her husband Martin Malone, and the three stood for some time as workmen sealed the tomb. Later they drove back to Hollywood in Polly's limousine and, as Dubrey wrote in her memoir: 'I sat silently, though Polly wept softly. She was dressed

Director Mervyn LeRoy and Marie during production on *Tugboat Annie* (1933). Photo courtesy of Sam Gill.

> in black, a color she never wears, purchased to do full honor to her old teammate and as a mark of her own sorrow. 'Marie was a great woman,' she said as she wiped her eyes. I nodded. 'Did I do anything wrong at the funeral?' she asked, like the child at heart she is. 'Why no, Polly! What makes you ask?' 'Well, Marie always told me to be more dignified,' she replied. 'I guess she was right. Anyway, I wanted her to approve of me. Maybe for once in their lives people can't say that Polly Moran was vulgar. I hope Marie knows.'

During her sixty-four years, Marie Dressler faced many challenges, but as she always did with a laugh opportunity, she wrestled them to the ground until they cried "uncle." Lack of money, education, and sometimes taste never stopped her. She barreled through stage productions, movies, and life with a no-nonsense "this is who I am" attitude and turned her deficits into assets. While the memories of her stage triumphs have passed with the people who saw them, her films live on, preserving her spirit and talents for future generations.

Max Comes Across: Linder in America

THE FIRST GREAT COMIC CREATOR of the cinema was Max Linder. Coming to films in their infancy, he quickly stood out from anarchic and roughhouse contemporaries such as Andre Deed and Fernando Guillame with a more sophisticated approach to material and the character of a dandified, everyman-about-town.

The son of wealthy vineyard owners, Gabriel-Maximillian Leurielle was born in 1883 and decided early that he wanted to be an actor. After conservatory study and repertory experience, he headed to Paris, where he adopted the name Max Linder. While playing small roles at the well-known Theatre de l'Ambigu and appearing in music halls, Linder began supplementing his income in 1905 by working as a day player at the Pathé Studio.

Alternating between background work, small bits, and occasional leads in dramas and costume pictures as well as comedies, by 1906 his soon-to-be-famous dapper but inept boulevardier persona began surfacing in films such as *Le Pendu* (1906), *Les Debuts d'un patiner* (1907's *The Skater's Debut*, his first big success), and *Pedicure par amour* (1908).

Star billing came his way in 1909 and during his career peak of 1910 to 1914, he turned out a new Max misadventure every two weeks. With prodigious invention, he laid the groundwork and created the blueprints for the comedians that would follow. Each film put Max through a specific situation that was built with complications and variations. Week to week would see Max trying to cure his hiccups, dealing with a difficult mother-in-law, taking up boxing, attempting to get unstuck from sticky flypaper, or more often than not, suffering from romantic complications.

Max Linder
GG

As his popularity grew, Linder signed increasingly lucrative contracts with Pathé and made regular personal appearances all over Europe, including an extended stay in Russia. Pathé distributed the comedies to the United States and the U.K. as well and his influence on American film comedy can be seen as early as 1909. Mack Sennett always acknowledged his debt to French comedies and in *The Curtain Pole* (1909), he not only wrote a script based on Linder's recipe for disaster, but does his own version of Max in the lead role.

The always elegant Max in a pose for his Essanany comedies.
Photo courtesy of Sam Gill

Directed by D.W. Griffith, Mack plays the excitable Frenchman Monsieur DuPont who, while visiting friends, accidentally breaks their curtain pole. After running out to get a new one, while hurrying back with the unwieldy pole he clobbers numerous innocent pedestrians, who then follow him like a comedic lynch mob, and when he hires a coach, the pole sticks out the window, knocking down lamp posts and causing more damage. By the time he returns to his friends, they've already replaced the pole.

Wearing a top hat, suit, gloves, a pointy putty nose, and equally pointy mustache and eyebrows, Sennett is definitely a coarsened version of Max as Monsieur DuPont, continually doffing his hat and kissing everyone in sight. Around the same time, Sennett also turns up in this character as a very animated cinema audience member in *Those Awful Hats* (1909) and while he didn't continue with the character, the principles of Linder's films were absorbed and built upon by Sennett and his American contemporaries.

Linder's creative peak was interrupted by the outbreak of World War I. Fiercely patriotic, Max stopped performing and put himself, and much of his income, at the disposal of the French cause. Using his own auto and airplane, Linder ran dispatches to the front and was hurt. Although the nature and severity of his injuries vary in different recountings–everything from being gassed to being shot through the lung, not to mention having been reported killed at the Battle of the Aisne–Max did suffer some kind of permanent lung damage. After being excused from service sometime in 1915, he resumed making films and entertained troops, but began having physical and mental breakdowns and was convalescing at a military hospital in Contrexville when he received overtures from the American film company Essanay.

Formed in Chicago in 1907 by George K. Spoor and Gilbert M. Anderson (the "S & A"), Essanay was strong on comedy from its very beginning. Its first full-time actor was Ben Turpin (who also filled in as carpenter, scene painter, prop man, and janitor) and its comedy output included George Ade Fables, the Sweedie Comedies, which starred Wallace Beery in drag as a big lummox Swedish girl, and the west coast-made Snakeville Comedies with Augustus Carney as "Alkali Ike" and an ensemble made up of Harry Todd, Margaret Joslin, and Victor Potel. While Spoor had stayed in Chicago, Anderson had gone out west and made his popular Broncho Billy films in Niles, CA. In 1915, the company had a coup when it snared Charlie Chaplin on the rebound after his halcyon first year in films at Key-

Linder working hard on his American debut in *Max Comes Across* (1917).
Photo courtesy of Sam Gill.

stone. Chaplin was with Essanay for about a year and turned out fourteen phenomenally successful films, which the company continued to recycle with later releases such as *The Essanay-Chaplin Revue* (1916) and *Triple Trouble* (1918). Although George Spoor was said to have been initially aghast at the immense salary Anderson offered Chaplin and the two had a very rocky relationship, he must have felt it was ultimately worth it, as he was the person actively courting Linder.

Since he was unable to return to active war service, Max stated that he accepted Essanay's offer as a way to furnish money for France's war effort and donated a large part of his salary. The war had devastated the French and European film industry, which enabled America to begin its path to worldwide movie domination. A one-year contract was arranged, for which Max would direct and star in twelve two-reel comedies and receive a salary of $260,000 (blown up to $400,000 by the press). Linder arrived in New York on November 7, 1916, where he was met at the dock by Spoor and immediately whisked off to Chicago to begin production. The newspapers made much out of the story of Max's difficult sea voyage:

being rammed by another boat and the panic that ensued as the passengers feared that they had been torpedoed, which, interestingly enough, also happened to be the plot of his first Essanay comedy.

Overall, the press had a field day, fueled by Essanay's publicity department, and items were rife about Linder as the comedy "Beau Brummel"–that he traveled with forty-six trunks of clothing "crammed with the very latest French sartorial cuts" and that "Max changes his attire every time he walks around the block." This also played into the company's ploy to build up Linder at Chaplin's expense, as there are numerous disdainful references to the low comedy and "baggy trousers, torn coat, and aged derby" of other comedians.

Max's impression of Chicago, the Essanay Studio, and George K. Spoor is said to have been very much as Chaplin's had been–not very favorable–but he set down to work at once on the scenario for the first

Racing for Title of Comedy King

Max gives Roscoe Arbuckle and Charlie Chaplin a run for their salaries in a 1917 newspaper cartoon.

film. Once the comic version of his rough voyage to America on the *S.S. Espagne* was chosen, elaborate sets, ship decks, cabins, and staterooms, some that rocked, were built and with interpreter Albert Petitmaitre and assistant director Leo White, shooting began in mid-December or early January of 1917. Two performers who were selected for the film would appear in all three of his Essanay shorts.

Albert Maupain had begun his career in early French films, but came to America and joined Essanay in 1915. A reliable character actor, after working for Linder he remained with Essanay and later appeared in features for Fox, Metro, Goldwyn, and the films of another French star in Hollywood, Leonce Perret. He returned to France after the war and had roles in films that included *Miracle of the Wolves* (1924) and *Napoleon* (1927) until the end of the silent era. For his leading lady, Linder chose eighteen year-old model and Broadway actress Martha Early (formerly Ehrlich). Despite their language difficulties, the pair clicked and in later interviews, Martha had extremely complimentary things to say about working with Max. After her three Linder films, she became a Ziegfeld Follies girl and changed her name to Martha Mansfield. Her big movie break came in the John Barrymore version of *Dr. Jekyll and Mr. Hyde* (1920) and she continued on with other popular pictures such as *The Little Red Schoolhouse* and *Potash and Perlmutter* (both 1923). Sadly, while shooting *The Warrens of Virginia* in 1923, her 1860s period dress caught fire on the set and she died of severe burns the next day.

Following some chilly location shooting on Lake Michigan in mid-January, *Max Comes Across* was completed and released on February 26, 1917. Although rumored to exist, the film is not available for viewing at this time. Critical reaction was mixed. For all the reviewers who found the film funny and inventive, there were almost an equal number that thought it fell short of expectations and that he had coarsened his humor for American tastes. It's clear that Essanay's scheme of having Max go head-to-head with Chaplin backfired, especially as Charlie had just hit a career peak with his Mutual Comedies and *Max Comes Across* just didn't compare as strongly.

Some of the most interesting remarks came from Julian Johnson of *Photoplay*, a fan of Linder's earlier work, who commented:

> This is a vitalized portrait of a man struggling to be funny, creating laughs from nothing, instead of letting laughs spring at ease from laughable situations and Linder today seems to

> me an affected, serious man who looks tremendously old when he permits his countenance a reposeful moment. The solemnity of war has written something across his features that all his smirks, and jumping, and mugging, and cross-eyed strains can't efface.

In many of the surviving Essanay publicity portraits, there's something of a "deer-in-the-headlights" look in Max's eyes, as if it was a Herculean effort to try and suggest the old gaiety and charm. It's apparent that all was not well–between Linder and Essanay, as well as with Max in general–and most of his interviews focus on his precarious health and descriptions of the horrors he had seen on the battlefields. Since Max's contract specified that he was to turn out a short a month, he embarked on his second production as soon as *Max Comes Across* was completed.

The plot has Max and his new wife return home from their wedding to receive a telegram informing them that Max's uncle has died, leaving him $3,000,000 with the stipulation that he remain a bachelor for life. He persuades his wife to consent to a divorce so they can get the money and

Francine Larrimore plays Max's spouse in *Max Wants a Divorce* (1917).
Photo courtesy of Sam Gill.

they set out to find a suitable lady to be the co-respondent. A date is set with a detective to catch Max with the "other woman," but all does not go as planned thanks to Max's jealous wife posing as a maid and a mix-up with some sanitarium inmates from next door. In the end, it all turns out to be the result of a typo and the money goes to Max only if he is married.

Speedily made, the finished *Max Wants a Divorce* was released on March 25 and received a much warmer reception than his first Essanay film. Screened today, it's charming and funny, plus a good deal more sophisticated than the average 1917 American comedy. Some of the strain in the previous short may have been Linder ill at ease in his new surroundings, as his direction here is very assured and smoothly effortless with many clever touches. Francine Larrimore, who plays Max's wife, is a great foil for him and has wonderful reactions as Max is flirting with the other woman so they can get their divorce, but is enjoying it a bit too much in her estimation. The ending gets a little frenetic with the inclusion of the sanitarium patients, but overall, it rates with his best films.

The grind of production and the cold Chicago winter were having an ill effect on Linder's already fragile health, so space was secured at the

Max Linder and Francine Larrimore during the shooting of *Max Wants a Divorce* (1917) at the Chicago Essanay studio. Photo courtesy of Sam Gill.

Thomas Ince Studio in Culver City, California for the next film. Essanay's publicity department worked overtime to assure Chicago that Linder really loved the city and it was only due to his health, in addition to lack of space at the studio, that was the reason for the California move. Never taking a break, the publicists also said that Max had added an additional six trunks of summer clothing to his already expansive retinue of forty-six. His staff, supporting players, and even many of the technical crew made the trip out west and despite the time taken for traveling and relocating at the new studio, the film was released on April 28.

Max plays the wastrel son of wealthy parents who comes home late from a night on the town once too often and is kicked out on his own. Distraught by his plight, Max decides to do himself in, but while failing at his second attempt, he finds an invitation to a society party. Max fits right in with his evening clothes and falls for the daughter of the house. The next day, he decides to get a job and ends up as a taxi driver. Of course, while out on the job, he meets up with his girl and her mother, so he pretends that the car is his, but they have an accident that leaves Max bouncing around on the overhead telephone wires.

Sadly *Max and a Taxi* doesn't compare well with *Max Wants a Divorce*. Where the earlier film was droll and effortless, Taxi is strained and forced. In its favor, it starts out promisingly with hijinks concerning a drunken Max and a horse carriage, plus a sequence where Linder reexamines his frequent theme of suicide, and unlike the Chicago films, it has loads of sunny California outdoor locations, but ultimately it doesn't add up to very much.

Although Linder appeared to like California and spent some time finally meeting and getting friendly with Charlie Chaplin, after *Max in a Taxi* his contract with Essanay was terminated. The press put the blame on his health and renewed problems from his war wounds, but privately it was said that mental as well as physical problems were the reason. Spoor claimed that the company lost in the ballpark of $87,000 on the contract with Linder.

After a period of recuperating in Arizona, Max sailed back to France in August of 1917. A number of news items expressed the possibility that when his health improved, Max would return to finish the balance of his Essanay films, but this, of course, never occurred. On his return to Paris, Linder opened a luxury cinema, the "Cinema Max," and introduced his countrymen to American stars, such as Mary Pickford, William S. Hart, and Douglas Fairbanks. After a couple of shorts, he returned to film-

Max trying to be a designated driver in 1917's *Max in a Taxi.*

making in a big way in 1919 with the starring feature *Le Petit Café* (*The Little Café*). Based on a play by Tristan Bernard, which was popular in Europe and America, where it was even adapted into a musical, Max plays a young man who becomes heir to two million francs, but because of a contract with his employer, must remain a waiter or forfeit a huge sum of his fortune. Max ends up slaving by day and living the high life at night. Thanks to a romance with the daughter of the café boss, all ends happily. Directed by Raymond Bernard, the film was a big hit in Europe and Pathé also released it in America to good reviews, but so-so business.

Despite this tepid response, Linder seemed determined to come back to the U.S. Although there had been rumors of his return since 1918, he didn't actually make the trip until the very end of 1919, when he formed a production unit with distribution through the Robertson-Cole Company. Setting up shop at the Maurice Tourneur studios at Universal City, Max began shooting the feature *Seven Years Bad Luck* (1921) with a staff that included assistant director Charles Dorian and gagman Al Davis. Detailing Max's misadventures in love and the problems he has after breaking a mir-

Max shares a cup with his bad luck omen in *Seven Years Bad Luck* (1921).
Photo courtesy of Sam Gill.

ror, the film's main setpiece, and what it's remembered for today, is Linder's staging of the popular "mirror routine."

Made famous by the Marx Brothers in *Duck Soup* (1933), the sketch dates back to stage plays of the Seventeenth and Nineteenth centuries and had been filmed many times before, by Harold Lloyd in *The Marathon* (1919) and later by Charley Chase with *Sittin' Pretty* (1924). The earliest American film version I've come across is Alice Guy Blache's 1912 Solax comedy *His Double*, where Darwin Karr impersonates his girlfriend's rival suitor and ends up doing the routine with him. In *Seven Years Bad Luck*, Max's valet has broken a large standing mirror and instead of incurring his boss's wrath, he grabs the cook, who looks like Max, to pretend to be his reflection until the repair person comes. Linder makes the deception more believable by giving Max a terrible hangover, so he attributes the oddness of his reflected image to his aching head. Max eventually discovers what's really going on, but gets interrupted by a phone call. While he's away, the glass is replaced and when Max returns, he throws a shoe at what he thinks is the cook, but ends up breaking the new mirror, leading to the bad luck of the film's title.

For this stay in California, Max embraced the local lifestyle and went "Hollywood." He bought a lavish home next door to Chaplin's and threw frequent parties with a gourmet chef and fine liquors. Besides rubbing elbows with industry heavyweights such as Thomas Ince, John Gilbert, Leatrice Joy, and Rudolph Valentino, Max became very close to Chaplin and the pair were seen together frequently at boxing matches and auto races. When working on films, they would share gags and ideas, helping each other to refine slapstick routines.

Critical reception was good for *Seven Years Bad Luck* and the film was profitable enough (particularly in Europe), so Max pressed on with another feature. Titled *Be My Wife* (1921), it concerns Max's trial and tribulations trying to wed his fiancée Alta Allen, not to mention their misunderstandings after tying the knot. Although the entire film is known to exist, what circulates is the first half hour, where Max is on the outs with Alta's aunt. The footage is fresh and funny with an abundance of inventive gags. The sequence climaxes with a wonderful routine where Max creates a false fight between himself and an imagined burglar that would be borrowed almost verbatim by Charley Chase for the ending of his short *Mighty Like a Moose* (1926). Linder has very good support from the comedy veterans Caroline Rankin, Lincoln Steadman, and Pal the dog,

Max and Charlie Chaplin pose by the lemon grove at the Chaplin Studio.

plus leading lady Alta Allen seems much more comfortable than in *Seven Years Bad Luck*. Linder had moved to Goldwyn Pictures to distribute the film, but felt that they did a poor job exploiting the picture, which had a mild box office performance.

For his last American film, Linder decided to try a different style. *The Three Must-Get-There's* (1922) is a direct parody of Douglas Fairbanks' recent hit *The Three Musketeers* (1921) and is a broad and wild burlesque, full of anachronisms and surreal juxtapositions of different eras and styles. Max plays Knockout Dart-in-Again, a young cavalier from the country who becomes an ally of the Three Must-Get-Theres and falls in love with Connie, the Queen's handmaiden. Dart-In-Again's main task is to travel to England to retrieve a brooch from the Queen's lover and is made a full Must-Get-There for his efforts.

A feature-length parody is very rare in silent comedy, but Linder pulls it off with a nimble and outright silly production where nothing is too absurd or ludicrous for use. The Queen's handmaidens play saxophones, telephones proliferate, and the names of the heroic trio, Walrus, Octopus, and Porpoise, are the norm. The cast of veteran slapstick regulars adds to the fun, with Bull Montana, Caroline Rankin, Al Cooke, Bynunski Hymen, and Harry Mann doing themselves proud. Max's love interest is a young Jobyna Ralston, who would soon be working opposite Paul Parrott at the Hal Roach Studio and then become Harold Lloyd's leading lady in classics such as *The Freshman* (1925) and *The Kid Brother* (1927). Of course, for full appreciation of the film, it helps if one is familiar with the Fairbanks film, but Max actually outdoes Doug on the swordplay, giving himself full opportunity to show off his excellent fencing skills.

Chaplin helped Linder arrange distribution through Allied Producers and Distributors, a United Artists subsidiary, but reviews were mixed and it did little business. Despite his best efforts, his attempt to firmly establish himself in American comedies really didn't work out. Part of the problem may have been that the screen character of Max was predominantly French, as opposed to the more universal personas of Chaplin, Arbuckle, Lloyd, and Keaton. Linder had been an innovator in the early Teens, which made him a bit of a figure from the past, and the comedians that had followed him, particularly Charley Chase and Raymond Griffith, used his ideas and style, but took them in different directions. His work was also undermined by his personal problems and bouts of depression.

In the fall of 1922, Linder sold his California property and returned to France. Still suffering from depression, he met eighteen year-old Ni-

A 1922 exhibitor ad for *The Three Must-Get-There's*.
Photo courtesy of Bruce Lawton.

nette Peters at the Swiss resort of Chamoix and they were married in August of 1923. Two more films were made–*Au Secours!* (Help! 1924), a surreal haunted castle short directed by Abel Gance, and the feature *Der Zirkuskonig* (*The King of the Circus* 1925), which was shot in Vienna and co-starred him with a young Vilma Banky. In 1924, Linder and his wife tried to kill themselves with an overdose of sleeping powders and despite the birth of a daughter in 1925, all was not well with the couple. Although he was working on an upcoming production, *Chevalier Barkas* (*The Knight Barkas*), Linder and his wife succeeded in their death wish and killed themselves on October 31, 1925, leaving four-month-old Maud Linder.

The effects of Linder's emotional turmoil are clearly visible in his face in this portrait used for publicity on *Be My Wife* (1921).

It's easy to attribute much of Linder's mental unrest to his World War I experiences, but even before the outbreak of the war, the screen character of Max seemed bipolar–either elated and walking on air, or absolutely depressed and dejected, looking for ways to kill himself. It's as if Linder seized on the manic-depressive tendencies in his own personality as subjects for his comedy. Although much of Linder's life was a sad story, its coda is more uplifting. His daughter Maud was raised by her grandparents under the family's real name of Leurielle, knowing nothing about her famous father. At age twenty, right at the end of World War II, she came across a film club that was showing *Seven Years Bad Luck* and went in. The next day, she resumed the name "Linder" and devoted herself to restoring her father's films and reputation. In the sixty-seven years since, she has done an amazing job. She has found scores of his missing films and packaged them for the public in cinema and television screenings, plus presented his story in feature compilations and documentaries, such as *In the Company of Max Linder* (1963) and *The Man in the Silk Hat* (1983), and books on the order of *Max Linder Etait Mon Pere* (*Max Linder was my Father* 1992). Her tireless work has given the screen's first great clown a new lease on the life that was ended too early.

Silent Partners: Comedy Teams of the Teens and Twenties Part Two: The 1920s

THIS SECTION CONTINUES *our look into comedy teams, going past the teens and into the 1920s, when the popularity of teams steadily grew and led to a near explosion at the end of the decade.*

A COUPLE OF SWELLS

Our first 1920s comic duo started at the tail end of 1919. The Hallroom Boys Comedies were based on the comic strip of the same name by Harold MacGill, which ran from 1906 to 1923 and chronicled the misadventures of the penniless playboys Percy and Ferdy in their quest to find and wed a Miss Millionbucks. Although there had been a few sporadic one-shot adaptations, such as *One-to-Three* (1914) with Wallace Beery and *The Fox Trot Craze* (1915), the series proper began with *Do it on $8 Per* (September 22, 1919). This was the offspring of the C.B.C. Film Sales Corp., which was founded by Jack Cohn, Joe Brandt, and the infamous Harry Cohn and would morph into Columbia Pictures in 1924.

Their first Percy and Ferdy was the well-known vaudeville team of Edward Flanagan and Neely Edwards, who had toured the country with their popular sketch *On and Off.* After *Breaking into Society* (March 9, 1920), Flanagan left, but Edwards stayed on and continued with Hugh Fay before eventually leaving to join Flannigan at the National Film Corp. for a few "Flannigan and Edwards" shorts. At this point, the Hallroom Boys series became a virtual revolving door for comics such as Harry McCoy, Jimmie Adams, George (a.k.a. Zip Monberg) Williams, Gilbert Wells, and Al Alt, but the mainstay Hallroom Boy was Sid Smith. Hard working and prolific, Smith was one of the diminutive and moustached comics that

The Hallroom Boys short *Tit for Tat* (1920) has Percy and Ferdy, in the persons of Hugh Fay (left) and Neely Edwards (right), conspiring about something. Photo courtesy of Eye Film Institute, Netherlands.

were as numerous as weeds in silent comedy. Starting his career in the Teens for Pathé and Selig, in the 1920s Smith bounced around constantly and worked for some of the biggest units such as Sennett, Jack White, Fox, and Christie, but also appeared in shorts at the other end for Grand Asher, Federated, Goodart, and even the bottom of the comedy barrel–William Pizor Productions. With the character of a bemused little fellow, Smith possessed a true ability to execute physical gags and crisp comic timing. Always a pleasant screen presence, his 1928 death at age thirty-six is said to have been from drinking bad bootleg booze at a weekend party.

C.B.C.'s earliest productions were the Hallroom Boys and Screen Snapshots newsreels (the latter of which ran until 1958). Distributing the shorts through outfits such as National Film Corp. and Federated, the leads were surrounded by expert supporting players, such as Polly Moran, Joseph "Baldy" Belmont, Joe Roberts, Jack Ackroyd, and Bud Jamison, not to mention behind-the-camera talent on the order of Herman Raymaker, Noel Mason Smith, Al Santell, Gilbert Pratt, Harry Edwards, and veteran comedy writer Jean Havez. In the beginning, the screen Percy and Ferdy were closer to the characters in the strip, but as the comedians became interchangeable, the shorts became standard slapstick romps. After something like seventy-nine entries, the series expired with the July 16, 1923 short *Seaside Simps*. In the early days, C.B. C. was jokingly referred to as "Corned Beef and Cabbage" by the industry, but after the changeover to Columbia, the sheer tenacity of Harry Cohn, with a little help from a director named Frank Capra, would make it one of the major studios of the 1930s and it still thrives today as Sony Pictures.

FAIR WEATHER FRIENDS

In the early part of the decade, there were a number of "transient teams" that were slapped together for a brief time. Comic Jimmie Adams had worked with Jack White at Fox Sunshine Comedies and when White began producing his own comedies in 1920, he hired Adams and paired him with Lige Conley. Headlining in this series was a break for Adams, who after working for Fox had spent time at Century Comedies playing

Jimmie Adams (left), Elinor Lynn (later known as Marion Mack), and Lige Conley (right) in the Mermaid Comedy *Free and Easy* (1921). Photo courtesy of Sam Gill.

second fiddle to Joe Martin the orangutan and the Century Lions. Lige Conley had grown up a couple of miles from the Mack Sennett Studio and after working as a cartoonist, began turning up after 1915 in Sennett, Hal Roach, Reelcraft, and Fox comedies.

A Fresh Start (1920) was not only the initial Adams & Conley opus, but also the very first Jack White Mermaid Comedy. The pair played convicts just released from prison who end up as waiters at a cabaret and get embroiled with a flirty wife, her murderously jealous husband, and rampaging lions. More pairings such as *Bang!* (1921) and *Free and Easy* (1921) followed, but were sporadic, as White also grafted Adams to Sid Smith at the same time for shorts like *Nonsense* (1920) and *High and Dry* (1921), as if it was a matter of who was available at the moment. Although these two teams were basically interchangeable, the films are funny thanks to the bountiful gags and talented performers.

A more unusual Jack White team was that of Lige Conley and black comic Spencer Bell. Working in comedy shorts was a thankless and often physically dangerous occupation for black comedians; stereotyped roles, skimpy pay, hazardous stunts, and little recognition was their lot in life. The

Spencer Bell (right) stands at attention to help out Lige Conley (center) as an unknown black actor looks on in *High Life* (1923). Photo courtesy of Sam Gill.

ranks of black supporting clowns included Edgar Blue (sometimes known as Blue Washington), Ray Turner, Curtis McHenry, and Henry Trice, but the most high-profiled of the group was Bell. Coming from a background of minstrel shows and vaudeville, Bell appeared on the Hollywood scene in the early 1920s and worked frequently for Larry Semon. His best opportunities came with Lige Conley in shorts such as *Wild Game* (1924) and *Below Zero* (1925), where they were often co-stars in everything but official billing. Although he had to put up with screen character names on the order of "Moonlight" and "Snowball," as Conley's right hand man, Bell had frequent chances to show his stuff–extreme athleticism, split-second timing, and some of the funniest legwork in pictures. After 1925, the pair only appeared together sporadically, but Bell worked everywhere–more shorts for Educational, Fox, and Sennett, plus features such as *The Outlaw Dog* (1927), *The Peacock Fan* (1929), and *Smart Money* (1931). He passed away in 1935.

While the above clowns were changing partners for Jack White, the Reelcraft Film Corporation was releasing a one-reel series with Bud Duncan, refugee from the popular teens' team of Ham and Bud. Launched by Schiller Productions in Yonkers, New York as a solo series, Duncan was soon paired with little Billy Gilbert for shorts such as *Scream Street*, *All Wet*, and *Stuck Up* (all 1921). This was not the Billy Gilbert well-known today for his appearances in sound films, but an ex-aeronaut and high diver who had started as a stuntman and bit comedian at Keystone in 1913. Branching out in 1916 to direct some of Harold Lloyd's earliest "glasses character" shorts (although Lloyd had dismissive things to say about Gilbert's work in his autobiography), he also worked in Fox Sunshine Comedies before this stint with Reelcraft.

Low-budget and crude, these Aladdin Comedies folded after a year with Bud Duncan concentrating on stage appearances before returning to films at the end of the decade for some Weiss Brothers Crackerjack Comedies and a series of Toots and Caspar shorts based on the popular comic strip. Billy Gilbert appeared in various features, plus shorts for Fox, Joe Rock, and Larry Semon, but mostly did bits in Sennett films in addition to acting as a studio prop man. When Republic Pictures took over the Sennett lot in 1935, Gilbert stayed on in the property department for many years until his retirement.

Former Hallroom Boy Neely Edwards had been busy appearing in shorts for the Special Pictures Corporation and Arrow's Speed Comedies in addition to working as support in features such as *Brewster's Millions*

Neely Edwards (left) and Bert Roach (right) as the tramp Nervy Ned and his hobo valet.

(1921) and *The Green Temptation* (1922), when he began headlining in a 1922 series for Universal. Starring as "Nervy Ned," a gentleman tramp, Edwards was paired with character comic Bert Roach, who played his hobo valet. Together in one-reelers on the order of *Society Hobos* and *Their Steady Job* (both 1922), the pair scrupulously avoided work and looked for easy money. Bert Roach had entered films in 1913 and worked steadily for L-Ko and Sennett, plus appeared in occasional features. In 1924, Edwards and Roach's teamwork continued, but morphed into a domestic series when comedienne Alice Howell was added to the mix (see Chapter 5). Neely and Alice played a comfortable middle-class married couple with Roach gumming up their lives as their goofy butler.

After the series ended in 1925, Alice Howell retired in 1927. Bert Roach did well in late 1920s features and had some prominent character bits in the early days of sound, but by the mid-1930s, he ended up in uncredited walk-ons, which he did until 1951. Neely Edwards' movie career also slowed down with the coming of sound, but he started a new leg of his career when he joined the cast of the popular stage show *The Drunkard* in 1933 and stayed with it during its legendary run of twenty-five years. He continued doing occasional bit parts in films, but Edwards retired when *The Drunkard* closed in 1959.

As an antidote to all the male buddy-buddy teamings was a number of male/female pairings. Two little-remembered romantic teams sprung up in 1921, the first being Billy Fletcher and Violet Joy in a series of Spotlight Comedies. These one-reelers were produced by Morris Schlank for distribution through the Arrow Film Corp. and centered on the comical doings of young newlyweds Fletcher and Joy, who are better known under different names. Fletcher is actually longtime character player Billy Bletcher, who began his career in the teens for Vim and Vitagraph. For some reason, it was decided to modify his name for this starring series (he also used Fletcher for some Universal Star Comedies made at the same time), but he soon returned to Bletcher and prolifically appeared as support in films, worked behind the scenes as a voice actor for Disney and others, plus made television appearances into the 1970s. After the Spotlights, Violet Joy became Vernon Dent's leading lady in his Folly Comedies for the Pacific Film Company and then changed her name to Duane Thompson. As that, she appeared in Christie comedies with Bobby Vernon and Walter Hiers in addition to shorts with Sid Smith, Jimmie Adams, and Edward Everett Horton. After some late 1920s features for Universal and Tiffany, her career ended with the arrival of sound.

Billy Fletcher and Violet Joy (better known as Billy Bletcher and Duane Thompson) in *Wanted, an Alibi* (1921), the first of their Spotlight Comedies for Arrow.

The other short-lived romantic series was the Alt-Howell Comedies produced by the Union Film Company and starring the vaudeville pair Alexander Alt and Helen Howell. Even more obscure today than the Spotlight Comedies, the Alt-Howell two-reelers were first distributed by the independent Reelcraft Pictures Corporation, but then switched to the even more independent Allied Distribution Corporation. Despite behind the scenes and in front of the camera help from veterans such as Al Martin and former Pokes and Jabs star Bobby Burns, survivors such as *Bungalow Love* and *The Lost Engagement Ring* (both 1921) are particularly uninspired.

Both players had appeared in vaudeville and Helen Howell had already been on film with "Smiling Billy" Parsons and in some of the Hallroom Boys comedies, first with Flannigan and Edwards and then Edwards and Hugh Fay. Although not one hundred percent verified, it appears that she was same Helen Howell who later played the ingénue in the Plum Center Comedies and became the first wife of director Frank Capra (1923-1928). Al Alt had embarked in films in the teens for the Thanhouser Company and after the Alt-Howell shorts, he moved on to the Hallroom Boys comedies and then had a long run for Century and Rayart. He also turned up in comedies for Samuel Bischoff and Jack White and after a few early sound shorts for RKO and Pathé, he produced some independent features. Continuing behind the camera, he became an assistant and second unit director on big films such as *Les Girls* (1957) and *Merry Andrew* (1958) and died in 1992.

In contrast to these young couples were the middle-aged marrieds in Arrows' Cruelly Weds Comedies. Paul Weigel and Lilie Leslie starred as a longtime wedded pair in a series of domestic situation comedies that used the shorts of Mr. and Mrs. Sidney Drew as inspiration. Produced, written, and directed by Sig Herzig, the only circulating entry today, *The Slyest Bidder* (1921), chronicles hubby Henry's adventures as an auction nut who can't keep himself from bidding and filling up their home with unwanted junk. Of course, wise wifie turns the tables to teach Henry a lesson. Stars Weigel and Leslie were established character players–Weigel in features such as *Bluebeard's Eighth Wife* (1923) and Harold Lloyd's *For Heaven's Sake* (1926), while Leslie was an Australian actress who had appeared in dramas as part of the Lubin stock company and later changed her name to Lila Leslie, where she often played Big Boy's mother in Jack White comedies such as *No Fare* (1928) and *Helter Skelter* (1929). Series auteur Sig Herzig spent most of the 1920s as writer of Christie Comedies and had a long career authoring movies and TV shows up to 1961.

A more traditionally slapstick male/female duo turned up a couple of years later in Jack White Cameo Comedies. Cliff Bowes and Virginia Vance appeared together in over sixty Cameos between 1923 and 1926. Bowes was a former swimming and diving champ and a veteran of the Mack Sennett studio who usually played the type of comedy patsy that sight gag difficulties always happened to. Virginia Vance was the blonde helpmate who always did her best to get Cliff out of the hot water that was always of his own making. Having gotten her start doing the same for Jimmie Adams in the very first Cameo Comedies, Vance later appeared in some features and was a regular in Sennett's Dan the Taxi Man series opposite Jack Cooper. She retired after marrying actor Bryant Washburn in 1929 and died at age forty in 1942. Cliff Bowes appeared in Cameos until his death, which, at age 34, was even younger than his co-star Vance when he had a stroke in 1929.

The capper for this group of early 1920s male/female pairings is the decidedly unromantic and definitely odd coupling of wizened, old Dan Mason with 6'3", three hundred pound Wilna Hervey in the Toonerville Trolley and Plum Center comedy series. Mason was a longtime stage veteran whose movie career began in 1913 as part of the ensemble in Edi-

Virginia Vance and Cliff Bowes have double trouble in *Head On* (1924).
Photo courtesy of Robert Arkus.

son comedies and in the latter teens, he moved on to supporting roles in features such as *Laughing Bill Hyde* (1918) with Will Rogers. Wilna Hervey (who sometimes appeared under the name Wilma Wild) was really a painter whose unusual size led her to movie work, where she started out doing bits in the comedies of Mr. and Mrs. Sidney Drew and other New York-based films.

In 1920, the Betzwood Film Company of Betzwood, Pennsylvannia launched a series of two-reelers based on Fontaine Fox's popular *Toonerville Trolley* comic strip. Mason was cast as the skipper, the cantankerous engineer of the trolley, and Hervey was his huge and powerful Swedish housekeeper Katrinka. The series lasted until 1922 and followed the misadventures of the eccentric denizens of Toonerville. It's when this series abruptly halted due to financial problems that Dan Mason himself conceived the idea of the Plum Center comedies, which was basically Toonerville with all the names changed to protect the not-so-innocent. Produced by Paul Gerson and distributed by FBO, the Plum Centers revolved around Mason as Pop Tuttle and Hervey as the large Tillie Olson.

When this series ended in 1923, Mason worked mostly in features, such as Johnny Hines' *Conductor 1492* (1924), *Rainbow Riley* (1926), and *Stepping Along* (1926). One of his last appearances was in Charley Bowers' Educational short *Hop Off* (1928) and he passed away the next year at age seventy-two. Wilna Hervey had only made movies to support her art pursuits, so her film career ended when the Plum Center series was over. In addition to appearing in these comedies with Dan Mason, she became the life partner of his daughter, Nan, and the two were together until Hervey's death in 1979.

ON THE ROACH LOT

The famous team that emerged from the Hal Roach Studio was, of course, Laurel & Hardy, but they were preceded by a few forgotten combos on the order of Hunky-Dorey, the Spat Family, and first and foremost by sheer quantity, Snub Pollard and Marie Mosquini. Snub Pollard, still one of the most recognizable faces of silent comedy, was born Harold Frasier in Australia in 1886. He came to America as part of the children's comic operetta troupe Pollard's Lilliputians and kept Pollard as his stage name after the group disbanded (as did fellow Lilliputian Daphne Pollard). Making his film debut for Essanay in 1914, Snub turned up in Chaplin comedies, such as *By the Sea* and *Police* (both 1915), and more importantly was a member of the general stock company in one-reelers

Snub Pollard and Marie Mosquini pose on the Hal Roach lot.

directed by Hal Roach. Soon Roach set up his own production unit and hired Snub to support his star comic Harold Lloyd. In 1919, Snub graduated to his own series, cranking out as many as forty a year. At first, his leading lady was a young Mildred Davis, but he was soon teamed with Marie Mosquini.

Mosquini had been born in Los Angeles and, at age fourteen, became the "girl Friday" for the fledgling Roach outfit. Besides her duties of answering phones, ordering props, checking out costumes, and even patching films, she began playing various bits in the comedies. These appearances increased and after being hooked up with Snub in 1920, she became a full-time actress. Snub's character was that of a goofy goon with a Fu Manchu moustache and Marie was usually his long-suffering wife or love interest. These breezy, anything-for-a-laugh shorts were close in spirit to the Mack Sennett school of comedy with Marie the only voice of reason or sanity in the madcap whirl.

After appearing in umpteen shorts together, they began going their separate ways in 1923. At that point, Marie began working with Will Rogers, Stan Laurel, and Paul Parrott and after leaving the Roach lot in 1924, she worked in Universal shorts with Charles Puffy and a few features, the most famous being *Seventh Heaven* (1927). In 1930, she retired from the movies when she married Dr. Lee De Forest of audion tube and Phonofilms fame. Snub's departure from Roach a little after Marie led to his involvement in another team that we'll get to soon.

In 1923, the Roach organization created a team that turned out to be one of the studio's rare misfires. The Spat Family comedies ran from 1923 to 1925 and starred Frank Butler and Laura Roessing as a quarreling husband and wife with Sidney D'Albrook completing the trio as the wife's obnoxious brother. Butler, who headlined as Tewksbury Spat, was a British and American stage veteran and D'Albrook a longtime character player before and after the Spats. The series chronicled the difficulties of the three (usually of their own making) while working on building a house, going on a camping trip, or putting on a play.

Surviving examples aren't particularly funny and are irritating due to the characters' constant bickering and battling. After the retirement of the Spats, Frank Butler moved behind the camera to become head of the Roach story department and later settled in at Paramount, possibly through the good graces of fellow Roach veteran Leo McCarey. There he wrote the scripts for *The Milky Way* (1936), *Road to Morocco* (1942), and *Going My Way* (1944), winning an Oscar for Best Screenplay for the latter.

As usual, everything is chaos when the Spats are involved. Sidney D'Albrook (bottom left), Frank Butler (center), and Laura Roessing leave destruction in their wake in *The Royal Four-Flush* (1925). Photo courtesy of Cole Johnson.

The last of the early Roach teams occurred when they spliced together the supporting character comedians Earl Mohan and Billy Engle to create Hunky-Dorey, who appeared in a series of nine one-reelers that lasted from the spring of 1924 to the fall of 1925. Earl Mohan was a longtime member of the studio's stock company, having started there in 1916 after working in vaudeville and the Sells-Floto Circus. Supporting every star comic on the lot, Mohan's specialty was a hilarious drunk character, which was memorably captured in Harold Lloyd's *Safety Last* (1923). Information on Billy Engle's background is more elusive. He was a native of Austria and a graduate of burlesque who began his film career in 1919. Small with a bald pate comb-over and usually a moustache, Engle was one of the most ubiquitous faces in silent comedy, appearing non-stop in shorts for Universal, Fox, Roach, and Christie.

One at a Time (1924) was their team debut short and introduced Mohan as the lousy boxer "Knockout Kelly" with Engle as his down-at-his-heels manager. They would return to these characters in other shorts like *The Bouncer* (1925), but in all their adventures, Billy was the brain and Earl the dumb brawn, whether they were working as inept tailors or Pullman porters. Sadly, audiences never warmed to these shorts, so after *All Wool* (Oct. 25, 1925), they went their separate ways. Engle then spent the rest of the silent era working mostly for Al Christie with his sound career consisting of uncredited bits into the 1950s. He died in Hollywood on November 28, 1966. Earl Mohan, never achieving the recognition he deserved for his comic talents, turned up much less frequently at Roach after the demise of Hunky-Dorey, but increased his appearances elsewhere. Besides many shorts for Educational and Fox, he was also support in features like *For Heaven's Sake* (1926) with Harold Lloyd and Buster Keaton's *The General* (1927), but died young at age thirty-nine on October 15, 1928.

OVER AT SENNETT

At the same time as the aforementioned Hal Roach teams, there were two "unofficial" pairings on the rival Mack Sennett lot. Harry Langdon was the comedy king's newest "find" and, by the end of 1924, was becoming a sensation. Extremely important as Langdon's foil was character comic Vernon Dent, one of the rocks of early film comedy, who was discovered singing in California nightclubs by comedian Hank Mann and promptly hired to be support in Mann's 1919 to 1921 series of Arrow comedies. After briefly graduating to his own series of Folly Comedies for the Pacific Film Co., Dent became a fixture at the Mack Sennett studio, where he supported everyone from Billy Bevan to Johnny Burke. A past master at supplying the comic gravity and tension necessary for a clown like Langdon to play off of, Dent was often the Goliath to Langdon's Little David. When Langdon left Sennett to embark on his own series of starring features for First National Pictures, Dent stayed at the Sennett Studio, but his character archetype remained a key ingredient in the Langdon formula, so much so that the role was filled in by Tom Murray in *Tramp, Tramp, Tramp* (1926), Arthur Thalasso for *The Strong Man* (1926) and *Three's A Crowd* ('27), and Bud Jamison in *The Chaser* (1928). When sound arrived, Langdon and Dent would be reunited in shorts for Educational, Paramount, and Columbia.

Sennett's other "unofficial" duo was Ralph Graves and Marvin Loback. Graves was an oddity on the Sennett lot–a handsome young leading man who had starred in numerous features and worked for D.W. Griffith in *Scarlet Days* (1919), *The Greatest Question* (1919), and *Dream Street* ('21). After appearing opposite Mabel Normand in the Sennett feature *The Ex-*

Budd Ross (left), Ralph Graves (center), and Marvin Loback (right) doing spittoon duty in the Sennett Comedy *A Yankee Doodle Duke* (1926). Photo courtesy of Steve Rydzewski.

tra Girl (1923), Graves remained at the studio for a two-year series of light comedies that were a distinct departure from the business as usual Sennett fare of grotesque and absurd zanies. For the first time, romance became an element of a Sennett comedy and new leading ladies, such as Alice Day and Thelma Parr, were brought in for Graves' love interests. Rotund Marvin Loback was also on hand as Ralph's buddy or shady business associate to bring in the more sight-gag related and traditional Sennett material to the films. After something like eighteen shorts together, the pair went their separate ways–Loback to more shorts and a soon-to-be-discussed partnership with Snub Pollard and Graves back to features, plus writing and directing, until 1949.

Sennett's experiment with the lighter elements in the Graves comedies led to an official team at the end of the 1920s–The Smith Family–which followed the trials and tribulations of Jimmy Smith, his wife Mabel, and their baby Bubbles. The trio was played by Raymond McKee, Ruth Hiatt, and Mary Ann Jackson, with the Sennett regulars Andy Clyde, Sunshine Hart, Irving Bacon, William McCall, Louise Carver, David Morris, Vernon Dent, and even Polly Moran filling in as support. Raymond McKee had graduated from an early stage career to shorts for Lubin, Edison, and C.C. Burr in addition to starring features such as *The Unbeliever* (1918), *Down to the Sea in Ships* (1922), and *Babbit* (1924) and had been in pictures for ten years when he began working for Sennett in 1924. Ruth Hiatt had been a child actor in the teens and before joining the Sennett organization in 1925, she appeared with Lloyd Hamilton and other stars in Educational Mermaid and Cameo comedies, plus had been a 1924 WAMPAS Baby Star. Mary Ann Jackson was a baby star, a two-year-old scene-stealer when the series began, who came from a family of performing children (see Chapter Seventeen).

Starting with *Smith's Baby* (1926), the series ran into 1929 and besides the three leads, their giant dog and various relatives were added to the mix, creating a 1920s domestic sitcom, with titles such as *Smith's Picnic* (1926), *Smith's New Home* (1927), and *Smith's Cook* (1927) being very self-explanatory. Although a bit more subdued than the usual Sennett fare, there was

In *Smith's Modiste Shop* (1927), Raymond McKee (left) gets the altitude on Villy Latimer as Ruth Hiatt (right) checks the width on Mamie Hicks and George Gray (center) takes notes. Photo courtesy of Sam Gill.

still plenty of slapstick and physical comedy, usually the result of something engineered by baby Bubbles. Ending in mid-1929, after this series, Raymond McKee moved on to some Jack White Talking Comedies before leaving films in the early 1930s, but was always busy writing episodes of radio shows, investing in California real estate and oil, not to mention having the Hollywood restaurant "Raymond McKee's Zulu Hut." Ruth Hiatt left films to marry after working in sound shorts with Lloyd Hamilton, the Three Stooges, and Our Gang and of course, Mary Ann Jackson became one of the stars of Our Gang on the Hal Roach lot.

ETHNIC PAIRS

In the previous decade, the predominant ethnic teams had been "Dutch comics" from the stage, such as Weber & Fields, Kolb & Dill, and their numerous imitators. The 1920s strain of racial duos came from the stage as well, but were based on hit Broadway plays. *Potash and Perlmutter* detailed the trials and tribulations of two Jewish knights of the garment industry and had opened to great success in 1913 starring Barney Bernard and Alexander Carr. Both comics had specialized in "Hebrew characters" for many years in vaudeville and book shows and continued on when the show was franchised into the sequels *Partners Again*, *His Honor Abe Potash*, and *Abe and Mawruss*.

Barney Bernard had made his film debut in 1916 with a couple of shorts for the Vitagraph Company, but in 1923, he and Carr transferred their partnership to the screen in the film version of *Potash and Perlmutter*. Produced by Samuel Goldwyn and directed by Clarence Badger, the story was a success again and led to two more movies–*In Hollywood with Potash and Perlmutter* (1924) and *Partners Again* (1926). Alexander Carr soldiered on as Mawress Perlmutter in the sequels, but Barney Barnard died at age forty-six before the second film was made, so he was replaced by another veteran stage comic, George Sidney.

Also a specialist in Jewish characters, Sidney had found fame as the star of the show *Busy Izzy*, which was followed by *Busy Izzy's Vacation* and *Busy Izzy's Boodle*. He even starred in a 1915 *Bizzy Izzy* short made in New York for American Gaumont's Casino Comedies, but didn't return to the screen until *In Hollywood with Potash and Perlmutter*. After the Potash and Perlmutter films, both he and Carr became popular movie character players, with Carr working up to Preston Sturges' 1940 film *Christmas in July*. George Sidney was even more in demand, which brings us to our next ethnic team, as in 1926, he was paired with Irish comedian Charles

George Sidney (left) and Alexander Carr (right) as Potash and Perlmutter in their third film outing *Partners Again* (1926).

Murray in *The Cohens and the Kellys.*

Starting his career at age ten in circuses and medicine shows, Charlie Murray hit big time vaudeville when he teamed with Ollie Mack and they became the Irish equivalent of Weber & Fields. After working together for over twenty years in hit shows like *Shooting the Chutes* and *The Sunny Side of Broadway*, the pair split up in 1910 and Charlie found his way to the infant film industry. By 1912, he was the leading comedian at the Biograph Company, where he created his screen persona of the layabout Irishman "Skelly," which he essentially played for the remainder of his career. He migrated to Keystone in 1914, where "Skelly" was renamed "Hogan" and Murray became one of Sennett's top comics until 1922, when he began freelancing in other shorts and numerous features.

The Cohens and the Kellys (1926) was a thinly veiled movie rip-off of Anne Nichol's hit play *Abie's Irish Rose.* Murray and Sidney's comic antics and battling as the heads of Irish and Jewish families whose oldest son and daughter fall in love and marry made them instant audience favorites together. Although two more silent Cohen and Kelly films were made, *The Cohens and Kellys in Paris* (1928) and *The Cohens and Kellys in*

Atlantic City ('29), Murray didn't appear in them. Instead, he and Sidney continued their feuding in four features for First National Pictures–*Sweet Daddies* (1926), *Lost at the Front* (1927), *The Life of Riley* (1927), and *Flying Romeos* (1928). When sound arrived, Murray did rejoin Sidney in *The Cohens and the Kellys in Scotland* (1930), *The Cohens and Kellys in Africa* (1930), *The Cohens and Kellys in Hollywood* (1932), and finally, *The Cohens and Kellys in Trouble* (1933), plus the pair made a few two-reelers together for the fledgling Columbia shorts department on the order of *Ten Baby Fingers* (1934) and *Back to the Soil* (1934). Both continued to appear separately as character players in features–Sidney until 1937 and Murray to 1938.

Over at the Fox Studio, a new series of East Side–West Side Comedies had been put together in 1925. This series was also based on the *Abie's Irish Rose* prototype, but instead of the battling heads of the families, it revolved around the children. The romantic couple was played by Barbara

George Sidney (left) and Charlie Murray (right) make noise in their silent comedy *The Life of Riley* (1927).

Luddy and Georgie Harris in five two-reelers that included *Pawnshop Politics* (1926) and *The Bathing Suitor* (1927). Luddy was a seventeen-year-old beauty and Harris a graduate of the English music hall. Scouted for Hollywood by Mack Sennett, he spent most of his time at Fox, where he was immediately typed as a Jewish character, even playing Max Davidson's son in *The Johnstown Flood* (1926).

After the series ended in 1927, Luddy became popular on the radio and in 1955 was the voice of Lady in the Disney animated classic *Lady and the Tramp*. This led to her becoming a Disney voice regular for *Sleeping Beauty* (1959), *101 Dalmatians* (1961), *Winnie the Pooh and the Honey Tree* ('66), and many more in addition to small parts in movies and TV shows until 1977. Following a few sound pictures in the U.S., Harris returned to England in the early 1930s and worked in features until the end of the decade. Years later, he was interviewed by Kevin Brownlow and David Gill for the installment of their *Hollywood* series (1980) dealing with silent comedy.

Mixed Doubles

The award for the largest number of pairings in the shortest amount of time goes to Al Cooke and Kit Guard, who were combined from 1923 to 1927 as the comic relief in series such as The Telephone Girl, The Go-Getters, The Pacemakers, Fighting Blood, The Adventures of Mazie, Wise-crackers, Fighting Hearts, The Beauty Parlor, and Bill Grimm's Progress. Usually working for FBO and often in support of star Alberta Vaughn, the pair played battling buddies who made as many problems as they solved for the leading characters.

The senior member of the team, Al Cooke, was born in America, but raised and educated in Paris and Switzerland. He started doing bits in films in 1916 and soon became part of the ensemble at the Mack Sennett Studio, where with his red nose and glassy eyes he specialized in inebriated gentlemen. Also appearing as King Louis XIII in Max Linder's feature *The Three Must-Get-Theres* (1922), plus full-length Sennett films such as *Love, Honor and Behave* (1920) and *A Small Town Idol* ('21), he really came to prominence in his first teaming with Kit Guard in 1923's The Telephone Girl comedies. Born in Denmark as Christen Klitgaard, Kit Guard had a varied early life as a sailor, blacksmith, professional boxer, and soldier before making his stage debut with the Alcazar Stock Company in San Francisco. He entered films after World War I service and can be spotted as a thug in the Marcel Perez comedy *Sweet Daddy*, shot in Yonkers, NY

Kit Guard (standing left) and Al Cooke (standing right) flank George O'Hara in an episode of *Fighting Blood* (1924) while Cliff Bowes and Billy Armstrong watch from the left front row. Photo courtesy of Robert Arkus.

in 1921. Also appearing in the popular serials *Bride 13* (1920) and *The Face at your Window* (1921), he became a "name" when he and Cooke were teamed in the Telephone Girl comedies.

During the next four years, the pair worked nonstop, even appearing together in the features *Her Father Said No* (1927) and *Legionnaires in Paris* (1927), but after their series of Bill Grimm's Progress comedies, they went their separate ways. No reason was given for their break and Cooke even pressed on with a series of Karnival Komedies, where he was briefly grafted to another comic, this time small and round-headed Barney Hellum, a Norwegian clown who had been a regular supporting player in Sennett comedies and would go on to star in a Barney Google series. Cooke went into sound for producer Larry Darmour, but by 1932, his career began to taper off and he died in 1935. Kit Guard worked as support in features and shorts, but by 1932, had been relegated to uncredited bit parts, which he continued doing in films and television programs until 1958.

Cowboy sidekicks were played by Pee Wee (Gilbert) Holmes and Ben Corbett in the W.C. Tuttle Western Comedies that were a subseries of Universal's Mustang Westerns. Holmes and Corbett played Dirty Shirt Jones and Magpie Simpkins, two always-feuding ranch hands in the mythical western 'burb of Piperock. Both were real cowboys–Holmes had been a rodeo rider and broke into films supporting Tom Mix and Dustin Farnum before starting to appear in comedy shorts for Fox in the early 1920s. Corbett hit the movies around 1915 and mostly worked for Universal. The series began in 1925 and its resident director was comedy pro Vin Moore.

The shorts were based on stories by Tuttle with the scenarios written by character comic Robert McKenzie, who had previous western experience as a mainstay of Essanay's Snakeville Comedies and with his family was regular support in the series. Although most of the shorts took place on the ranch with the boys pulling pranks and one-upping each other, usually over a girl, they did occasionally try to break things up in an entry like *When East Meets West* (1926) that has the boys hypnotized by a traveling fakir and imagining they're in the street bazaars and harems of Turkey.

The series ran from 1925 into 1927. Afterwards, Pee Wee and Ben continued as supporting comics in western features, but because they

Ben Corbett (left) and Pee Wee Holmes (right) team up with Joe Martin the orangutan in *When East Meets West* (1926). Photo courtesy of Robert S. Birchard.

were real cowboys and not experienced actors, they didn't fare as well in sound films and were demoted to small bits. Both continued working until their deaths, Holmes fairly young in 1936 and Corbett in 1961.

A temporary team that gets a good amount of attention today due to the participation of Oliver Hardy is the 1925 pairing of Hardy with goofy Bobby Ray. As Laurel and Hardy fans know, in the teens and most of the 1920s, "Babe" Hardy was an ace supporting player working with stars such as Billy West and Larry Semon and had even been partnered at Vim in 1916 with Billy Ruge as the short-lived Plump and Runt. In 1925, Hardy rejoined Billy West for a number of Broadway Comedy two-reelers that West was starring in and producing for his Cumberland Productions with distribution by Arrow. At the same time, West was producing a series of Mirthquake Comedies for comic Bobby Ray and Babe ended up grafted to Ray for at least four of the shorts.

Bobby Ray began his career as a child on the stage under his real name of Bobby Feuhrer. Working with the likes of Maude Adams in *Peter Pan*, his movie debut came in 1914, when he replaced Augustus Carney in Universal's Universal Ike comedies. Carney and Universal had a disagreement, so Universal Ike became Universal Ike, Jr., with Bobby taking over. From there, he moved over to the Reliance Company's "Komic Comedy" brand, first as support and then stepping into the lead in the unit's Bill the Office Boy series. In the later teens, Ray can be spotted as part of the ensemble supporting Larry Semon and he had his first starring shorts in a 1920 series of low-budget and crude Tusun Comedies from the independent Russell-Greiver–Russell outfit. He seems to have returned to the supporting ranks until Billy West tapped him for this series in 1925.

The Hardy and Ray shorts–*Stick Around*, *Hey, Taxi*, *Hop to It*, and *They All Fall* (all 1925)–are interesting and definite Laurel and Hardy forerunners. In most, Hardy is the slow-burning boss with Ray as the inept bonehead who gets Babe into hot water. Both are dumb and although Babe is a bit brighter, he's not as smart as he thinks he is. In *Stick Around*, where they play bungling paperhangers, they even wear derbies. Since Hardy was often busy working on Billy West's set, Harry McCoy often turned up with Ray and in one, *Cagey Love* (1925), Edgar Kennedy is the tough boss, but without the real teamwork as with Hardy.

After this group of shorts, Babe Hardy began working as support at the Hal Roach Studio. Bobby Ray moved over to Rayart for a series of Morris Schlank-produced Radiant Comedies, which starred him in two-reelers such as *The Stupid Prince* (1926) and *Baby Faces* (1927), plus under

Bobby Ray (center) and Oliver Hardy (right) fight over Marjorie Beebe's business in *Hey Taxi* (1925). Photo courtesy of Jim Kerkhoff.

his real name, he directed others with comedian Al Alt to end of the 1920s. With the changeover to sound, he became an assistant director on B movies for studios such as PRC and Monogram in addition to TV shows, such as *I Led Three Lives* (1953—1956), right up to his death in 1957.

A low-budget duo was put together by Gene "Fatty" Layman (sometimes Laymon) for a few two-reelers distributed by Tennek/Sava Films, which were known as Two Star Comedies. Layman was one of the many fat men who wanted to fill the plus-sized trousers left vacant when Roscoe "Fatty" Arbuckle had to leave the screen because of scandal, so he combined his large person with short and skinny Charles Dorety. In the surviving shorts *The Inventors* (1926) and *Are Golfers Cuckoo?* (1926), the pair seem to be working from the late teens Arbuckle/Keaton prototype, but the lack of material and money doomed the films to obscurity. Dorety had been a dancer and comic in vaudeville and after beginning his film career at Fox Sunshine Comedies, he bounced around to Bulls Eye and Lehrman First National Specials before a stint headlining in a series for Century Comedies. Sadly, his lack of a definable character and approach to comedy caused him to end up as an uncredited bit player, which he did until 1955.

Information is scarce on Gene Layman's life and career, but he surfaced in films around 1920, appearing in the J. Stuart Blackton drama *The Forbidden Valley* before producing these shorts with Dorety. From there, he went on to being a regular in Century Comedies' forgotten Keeping Up with the Joneses two-reel series, where in blackface and drag, he played the family's black cook Bella Donna. After sound arrived, he turned up in a few minor westerns and crime dramas before he disappeared from films after 1934. An interesting sidebar to Layman and Dorety's screen teamwork was their forming of H.I.L. Productions in 1928, which saw them going to different communities and making shorts that starred Layman with local residents. Dorety would direct and edit the footage, which would have a "premiere" in the town at the end of the week. This enterprise seems to have ended once sound was added to the technical mix.

THREE-WAY STRETCH

Probably the most unusual teams of the 1920s were the Fox Monkeys and A Ton of Fun. The Fox Monkeys were formed in 1923 in the tradition of earlier primate partners, such as Napoleon & Sally, with this simian trio consisting of Max, Moritz, and little Pep. Starting with *Circus Pals* (1923) and going on through *Jungle Pals* (1923) and *School Pals* (1924), the monks' specialty was disrupting the natural human order of things, such as Jean Arthur's modiste shop in *Monks a la Mode* (1923). Trained by Reuben Gastang and Charles Judge, the chimps' films benefitted from the support of regular comedy players such as Jack Duffy, Otto Fries, Stanley Blystone, and Merta Sterling and as the series went on, they moved into genre parodies on the order of *Westward, Whoa!* (1924) and *Grief in Bagdad* (1925). The peak of their short career came in their 1924 feature *Darwin Was Right*. Most of their outings were handled by Lewis Seiler, who had started in the business as a gagman in 1919 and graduated to directing with the monkey shorts. After helming their feature, he moved on to two-reelers and features with humans and worked nonstop on pictures like *It All Came True* (1940) and *Guadalcanal Diary* (1943) until 1958. After their feature, the monkeys' appearances tapered off and finally ended in mid-1925.

A main component of silent comedy was physical grotesquery, but the A Ton of Fun comedies ran with the idea and never looked back. Frank "Fatty" Alexander, Hillard "Fatt" Karr, and Bill "Kewpie" Ross were the three very plus-sized comics who made up the Ton, with the idea being that if one fat guy was funny, then three would be a riot. Thirty-six

Max, Moritz, and little Pep get the drop on Stanley Blystone in their feature *Darwin Was Right* (1924). Photo courtesy of Sam Gill.

two-reelers were produced from 1925 to 1928 by Joe Rock for his Standard Cinema Corporation. Alexander and Karr were longtime comedy veterans. Alexander had worked for Mack Sennett, Century, and Vitagraph in addition to falling into countless vats of suds and goo as one of Larry Semon's main foils for almost ten years. Hilliard Karr had started his career in Florida as "Funny Fatty Filbert" in Josh Binney Comedies and along the way, spent time at Fox and Universal before teaming up with these other two hefty fellows.

The usual format for the shorts consisted of putting the Fatties in situations and locations where fat men should fear to tread and then milking all the weight-related gags possible, reflected in titles such as *Tanks of the Wabash* (1927) and *Wanderers of the Waistline* (1927). Former Sennett girl Lois Boyd was their regular leading lady, who often had to choose between her three high-calorie suitors. Sometimes presented as siblings ("the Barrel Brothers") or as three fat buddies who hang out together, the result was a clever and fun series.

BLOOD BROTHERS

With the exception of Gordon and William Dooley, stage acrobats who made a couple of stray shorts such as *The Palm Missed* (1921) and *All Balled Up* (1921) for Reelcraft, the only team of the 1920s who were actually related were the brothers Lupino Lane and Wallace Lupino. Both were veterans of the English music hall and Lupino Lane became a huge star and was brought to America to appear on Broadway (see Chapter Fifteen). Hollywood also beckoned and in 1925, he began a series of starring shorts for producer Jack White with brother Wallace brought along to play his villain, buddy, or rival. Where Lupino Lane was an acrobat and pure clown, Wallace was a versatile character actor whose roles in support of his brother included Moroccan sheiks, fiery gauchos, and in *Listen Sister* (1928), even a girl's boarding school matron. Besides working with other comics on the lot, Jack White also starred Wallace in his own one- and two-reelers. In 1930, the family returned to England, where the brothers continued appearing together in films and on stage in their blockbuster hit *Me and My Girl.*

The high-calorie comedians Hilliard "Fatt" Karr (back), Bill "Kewpie" Ross (right), and Frank "Fatty" Alexander (front left) posing in character and in an auto for their 1925 comedy *All Tied Up*. Photo courtesy of Steve Rydzewski.

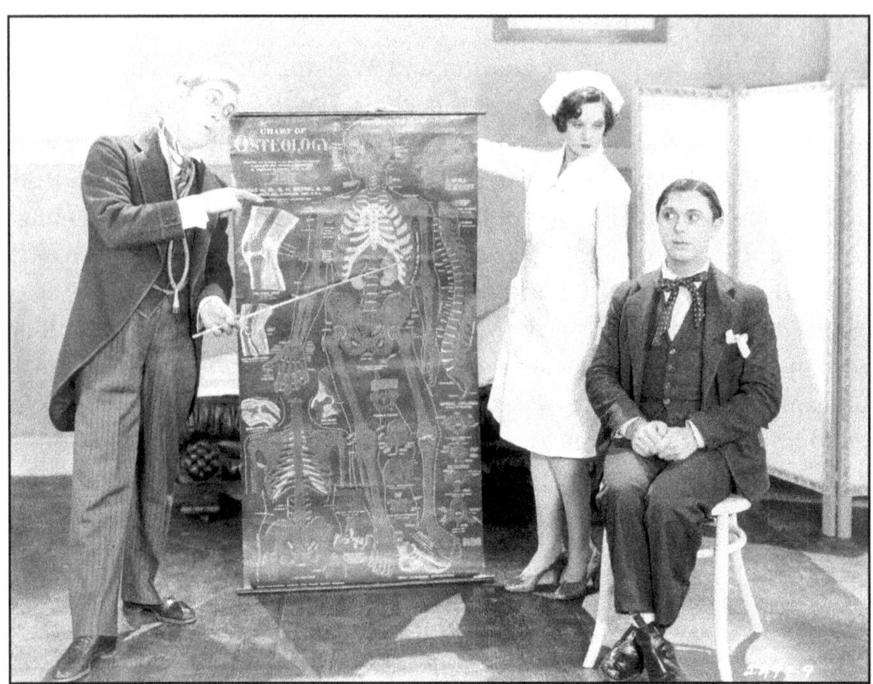

Doctor Wallace Lupino (left) attempts to examine Lupino Lane (right) with the help of nurse Muriel Evans in *Good Night Nurse* (1929). Photo courtesy of Robert Arkus.

THE BIG COMBO

In early 1926, Paramount Pictures had a smash hit on their hands with the film *Behind the Front*, which made a hot commodity out of the mismatched duo of Wallace Beery and Raymond Hatton. While remembered today for his 1930s MGM classics, such as *Dinner at Eight* (1933), much of Wallace Beery's early career was spent in silent slapstick. He first came to prominence playing a big lummox Swedish girl in Essanay's Sweedie comedies and besides working briefly for Mack Sennett, he also directed comedies for Essanay and Universal. By the late teens, Beery's comedy skills gave him the opportunity to break into features as a busy character player in films such as *The Three Ages* (1923) and *The Red Lily* (1924).

Raymond Hatton's early film work was at Biograph for D.W. Griffith and a number of 1913 Keystones, such as *Their First Execution*, *That Ragtime Band*, and *Barney Oldfield's Race for a Life*. By 1915, he had hooked up with Cecil B. De Mille, becoming a regular member of the director's stock company with important roles in *Joan the Woman* (1917), *Male and Female* (1919), and the starring lead in *The Whispering Chorus* (1918). In the 1920s, he was a steady supporting player in comedies such as *Head Over Heels* (1922) and dramas on the order of *The Hunchback of Notre Dame* (1923).

Paramount, knowing a good box office thing when they saw it, rushed them into a second outing, *We're in the Navy Now* (1926), and kept them coming for a total of seven. The basic storyline consisted of the slick Hatton taking advantage of the dumb and gullible Beery and a solid group of comedy pros worked on the productions. The first three were directed by Eddie Sutherland, with Frank Strayer, Ralph Cedar, and F. Richard Jones

Wallace Beery (left) and Raymond Hatton (right) in their second starring comedy feature *We're in the Navy Now* (1926).

taking the reins on later entries, while the scripts and titles were the products of the likes of Monty Brice, Ralph Spence, George Marion Jr., Grover Jones, Gilbert Pratt, and Frank Butler. On screen, the two were surrounded by strong supporting comics, such as Tom Kennedy, Chester Conklin, Zasu Pitts, Max Asher, and Ford Sterling.

Following their last opus together, 1928's *The Big Killing*, Raymond Hatton went back to the supporting ranks. Still busy in the early days of talkies, his roles got progressively smaller and by the 1940s, he'd become a fixture of low-budget westerns. He continued working in movies and TV until his last appearance in *In Cold Blood* (1967). Sound, on the other hand, gave Wallace Beery's career a shot in the arm and he became one of MGM's top stars with pictures such as *The Big House* (1930), *The Champ* (1931), and *Viva Villa* (1934). Beery remained a headliner at the studio up to his death in 1949 and his comedy chops continued to come in handy in his pairings with Marie Dressler and Marjorie Main.

Behind the Front and *We're in the Navy Now* were two of the top box office hits of 1926, so other producers, getting a whiff of the money to be made, were now open to get on the comedy team gravy train. On the Hal Roach lot, two long-experienced screen comics began appearing together frequently in the fall of 1926. Their natural timing and chemistry had even been apparent in an early and isolated film together, *The Lucky Dog*, in 1921, and by mid-1927, they became an official team. This is, of course, Stan Laurel and Oliver Hardy, who ended up as the best-known and most beloved team in screen history. Since they have volumes devoted to their films and lives, we don't need to go into details here, but their popularity, following on the heels of the Beery and Hatton films, opened the floodgates for a gold rush of teams in the late 1920s.

CARBON COPIES

Like Stan & Ollie, another pairing in the Beery & Hatton mold was the joining of mousey George K. Arthur with big lug Karl Dane. Both had worked their way up to become popular character players at the MGM Studio, Arthur by way of England and starring American films, such as *Hollywood* (1923) and *The Salvation Hunters* (1925), while Dane came from Sweden in 1918 and made a big impression in the smash hit *The Big Parade* (1925). *Rookies* (1927) was their first together and the 5'6" Arthur and 6'3" Dane continued the "Mutt and Jeff" tradition of tall and small in a total of seven comedies, which also included *Detectives* (1928) and *China Bound* (1929).

George K. Arthur (as baby) and Karl Dane in a publicity shot for *Baby Mine* (1928). Photo courtesy of Louie Despres.

The arrival of sound effected them drastically, especially Dane because of his thick Swedish accent. They continued their partnership is a series of low-budget talkie shorts, such as *Dizzy Dates* (1930) and *A Put up Job* (1931) for Paramount and Larry Darmour Productions, but afterward went their separate ways. Due to his inability to get work, Dane shot himself in 1934. George K. Arthur fared much better with bits in features like *Riptide* (1934) before his career eventually wound down. Earlier in his career, he had produced *The Salvation Hunters* to showcase himself and he later returned to producing with a number of well-received short films.

Although Paramount had Beery and Hatton, they must have thought the more the merrier, as they briefly spliced together the well-known comics W.C. Fields and Chester Conklin. Fields, still a comedy icon today for his stage and film appearances, had made his film debut in 1915, but it wasn't until 1925's *Sally of the Sawdust* that he made a real impression on moviegoers. Soon signed by Paramount, Fields headlined in Astoria, New York-made features such as *It's the Old Army Game* (1926) and *So's Your Old Man* (1926), but when the studio closed its Astoria plant in the spring of 1927, W.C. was brought to Hollywood. Not knowing what to do with him, someone decided to pair him with former Keystone player Chester Conklin.

After making a name for himself during five years of working for Mack Sennett, plus starring in shorts for Fox, Special Pictures, and Educational, in the early 1920s, Conklin branched out to supporting character roles in high profile features such as *Greed* (1923), *A Woman of the World* (1925), and *The Duchess of Buffalo* (1926). Today, the three features that starred Fields and Conklin–*Two Flaming Youths* (1927), *Tillie's Punctured Romance* (1928), and *Fools for Luck* (1928)–are lost. Only a snippet of them together from the Paramount publicity short reel *A Trip through the Paramount Studio* (1927) survives, but it's impossible to judge their teamwork from this. At any rate, their films weren't particularly successful and Paramount even dropped Fields' contract. Of course, he was back after the move to sound and both he and Conklin enjoyed many more years entertaining audiences.

Warner Brothers decided to combine veteran comics Louise Fazenda and Clyde Cook for five films starting with *Simple Sis* in mid-1926. Fa-

In a publicity shot for *Fools for Luck* (1928), W.C. Fields and Chester Conklin attempt to determine whose moustache looks the least real.

zenda had become a comedy star with a pig-tailed bumpkin character for Mack Sennett and eccentric clown Clyde Cook had toured the world on stage as "the Kangaroo Boy" before ending up in shorts for Fox Sunshine Comedies and Hal Roach. Cook had also made the jump to features and he and Fazenda first appeared together as comic relief in the Warner's drama *Miss Nobody* (1926). More outings, such as *A Sailor's Sweetheart* (1927) and *Pay as You Exit* (1928), followed *Simple Sis* (1926), where they were often joined by William Demarest and a young Myrna Loy. Although popular, their teamwork has been overlooked due to the unavailability of the films. With the arrival of sound, both Fazenda and Cook continued on as memorable supporting players for many years.

A footnote in the spawn of co-joined character players is the duo of Sammy Cohen and Ted McNamara. Originally spliced as comic relief in the World War I saga *What Price Glory?* (1926), the Fox Studio decided to jump on the team bandwagon and paired them again in *Upstream* (1927) and *Colleen* (1927) before launching their own starring vehicles *The Gay Retreat* (1927) and *Why Sailors Go Wrong* (1928). They were a repetition of the popular Irish/Jewish theme, but instead of boy and girlfriend, they were battling buddies–rival taxi drivers or sailors. Cohen had been an eccentric dancer in musical comedies before being spotted by director Marshall Neilan, who cast him in his first film *The Skyrocket* (1926). McNamara, in spite of specializing in Irish characters, was Australian by birth and had been a member of the juvenile Pollard's Lilliputians Company that also began the careers of Snub Pollard, Daphne Pollard, Billy Bevan, and others.

Ted McNamara died of pneumonia at thirty-six just after completing *Why Sailors Go Wrong*. Fox attempted to keep the franchise going, pairing Cohen with ugly Jack Pennick in *Plastered in Paris* (1928) and Harry Sweet in *Homesick* (1928), but the arrival of sound ended the series and saw Sammy Cohen's career slow down. His later film work included bits until 1946, with his best opportunity coming as soldier Mike Murphy in *The Fighting 69th* (1940).

THE TERRIBLE TWOS

Beery and Hatton's films helped beget Laurel & Hardy and in turn, Stan and Ollie's popularity sired a crop of "Fat and Skinny" combinations. Snub Pollard, after being phased out from the Hal Roach Studio, his home for nearly a decade, went on a successful vaudeville tour and in 1926 started a new starring series for Weiss Brothers Artclass Pictures. Unfortunately, this group of two-reelers was short-lived, but he was back at Weiss for another round the next year, this time teamed with corpulent Marvin Loback for a bald attempt to cash in on the thick and thin popularity of Hal Roach's duo. Most of the Pollard/Loback shorts, such as *Double Trouble* (1927) and *Men about Town* (1928), used L&H material, but *Sock and Run* (1929) in particular is like a tour through Stan and Ollie's late 1920s gag book. The first reel alone recreates routines from *Putting Pants on Philip* (1927), *You're Darn Tootin'* (1928), and *Should Married Men Go Home?* (1928) while the second plunders the prizefight material from the surviving first reel of *The Battle of the Century* (1927).

Snub, with his droopy Fu Manchu moustache, is still remembered today, but his oversized buddy Marvin is completely forgotten. Loback was an adept comic foil who found a ready place in silent comedy due to the fact that his extreme weight made him a walking sight-gag. He first began turning up around 1917 in L-Ko, Sennett, Triangle, and Harold Lloyd Comedies. A good part in the Universal's special *The Geezer of Berlin* (1918) gave him some visibility, leading him to become part of the regular stock company on both the Sennett and Roach lots. As earlier mentioned, he had been "unofficially" teamed with Ralph Graves for Sennett from 1924 to 1926, after which he began appearing for Weiss Brothers–he's particularly funny in drag as Poodles Hanneford's blimp girlfriend in *Why Detectives Go Wrong* (1928)–but was mostly hooked up with Snub. This series was the last major roles for he and Snub, as they both spent the rest of their careers doing bits in shorts and features up to their respective deaths–Loback in 1938 and Snub in 1962.

In late 1927, producer Jack White began casting around for a pair to join the team sweepstakes and tried out several one-shot variations with the likes of Eddie Quillan and George Davis, Monty Collins and George Davis, Wallace Lupino and Fred Spencer, and others before coming up with the combination of Vernon Dent and Monty Collins. Dent had been freelancing at other comedy units due to a hiatus at the Mack Sennett Studio and appeared in a number of White's shorts. Monty Collins had recently been promoted to star status by White, first in one-reel Cameo comedies and then bumped up to two-reel Mermaids. Collins was the son of an old vaudevillian (Monty Sr.) who worked in films and supported Arbuckle and Keaton, most memorably in *The Play House* (1921) as half of the pair of one-armed audience members. Young Monty had his own stage background and began turning up in films in the mid-1920s. Often cast as a henpecked husband, Collins was nervous and skinny with a long nose, bulging Adam's apple, and bowl-cut bangs.

Snub Pollard (left) and Marvin Loback (right) make like "Two Tars" in their 1929 Weiss Brothers Comedy *Here Comes a Sailor*. Photo courtesy the Eye Film Institute, Netherlands.

First teamed in *Social Prestige* (December 23, 1928) and continuing with *Whoopee Boys*, *Parlor Pests*, and *Those Two Boys* (all 1929), the duo played rowdy working-class types who become millionaires thanks to a lottery or striking oil and end up disrupting polite society events. Their Laurel and Hardy borrowings include situations from *The Second Hundred Years* (1927), *From Soup to Nuts* (1928), and *Their Purple Moment* (1928), plus the basic destruction motif of *You're Darn Tootin'* (1928) and *Two Tars* (1928). In advertising, much was made of their different physiques, or as an Educational press sheet put it, "Collins is slender while Dent is fat," and although definite Laurel and Hardy knock-offs, the surviving films are entertaining thanks to Collins and Dent's sizeable comedy talents.

Their joint association bridged the changeover to sound, where they continued their rough mayhem in *Ticklish Business*, *Hot Sports*, and *The Talkies* (all 1929) before going their separate ways. Both ended up working constantly for concerns such as Educational, Sennett, and Vitaphone and finally as part of the comedy ensemble at the Columbia Pictures shorts Department, where they made life difficult for the Three Stooges, Harry Langdon, Andy Clyde, and others for many years. Collin's last credit before his death from a heart attack in 1951 was as gagman on Laurel and

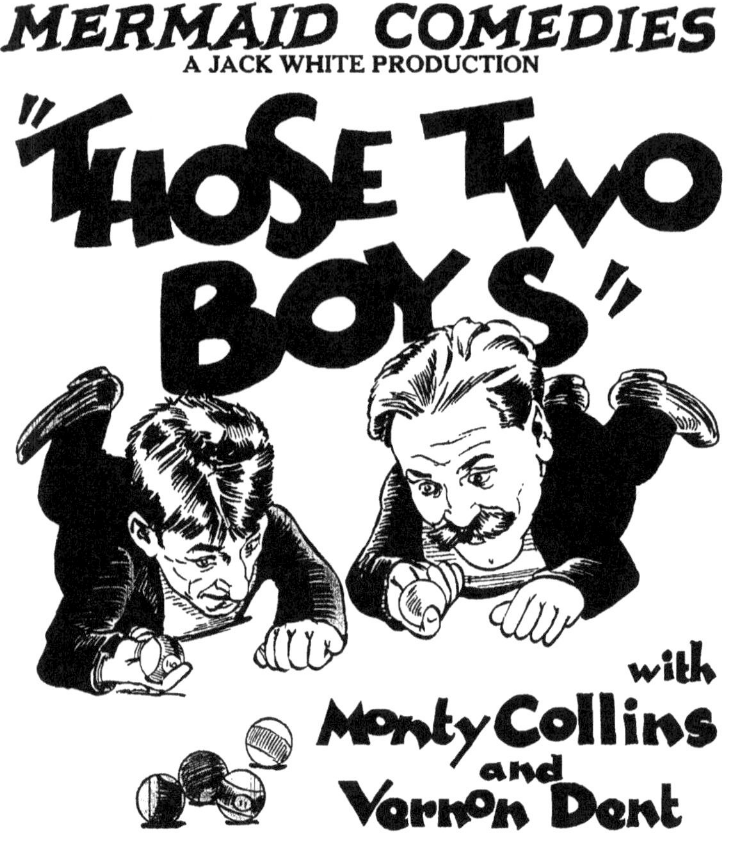

Educational Pictures press sheet cover illustration with Monty Collins (left) and Vernon Dent (right) from *Those Two Boys* (1929).

Hardy's *Atoll K* (1950). Vernon Dent retired due to ill health in 1954, although his last appearance (via stock footage) was with the Stooges in *Guns A-Poppin* (1957), and he died in 1963.

A pair that was slapped together as part of the late 1920s rush to put popular comic strips on the screen was the Stern Brothers Mike and Ike series. Based on the newspaper strip by the famous Rube Goldberg, whose comic adventures of identical twins ran from 1907 into the 1940s, the pair was first played by Charles King and Charles Dorety. Although they sported identical moustaches and clothing, they were hardly twins and the shorts were just the usual Universal shorts slapstick shenanigans. After the first few releases, King and Dorety were replaced by Joe Young and Ned La Salle, who played the brothers until the series ran its course with *Good Skates* in 1929.

LADIES LAST

On the subject of silent female comedy teams, the sad fact is there were barely any. While there were scads of male/female pairings, such as the Drews, John Bunny & Flora Finch, and Harry Myers & Rosemary Theby, only two female duos stand out. The first is the combo of Marie Dressler and Polly Moran, but during the silent days, this only consisted of two films–*The Callahans and the Murphys* (1927), pulled out of distribution because of protests over how it portrayed the Irish, and *Bringing up Father* (1928), adapted from the George McManus comic strip. It wasn't until early sound with *Dangerous Females* (1929) and *Caught Short* (1930) that these comedy warhorses truly became a unit. This leaves the union of Anita Garvin and Marion Byron, who were brought together by producer Hal Roach in the final days of silents for only three shorts, as the genuine female team. Both were ex-showgirls and while Garvin had been an excellent supporting player for a number of years in Christie, Jack White, and Roach comedies, Byron was a newer recruit whose biggest role had been the female lead in Keaton's *Steamboat Bill Jr.* (1928).

Charles King (second from right) and Charles Dorety (far right) in harness for an unidentified Mike and Ike Comedy. Photo courtesy of Sam Gill.

In 1928, the Roach studio was enjoying a huge success with the teaming of Laurel & Hardy. Hoping that lightning might strike twice, the girls were put together as a female equivalent. Where Stan and Ollie had the "fat and skinny" physical contrast going, the girls had "tall and small." Garvin, with her worldly-wise manner and already proven slow-burn, was a shoo-in for the "Hardy" role and sweet, innocent, and slightly ditzy Marion was given the "Laurel" part. Their first two films together, *Feed 'Em and Weep* (1928) and *Going Gaga* (1929), are strongly based on the L&H blueprint, but their last and most well-known film, *A Pair of Tights* (1929), takes the team in a different direction that moves away from L&H

Marion Byron (left) and Anita Garvin (right) try to use their feminine wiles to hitch a ride in their first teaming, *Feed 'Em and Weep* (1928). Photo courtesy of Cole Johnson.

hand-me-downs and develops a more female point of view. The premise is the troubles that single girls have on dates, so the things they have to deal with–lack of money, tightwad boyfriends, overbearing suitors–feel more organic and grounded in reality than their previous shorts. Sadly, they never got to develop the single girls theme any further, as Marion Byron left the Roach lot, and they went their separate ways.

CONCLUSION

With the arrival of sound, most of the silent teams split up. Some of the halves, such as W.C. Fields and Wallace Beery, became bigger stars while many others ended up as supporting character players. Laurel & Hardy made the transition to talkies without a hitch and became more popular than ever, as did Marie Dressler and Polly Moran before Dressler's premature death brought their teamwork to an end in 1934. The new medium brought a rush of well-seasoned stage performers to films, so teams continued to proliferate in the persons of Clark & McCullough, Burns & Allen, Wheeler & Woolsey, Olson & Johnson, The Ritz Brothers, and of course, The Three Stooges. Even the girls got their chance with the combos of Thelma Todd/Zasu Pitts and Thelma Todd/Patsy Kelly. Over the years, cinematic comedy teams would continue with major pairings such as Abbott & Costello or Martin & Lewis, not to mention more minor league combos on the order of Brown & Carney, Quillan & Vernon, and many more.

Keaton and the Silent Comedy Grapevine

IDEAS NEVER EXIST IN A VACUUM, particularly in the world of silent comedy. Ideas, gags, and whole routines turn up again and again in myriad films. A case in point is the routine of a comic battling a live oyster in his bowl of oyster stew. This bit got passed on from Billy Bevan to Billy Dooley, Clyde Cook, Curly Howard, and Lou Costello, winding its way from the silent days to early television. Who knows where the idea originally came from? Silent film comedy took advantage of, and recorded for posterity, the comedy vocabulary that had been developed by the Commedia dell 'Arte, British variety and pantomime, and American vaudeville. All the silent comedians and their collaborators borrowed from each other, but the true test of a clown was the personal spin that they brought to the material to make it their own.

Buster Keaton was one of the most original performers and comedy creators of the era, but even he was a product of his influences. In his early stage years, this was his father Joe, not to mention all the other acts he observed during their years of crisscrossing the country while touring and performing. When Buster moved into films, his first important collaborators were Roscoe "Fatty" Arbuckle and Eddie Cline, through whom he was influenced by Mack Sennett. Keaton learned film basics from Arbuckle, who had been taught them by Sennett. Eddie Cline had also started his career with Sennett and was likely responsible for ex-Sennett bathing girls Virginia Fox and Sybil Seely (formerly Sibye Trevilla) becoming Buster's first regular leading ladies.

After his film apprenticeship with Roscoe Arbuckle, Buster began his own starring series of shorts in 1920 and quickly became one of the industry's top comics. As such, he then influenced what many of the other film clowns were doing. At that time, Charlie Chaplin was the most popu-

Newspaper cartoon of Joe and Buster Keaton from their vaudeville days.

lar film comedian, so much so that there were out and out mimics on the order of Billy West, Ray Hughes, Harry Mann, and Al Joy cranking out shorts to trick unsuspecting movie patrons that they were Charlie. During Buster's heyday, there were two active "Keaton Clones" who were perhaps not as brazen as say Billy West, but can still be classified as more than just "Keatonesque."

Charles Dorety was a workman comic who toiled away for companies such as Bulls Eye and Century, even making fleeting appearances with Arbuckle and Keaton in *The Garage* (1920) and in Keaton's *The High Sign* (1921), but never developed his own comic style or identifiable character. There are two surviving silent shorts with Dorety "doing" Buster–*A Twilight Baby* (1920) and *Third Class Male* (1921). When screened today, these shorts elicit a gasp on Dorety's initial appearance, as the flat porkpie hat, deadpan demeanor, and stumpy body language are all there, but it's hard to judge how regularly he did Buster thanks to the loss of most of his films. There are also photos of Dorety in the porkpie hat and Buster out-

On the left is a frame scan of Charles Dorety from the Century Comedy *Third Class Male* (1921) and on the right an ad of George Chandler from the *1929 Standard Casting Directory*, both of which illustrate their work as Keaton clones. Photo courtesy of Billy Rose Theatre Division, The New York Public Library for the Performing Arts, Astor, Lenox and Tilden Foundations.

fit, but with the addition of a brush mustache. By the time sound rolled in, Dorety was demoted to small bit parts and even in one of these, the Roscoe Arbuckle directed *Crashing Hollywood* (1931), he turns up as a Keaton impersonator at a Hollywood party.

The other ersatz Buster was character actor George Chandler, best remembered today as W.C. Fields' son Chester in *The Fatal Glass of Beer* (1933) and as Uncle Petrie on TV's *Lassie*. After working in vaudeville, where he was billed as "The Musical Nut," Chandler was headlined by Universal in a 1928/1929 series of Tenderfoot Thrillers two-reelers which featured him as a Keatonesque eastern dude, usually named Cuthbert or Bertie, who comedically had to prove his manliness out west in titles such as *Saps and Saddles* (1928) and *A Tenderfoot Terror* (1929). Described as "that engaging boob," sadly none of these are known to be available today, but contemporary reviewers referred to his "characterization (a la Keaton)" and that he was "featured in a Buster Keaton type of role." What do survive are some early sound Keatonish appearances in 1931 Arbuckle-directed shorts, such as *The Back Page* and *The Lure of Hollywood*, not to mention the aforementioned *Crashing Hollywood*, which brought Dorety and Chandler together for some Keaton aping in stereo. Chandler soon dropped the Buster mannerisms and became a ubiquitous character player and later president of Screen Actors Guild.

STRAIGHT OUT OF THE FUNNY PAGES

In addition to these imitators, Keaton had a strong overlap of style and material with five of his movie contemporaries. The first two–Larry Semon and Charley Bowers-share the streak of surrealism that runs through many of Buster's films. Both came from a background of cartoons and newspaper comics, which is another possible influence on the young Buster, as there are certain images in his films that bear striking similarities to episodes in Windsor McCay's 1904 to 1911 strip *Dream of the Rarebit Fiend*.

Larry Semon began in films a year before Keaton, hired by the Vitagraph Company to write and direct one-reelers for fat comic Hughie Mack. He soon began starring in them himself before graduating to two-reels and increasing fame. His screen character was pure clown with windup toy movements, chest-high balloon trousers, clodhopper shoes, and a bowler hat, topped off with heavy white make-up on his horse face that made him look like a slapstick version of Nosferatu. All of the above merged together in the character of a happy dumbbell caught up in a whirlwind of chaos. As a director, the plots of his films were just excuses to set his gags in motion and his fondness for explosions, chases, crashes, and spectacular falls from high places created in his best films a mad, surreal world.

Like Buster, Semon was known for the bone-breaking stunts he performed in his films–leaping from speeding trains, swinging from water towers, diving head first into vats of goo–but the difference was that most of them weren't really done by Semon. Bill Hauber, a Mack Sennett veteran and one of silent comedies' "unknown soldiers," performed them for

Larry Semon circa 1920 at the peak of his fame.

Larry from 1918 to 1925. Director Norman Taurog later said:

"When we made a picture with Larry, he'd go to New York and we made the picture. When he came back, we fitted him in all the close ups. That's the truth. Bill Hauber, who used to double for him all the time, was close to him and that great and could do him that well."

Semon was one of the kings of the comedy short, but in the mid-1920's when Keaton, Chaplin, and Harold Lloyd successfully moved into features, Larry decided that he should, too. Unlike Buster, his screen persona was too one-dimensional and he was unable to develop feature length story lines. Keaton was aware of the important differences between himself and Semon and talked about it in his 1960 autobiography, *My Wonderful World of Slapstick*:

> During the years we were trying to figure out what made movie fans laugh, and why, there was an extraordinary silent-pictures comic who made many successful one-reel and two-reel pictures. His name was Larry Semon, and he was so weird looking that he could have posed as either a pinhead or a Man from

Charley Bowers upstages his radio mate in his Whirlwind Comedy *He Couldn't Help It* (1927).

> Outer Space. His movies were combinations of cartoon gags, fantastic gags, and farcical plots. Chaplin, Lloyd, and myself just couldn't make two-reelers as packed with laughs as Larry's. But when an audience got half a block from the theatre, after being convulsed by Semon's whamios, they couldn't have told you what they had laughed at. I would say this was because they were impossible gags. Only things that one could imagine happening to real people, I guess, remain in a person's memory.

When his features crashed and he had to return to shorts, Semon panicked and began repeating his old gags ad nauseum. This bankrupted him financially and emotionally, which led to a nervous breakdown and his death from pneumonia in 1928.

Charley Bowers had a background in circuses and newspaper cartooning when he entered the film industry in the teens as an animator, producing Mutt and Jeffs and other cartoons. In the mid-1920s, he began making and starring in live-action comedy shorts with amazing stop-action animation effects. *Egged On*, *Now You Tell One*, *A Wild Roomer* (all 1926), and *There It Is* (1928) reveal Bowers to be the heir of George Melies, making the impossible come true before our eyes–eggs hatch into miniature Model Ts, a manservant machine runs rampant down real city streets, and plants grows so fast that they shoot up a farmer's pant leg and impale him in midair.

Mixing the unbelievable with the everyday was Bowers stock-in-trade and something that he shared with Buster, particularly in his shorts and the feature *Sherlock Jr.* (1924). As a performer, Bowers actually looked like the love-child of Keaton and Larry Semon–small with the features of both, plus Buster's solemn demeanor. Bowers' heyday was brief; in three years, he turned out sixteen of these little gems, but with the arrival of sound, his output grew sporadic and after his death in 1946, his reputation fell into total obscurity. In another parallel to Keaton, many of his films that had been lost for decades have started to resurface and a high profile DVD release has started the ball rolling on the reexamination of his work and unique vision.

THE ROUGH AND THE READY

The three other clowns that share traits with Buster have stunts and strenuous physical business in common with him. The first is Keaton's pal and former teammate, Al St John. Most viewers know Al as the evil country gremlin that he played in support of his uncle Roscoe Arbuckle, first at Keystone and then Comique, who had a reputation for wild and wooly physical stunts second only to Buster (see Chapter Eleven).

Al and Buster worked together in front of and behind the camera in Arbuckle's 1917 to 1920 comedies for Comique, where the three of them played a game of "who can top who" in physical roughhouse. Then, in 1920, when Arbuckle moved into features and Buster embarked on his series of shorts, Al went out on his own, too. First, he starred in a string of shorts produced by Warner Brothers and after two seasons, settled into a four-year run with Fox. Today, there's only a handful of survivors from these years, such as *The Paper Hangers* (1921), *Special Delivery*, *The Studio Rube*, and *Out of Place* (all 1922), but they show that Al dramatically dropped his over-the-top approach and went with a cool and underacted style very much like Buster.

The Keaton similarities become even stronger in 1924 when St John teamed up again with his Uncle Roscoe to do a series of Tuxedo comedies for Educational release. Although Arbuckle had been exonerated in his famous rape trials, due to the scandal, he could not appear before the cameras and was writing and directing. The pair made seven shorts together, which got rid of the last remnants of Al's country boob character and made him the clean-cut (but still bumbling) man-about-town or young hubby.

After this group, uncle and nephew went their separate ways with Al continuing this character in a series of shorts for producer Jack White until 1929. In the sound era, Al became a staple in low-budget westerns with a sidekick character known as "Fuzzy." Just as Buster would rework and recreate his old routines on television in the 50s and 60s, Al did the same thing in the 40s and 50s (with a beard and without his teeth) to provide comic relief to the two-gun heroics of Buster Crabbe, Don "Red" Barry, and Lash LaRue. He and Buster even worked together again in the Educational short *Love Nest on Wheels* (1937), where they reworked bits from Arbuckle's *The Bell Boy* (1918), and the feature *Lil' Abner* (1940). As "Fuzzy," Al became such a favorite of kids around the world that his westerns were cut down to two reels for European television and became "Fuzzy shorts" with titles like *Fuzzy der Meister Cowboy* and *Fuzzy der Sheriff*. Al retired from the screen in 1952, but continued making popular personal appearances until his death in 1963.

Our next comic, Lige Conley, was billed by producer Jack White as "The Speed Boy of Comedy" and while not a particularly original comedian, his breezy personality and ability to perform stunts were the springboards for a six-year starring series of lightning-paced action comedies. Born Elijah Crommie in 1899, he grew up a couple of miles from Mack Sennett's studio and in 1915 began turning up in Sennett, Hal Roach, Reelcraft, and Fox comedies. Jack White began starring Lige in 1920, first teamed with Jimmie Adams and then on his own.

The title of his best remembered short, *Fast and Furious* (1924), is a good description of his entire series. Almost all of Conley's comedies feature one big action sequence where as many physical obstacles as human-

Al St John scanning the horizon in a very Keatonish way in his 1921 Fox Comedy *The Happy Pest*. Photo courtesy of Louie Despres.

ly possible are thrown in his way. In *Neck and Neck* (1924), it's a gigantic traffic jam that has him ending up sprinting from the top of car to car. Haunted houses, skyscrapers, and even movie studios were backdrops for his adventures, plus he was sent into the wild blue yonder in shorts such as *Treasure Bound* (1922) and *Air Pockets* (1924). Sports or some variety of race were also good for climaxes in *The Steeplechaser* (1922), *Backfire* (1923), *Three Strikes* (1923), *Pigskin* (1924), *Cheap Skates* (1925), and *Lickety Split* (1926).

Fast and Furious is his most elaborate short where the entire second reel is a nonstop chase (reworked from Larry Semon's 1922 *The Show* by director Norman Taurog) that involves horses, autos, motorcycles, railroad handcars, and a speeding locomotive. Three specific Keaton borrowings are one view–Lige rides on the handlebars of a driverless motorcycle a la *Sherlock Jr.* (six months after that film's April 1924 release), a collapsing auto from *The Three Ages* (1923), not to mention the gag from *The Goat* (1922) where Lige thinks he's climbing on to a car's rear spare tire, but when the car takes off, it's really a standing sign for an auto shop.

Lige Conley takes to the air as Stanley Blystone (left), Eddie Boland (third from right), Estelle Bradley (second from right), and Babe London (far right) look on amazed in *Cheap Skates* (1925). Photo courtesy of Sam Gill.

Conley's series for Jack White ended in 1926 and although he made a few starring shorts for Fox and Sennett, he soon lost his star status and drifted behind the camera writing gags. After the arrival of sound, he's known to have made a few appearances with Lloyd Hamilton, but then disappears. Sporadically working behind the scenes, while helping a stalled auto he was struck and killed by a car in 1937.

Our last comic to give Buster a run for his money as a silent comedy athlete was Lupino Lane. Part of the British invasion of American slapstick films that began with the arrival of Charlie Chaplin in 1914 and continued with the likes of Billie Ritchie, Billie Reeves, Jimmy Aubrey, Sydney Chaplin, and countless supporting players, Lane, like Keaton, was raised on stage, in his case English pantomime and variety, where he received a thorough training in tumbling, juggling, and mime. Lane was a member of the British theatrical clan the Lupinos, which began its reign in the 1600s, and was known as "Little Nipper' as a child. Besides appearing on stage, he began working in British films in 1913 and when he hit international fame, he came to America in the early 1920s. Between appearances on Broadway, he made a few films for Fox, such as *The Pirate* (1922) and the feature *A Friendly Husband* (1923).

In 1925, he embarked on a series of lightning-paced action comedies for producer Jack White, where he used all the stunts and physical tricks he had learned on stage. Doing some of the most seemingly bone-crunching flips and falls ever put on film, Lane even defies gravity when he runs up one side and down the other of an archway (not just once, but twice) in *Maid in Morocco* (1925), plus pops in and out of a maze of trapdoors in the blink of an eye in *Sword Points* (1928). Other shorts, such as *Time Flies* (1926), *Naughty Boy* (1927), and *Roaming Romeo* (1928), are marvels of comic action with Lane as the diminutive dervish who sets all the other elements spinning.

His most direct borrowing from Buster is the basic premise for *Only Me* (1929), where he takes the opening of *The Playhouse* (1922) and expands it to the entire short, playing twenty-four different characters as the audience and all the acts of a low-rent vaudeville theatre, but Lane also benefitted from the direction of Keaton mentor Roscoe Arbuckle in his early comedies *The Fighting Dude* (1925), *Fool's Luck* (1926), and *His Private Life* (1926).

Lane continued his series for Jack White into the beginning of sound. Making a very successful transition to the new medium, he appeared in Ernst Lubitisch's *The Love Parade* (1929) and other big Hol-

Lupino Lane (right) does his best to pretend the cop isn't there in *Who's Afraid?* (1927). Photo courtesy of Robert Arkus.

lywood features. Homesick, he and his family returned to England in 1930, where he continued making films, and had his greatest stage success in the late 1930s with the original production of *Me and My Girl.* Like *Hello Dolly* to Carol Channing, *Me and My Girl* became Lane's show and he toured in it all through the second World War and after until his death in 1959.

STILL THE HEADLINER

Lupino Lane and the rest of the aforementioned comedians were successful and popular in their day, but for the most part are now forgotten except by the staunchest of film buffs. Only Buster has remained "current," still selling DVDs and making new fans. Thanks to a combination of his singular wit and creativity, astounding physical prowess, Trojan work ethic, and prodigious skills as a filmmaker, Keaton's work has withstood the test of time and earned an enduring spot in the popular arts.

George Rowe: The Cock-Eyed Wonder

In the Teens and 1920s, the Hal Roach Studio had one of the best collections of comedy characters actors in Hollywood. These second, third, and even fourth bananas appeared in countless Roach one and two-reelers (often more than once in a single short) and helped create the universe that surrounded Harold Lloyd, Snub Pollard, Charley Chase, Our Gang, and Laurel & Hardy. Some, like Edgar Kennedy and James Finlayson, became stars or near stars in their own right while others, such as Anita Garvin, Spec O'Donnell, Charlie Hall, and Tiny Sanford, are still remembered and celebrated. But there's a large group made up of the likes of Mark Jones, Helen Gilmore, Earl Mohan, Vera White, Sammy Brooks, Billy Engle, and eternally old Gus Leonard that have never gotten their due. A key member of this neglected group is George Rowe, an odd cross-eyed little man who had the air of having been dropped off on earth by accident like E.T.

Rowe looked like he was from another planet, too, or could pass for L. Frank Baum's Scarecrow of Oz, as he was made up of odd mismatching parts. The tiny head that almost tapered to a point, adorned with jug-handle ears and covered with middle-parted thick black hair that seemed to start right at his eyebrows. A moth-eaten toothbrush moustache, plus a long chicken neck that led to a small scrawny and undernourished body. Of course, his most prominent features were his eyes, whose pupils looked like magnets that were attracted to each other. Add it all together and you get the selective breeding poster child.

While items have turned up about obscure performers like Jess Devorska having been a former Russian opera singer or that Barney Hellum's real name was Bjarne Hellum and that he was a noted Norwegian comedian before signing with Mack Sennett, sadly today George Rowe is

Close-up frame scan of George as a gypsy from the 1921 Eddie Boland comedy *On Their Way*. Photo courtesy of Robert Arkus.

as much of a man of mystery as he was on the screen eighty years ago, but not because of lack of interest. Film historian Sam Gill attempted to locate him over thirty years ago–"I tried to track him down in the summer of 1966, because Eddie Baker told me he had seen George Rowe on Hollywood Boulevard just a few months before, but that he didn't have a phone number or address for him. I never could find a phone number or address either, and no one else seemed to know where he might be living. I was so close. I wanted to talk to Rowe about his experiences working with Hal Roach and all the other great personnel there; but no such luck."

Unfortunately, George Rowe is a very popular name. A check of the *California Death Index* gives eight likely George Rowes who died between 1966 and 1981. The 1920 and 1930 census records also list many George Rowes in California, but all with the occupations of mechanic, laborer, oil driller, etc.–not a picture player among them. The *Social Security Death Index* also has multiple GRs, any of whom might be our boy, and the second edition of Eugene Michael Vazzana's *Silent Film Necrology* has a George Rowe included with the dates of 1871 to 1923, but the source obit for this listing, from the November 15, 1923 issue of *Variety*, is actually for a George Roux. There was even a George Fawcett Rowe who lived from 1824 to 1889 and was a famous New York stage actor.

A glimmer of hope came when film historian Brent Walker, while checking old L.A. City Directories, found three photoplayers listed among many George Rowes-

1922: Rowe, Geo. H. photoplayer at 627 W. 92nd Street
1924: Rowe, Geo., photoplayer at 7276 Jasmine Avenue
1925: Rowe, Geo. B., photoplayer at 1217 W. 38th Place

Brent said that the other George Rowes were usually listed as machinists, clerks, or had no occupations listed at all. He also added:

> You may notice the discrepancy between George H. and George B., but I would imagine it was the same person and one of the initials is incorrect. Names listed in the City Di-

From left to right there's Paul Parrott, Charles Stevenson, unknown, Sidney D'Albrook, George, and Sunshine Sammy Morrison pulling a heist in the 1922 Roach Comedy *Loose Change*. Photo courtesy of Cole Johnson.

> rectory do change from year to year. The 1922 address is in south central L.A., the Jasmine address is definitely our boy because it's smack dab in the middle of Culver City/Palms area (where the Roach lot was). The 1925 address is near U.S.C. and Exposition Park. The City Directories end in 1942, and then the phone directories pick up, but I looked at a 1955 phone directory and by that time they weren't listing jobs anymore and there were a ton of George Rowes.

George B. Rowe seems very likely to be his full name, as certain references and listings for him exist under the name Ben Rowe, but searches of that name with all the possible variations and combinations of George and Ben together has led to the same brick walls. Looking for "the" George Rowe has been frustrating, very much like being the cop that chases Charlie Chaplin through the hall of mirrors in *The Circus* (1928). So we're still stuck with nothing but questions–Was he from vaudeville? Could he have possibly been British? Did he also work as a gagman at the Roach lot? Was he actually cross-eyed or was it only a shtick he did on camera?

He seems to have entered the Hollywood scene at the very end of 1919 and made his home on the Roach lot. Turning up in a gazillion of their shorts, he did everything from major supporting roles to quick walk-on bits. Some of his fleeting appearances look like somebody went and grabbed him from another set for five minutes, as in Paul Parrott's *Friday the 13th* (1922), where George shows up as a justice of the peace at the very end of the picture, seemingly so they can use the gag of having his name be "I.C. Cross." Of course, the gags are often about his skewed vision as when he happily takes the controls of the trolley in *Trolley Troubles* (1921) and mows down cops, veers through traffic, and crashes through someone's living room or when he's a member of a Russian firing squad ordered to shoot Stan Laurel in *Frozen Hearts* (1923) and hits everything in the room but Stan.

His true domain was the one-reelers that starred Snub Pollard, Eddie Boland, or Paul Parrott, where he fit perfectly in that world of slapstick surrealism and absurdity. In *Punch the Clock* (1922), Snub has slept overnight in the doorway of the factory where he works because if he's late once more, he'll get the sack. Afraid to leave his post, Snub asks a bypassing George to get him a cup of coffee at the diner across the street. While George is gone, irate husband Eddie Baker comes by and mistakes Snub for his wife's lover. Eddie pummels Snub and chases him all over the

George looking inscrutable in support of Eddie Boland (right) in the unfortunately named Roach Comedy *The Chink* (1921). Photo courtesy of Eye Film Institute, Netherlands.

neighborhood. But every time there's a lull in the chase, faithful George magically appears holding a cup of coffee for Snub. Wherever Snub is chased, George is silently there with that coffee.

In addition to playing an oddball that just happens to wander on the scene and calls attention to himself by his eccentricity, Rowe sometimes plays a rival for the affections of the leading lady as in *The High Rollers* (1922); in shorts like *Call a Taxi* (1920), he's practically on equal footing with Snub and Sunshine Sammy as part of a comedy trio. At the same time, he seems to have been too gooney for the more realistic world of the Harold Lloyd films, although he does turn up in a small bit as a henpecked husband in *Never Weaken* (1921) and in the background of *Grandma's Boy* (1922). And while his on-screen time was often brief, he made the most of the footage given to him and always got his laughs. In *Light Showers* (1922), he's a guest at a party given by Snub and Marie Mosquini at their flooded house. Water is leaking in all over and when George is leaning at the piano listening to the music, a stream of water sprouts from the floor and dampens his protruding rear-end. The close-up of Rowe's very slow realization of what's going on is one of the funniest things in the short.

Besides his eyes, his comic vocabulary consisted of an ear-to-ear Cheshire cat grin and a deadpan that bordered on the comatose. A good example of the latter is in *Money to Burn* (1920), where Rowe comes into the tailor shop where Snub Pollard and Sunshine Sammy work. Standing catatonically in the center of the room, he gives not a flicker of response

George prominently featured in an early 1920s exhibitor ad for Hal Roach one-reelers. Photo courtesy of Bruce Lawton.

as everyone asks him what he wants. Finally, to make sure that he's alive, they jab him with a pin and he blurts out that he wants to buy a suit coat. As they try different jackets on him, they have to keep sticking him so he'll bark out his response and ultimately they sell him one with the hanger still in the back. The wonderful button to this routine has George out in front of the shop in his spiffy new jacket and he actually stirs himself to flirt with a cute girl. As they chat, the hanger protruding from the back of his collar hooks on a pipe that is sticking out of the back of a nearby truck. Suddenly, the truck speeds off and George is dragged down the street in a beautiful deep focus long shot worthy of Orson Welles and Gregg Toland.

Although he was a full-time member of the Roach stock company, he does turn up elsewhere. In the Chester Comedy *Beat It* (1921) starring Snooky the chimp, George is sitting at a table next to a large man in drag a la Henry Bergman in the crummy cabaret where Snooky is a waiter and drummer in the pit band. Really just background with no business, George was probably keeping at least one eye on Snooky and soaking up some of her timing and comedy expertise. Also that year, he had a small part in one of Henry Lehrman's First National Comedy Specials, *The Punch of the Irish*. As a guest at the society party given by Billy Engle and his wife (Frank J. Coleman in drag), he has some business and nice close-ups while he rubs elbows with Phil Dunham and Virginia Rappe.

By 1921, Rowe was a fixture on the Roach lot. So much so that some Roach exhibitor ads included his picture captioned as "Cross-eyed Slim" and more than one item in the Motion Picture News refers to him being known as "the wall-eyed gink." The following year brought George's first and only starring short, *High Tide* (1922). In it, he played Professor Pepper from Salt Lake, who, with his sidekick Sunshine Sammy, rescues castaways Ethel Broadhurst and Mark Jones from cannibals on a desert island. Whether this was just a one-shot or a pilot for a potential series is unknown, but with Rowe's otherworldly persona, it seems likely that that the nutty inventor character would have worked well for him, the way it did later for Snub Pollard and Charley Bowers. Amazingly, this film, considered lost and unseen for years, turned up recently on eBay and was acquired by Lobster Films. Almost at the same time, a version that had been part of the German TV package of *The Mischief Makers* also surfaced.

Von Kannibalen Wird Gerwarnt begins with Our Gang footage from *Young Sherlocks* (1922) that has Sunshine Sammy outside the bakery shop, where baker George Rowe is replacing a gas pipe. Sammy gets a big dose of gas and stumbles in slow motion over to the Gang's secret headquarters and literally drops into the middle of their "secret society" meeting. A title card (in English) says, "Still in a daze....Sammy tells a story about his adventures in Africa." We then cut to *High Tide*, opening with natives dancing around a big stewpot. An odd-looking one-man submarine suit walks up on shore and George, along with assistant Sammy, get out prepared for a hunting trip. At the same time, shipwrecked Ethel Broadhurst and her father Mark Jones wash up on shore and are discovered by George, who is going to rescue them as soon as he finishes hunting. While George and Sammy have misadventures hunting, Ethel and Mark are captured by the natives and are put on the menu for lunch. After George stumbles into the culinary preparations and gets put aside for dessert, Sammy switches places with one of the cannibal kids and saves the day. When the escapees beat a path to the one-man submarine suit, there's not enough room for Sammy, so he gets carried into the surf under an arm. Here we cut back to the ending of *Young Sherlocks*, where Sammy's mother tracks him down for neglecting his chores to provide the button for the episode.

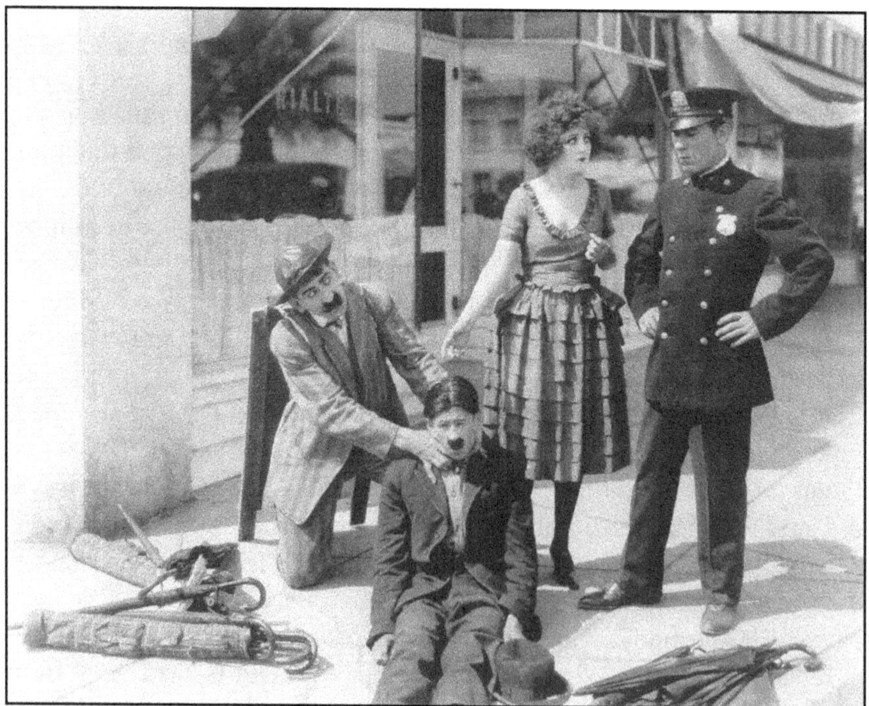

Ethel Broadhurst seeks the help of a police officer as Paul Parrott throttles George in *Soft Pedal* (1926). Photo courtesy of Cole Johnson.

It's difficult and unfair to judge *High Tide* by this truncated version without intertitles and possibly missing footage, but a strong air of deadpan absurdity survives. The walking submarine suit is a living dadaist sculpture and George as the star is just as goofy and goony as always. He's a totally unheroic hero and it's his assistant Sammy who repeatedly saves his butt. Hopefully, the complete version will eventually circulate and become available.

Possibly Rowe's best performance is in the Paul Parrott short *Post No Bills* (1923). Parrott is the co-owner of a neighborhood movie theatre and George is the press agent who's taken the day off to get married. The blushing bride is Helen Gilmore, who looks to be about sixty-four years old and is three times as tall and wide as her optically challenged bridegroom. So nervous that his heart is flopping around in his chest like a beached flounder, George finds that he's neglected to get a marriage license. The bride-to-be prostrate with grief, he bravely sets out to save the day and get the license (although it would help if he'd open the door before dashing through the doorway). The rest of the short intercuts George's misadventures securing the license with Parrott's maniacal papering of the town with theatre flyers. When Rowe arrives at the license bureau, he tries to butt ahead in the line, but is soundly beaten for his cheek by little Sammy Brooks. Later, when he's running back to the ceremony with license in hand, he has a run-in with Parrott, who's tripping up pedestrians with banana peels and sticking flyers on their posteriors. Finally George triumphantly arrives back to his bride like the cave man home from the successful hunt, but when he hands the minister the goods, it turns out to be one of Parrott's flyers. Gilmore swoons for the umpteenth time and when George turns to comfort her, it's found that the license has been pasted to his seat and the ceremony proceeds for this match made in slapstick heaven.

Rowe's 1923 Roach contract still exists and besides proving that he could sign his name, it also tells us that his salary was $150 a week. While hardly in the Mary Pickford or Charlie Chaplin league, it's not too shabby compared to what the average Joe was making in 1923. Besides his re-signing, another important event that happened that year was the beginning of his harmonious working relationship with Stan Laurel. Laurel, fresh from a successful series of two-reelers produced by G.M. "Broncho Billy" Anderson and distributed by Metro Pictures, began working early in the year at Roach on one-reelers that would alternate with Paul Parrott's. This was Stan's second stint at the studio and while he was becom-

William Gillespie (left) and George suffer through Frank Butler's (center) sour notes in *Tol'Able Romeo* (1925). Photo courtesy of Cole Johnson.

ing a name comedian, he was still searching to find the right approach to movie comedy. At this point, his screen character hadn't jelled and he was working too hard, often laughing at his own antics as if to nudge the audience to laugh, too.

Laurel seems to have appreciated George's zaniness and highlights his performances, using him in twenty of the twenty-five comedies he made during this stay at Roach. In *Short Orders* (1923), Stan's the waiter and George the chef in a crummy diner and they exhibit real teamwork in the scenes where they unorthodoxly prepare the meals–i.e. cutting meat with a giant redwood tree saw and the catching and slicing of limburger cheese that's so strong it jumps around on the table. Thanks to Robert Youngson, *Kill or Cure* (1923) contains one of Rowe's best known performances as the deaf man who stands and blankly watches as Laurel goes through his entire salesman spiel. George looks at his most cretinous in this bit and doesn't bat an eye or move a muscle until William Gillespie comes up and signs that it's time to eat. When they leave, it reveals the Deaf Institute sign on the gate, so Stan improvises his own version of sign language for the next passerby, battle-axe Helen Gilmore, and gets pounded for his performance. George also has good roles and business in *Postage Due*, *Near Dublin*, and *Rupert of Hee Haw* (all 1924). Although promoted to two-reelers midway through the series, Stan was let go by Roach in early 1924. The story goes that Stan's relationship with his common-law-wife Mae was affecting his abilities in front of the camera, but he would return to Roach in a year Mae-less and with a successful series for Joe Rock under his belt.

By 1925, a change was going on at the Roach studio. The style of the films was becoming more realistic, favoring stronger story lines and a slower pace. At this time, Our Gang and Charley Chase were the biggest attractions on the lot, which set the tone for more identifiable characters and use of clever sight gags with less out-and-out slapstick. The antic and cartoony comedies of Pollard and Parrott type were being phased out and George Rowe with them. Despite his reputation as a benevolent boss, Hal Roach never had a problem getting rid of performers if he felt their usefulness was over. Good examples of this are the abrupt terminations of Edna Marion, Viola Richard, and Dorothy Coburn in 1928 and Charley

Charley Chase is flanked by janitor George (left of Charley) and Jack Gavin (large man on right) in his 1924 one-reeler *Stolen Goods*. Photo courtesy of Cole Johnson.

Chase's firing in 1936. Handwritten on the envelope that contains Rowe's 1923 contract is "Employment terminated June 27, 1925 by verbal agreement," even though there was still four and a half months to go on the contract. After leaving the studio, George continued to show up in Roach releases for almost an entire year until mid-1926, mostly in a series of Parrott shorts originally shot in 1921 and 1922. Ironically, one of his best parts as Jimmy Finlayson's cameraman and co-star in the short *Unfriendly Enemies* (1925) was shot just a month before his termination and was directed by his buddy Stan Laurel, who had just returned for his third and permanent stay on the Roach lot.

Snub Pollard, after his heave-ho from Roach, did a twelve-month tour of vaudeville and then signed with Weiss Brothers Artclass Pictures Corporation in 1926 for a new starring series of two-reelers that ultimately teamed him with another ex-Roach employee, Marvin "Fatty" Loback. When Paul Parrott's series was curtailed, he starred in a few shorts for Fox, but then returned to Roach and moved behind the camera as director James Parrott. As such, he directed tons of Roach comedies until he was let go in the early 1930s, although he later returned to contribute gags for some Laurel & Hardy features. What Rowe did on his exit was a mystery until recently, when an ad turned up in a June 22, 1926 *Salem Capital Journal* for the stage show *Movie Makers of Hollywood*. This was an extra added attraction that would appear after or between films and top-billed in the company is "George Rowe, famous Pathé Comedian." The Salem referred to is Salem, Oregon, so this looks like some kind of west coast tour of local cinemas of a sketch that promised to show the "behind the scenes of cinema wonderland" with George probably as the main comic relief. He may have also appeared in shorts for other studios or even done bits in features. With so many films missing, it's hard to say, but so far there have been no definite sightings of him during this period.

His next blip on the cinematic radar occurs in 1928 with a quick cameo as a cross-eyed pedestrian in Laurel & Hardy's *You're Darn Tootin.'* After this, he turns up very briefly in two non-Roach shorts. In *All Washed Up* (June 2, 1928), a Larry Darmour-produced comedy starring Al Cooke, a group of thugs are trying to kill Al. George is one of them and there's a quick shot of him sticking his head out of a window after he's dropped barrels and rocks on Cooke and Barney Hellum. The other appearance is the Christie comedy *Loose Change* (June 10, 1928), where Rowe is one of four people standing and watching Jack Duffy's antics getting off a train at a station. In this one-minute scene, he's dressed in a nice

This ad turned up in the June 22, 1926 copy of the *Salem (Oregon) Capital Journal*, and helps to fill in some of the mystery of what Rowe did after leaving the Hal Roach Studio. Photo courtesy of Cole Johnson.

suit and hat, but unfortunately, the camera never gets close enough to see if his eyes are crossed or not. *Two Tars* (November 3, 1928) may be his last known appearance. He's often listed as being in the film and while he isn't visible after repeated viewings, he may have been one of the background motorists. After this brief period of return in 1928, he seems to disappear from films altogether and permanently.

It's really too bad that he doesn't show up in at least one Roach talkie, as it would be fascinating to hear his voice. But like fellow oddball Larry Semon, what kind of voice could possibly match that image? While it's a shame that Eddie Baker didn't get his phone number and address back in 1966 so that Sam Gill could have contacted him and gotten the inside dope on his life and career (as Sam's been able to do with many silent comedy veterans), in some ways, the mystery makes Rowe more intriguing and gives an extra zing to when he pops up unexpectedly in a short that's similar to the feeling you get when you find all the Ninas in an Al Hirschfeld drawing. Although we may never find out the details of his life, at least we still have many of the appearances he made during his short film career to laugh at and enjoy.

Hal Roach Presents His Silent Rascals

BABY BOOMERS WHO GREW UP watching The Little Rascals daily on television are usually amazed to discover that their beloved series was not only originally called Our Gang, but that most of their favorite gags, plots, and even characters were first created in the 1920s and then reworked in the sound films. In 1922, producer Hal Roach had an idea for some kid comedies and thought "maybe I can make a dozen of these things before I wear out the idea." When Our Gang ceased production in 1944, it was one of the longest running series in film comedy history.

Hal Roach is primarily remembered today for his films with Our Gang and Laurel & Hardy, two of his greatest successes that started in silents and continued into the sound era. But it was his association with Harold Lloyd that created his studio and set the theme–recognizable people in outlandish, but identifiable situations–that became the trademark and philosophy of a Hal Roach comedy.

Compared to his fellow early Hollywood moguls, Roach himself was something of an everyman. Adolph Zukor, William Fox, Samuel Goldwyn, and Louis B. Mayer had all been successful merchants who switched from selling furs, gloves, and even junk to a new product–movies. Roach, on the other hand, had been a muleskinner, prospector, and cowboy before he entered the film industry at the bottom rung as an extra. After working at various studios and striking up a friendship with fellow extra Harold Lloyd, Roach received a small inheritance in 1914 and decided to create his own production unit. The first person he hired was Lloyd because "he was the hardest working actor I had ever seen."

Four bloodthirsty pirates (left to right)–Sunshine Sammy Morrison, Jack Davis, Mickey Daniels and Jackie Condon–on the high seas in *Saturday Morning* (1922). Photo courtesy of Sam Gill.

At that time, comedies were cheap and easy to make. All that was needed were a few characters and a park or some other public place. So after a few false starts, Roach and Lloyd settled down to the production of Lonesome Luke Comedies. Although neither had had much experience with comedy, they studied and strived to improve and refine their work. With the development of Lloyd's "Glasses character," his popularity soared and Roach expanded his operations as their success grew. A new studio was built in 1920 and a popular series had been created starring Lloyd's former second banana Snub Pollard. But other new series that were tried out with Dee Lampton, Eddie Boland, Toto, Beatrice La Plante, and the young Stan Laurel were uneven and largely unsuccessful. Roach needed another comic star to build a series around and he turned out to be already under contract.

Ernest Frederic Morrison, better known as "Sunshine Sammy," was the son of a chef and born in 1912. He entered films in 1917 and gained a good deal of attention as the comic relief in a number of Pathé features that starred Baby Marie Osborne. Sammy's popularity quickly grew and

Sunshine Sammy supporting May Allison in *Peggy Does her Darndest* (1919).
Photo courtesy of Sam Gill.

in 1918, he appeared in the Fatty Arbuckle two-reeler *The Sheriff* and a few shorts of his own, known as the "Sambo" series. The August 24, 1818 issue of the *Motion Picture News* reported:

"The first two-reel Pathé-Diando Comedy featuring the little Negro who is known as Sunshine Sammy has been completed under the direction of Walter McNamara, and is titled "*Black Cupid*." Sunshine Sammy has played in many of the Baby Marie Osborne pictures."

Roach signed him in 1919, making Sammy the first black performer to be signed to a long-term Hollywood contract and, outside of his future Our Gang cohort Farina, probably the only black silent comedy star. Black stage comic Bert Williams only starred in a couple of early shorts before his premature death in 1922 and although talented black comedians like Spencer Bell and Ray Turner turn up in tons of shorts, they were rarely allowed to do anything but be scared or whip out giant razors or dice to shoot craps with. But on the Roach lot, Sammy was allowed to be what he really was–a tough, smart kid with an infectious personality and smile. Sammy said in late interviews that there was no prejudice on the Roach lot, but sadly, that wasn't the case with the rest of the film industry. Many of the reviews or items that appeared in the contemporary exhibitor magazines often refer to him as "Sambo" or "Sunshine Sambo" and one Pathé exhibitor ad for a 1918 Baby Marie feature had the jaw-dropping line, "If there are patrons in your audience who do not like children, they'll love them when they see Baby Marie Osborn and the funny little coon in the Pathé photoplay *A Daughter of the West*."

Most of Sammy's time at Roach was spent giving Snub Pollard, Eddie Boland, and Paul Parrott a run for their money. Even Harold Lloyd was no match for Sammy's crack comic timing, which can be seen from his memorable appearance in *Get Out and Get Under* (1920). A major film event of 1921 was the release of Charlie Chaplin's *The Kid*, which made an international star out of little Jackie Coogan. Roach seized the opportunity to star Sammy, but it took a couple of tries to get it just right. The unfortunately titled *The Pickaninny* (Dec. 4, 1922) was the pilot film and followed Sammy's misadventures as a delivery boy at a country store, but too much time was spent on the adults and the film made little impression. Hal Roach later told the story of watching a group of kids fighting over sticks and being amazed at how long it held his attention. He then took Sammy and surrounded him with other kids, focusing on their feel-

Sunshine Sammy in the Eddie Boland comedy *The Chink* (1921).
Photo courtesy of Eye Film Institute, Netherlands.

ings and views of the world, and assembled a top-notch crew behind the scenes to create the series.

Charles Parrott had come to the studio in 1921 to direct the Snub Pollard comedies. Originally entering films in 1914 after a career in vaudeville, he briefly worked for Al Christie and then ended up at Mack Sennett's Keystone. Initially a performer at Keystone, he also moved behind the camera, directing and writing. Leaving Sennett in 1916, he moved around, directing at almost every comedy unit that existed at that time–Fox, L-Ko, King Bee, Bulls Eye, Reelcraft, Paramount, Jack White, and finally Roach. Impressed with his taste and creativity, Roach soon made Parrott the director-general of the studio, where he refined the use of realistic characters that Roach and Lloyd had started and added strong storylines and a sense of the absurd that put an extra zing into the proceedings. Eventually, he would return to performing in 1924 as Charley Chase, but in 1922, he was given the task of fleshing out Roach's idea for a group of kid comedies.

Over the years, Parrott would bring a lot of comedy talent to the studio–people like Oliver Hardy, Mae Busch, and Harry Bernard–and for this project, he tapped a scenario writer that he had worked with on a series of Paramount comedies for Mr. & Mrs. Carter De Haven. Robert McGowan was a former fireman who decided that he wanted to write movie stories after being involved in running a nickelodeon. Arriving in Hollywood in 1913, he broke into the business doing behind the camera technical jobs, working his way up to writing scripts for Nestor and Christie comedies and occasionally directing. At the time of his joining Roach, he had been writing Eddie Lyon's comedies for Arrow. McGowan loved kids and made the filming fun for them, but carefully kept his own children out of the business. He soon became Our Gang's guiding light and supervised the shorts until 1933.

Other individuals played important parts in the formation of the series. Harley M. "Beanie" Walker was in charge of naming and writing the titles for the films. This ex-sportswriter, whose pithy concoctions are revered by fans today, began as Roach's title writer in 1917 and became one of the best in the business. His capturing of the "kid's angle" and the way they talk made a great contribution to the wit and polish of the shorts. Walker stayed at Roach until 1932 and then worked on Universal shorts and Paramount features until his death in 1937.

Now we come to the overlooked and forgotten Tom McNamara. Not much is known about McNamara, but he was a San Francisco-born car-

An illustration of Tom McNamara's cartooning skills in his ad from the *1921/22 Film Daily Yearbook*.

toonist who had done comic strips, such as *The Sandlot League* and *Us Boys*, that focused on kids. Involved with films since 1917, he had written titles for the features *The Gilded Lily* and *Little Italy* (both 1921) before joining the Roach organization to work on Our Gang. His exact contribution and influence on the series is hard to discern today, but his input at the beginning appears to have been almost as important as Robert McGowan's. He not only worked with H.M. Walker on stories and titles, but co-directed five shorts with McGowan and even piloted *The Cobbler* and *Boys to Board* (both 1923) on his own. He abruptly left the series and the Roach studio in early 1923 and afterwards wrote screenplays for the features *Up the Ladder* (1925) and *Little Orphan Annie* (1932), plus worked on story and gags for Mary Pickford's *Little Annie Rooney* (1925) and *Sparrows* (1926). Also continuing his output of comics, he drew stories for National and Fawcett publications into the 1930s and 40s and worked as a writer for theatrical productions before passing away in 1964.

This unit of talented collaborators set to work and soon:

> **PATHE SETS SEPT. 10 AS RELEASE DATE FOR ONE TERRIBLE DAY**. Pathé makes the long anticipated announcement that Hal Roach's new idea in two-reel comedies bearing the trademark of "Our Gang" has been successfully worked out and is ready for its first public demonstration. *One Terrible Day*, the first of the series involving children and their animal friends in strained relations with the adult community, is scheduled for release on Sept. 10. Upon this occasion the Hal Roach "zoo" is relied upon to justify itself—Dinah the mule, Cork the pony, Bill the bulldog and a flock of educated geese being ably supported by Sunshine Sammy, "Roosevelt Pershing Smith" (as little Jackie Condon insists on being called), and such other trouble-makers as Mickey Daniels, Jack Davis, Peggy Cartwright, Winston Doty, Weston Doty and Dick Cartwright. (*Exhibitor's Trade Review*, September 9, 1922)

Although not the first film shot, *One Terrible Day* (September 10, 1922) was the first released and a good choice to introduce the Gang. The simple premise–a rich lady takes the underprivileged Gang on a day's outing to her country home and gets more than she bargained for–gave the kids plenty of room to show their stuff and they come across as uncontrollable forces of nature as they use her fancy fountain for a "swimmin' hole" or play bullfighter with her confused cow. Exhibitor and public enthusiasm was immediate and the next releases were welcomed with open arms.

Our Gang (November 5, 1922), the original film made, was released third, as Roach felt it needed some fine tuning. At one time considered lost, over the years fragments and shortened "toy film" versions of this initial entry have surfaced, which almost add up to the entire film. Two story threads–a little girl whose widowed mother's grocery store may be repossessed by a mean landlord and that of a pampered rich boy who gets

Roy Brooks (left), Mollie Thompson (right), and Vera White (far right) try to cope with the Gang in *One Terrible Day* (1922). Photo courtesy of Sam Gill.

a he-man makeover by the Gang–come together in the last part of the film as the kids use their unusual methods to operate and get customers for the store. The melodramatic plot device of the mother's impending mortgage is treaded on very lightly with the main focus on the interaction of the kids and their unique solutions to the problems they encounter. The spontaneity of the films and the high quality of the gags in other strong early releases, such as *Young Sherlocks*, *Saturday Morning* (both 1922), and *The Champeen* (1923), nailed their success and assured the continuation of the series.

As to the kids themselves, Roach's idea had been for a "cast of just kids, tattered and full of spirits," and the first group of regulars that eventually formed around Sunshine Sammy was found mostly through friends and studio employees. Staff still-photographer Gene Korman loaned his daughter Mary and recommended family friend Mickey Daniels. Allen "Farina" Hoskins, originally called "Maple," was discovered by Sunshine Sammy and his dad. Jack Davis was Harold Lloyd's brother-in-law. Chubby Joe Cobb and his dad showed up at the studio during a vacation with the result that Joe was promptly put into the Snub Pollard two-reeler *A Tough Winter* (1923) and then ensconced in the Gang. Outside of Sunshine Sammy, the kid with the most acting experience was probably four-year-old Jackie Condon, referred to as "duster head" by Mickey in *July Days* (1923), who had been appearing in films since he was a baby. These kids became the archetypes that were repeated during Our Gang's long run–a feisty, freckle-faced kid and the pretty heroine that he has a crush on, a good-natured fat boy, and a wise black kid (usually named after a breakfast cereal). There were also a number of early kids–Peggy Cartwright, Winston and Weston Doty, Monty O'Grady, Anna Mae Bilson, Dick Cartwright–who quickly fell by the wayside, while the title of "kid most taken for granted" goes to Andy Samuel. Andy appeared in a total of nineteen shorts in three years and his moment of glory was his Charlie Chaplin imitation in *The Big Show* (February 25, 1923).

Another reason for the success of the series was the great supporting appearances by members of the Hal Roach stock company. Charlie Hall, Lyle Tayo, Earl Mohan, Vera White, Noah Young, George Rowe, Pat Kelly, Dick Gilbert, Anita Garvin, and even Oliver Hardy showed up from time to time and brightened the proceedings. Character comic William Gillespie

Paul Jacobs comforts Violet Radcliffe in *Little Billy's City Cousin* (1914).
Photo courtesy of Sam Gill.

probably appeared in the most shorts, but by far the most important of the adult actors to work with the Gang was Mickey's dad Richard Daniels. Short and a little on the wizened side, the senior Daniels usually played a kindly, older grandfather type of figure who, while being busy being a cobbler, a blacksmith, or a groundskeeper in shorts like *July Days* (1923) or *Mary, Queen of Tots* (1925), always found time to build the Gang go-carts or help them with their problems. Although Daniels appeared in other Roach films and in Harold Lloyd features such as *Girl Shy* (1924) and *For Heaven's Sake* (1926), his most memorable work was with Our Gang.

Portrait of the Powers Kids Matty Roubert and Baby Early circa 1912.

The immediate success that met Our Gang was remarkable, especially as Roach's idea wasn't all that original. Besides the aforementioned Baby Marie Osborne and Jackie Coogan, there had been plenty of Our Gang antecedents. Starting with the one-reel *Just Kids* in 1913, Henry Lehrman had initiated a series for Mack Sennett that became known as Keystone Kids, which led to a number of films like *Little Billy's Triumph* and *Little Billy's City Cousin* (both 1914) that starred three-year-old Paul Jacobs as the title character. When Lehrman left Keystone to become part of The Sterling Film Co., he took Jacobs and director Robert Thornby with him. The forgotten Bobby Connelly began working for Vitagraph in 1913 and eventually starred in two series for them: Sonny Jim in 1914 and the Bobby films two years later before dying at age thirteen in 1922. The Edison Company starred ten-year-old Andy Clark as an easy-going messenger boy in their 1914 Andy series.

Around the same time, Universal created two series built around talented kids. Matty Roubert, born in 1907, had appeared in pictures for Vitagraph and Biograph before turning up regularly in comedies for producer Pat Powers, where he was usually teamed with a little girl named Baby Early. Known as the Powers Kids, they spent most of their time as pint-sized troublemakers in shorts such as *Injuns* (1912) and *Having Their Picture Took* (1913). In 1914, Universal dubbed him Universal Boy and began turning out one-reelers that included *Universal Boy as the Newsboy's Friend* and *Universal Boy in Cupid and Fishes.* After this, Roubert continued working through the teens and had a later series, Romances of Youth, that was distributed by Reelcraft in 1920. Universal's other kid star was Bobby Fuehrer. Born in 1900, he had acted on stage with stars such as Maude Adams and was tapped by the "Big U" to replace Augustus Carney. After becoming a big star as Alkali Ike in Essanay's Snakeville Comedies, Carney had jumped ship to work for Carl Laemmle as Universal Ike. The arrangement didn't last long, though, and after Carney walked, Bobby took over as Universal Ike, Jr. Following eighteen entries on the order of *Universal Ike Junior and the Vampire* and *Universal Ike Junior is Kept from Being an Actor*, Bobby hightailed it over to D. W. Griffith's Majestic/Fine Arts Co., where he became part of their Bill the Office Boy comedies. In the 1920s, an older Fuehrer changed his name to Bobby Ray and starred in comedies for Arrow and Rayart, plus directed as Robert Furer.

Other kid comedies were the "Children's Pictures—By Children—For Children" made by the Juvenile Film Corporation in 1916 and released on the states' rights market. Titles such as *Chip's Backyard Barnstormers* and *Chip's Rivals* (both 1916) were helmed by James A. Fitzpatrick (of later Traveltalks fame) and starred Joseph Monahan, who seems to have managed to include his imitation of Charlie Chaplin in practically every film. Chester and Sidney Franklin began a group of kids' films under the auspices of D. W. Griffith, first at Majestic and then his Fine Arts Studio. These started as shorts like *The Doll-House Mystery* (1915) and moved on to features such as *Sister of Six* (1916). From here, the brothers went to the Fox Studio for a series of elaborate feature-length fairy tale and adventure epics that starred kids. The talented child ensemble (Francis Carpenter, Virginia Lee Corbin, Violet Radcliffe, Buddy and Gertrude Messinger, George E. Stone, Raymond Lee, Lewis Sargent) played their roles straight, but the Franklins inserted witty spoofs of the genre and the acting of popular stars of the day, such as Theda Bara, William Farnum, etc., which make surviving examples like *Aladdin and his Wonderful Lamp* (1917) and *Ali Baba and the Forty Thieves* (1918) still great fun today.

Fox also had a kiddie team in the sisters Jane and Katherine Lee. After supporting stars like Annette Kellerman, Theda Bara, and Stuart Holmes, the studio put them into their own features, such as *Two Lit-*

The Fox Kiddies Jane (left) and Katherine (right) Lee get ready to deliver a pie to the Kaiser in their World War I comedy *Swat the Spy* (1918). Photo courtesy of Sam Gill.

tle Imps (1917) and *Swat the Spy* (1918). Some were helmed by comedy veteran Arvid E. Gillstrom and most had topical World War I themes that consisted of the moppets shaming their elders into doing their civic wartime duty. According to the *Moving Picture World*, Fox brought them back in 1922 "in re-edited versions of some of their former successes. The pictures have been edited by Ralph Spence and cut down to two reels. The first of the series is called *A Pair of Aces*, and is made up of situations and bits of business culled from several of the original features."

An overlooked kid series that derived from a forgotten newspaper comic strip was the Paramount-Briggs Comedies produced in 1919, which were based on the cartoons of Clare Briggs that appeared in the *New York Tribune* and five hundred other newspapers around the country. The stories revolved around young Skinnay, his best girl (known as "her"), his pal Bud, and Skinnay's family. Not a long lasting series, around eighteen, such as *Skinny, School and Scandal*, and *The Fotygraph Gallery* were produced, with the leads played by brother and sister Johnny and Rosemary Carr and the company under the direction of John William Kellette.

1920 saw the rise of Edward Peil, Jr., who under the name of Johnny

Johnny Jones confronts a figment caused by his overeating in *Edgar's Feast Day* (1921). Photo courtesy of Sam Gill.

Jones became a popular kid star in a series of Goldwyn-produced two-reelers based on stories by Booth Tarkington. The Adventures and Emotions of Edgar Pomeroy lasted two years and the only known survivor, *Edgar's Feast Day* (1921), has Edgar and his buddy gorging themselves on ice cream and then having a terrible nightmare where they are chased by giant pieces of food. From here, Johnny moved to Pathé's Johnny Jones Comedies, where he was supported by Gertrude Messinger and Ben Alexander in comedies that followed "the adventures of Johnny and his kid pals in juvenile business," then appeared in a few late 1920s features under

Baby Peggy in disguise on a hot case in her Century Comedy *The Kid Reporter* (1923).

his real name. Pathé also produced another boy's series, The Adventures of Bob and Bill, about a pair of twins–Robert and William Bradbury–and their relationship to animals.

Universal's Century Comedies, run by Abe and Julius Stern, specialized in animals and kid stars in the 1920s (no doubt due to the lower salaries involved). In addition to the Century Lions, their feral stars included Mr. & Mrs. Joe Martin (orangutans), Queenie the horse, and the dogs Brownie and Pal. In 1921, a baby that had appeared as an unbilled sidekick to Brownie got spun off into her own series and little Peggy Montgomery became very well-known as Baby Peggy. The Sterns put together a unit that turned out Peggy's shorts through 1924, which was made up of talented comedy creators, such as Fred Hibbard, Arvid E. Gillstrom, and Alf Goulding, and surrounded her with regular supporting players like Blanche Payson, Dick Smith, Max Asher, James T. Kelly, William Irving, and giant Jack Earle. In the beginning, the focus was on plots where Peggy was an orphan or lost immigrant child, but by 1923 had switched to Hollywood spoofs like *Peg O' the Movies* and *Carmen Jr.* or new versions of fairy tales, such as *Hansel and Gretel* (1923) and *Jack and the Beanstalk* (1924). Peggy also starred in features like *The Darling of New York* (1923) and *Captain January* (1924) before her career faded in the late 1920s.

At the same time, the studio also developed a couple of brief series starring boys. Lewis Sargent, who had appeared in some of the Franklin kid pictures and made a name for himself playing Huck in William Desmond Taylor's *Huckleberry Finn* (1920), spent the 1922/23 season in a number of Messenger Boy one-reelers written and directed by W. Scott Darling. Johnny Fox starred in shorts like *Fresh Kid* and *Ginger Face* (both 1922) and was Universal's answer to freckle-faced feature star Wesley Barry. It was Barry's popularity that helped to bring a horde of spreckled urchins like Mickey Daniels, Spec O'Donnell, Leon Holmes, and Jack McHugh to the screen.

Now we arrive at what appears to be Our Gang's direct forerunner–Campbell Comedies. William S. Campbell started his directing career in the mid-teens for Mack Sennett and then moved on to Fox Sunshine Comedies and Universal. In 1920, he helmed the comedies starring Snooky the Human-Zee, which were produced by Chester Comedies and released by Educational Pictures. This series revolved around the adventures of a chimp and a little girl, usually Ida Mae McKenzie, who repeatedly rescued and took care of a number of unnamed babies and toddlers. In 1921, Campbell went into business for himself, producing and direct-

Josephine acts as Laurence Licalvi's simian alarm clock in the Campbell Comedy *A Rag Doll Romance* (1922). Photo courtesy of Eye Film Institute, Netherlands.

ing two-reelers that continued the theme of kids and animals. Starring kids like John Henry Jr., Doreen Turner, Coy Watson Jr., and Laurence Licalvi, Campbell put the main focus on the children and had Josephine the monkey and "the famous Campbell dog" as their helpmates.

Only two or three of the shorts are known to survive today. *Schoolday Love* (January 29, 1922) has Coy Watson, Jr., driving around in a dog-powered auto and getting into trouble at school in true Our Gang style. The only title to really circulate, *Monkey Shines* (February 26, 1922), has a young shoeshine boy trying to make enough money to take care of his widowed and consumptive mother. His monkey and dog companions come up with a scheme where they fill a hole in the sidewalk with mud and cover it with a newspaper. Soon a line of muddy-footed innocent pedestrians are waiting for Laurence's services, but the local cop gets wise and gives chase. It all ends happily as the cop has a young daughter who is rescued from a train by Laurence and then the cop meets and eventually marries the boy's mother. As sentimental as the plot sounds, the focus is on the comedy and the animals are given plenty of footage–getting up in the morning and doing their daily ablutions, etc. Also, the presence of comedy regulars, such as Eddie Borden, James Donnelly, and Silas Wilcox, ensures a lighter tone.

The series only lasted through eleven shorts, but it seems that Hal Roach was aware of them, particularly as the animals were owned and trained by Tony Campanaro, who began working for Roach around the time that the Campbells ended. Originally, animals were going to play a much larger role in Our Gang. The second short, *The Firefighters* (October 8, 1922), opens with a short sequence about a flirty duck and his angry wife (which often circulates today under the title *Flappers*). Although their animal friends remain a constant element in the Gang's adventures, Roach soon took the animal idea and spun it off into its own series–the highly surreal Dippy-Doo-Dad Comedies.

By late 1923, Mickey Daniels had become the leader of the Gang, even pulling focus from Sunshine Sammy, who didn't seem quite as remarkable as he got a little bigger and older. Mickey's scrappy persona, combined with his expressive face and expert comic timing, made him a natural underdog that audiences could really empathize with. Also, his ongoing relationship and real chemistry with Mary Kornman brought out

Joe Cobb, Jackie Condon, Mary Kornman, Mickey Daniels, and Farina Hoskins set off for plunder in *Buried Treasure* (1926). Photo courtesy of Robert Arkus.

his sensitive side, making him a more dimensional character. As to Mary herself, besides sometimes being a real flirt, she was often the voice of reason that made the boys stop and almost think over the consequences of the latest scheme they were hatching. Cute, with a little pug nose, Mary was slender and very long-legged and was soon taller than many of the guys in the Gang. Both Mary and Mickey tried to find continued movie success as adults, but outside of Roach's early 1930s Boy Friends Comedies, it proved elusive and they eventually drifted out of films.

Our Gang had proved to be a winner right out of the starting gate and kept up a very impressive level of consistency. A number of the shorts rate among the best silent comedies being made at that time. *The Sun Down Limited* (September 21, 1924) takes the idea of the Gang building a train to an amazing level with an incredibly detailed railway system complete with working depot and telegraph office. This short in particular fully creates an "Our Gang alternate universe"–as there are very few adults in the film, it's mostly the kids functioning in a world of their own creation.

Ask Grandma (May 31, 1925) is the story of Mickey's difficulties with an overbearing mother who won't let him just be himself. She makes him take ballet lessons, dress like Little Lord Fauntleroy, and adhere to a long list of etiquette rules (all beginning with "Don't"). His grandma helps him out, playing baseball and boxing with him in addition to advising him to follow his natural instincts. When his crush on Mary leads him into a fight with bully Johnny, Mickey proves himself and his mother sees the error of her ways. Veteran character actress Florence Lee is wonderful as grandma and brings a perfect combination of heart and moxie to the role. While it's the story of Mickey's plight that's stressed in this entry, the usual slapstick sight gags aren't ignored, either. When grandma gets ready to play ball, she limbers up with silent speed backflips and somersaults (as a later grandma does in 1931's *Fly My Kite*) and when she reminds Mickey's mother about what a tomboy she was as a kid, there's a flashback sequence with Mickey in drag as his mom, complete with pigtails and a bonnet.

Thundering Fleas (July 18, 1926) is all sight gags, hung on the tale of an educated flea who finds Farina's dog more inviting than the performing life, so he escapes from the flea circus and gathers plenty of friends who all end up infesting Mary's older sister's wedding ceremony for the big climax of the film. Besides the usual top-notch gags, there's cute animation of flea life and funny cameos from Jimmy Finlayson, Jerry Mandy, Martha Sleeper, Oliver Hardy, and Charley Chase (wearing a huge moustache with a life of its own). Other highlights from this period include *No*

Noise (September 23, 1923), *Seein' Things*, *High Society* (both 1924), and *One Wild Ride* (1925).

Many shorts, like *The Sun Down Limited*, *Tire Trouble* (both 1924) and *Better Movies* (1925), feature the Gang's awe-inspiring, homemade versions of working railroads, pirate ships, goat-powered fire trucks, and secret clubhouses. Before becoming a fireman, the young Robert McGowan had wanted to be an inventor and the Gang's adventures gave him free reign to imagine incredible contraptions, which were then built by unsung technical wizard Charley Oelze. After a background spent in circuses and cattle ranches, Oelze had been a cowboy movie extra and eventually was in charge of the extras waiting to be picked for scenes at Universal. When his fellow extra and friend Hal Roach started his own studio, Charley was hired as property man and remained with the organization for almost thirty-five years as an assistant director and jack-of-all-trades troubleshooter.

As mentioned earlier, there had been a slew of kid comedies before Our Gang, but its huge success created a veritable boom. Again Universal and Century led the way with a flock of child-oriented shorts. Melvin Joe Messinger, better known as Buddy, had been in films since the age of nine

James "Bubbles" Berry (left), Martha Sleeper, and Buddy Messinger (right) enjoy the results of a whitewash malfunction in the Century Comedy *BuddingYouth* (1924).

in 1916. During 1922 to 1925, he starred in a series for Century, where he was supported by some soon to be well-known kids like Martha Sleeper, Spec O'Donnell, and James "Bubbles" Berry. After this group of films, Buddy went over to Bray for a series of Sunkist Comedies about college hijinks that teamed him with a chimp named Mr. X. Little Arthur Trimble had been starring in independent shorts since the early 1920s and joined Universal around 1924. The next year, the studio launched him in their adaptation of R.F. Outcault's famous comic strip *Buster Brown*. Buster had originally been brought to the screen in 1903 and then again in 1914 by the Edison Company and in this new edition, Trimble had support from Doreen Turner as Mary Jane and Pete the pup as Tige. The results were mostly lackluster with most of the laughs coming from Pete's antics. The series managed to last until 1929 and its main director, Gus Meins, went on to join the Our Gang family in the 1930s.

On the tails of Buster Brown, the studio made another bid to cover the kid comedy market with a version of another newspaper strip, George MacManus' *The Newlyweds and their Baby*. Starting in 1926, the fairly frightening Sunny McKeen starred as the said baby Snookums, who made

It's Alive! Sunny McKeen proves that he was hatched and not born in this Easter publicity photo for the Stern Brothers' The Newlyweds and their Baby series. Photo courtesy of Sam Gill.

life a living hell for his not-too-bright parents (and the general audience). McKeen as Snookums was practically bald except for one foot-long hair that stuck straight up from the top of his head that made him look like a living tampon. Basically as unfunny as the Buster Browns, this series had at least a bizarre quality and tastelessness going for it. A good example is *The Newlyweds Christmas Party* (December 5, 1927), which has Snookums inviting the local poor kids to the festivities. When Santa arrives, he gives them racially stereotypical gifts–a Jewish kid gets a ham hock, an ironing board goes to the Chinese boy, an Irish tough gets some bricks, and the black kid is given a live chicken, which causes him to start to lick his lips and look for a place to end its life. The series briefly made the transition to sound, where it was renamed Sunny Jim Comedies, but Sunny McKeen died at age eight in 1933 from blood poisoning.

In 1923, Jack White Comedies jumped on the gang bandwagon with a series called Juvenile Comedies. This group of ragtag urchins was made up of Mickey Bennett, Ben Alexander, Johnny Fox, Jack McHugh, Harry "Ginger" Spear, and Bobby Gordon, but the youngest member soon gathered all the attention and became the star. Malcolm Sebastian (originally Sabiston) was born in Hollywood in November of 1923 and according to studio publicity, made his screen debut at the age of three months in the feature *Three Weeks* (1924). Jules White, brother of Jack and later film mentor of the Three Stooges, is credited with discovering Malcolm and outfitting him in a large bowler hat, shoes, and a diaper (which thankfully was replaced with ragged clothing as he got older). Dubbed "Big Boy," his first appearance was in *Baby Blues* (1925) and by 1927, the series became Big Boy Comedies and focused on his adventures. The plots owed a lot to Jackie Coogan films, usually presenting Big Boy as an orphan or a poor kid living with a widowed mother or grandmother. Malcolm was a good little actor and played his scenes very seriously, making the comedy funnier. When the series ended in 1929, Malcolm made a talkie appearance with the Gang in *Shivering Shakespeare* (1930), then retired from the screen. He spent his adult life managing restaurants and golf courses in the San Diego area and made a few appearances at film conventions before his death in July 2006.

Of course, Our Gang fever even reached the lower-budgeted independent companies and a number of series were out and out clones. 1924 saw two short-lived entries, the elusive Kahn Kids Comedies from Screen Arts Distributors and M.J. Winkler's Reg'lar Kids. Today, Margaret J. Winkler is remembered as the distributor of animation, such as the early Felix

1925 exhibitor ad for the modestly budgeted Hey Fellas! Series.

the Cat and Disney's Alice in Cartoonland series, but Reg'lar Kids was a live action rip-off which had Spec O'Donnell, Carter De Haven Jr., and adult Billy Franey as regulars in the onscreen crew. The shorts, helmed by Brian Foy and Monte Brice, lasted into 1925.

McKnight-Womack Productions began a series of Hey Fellas two-reelers in 1925, which were described as "the doin's and disasters of Young America." In an attempt to get close to Our Gang, Mickey Daniels' brother Cliff was cast as leader of the group and regular Roach pug-ugly character player Dick Gilbert turns up in support. Probably the most interesting aspect of this short-lived series is that future voice of Goofy and Walt Disney gagman Pinto Colvig was responsible for the titles and gags. Longer lasting, possibly due to being made on an even cheaper budget, were the

Bray Company's McDougall Alley Kids Comedies. Having been a pioneer in film animation, the Bray Company made a move into live action shorts in the late 20s and despite taking advantage of comedy pros like Jack Cooper, Robert McKenzie, Andy Clyde, and William Irving, their batting average was pretty poor. For the McDougalls, any creativity seems to have been used up when they thought of the names "Oatmeal" for the black kid and "Free Gin" for the Asian one. It was all downhill from there, but the series managed to hang on until late 1928.

Another kiddie series came from William Pizor (rhymes with "eyesore") Productions–maker of the ultimate rock bottom comedy shorts. The hallmarks of Pizor films were non-existent gags, shoddy production values, and plodding direction. The one big name he used was Sid Smith,

Little Jerry Madden and his toy menagerie pose for Fox Animal Comedies.

between his various stints at majors such as Sennett, Fox, and Christie, and the stable of "stars" developed by Pizor–Teddy Reavis, Fred Parker, and Lloyd Hamilton clone Art Hammond–maybe weren't half bad, but they never had a chance in these dire productions. Pizor's kid films starred an effete Arthur Trimble type named Jackie Daily, whose shorts, like *Wild and Wooly* and *Irish Luck* (both 1927), with their mind-numbing pace and arid entertainment value, lived up (or down) to the usual Pizor standards.

The Fox Studio made their entry in the Our Gang sweepstakes with a 1926 series titled Animal Comedies. Initially, these shorts starred Jerry Madden, a three-year-old Big Boy clone with a sad face and too-big clothes, who played an orphan trying to make his way in an unfriendly world with the help of his animal friends. After a few of these, such as *Jerry the Giant*, *Napoleon Jr.* (both 1926), and *A Dog's Pal* (1927), little Jerry left the series. He was replaced by adult Gene Cameron for a couple of shorts, where he played second fiddle to a kangaroo, like *A Kangaroo Detective* (1927), but when Cameron was killed in an auto accident, the series mutated into a total Our Gang rip-off. Starting with *Captain Kidd's Kittens* (1927), the usual group of kids–freckle-faced tough guy, fat boy, young Asian, black kid, etc.–were put through about five adventures that included *Wild Puppies* (1927) and *The Elephant's Elbows* (1928) by director Clyde Carruth. In spite of the participation of talented kid actors like Coy Watson Jr., Jack McHugh, and Leon Holmes, the series was mundane with weak gags and characters. The best that can be said about this group of comedies is that at least they had decent budgets and a little studio polish, which put them on a slightly higher level than the Hey Fellas or McDougall Alley shorts.

In the last part of the 1920s, three other kid-related comic strips hit the screen. Martin Branner's *Winnie Winkle* was brought to movie life in 1926 by West Brothers Productions (comedian Billy West and his brother George) and Artclass Pictures as a vehicle to showcase West's wife and longtime co-star Ethlyn Gibson. As in the strip, the movie Winnie was supported by her little brother Perry Winkle and ersatz Our Gang squad The Rinky-Dinks. These anemic characters consisted of Spud, Spike, and Chink, with the make-up on the Caucasian kid playing Chink looking like something out of a bad community theatre production of Gilbert & Sullivan's *The Mikado*. The behind the camera contributions of comedy vets like Hugh Fay, Arvid E. Gillstrom, and Ralph Cedar didn't seem to help the series, which petered out in early 1928.

Better luck was had with a character from Fontaine Fox's strip *Toonerville Folks*. Mickey (Himself) McGuire was a tough Irish kid and the self-styled leader of Tomboy Taylor, Hambone Johnson, and Teeth McDuff in their adventures and battles with rich kid nemesis Stinky Davis. Producer Larry Darmour started the series rolling in 1927 and cast a then unknown Mickey Rooney (Joe Yule Jr.) in the lead. This was Rooney's first step to becoming one of the most popular entertainers of the 1930s and 40s and years later, just the fact that he was in the films kept them accessible and in circulation. The series was fairly low-budget, but since Mickey was a poor kid anyway, the cheap sets and the constant use of outdoor and found locations worked in its favor. As the gags were rarely more than just routine, the comedy burden fell on Rooney's shoulders and he proved himself a real trooper with an engaging and energetic performance of a pint-sized wheeler-dealer. The other kids never make much of an impression, although little Kendall McComas later ended up as "Breezy Brisbane" in a few sound Our Gang shorts like *Readin' and Writin'* and *Spanky* (both 1932). Directors Al Herman and Earl Montgomery kept the McGuire's pace moving and Mickey's homemade cars, wagons, and other contraptions show real invention and wit and are almost as good as Charley Oe-

Smitty series regulars Donald Haines (left), Betty Jane Graham, and Jackie Coombs (right) in their 1928 comedy *Camping Out*. Photo courtesy of Sam Gill.

zle's for Our Gang. The series continued into sound and lasted until 1933, when Rooney moved on to bigger and better things.

Our last comic strip transfer to cover is the Smitty Comedies. Created by Walter Berndt in 1922 about an office boy and his friends, the Van Buren Company began the film version in 1928 with freckle-faced Donald Haines as Smitty and George Marshall as director.

The shorts were distributed by Pathé and co-starred Jackie Combs, Betty Jane Graham, and Billy Bruce. A selling gimmick for this series was star cameos, or "Big Seat Selling Names In Each Comedy" in Pathé exhibitor ads. The first release, *No Picnic* (1928), boasted boxing champ Jack Dempsey as the guest star and later ones included the likes of Billy Bevan and Lloyd Hamilton. The series was short-lived and quickly forgotten, but star Donald Haines spent a couple of years in the early 1930s as a member of Our Gang. He continued working in films until World War II service and his death in 1942.

Mid-1926 started the "second phase" of Our Gang where the original kids begin to be replaced by younger versions of themselves. Jack Davis was the first of the early Gang to leave, packed off to military school by his brother-in-law Harold Lloyd in late 1923, with the next to go the catalyst for the series, Sunshine Sammy. *Cradle Robbers* (June 1, 1924) was his last short when he left movies altogether to headline in his own vaudeville act. Billed as "Sunshine Sammy –Our Gang star," he sang and danced his way across the country. With the exception of an MGM musical short, *Stepping Along* (1929), Sammy didn't return to the screen until 1940 to spend three years as part of another gang–the East Side Kids. After a number of cheaply-made adventures like *Spooks Run Wild* (1941) and *Clancy Street Boys* (1943), Sammy joined the army and entertained the troops during World War II as part of the USO. Later leaving show business, he spent the last part of his life being feted for his contributions to black film history.

When Sammy left the Gang, Farina moved into his spot, which finally brought an end to the question of his mysterious gender. Many of the early shorts refer to Farina as "she" and his usual outfit was a sack-like dress (the mystery and dress were later inherited by Buckwheat in the 1930s). An item from a June 1925 issue of *Motion Picture News* suggests that Farina himself was very aware of the confusion:

"Farina, of the Hal Roach "Our Gang" comedies, has resorted to diplomacy. For a long time Farina has protested wildly against having to be a girl in the screen plays. But they told him that somebody had to be a girl.

The other day Farina turned up with his fifteen-month old sister. Now he hopes that he can be a boy in pictures."

His sister Jannie had actually begun appearing earlier in 1924 and it was announced in the fall of 1926 that she had officially joined the Gang and was dubbed "Aroma," but she was most commonly nicknamed "Mango." Robert McGowan had developed a system for adding new kids that had them spend a few months as a sort of background Gang member to gather screen time and experience. Jay R. Smith replaced Mickey Daniels this way and, later, Bobby "Wheezer" Hutchins would do the same when Jackie Condon was getting a bit long in the tooth at ten years old.

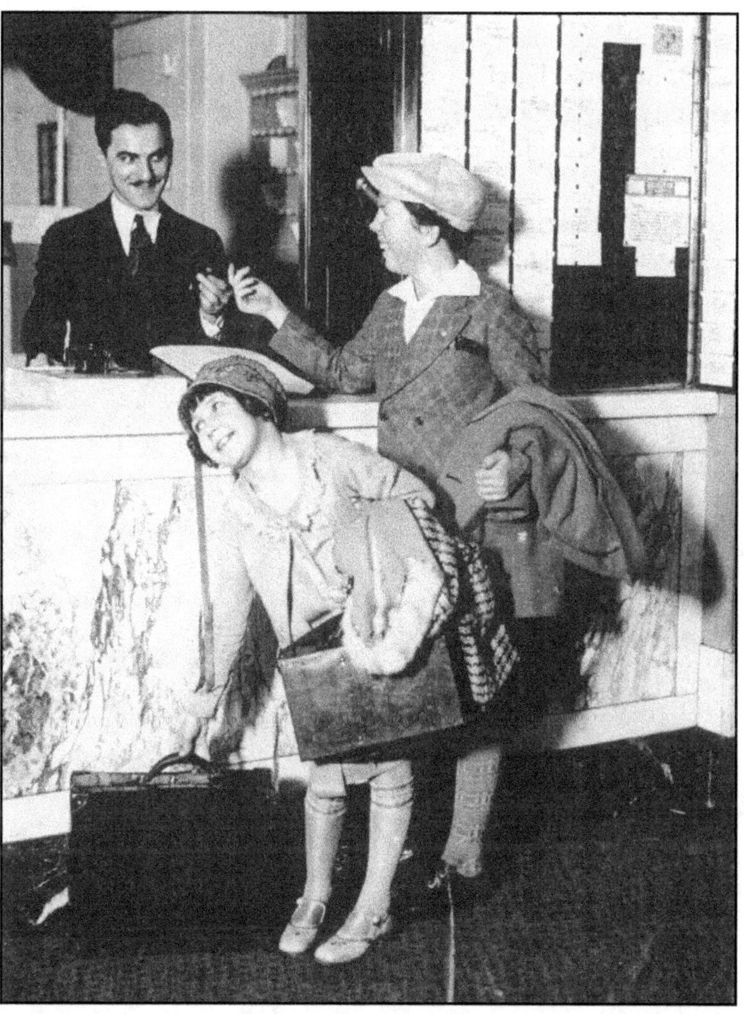

Like Sunshine Sammy, Mickey Daniels appeared in vaudeville after he left Our Gang. Here he is in a publicity shot with his stage partner Peggy Eames.

Other new kids who came into the series include Johnny Downs, Eugene "Pineapple" Jackson, Scooter Lowry, and Bobby "Bonedust" Young, who would come and go into the early 1930s. Harry Spear arrived from Jack White Comedies, where as "Ginger," he had been a regular in their Juvenile Comedies besides appearances like the one where he shoots Lupino Lane in the rear with an arrow in *Who's Afraid* (1927). When Mary Kornman got too old, a new blond heartthrob was needed and four-year-old Jean Darling filled the bill.

During this transitional period, the anchors for the series became Farina and Joe Cobb. Both had started early, staying with the Gang nearly a decade each, and were favorites of Hal Roach, which accounts for their longevity. When Farina made his debut in the second release *Fire Fighters* (1922), he could barely walk and in his first films he spent a lot of time getting knocked down by the other kids, but that never stopped him from getting in the middle of things. Nothing ever seemed to stop Farina, especially when he was little. When he got older, he was always the most sensible and pragmatic of the kids with a well-developed reflex for self-preservation. Besides his dead-on comedy abilities, he was quite a good

Farina has found a friend in the Gang's 1926 adventure *Buried Treasure.*

actor and, in shorts like *Love My Dog* (April 17, 1927), could do truly heart wrenching crying scenes. After leaving the series in 1931, he was very good as Joe E. Brown's assistant in *You Said a Mouthful* (1932) and in a dramatic part in *Mayor of Hell* (1933) with James Cagney, but his career sputtered out in the mid 1930s.

Joe Cobb could be the prototype of Poppin' Fresh, the Pillsbury Doughboy, with his round white face and shy smile. He seemed to be made all out of circles and was as big around as tall. It generally took a lot to rile Joe, but when it happened, he was a wild man ready to lick the entire world. After making the transition to sound with the Gang, his advancing age made it time for him to retire, but he still turned up from time to time with the 1930s kids in shorts like *Fish Hooky* (1933) and *Pay as You Exit* (1936). Also working as a master of ceremonies for Our Gang publicity tours, he did small bits in features before quitting acting in 1942 and joining the aviation industry. Joe pretty much remained the same height he had been while in the Gang and he passed away in 2002.

At the end of 1926, Robert McGowan decided to lighten his load a bit and while he continued to direct some of the shorts (while producing and supervising the overall series for Roach), he also took advantage of the usual brand of Hollywood nepotism and brought his nephew and namesake Robert Anthony McGowan in to share the directorial chores. The younger McGowan worked under the name Anthony Mack and started directing with *Telling Whoppers* (December 19, 1926), at first in tandem with his uncle or Charley Oezle. On his own, he piloted fifteen shorts, which were for the most part lackluster, although he did helm two which are the oddest in the series entire history. *Dog Heaven* (December 17, 1927) starts with Pete the pup hanging himself in graphic detail and then relating the story of woe that drove him to it to the canine pal that saved his life. In *Cat, Dog and Co.* (September 14, 1929), Wheezer is happily torturing all the animals he sees until he has a terrible nightmare where he's captured and put on trial by giant animals for his acts of cruelty. Mack's last directorial effort was the early talkie *Boxing Gloves* (September 9, 1929), but wasn't the end of his association with Our Gang. Nine years later, when the series moved over to MGM, Mack, under his real name of Robert A. McGowan, co-wrote the screenplays for practically all of those dismal shorts. It's hoped that the giant animals from *Cat, Dog and Co.* had the opportunity to put him on trial for cruelty to audiences.

The turnover of the late 1920s brought two very important newcomers to the Gang–one human and the other animal. The animal was, of

Pete and Pal appearing together in the June 1926 issue of the *Movie Home Journal*. The original caption says: "Yes sir that's my baby! Introducing Pete (right) the dog with the sense of humor, and his father Pal, also a noted star." Photo courtesy of Billy Rose Theatre Division, The New York Public Library for the Performing Arts, Astor, Lenox and Tilden Foundations.

course, Pete the pup, who made his Our Gang debut in *Olympic Games* (September 11, 1927). Pete was owned by a French-born former actor/wrestler named Harry Lucenay and his father was Pal, another of Lucenay's dogs. Pal was a star in his own series of Century Comedies in 1923 and 1924 and also worked with the likes of Buster Keaton, Monty Banks, Big Boy, and other popular comics. A picture from the *Movie Home Journal* has father and son posing together, presenting Pete as an up and comer.

At any rate, Lucenay started Pete in films when he was six months old and by the time he joined the Gang, he was a seasoned pro. His earliest known appearance seems to be Lupino Lane's Fox feature *A Friendly Husband* (January 1, 1923). By 1925 Pete was working regularly, turning up in films like Harold Lloyd's *The Freshman* and as the title character in *Dynamite Doggie* opposite Al St John. Along the way, he appeared with

Harry Langdon, Ben Turpin, A Ton of Fun, and in a couple of Stan Laurel comedies for Joe Rock, such as *Somewhere in Wrong* and *Dr. Pyckle and Mr. Pride* (both 1925). In fact, it was Laurel who first used Pete at Roach in his directorial effort *Yes, Yes Nanette* (1925). In the fall of that year, starting with *Educating Buster* (September 23, 1925), Pete began co-starring as Tige in Universal's Buster Brown series, supplying all the laughs and stealing the show from effeminate Arthur Trimble. Reviewers, exhibitors, and the public went crazy over him and he stayed with the series for two years until Roach came up with a better offer.

Baby Mary Ann Jackson is presented her own miniature director's chair by her Smith Family co-star Ruth Hiatt.

Our Gang had had various dogs before, but none of them with an ounce of the personality and charm that Pete had. Unfortunately, Harry Lucenay seems to have been a very disagreeable and difficult person and according to *Photoplay*, the original Pete was poisoned in 1930. This appears to have been due to some kind of grudge, but Lucenay had been breeding Pete's sons and was ready with a replacement. This was when Pete's famous eye ring started changing eyes. Lucenay later had a falling out with Roach, making *The Pooch* (June 11, 1932) the last of the series with any of Pete's actual progeny. Lucenay then took his dogs to the east coast, where they made personal appearances and worked in the Fatty Arbuckle short *Buzzin' Around* (1932). This brings us to the great Pete mystery–the origin of his eye ring. According to Hal Roach, it was made with some kind of permanent dye for Pete's stint in the Buster Brown comedies, but the ring is already in place in his earlier appearances that survive. Whether he was born with it or it was created for a very early appearance, we'll never know. Probably Harry Lucenay was the only one with the facts, but he was shot and killed during a card game in 1944.

The important new human was Mary Ann Jackson. Although new to the Gang and only five years old, Mary Ann was already a comedy veteran, having been one of the stars of Mack Sennett's Smith Family comedies. Born on January 14, 1923, the particulars of her film debut were recorded in the August 1, 1925 issue of the *Moving Picture World*:

> Two-year-old Mary Ann Jackson is the child actress who has been engaged by Sennett. She is probably the youngest actress in Hollywood, at least the only baby to boast of a real contract. Mary Ann was discovered on the set one day when she came to the studio to watch her brother work. An added scene in the picture called for a baby to walk through some custard pies on a table. Mary Ann got her chance, and never were pies trod upon with such dignity and poise. So Mary Ann will be a Sennett starlet for some time to come. She is the sister of Peaches and Bobby Jackson, well-known screen children.

Practically Mary Ann's entire family was in the movies. Older sister Peaches had a sizeable career with important roles in features like D. W. Griffith's *The Greatest Thing in Life* (1918) and *Circus Days* (1923) with Jackie Coogan. Oddly enough, her career wound down the time that

Mary Ann's started. Brothers Bobby and Dick worked, too, with Dick making appearances with Our Gang during 1931 to 33. Finally, Charlotte, the mother of the brood, had good roles in features until 1922, when she may have retired to take care of her growing family.

Starting with Sennett in 1925, Mary Ann served at first as a sort of all-purpose scene-stealer, but in July of 1926, she became co-starred with Raymond McKee and Ruth Hiatt in the studio's attempt to try out a more situational type of comedy about the misadventures of a middle-class family. The first Smith Family release was *Smith's Baby* (July 25, 1926) and for the next three years, Mary Ann made life difficult for her screen parents while swiping most of the laughs and audience attention. Switching over to Roach and Our Gang with the film *Crazy House* (June 2, 1928), she was actually appearing in both series simultaneously, as a number of her previously shot Smith comedies continued to be released until March of 1929.

With her feisty tomboy manner, black pageboy hairdo, and tons of freckles, Mary Ann was the perfect contrast to Jean Darling's curly coquetry, plus her deft comic timing and extremely expressive face enabled

The regulars of the late silent Our Gang are from left to right: Joe Cobb, Harry Spear, Allen "Farina" Hoskins, Jean Darling, Mary Ann Jackson, Bobby "Wheezer" Hutchins, and Pete the pup. Photo courtesy of Robert Arkus.

her to more than hold her own with longtime Gangsters like Farina and Joe Cobb. Mary Ann's ace in the hole was a big take of surprise that was the perfect embodiment of the sound "boing." Although a no-nonsense tomboy, she was often pining away with unrequited love for Harry or Joe and was frequently saddled with Wheezer as the younger brother that she had to look out for. After her last Gang short, *Fly My Kite* (May 30, 1931), she made a few film appearances here and there, but mostly devoted herself to family life before passing away in December of 2003.

The last part of the silent era saw Robert McGowan experimenting with some offbeat ideas, which resulted in two shorts that play with film technique in a way that would be at home in European art films. *The Spanking Age* (December 15, 1928) is the story of Mary Ann and Wheezer having to live with a mean stepmother, but it's shot with the camera at the kid's level, so the adults are never seen above the waist. The other, *Wiggle Your Ears* (April 6, 1929), is shot entirely in close-ups, making it a comic equivalent to Dreyer's *The Passion of Joan of Arc* (1928) in a story of a puppy love triangle with Harry, Jean, and Mary Ann.

When sound took over the film industry, Hal Roach was in an enviable position. His Laurel & Hardy, Our Gang, and Charley Chase series made the transition without a hitch and actually became more popular. The challenges of the new medium seemed to reinvigorate Robert McGowan. He kept the focus on the Gang's world and reworked a lot of the plots and themes from the silents. Now he was able to capture the kids' own patterns of speech and their natural mispronunciations added to the comedy (later taken to its zenith with Buckwheat and Porky). Sound effects were also used creatively, so in shorts like *Birthday Blues* (1932), the Gang could make a giant breathing cake that goes "weee-woooow!!" New crops of kids continued to give the series a transfusion and keep it fresh, with Jackie Cooper, Dickie Moore, "Chubby" Chaney, and "Stymie" Beard being some of the most memorable. "Spanky" MacFarland joined in 1931 and probably became the ultimate and best-remembered Little Rascal in the series' history. In fact, the mid-1930s group led by Spanky and made up of Alfalfa, Darla, Buckwheat, Porky, Butch, and Woim, is the best-known and loved due to constant television exposure.

Roach kept Our Gang going until 1938. At that time, short subjects were becoming unprofitable due to the rise of double features. Having decided to concentrate on features, all of Roach's shorts stars were given trial feature films. Laurel & Hardy moved easily, but others, like Charley Chase, were let go. Our Gang's full-length *General Spanky* (1936) must

Silent and sound Gangs come together in the persons of Johnny Downs (left) and Spanky McFarland (right) at a 1937 Our Gang reunion. Photo courtesy of Sam Gill.

not have met Roach's expectations, for in 1938, he sold the series and all the kids' contracts to MGM. It's better not to say anything about these later shorts, which MGM used as a sort of soap box to tell children how they should behave instead of for entertainment. Luckily, television revived the Roach films and DVD and video has helped to keep them alive and kicking to this day.

Laurel and Harry

HARRY LANGDON WAS THE SILENT COMEDY comet that shot across the motion picture skies in the mid-1920s. Although his trajectory was brief and he crashed before the end of the silent era, while he blazed brightly, his influence echoed throughout the genre. Around 1925, a wave of pasty-faced innocents sprang up everywhere–Billy Dooley cavorted for Christie comedies, Arthur Stone was on the Hal Roach lot, and Mack Sennett soon tried to fill the gap caused by Langdon leaving him by putting Eddie Quillan and Johnny Burke through suspiciously similar paces. Even an old timer like Larry Semon, whose films were known for their wild gags, frenetic speed, crashes, and explosions, suddenly began standing still in indecision and blinking slowly. Langdon was in the air, but his most important and fruitful effect was on a transplanted British comic who was struggling to find the right screen persona.

In 1924, Stan Laurel had been in films for seven years, but hadn't met with exactly wild success. Popular enough to have had starring series for producers such as Hal Roach and G.M. Anderson, his film career to this point had been a search to find the right comic character, as it changed from film to film. Sometimes he'd be a brash go-getter, another time a mama's boy, then the next time he'd combine the two into sort of an aggressive milquetoast. He worked too hard, laughing at his own antics as if to nudge the audience to laugh along. Since his persona hadn't gelled, the pace was kept breakneck and the shorts were built around occupations, locations, or movie parodies.

When Harry's initial surge of popularity hit the film industry, Stan was making a series of two-reelers for producer Joe Rock. By the end of 1924, in shorts such as *West of Hot Dog* and *Somewhere in Wrong*, you can see his style start to change. The pace of the films is less frenetic and Stan

Stan Laurel makes for a very Harry Langdonish cop in his 1924 Joe Rock-produced *A Mandarin Mix-up.*

develops slower, more hesitant body rhythms and hand gestures. Much of his brashness has dissolved and he becomes wistful. He's now shy with women and people in authority, plus begins to make his crying routine more organic. Seeing Langdon's work on the screen definitely seems to have prompted Stan to explore and exploit his own inner man-child and made him realize that faster doesn't always mean funnier. It was just a couple of years after absorbing and developing his own spin on these Langdon traits that the character which we know and love as "Stanley" would be born at the Hal Roach studio.

In the years that ensued, Harry and Stan's lives and careers would intersect. They became friends and later full-fledged collaborators when Harry joined the writing staff on the L & H features from *Block-Heads* (1938) to *Saps at Sea* (1940), not forgetting that Hal Roach even used Langdon as a cudgel to get an errant Stan back in line during a contract dispute, which resulted in *Zenobia* (1939). The final word belongs to Stan, who had this to say about Harry to John McCabe for the publication of *Mr. Laurel & Mr. Hardy*: "A great comedian who had it in him to be a great actor, like Chaplin."

Papa's Family

MAX DAVIDSON HAD BEEN APPEARING in movies since the early teens when he scored a notable success appearing with Jackie Coogan in the features *The Rag Man* and *Old Clothes* (both 1925), which led to him soon starring in his own series of shorts for Hal Roach. While long specializing in playing stereotypical Jewish tailors and merchants, at Roach Max was able to flesh out the character and surround it with a screen family made up of excellent comedy performers. As Davidson was already well into middle age, his shorts weren't built around the quest for success or obtaining the leading lady and as a performer, he didn't move with the balletic grace of Chaplin or do tremendous stunts and falls like Keaton. Max's comedic focus was on his face and shoulders, where he had developed a repertoire of shrugs, lifted eyebrows, and tilts of the head, so he needed a dysfunctional family to keep him in cinematic hot water in order to portray the mounting frustrations of his put-upon papa.

In his surviving Roach comedies, there are four main performers who are regular and recurring irritants in papa's life. First and foremost is Walter "Spec" O'Donnell, who bedeviled Max in eight episodes and always lived up to his *Call of the Cuckoos* (1927) description of "Love's Greatest Mistake." Born in 1911, the popularity of freckle-faced movie urchins such as Wesley Barry and Mickey Daniels brought Spec into films in 1923–he even played Barry's younger brother in *The Country Kid* (1923). While Spec appeared in many features all through the 1920s, most memorably Mary Pickford's *Little Annie Rooney* (1925) and *Sparrows* (1926), his special niche was in comedy shorts. Starting in the live-action segments of a number of Walt Disney's first Alice in Cartoonland cartoons, he moved

Late 1920s portrait of Max Davidson. Photo courtesy of Louie Despres.

on as support (with Martha Sleeper) in Buddy Messinger's series of kid comedies for Century. In 1926, he found a home at the Hal Roach studio and during his four years there, made screen life difficult for Charley Chase, James Finlayson, Marion Byron, and most consistently Max.

Screen freckles usually denoted fresh and fun-loving characters, but Spec's spots came with an icy heart, a malevolent grin, and beady eyes that loved to see his screen father squirm. Whether it's showing up in drag to be the maid in *Don't Tell Everything* (1927) or inadvertently killing and roasting the prize rooster in *Pass the Gravy* (1928), Spec's very existence seems designed to keep Max in constant conniptions. O'Donnell's work with Davidson was the peak of his career, as when sound arrived he was demoted to uncredited and usually silent bit parts. This may be because his voice didn't fit his sly and wise-ass screen image, as he does have a line in 1938's *Angels with Dirty Faces* and his slow, stilted delivery is reminiscent of Mickey Mouse's pal Goofy. Nevertheless, Spec, who never really looked very different than he did in the 1920s, steadily turned up as newsboys, office boys, messengers, and elevator boys into the 1950s. His last screen role was as an elderly millionaire in Sam Peckinpah's *Convoy* (1978) and he passed away in 1986.

In contrast to his sons or stepsons, Max's screen daughters are always his pride and joy, but they still cause him a lot of aggravation, particularly when they take up with boys he doesn't approve of or assumes aren't Jewish (whom he refers to as "Irishers"). Vivacious Martha Sleeper played Max's daughter in four shorts and drove him to distraction in entries such as *Flaming Fathers* (1927), where Davidson follows her to the beach to keep her from eloping and of course suffers one embarrassment after another. Sleeper began her career as a child dancer in New York. A trip to Hollywood led to movies in 1923, where she was soon featured

Spec O'Donnell (left) and Max being observed by Lillian Elliott in *Don't Tell Everything* (1927). Photo courtesy of Robert Arkus.

at age twelve in Buddy Messinger's kid comedies at Century. Producer Hal Roach quickly signed her and looking very mature for her age, she became Charley Chase's leading lady in shorts such as *The Rat's Knuckles* (1924) and *Bad Boy* (1925).

Her sharp sense of timing and willingness to join the physical knock-about in shorts like *Pass the Gravy* (1928) kept her busy all over the lot and even resulted in one delightful Martha Sleeper starring comedy–1925's *Sure Mike*. Her five years with Roach is what she's remembered for today, as her later work in silent and sound features was lackluster and made no use of her skills as a comedienne. Frustrated by the Hollywood system, she moved to New York in 1935 and spent a decade on the Broadway stage. At the same time, she became known for designing jewelry and clothing, devoting the latter part of her life to these pursuits. Living for many years in Puerto Rico, she occasionally appeared in local theatre productions and died in 1983.

Another major source of discomfort in Max's onscreen life was his Mrs.—better known as Mama. Actress Lillian Elliott memorably essayed the role three times in the Roach comedies, often as a flirty rich widow who can't stand Max's bratty son or has devil's spawn sons of her own

Martha Sleeper and her frequent co-star Charley Case in *Mum's the Word* (1926).

who don't relish the prospect of Max as a stepfather and do their best to frighten him off. Elliott acts so giddy at the beginning of *Should Second Husbands Come First?* (1927) that her eldest son describes her as having "birds on her aerial." A longtime stage performer, Elliott was known as "the leading exponent of German dialect on the American stage" and appeared in musicals such as *Hanky Panky* in addition to dramas like *Help Wanted*. It was the 1915 film version of the latter play that was her first movie role, although it wasn't until the 1920s that she became a regular film player. She first appeared with Max in the Jackie Coogan feature *Old Clothes* (1925) before she turns up as Widow Finkelheimer in *Don't Tell Everything* (1927). Small and plump, she was frequently coquettish with Max, but also possessed a withering glare, which she makes good use of when she suspects that Max is fooling around with the "maid." During the sound era, she made a few more appearances on the Roach lot–*Hasty Marriage* (1931) with Charley Chase and Our Gang's *Free Eats* (1932)–but was mostly seen in features in small roles as landladies, mothers, or society matrons. Married for many years to actor James Corrigan, she was the mother of popular 1940s and 50s character actor Lloyd Corrigan and she retired in 1943.

The fourth cause of consternation for Max was character comic Jess DeVorska. Skinny, jug-eared, and always slow-witted, whether he was playing Davidson's son, stepson, or a suitor for his daughter, Max usually winces just taking a look at him. Born in Lithuania, after immigrating to the United States in 1914, he began appearing on stage and in vaudeville as an actor, dancer, and, according to some accounts, even an opera singer. He entered films in 1926 and was immediately typed as a Jewish character with names such as Kohn, Levine, or Goldfarb. *Why Girls Say No* (1927) was his first short with Davidson, where he played the disgruntled hanger-on Mr. Ginsberg, which was followed by *Jewish Prudence* (1927). This time, Devorska graduates to playing Max's reluctant truck-driving son, but his bid for screen immortality comes in *Don't Tell Everything* (1927), where he is absolutely hilarious as the shyly inept mechanic who decimates Max's Model T, then comes back to haunt him and eventually turns out to be his new stepson. 1927 was Devorska's peak year, as in addition to the Davidson shorts, he starred in the FBO feature *Jake the Plumber*. Cast as a young plumber's apprentice who, in the film's big climax, ends up having to take the place of a drugged jockey and ride a horse to victory, this was Devorska's only leading role and is sadly considered a lost film. Afterwards, he had some good supporting roles in early talkies

An exhibitor ad for Jess Devorska's only starring feature *Jake the Plumber* (1927).

such as *Around the Corner* (1930) and *The Last Parade* (1931), still cast as a Jewish type, but they soon tapered down to smaller, uncredited bits before his career ended in the mid-1930s. Little is known about his later life, but he served in the United States Navy in both World War I and II and died at the amazing age of 101 in 1999.

While Jess Devorska, Spec O'Donnell, Martha Sleeper, and Lillian Elliott are the players closely associated with the Davidson series, there's another who has been completely forgotten, one whose contribution is totally overlooked due to the unavailability of the shorts he appeared in. Gene Morgan made six 1928 comedies with Max, but only the first one, *Pass the Gravy*, is in circulation to give us a look at him today. Playing Martha Sleeper's fiancée and son of Max's blustery neighbor, Morgan spends a good deal of the short panic-stricken and trying to warn Max on the sly that the chicken dinner is none other than the prizewinning Brigham. Born Eugene Schwartzkopf, Morgan began his career on stage as a boy in Toledo, Ohio. As Gene "Rags" Morgan, he was a dancer, singer, and blackface comedian who by the 1920s had branched out to being an orchestra leader billed as "King of Mirth." He started appearing in films in the early 1920s with some Folly Comedies for the Pacific Film Co and as the middle

Max Reacts to Gene Morgan and an unidentified lady's confrontation on the floor in *Dumb Daddies* (1928). Photo courtesy of Louie Despres.

of the decade rolled around, he was doing bit roles for Roach and Al Christie. Signed to a starring Roach contract in 1928, he spent most of his time in the Davidson shorts–*Dumb Daddies, Came the Dawn, Blow by Blow, That Night* and *Do Gentlemen Snore?*–but at this moment it's impossible to judge his real contribution to the series since the films are sadly unavailable. His work at Roach ended with the early days of sound, but he continued as a regular character actor in features playing reporters, photographers, drunks, and hotel clerks–sometimes fresh and often befuddled. On contract to Columbia Pictures from 1935 to 1940, he also had a side career on radio as a popular master of ceremonies and orchestra leader. He died of a heart attack in 1940 after making a couple of return appearances at the Roach Studio in *Saps at Sea* and *Captain Caution.*

Besides the aforementioned Davidson regulars, there were a few "distant relatives"–performers who made only one or two memorably irksome appearances. Cute Marion Byron plays Max's daughter in *The Boyfriend* (1928) and her choice of the title character make Max and Mama pretend to be insane to drive him away. Johnny Fox had been in features like *The Covered Wagon* (1923) and comedy shorts for Century and Jack White before turning up as Max's dense Charleston-loving son in *Jewish Prudence* (1927). Bert Sprotte, a longtime Hollywood character actor, played the murderous neighbor Schultz in *Pass the Gravy* (1928) and an actual killer in the missing *Tell it to the Judge* (1928). Two other Mamas did their best to keep Max in line–Rosa Rosanova is particularly combative in *Flaming Fathers* (1927) and Anne Brody bookends the series as Mama in *Why Girls Say No* (1927) and *Hurdy Gurdy* (1929). Perhaps the funniest single performance comes from future director David Butler as Lillian Elliott's older son in *Should Second Husbands Come First?* (1927). Determined not to have Max for a stepfather (whom he claims looks like an Airedale), with his younger brother Spec, he tries to scare the old man away with hints of insanity, threats of poison, and, finally, the appearance of Spec in drag as a "wronged woman" from Max's past. As a performer, Butler was too good-looking to be a total comedian, but too goofy to be a leading man, so he usually played the leading character's best friend until he moved behind the camera in 1928. His career as a director encompassed comedies and musicals, continued into television, and lasted until 1967.

Hurdy Gurdy (1929) was the last short with Max as Papa. Later in life, Hal Roach claimed that the Davidson series was discontinued due to protests from theatre owners and Jewish groups, but as this has never been substantiated, it may be that the series just ran its course. In the sound era,

Thelma Todd and Eddie Dunn (left) are confronted by the group led by Max that includes Oscar Apfel (left of Max), Edgar Kennedy (in back as cop), Ann Brody (front right of Max), and Gertrude Messinger (behind Brody) in *Hurdy Gurdy* (1929). Photo courtesy of Robert Arkus.

the closest equivalent to the Davidson comedies seems to be The Average Man series that Edgar Kennedy headlined for RKO, which had most of the same comedians playing his relatives for almost twenty years. After *The Boyfriend* (1928), Davidson finished his days at the Roach studio the way he had begun–back to the All Star shorts and as support for comics like Charley Chase and Harry Langdon in comedies such as *Great Gobs* (1929) and *The Shrimp* (1930). His voice and accent fit his already well-established screen persona perfectly, so Max did well in the early days of talkies in features like *So this is College* and *The Lottery Bride* (both 1929), but oddly was soon demoted to bit parts, rarely having lines, for the rest of his career. But while it lasted, his starring series following the misadventures of an American Jewish family ranked alongside the likes of *The General* (1927), *The Kid Brother* (1927), *Big Business* (1929), and *City Lights* (1931) as part of the very peak of silent film comedy.

It's a Gift: W. C. Fields in the Movies

William Claude Dukenfield was born January 29, 1880, ironically enough in "the City of Brotherly Love"–Philadelphia, Pennsylvania. Early on, the young Fields was spellbound by the jugglers that he saw in local vaudeville. Trying it on his own, he found that he had "a fatal facility for it." He left home and supported himself with odd jobs while he looked for bookings, soon developing an act as a tramp juggler, which saved on fancy costume and prop costs. The act was silent and Fields added comedy by planning mistakes and reacting with funny displays of anger. In time, the routine became about man and his ongoing battle with inanimate objects. By 1900, Fields had signed with the prestigious Keith Orpheum Circuit and toured the world. For the next fifteen years, while continuing to juggle, he developed more material, such as his famous golf and pool routines, and in 1915, made the leap to Broadway when he was signed for the Ziegfeld Follies.

That year brought another milestone–his first films. Two shorts, *Pool Sharks* and *His Lordship's Dilemma*, were shot in Flushing, New York for the Gaumont Company's Casino Star series.

Although the second film is lost, *Pool Sharks* still exists and gives a fascinating look at the thirty-five-year-old Fields. He's slim, but immediately recognizable with a high top hat, white gloves, and a cane and while most of the film consists of slapping, eye-gouging, and whacking with pool cues, there are a few flashes of his black wit and dexterity with props that give us a glimpse of the Fields to come. Unhappy with the results of these shorts and under pressure from Flo Ziegfeld about his daytime moonlighting, he gave up on films and concentrated on his stage work.

Fields and Budd Ross (left) demonstrate *His Lordship's Dilemma* (1915). Photo courtesy of Robert Arkus.

After seven years with the Follies, he made a big splash on Broadway in the 1923 book musical *Poppy*. The character of huckster and conman Professor Eustace McGargle became a classic Fields persona and over his career would alternate with his character of the put-upon and henpecked family man. In 1925, famous director D. W. Griffith made *Poppy* into a film to highlight his protégé Carol Dempster and luckily, Fields was brought along to recreate his role. Rechristened *Sally of the Sawdust*, Griffith let Fields kick a dog, disguise himself as an Indian, and do whatever material he wanted. The problem was that the focus of the film is on Carol Dempster, so much of Field's footage was cut, truncated, or diluted with frequent reaction shots of Dempster. Despite the watering down of his role, Fields still stole the picture and it marked the real beginning of his movie career. After being brought in to provide comic relief for Griffith's next film *That Royle Girl* (1925), Paramount Pictures offered him $4,000 a week to make three pictures a year for five years.

Based at Paramount's Astoria Studio (today the Kaufman-Astoria Studio), *It's the Old Army Game* (1926) was his first for the company, shot in Astoria and on a month's location trip to Ocala, Florida. Next, Fields made *So's Your Old Man* (1926), which presents the first of his downtrodden husbands. Directed by ex-animator and good friend Gregory La Cava, Fields has full scope for his comedy and delivers deftly played dramatic moments. Much of the picture was shot on atmospheric Queens locations around the Astoria Studio, plus W.C. gets his famous golf routine on film, which gives us a good look at his stage foil and valet William "Shorty" Blanche, who plays his troublesome caddy.

Fields followed this up in rapid succession with *The Potters* and *Running Wild* (both 1927). In the latter, Fields plays a worm that turns into a lion thanks to hypnosis and was again directed by Gregory La Cava. It's said that the pair fought so much while making their two films together that they decided to preserve their friendship by never doing it again. The spring of 1927 saw Paramount close its Astoria studio and Fields was

Cameraman Alvin Wycoff, director Edward Sutherland, and Fields shooting *It's the Old Army Game* (1926). Photo courtesy of Bruce Lawton.

packed off to Hollywood, where he was teamed with ex-Mack Sennett comic Chester Conklin in *Two Flaming Youths* (1927), a remake of *Tillie's Punctured Romance* (1928), and *Fools for Luck* (1928). Sadly, none of these three are known to survive today. Despite being given a lot of freedom and using large amounts of his proven stage material, 1920s audiences didn't warm up to Fields' silent Paramount features. It may have been that his humor was too dark for 1920s movie audiences or perhaps it was the unappealing clip-on moustache that he brought with him from the stage. His contract had a two-year option and after *Fools for Luck*, Paramount chose not to renew it. Fields went bitterly back to the stage, blaming Paramount for the film's problems.

At the same time, sound arrived in films and shook up the entire industry. Stage performers who could handle dialogue were in demand and this provided W.C. with his entry back into films. On the East Coast, he made his sound debut in the two-reel *The Golf Specialist* (1930), which introduced his nasal bray and muttered asides to movie audiences. Returning to Hollywood in 1931, he worked in three features and then made four shorts for producer Mack Sennett. These shorts–*The Dentist* (1932), *The Fatal Glass of Beer*, *The Pharmacist*, and *The Barber Shop* (all 1933)–crystallized his film persona and set the direction for the rest of his career. By turns belligerent, henpecked, and blustering, sound helped make the Fields character a three-dimensional everyman who expressed what many in the audience felt in their hearts, but couldn't bring themselves to say. As before, the Sennett shorts were based on his earlier stage sketches and material, but this time, it clicked 100% on film.

Paramount came back with another offer and Fields was soon at his creative peak, turning out comic masterpieces such as *You're Telling Me* (1934) and *It's a Gift* (1934). The first was a remake of *So's Your Old Man* in sound and the story of W.C. trying to make good with his inventions fits in well with the depression era setting. Well-directed by Mack Sennett veteran Erle C. Kenton, the film is a nice lead-in for the features that followed. Much of the material in *It's a Gift* was taken from the 1925 stage revue *The Comic Supplement* that was written by J.P. McEvoy and starred in and reworked by Fields. Producer Flo Ziegfeld never brought the show into New York, instead taking key scenes and sticking them into the 1925 edition of the Follies. While some of the routines first hit the screen in *It's the Old Army Game*, Fields captured their ultimate version in *It's a Gift*.

Other Fields classics include *The Old Fashioned Way* (1934) and *The Man on the Flying Trapeze* (1935). Adding to the quality of these films

Fields, unknown, and a boom mike in a production shot from *It's a Gift* (1934).

was the regular stock company of players that Fields had gathered and would use multiple times, such as Kathleen Howard, Tammany Young, Elise Cavanna, Grady Sutton, and Jan Duggan. During this period, W. C. was providing the scripts for many of the pictures under increasingly outlandish pseudonyms–Charles Bogle, Mahatma Kane Jeeves, and Otis Criblecoblis. He was even loaned to MGM to play a memorable Mr. Micawber in their prestigious production of *David Copperfield* (1935), but this winning streak was derailed by the complete collapse of his health in 1936. Barely able to finish his sound remake of *Poppy* (1936), Fields' years of drinking had caught up with him and he spent the next two years in and out of hospitals. The only work he was able to do during this time was on radio, which was extremely popular and famous for his on-air feud with dummy Charlie McCarthy.

By 1939, his health had stabilized enough that he signed a contract with Universal Pictures and was able to complete three late masterworks–*My Little Chickadee* (1940), *The Bank Dick* (1940), and *Never Give a Sucker an Even Break* (1941). Older and heavier, his illness had coarsened his approach a bit, making his targets broader and his style a little more cartoony, but it also unleashed a more surreal sensibility and gave him the chance to work with director Eddie Cline, an old comedy pro. After *Sucker*, Universal didn't renew his contract and Fields' rapidly declining health limited him to "guest appearances" in other people's films. Features such as *Follow the Boys* (1944) and *Song of the Open Road* (1944) saw a still funny but slowed-down Fields, looking very much worse for wear even with professional make-up jobs. His last appearance was in *Sensations of 1945* (1944), redoing an old piece he had performed in the 1928 Earl Carroll Vanities, and he died at age sixty-five on Christmas Day, 1946.

Appendix: Selected Filmographies

Filmography Key:

Prod=Producer, Dist=Distributor, C=Cast, A=Author,
Sc=Scenario, PH=Photographer, WT=Working Title
Films marked with an asterisk are known to exist
ACAD=Academy Film Archive, Beverly Hills, California
CAN=National Film, Television and Sound Archives, Ottawa
CF=Cinteca del Friuli, Italy
CI=Cineteca Italiana, Milan
CQ=La Cinematheque Quebecoise, Canada
CUBA=Cinemateca de Cuba
DF=Det Danske Filmmuseum, Denmark
EYE=Eye Film Institute Netherlands, Amsterdam
FAN=Cinematheque Francaise, Paris
FCA=Fundacion Cinematea Argentina, Buenos Aires
GEH=George Eastman House, Rochester, New York
LOB=Lobster Films, Paris
LOC=Library of Congress, Washington, DC
MC=Museo de Cinema, Turin
MoMA=Museum of Modern Art, New York
MUN=Filmmuseum, Munchen
NFA/BFI=National Film Archive, London
NFC=National Museum of Modern Art, Tokyo
NFTS=National Film, Television & Sound Archive, Ottawa
RFA=Royal Film Archive of Belgium
UCLA=University of California, Los Angeles

*denotes that a film is known to exist

BILLIE RITCHIE FILMOGRAPHY

L-Ko Komedies

Prod: Henry "Pathé" Lehrman. Dist: Universal Pictures.

Love and Surgery* (10/25/1914) Dir: Henry Lehrman. 2 rls. Cast: Billie Ritchie, Gertrude Selby, Henry Bergman, Henry Lehrman, Eva Nelson. (LOC)

Partners in Crime* (11/1/1914) 1 rl. Cast: Billie Ritchie, Henry Bergman, Gertrude Selby, Henry Lehrman. (LOB)

The Fatal Marriage (11/8/1914) Dir: Henry Lehrman. 1 rl. Cast: Billie Ritchie, Gertrude Selby, Henry Lehrman, Henry Bergman, Charles Inslee.

Lizzie's Escape (11/15/1914) Dir: Henry Lehrman. 1 rl. Cast: Billie Ritchie, Henry Lehrman, Gertrude Selby.

The Groom's Doom (11/22/1914) 1 rl. Cast: Billie Ritchie.

The Rural Demons* (12/13/1914) Dir: Henry Lehrman. 1 rl. Cast: Billie Ritchie, Gertrude Selby, Henry Lehrman. (LOC)

Billie Ritchie and Eva Nelson tear up the dance floor as Peggy Pearce (left in dots) and Bert Roach (center in cowboy hat) cheer them on in *Live Wires and Love Sparks* (1916). Photo courtesy of Robert Arkus.

The Manicure Girl (12/27/1914) 1 rl. Cast: Billie Ritchie, Louise Orth, Charles Dudley, Hank Mann.

Through a Knot Hole (1/10/1915) 1 rl. Cast: Billie Ritchie.

Cupid in a Hospital* (1/6/1915) Dir: Henry Lehrman. 1 rl. Cast: Billie Ritchie, Hank Mann, Louise Orth, Charles Dudley, Eddie Polo, Eva Nelson. (LOC)

Thou Shalt Not Flirt (1/13/1915) Dir: Henry Lehrman. 1 rl. Cast: Billie Ritchie, Louise Orth, Henry Lehrman.

The Death of Simon Legree (1/24/1915) Dir: Henry Lehrman. 1 rl. Cast: Billie Ritchie, Louise Orth.

After Her Millions (1/31/1915) Dir: Henry Lehrman. 3 rls. Cast: Billie Ritchie, Gertrude Selby, Henry Lehrman.

Father Was a Loafer (2/10/1915) Dir: Henry Lehrman. 1 rl. Cast: Billie Ritchie, Gertrude Selby, Louise Orth, Eva Nelson, Alice Howell, Hank Mann.

All Aboard (2/12/1915) Dir: Henry Lehrman. 2 rls. Cast: Billie Ritchie.

Almost a Scandal* (2/17/1915) 1 rl. Cast: Billie Ritchie, Louise Orth, Henry Bergman, Hank Mann, John Rand, Eva Nelson. (EYE)

The Avenging Dentist (2/28/1915) Dir: Harry Edwards. 2 rls. Cast: Billie Ritchie, Louise Orth, Henry Bergman.

Bill's New Pal (3/3/1915) Dir: Harry Edwards. 1 rl. Cast: Billie Ritchie, Gertrude Selby, Henry Bergman, Louise Orth.

In and Out of Society (3/7/1915) 1 reel. Cast: Billie Ritchie, Peggy Pearce, Dick Smith.

Hearts and Flames (3/31/1915) Dir & A: Harry Edwards. 2 rls. Cast: Billie Ritchie, Louise Orth, Henry Bergman, Bob Mack, Eva Nelson.

The Fatal Note (4/7/1915) Dir & A: Harry Edwards. 1 rl. Cast: Billie Ritchie, Peggy Pearce.

Poor Policy* (4/25/1915) Dir & A: Harry Edwards. 1 rl. Cast: Billie Ritchie, Henry Bergman, Peggy Pearce. (LOC)

Father Was Neutral (5/5/1915) Dir & A: Harry Edwards. 1 rl. Cast: Billie Ritchie, Peggy Pearce, Henry Bergman.

Love and Sour Notes* (5/19/1915) Dir: John G. Blystone. 1 rl. Cast: Billie Ritchie, Peggy Pearce, Fatty Voss, Henry Bergman, Frank J. Coleman. (MoMA)

Bill's Blighted Career* (6/9/1915) Dir: Harry Edwards. 2 rls. Cast: Billie Ritchie, Peggy Pearce, Henry Bergman. (NFA/BFI)

The Curse of Work (7/4/1915) Dir: Harry Edwards. 2 rls. Cast: Billie Ritchie, Louise Orth, Henry Bergman.

A Doomed Hero (7/18/1915) 2 rls. Cast: Billie Ritchie, Peggy Pearce, Henry Bergman, Dick Smith.

Life and Moving Pictures (7/28/1915) Dir: Henry Lehrman. 2 rls. Cast: Billie Ritchie, Harry Gribbon, Mae Emory, Henry Lehrman, Alice Howell, Gertrude Selby, Dick Smith, Eva Nelson.

Hello Bill (8/11/1915) 1 rl. Cast: Billie Ritchie, Louise Orth, Reggie Morris.

A Vendetta in a Hospital* (9/8/1915) 3 rls. Cast: Billie Ritchie, Gene Rogers, Henry Bergman, Louise Orth, Hank Mann, Raymond Griffith.

Married on Credit* (9/29/1915) 1 rl. Cast: Billie Ritchie, Louise Orth, Henry Bergman, Gene Rogers, Fatty Voss. (GEH)

Room and Board—A Dollar and a Half (10/20/1915) Dir: Henry Lehrman. 1 rl. Cast: Billie Ritchie, Louise Orth, Henry Bergman, Alice Howell.

Silk Hose and High Pressure* (11/8/1915) Dir: Henry Lehrman. 3 rls. Cast: Billie Ritchie, Gene Rogers, Henry Bergman, Alice Howell, Louise Orth, Eva Nelson, Henry Lehrman. (LOC)

Stolen Hearts and Nickels (11/24/1915) 1 rl. Cast: Billie Ritchie, Reggie Morris, Louise Orth, Eva Nelson.

Sin on the Sabbath* (12/8/1915) 2 rls. Cast: Billie Ritchie, Louise Orth, Gebe Rogers, Alice Howell, Reggie Morris. (MoMA)

Billie's Reformation (1/9/1916) 3 rls. Cast: Billie Ritchie, Louise Orth, Reggie Morris, Gene Rogers, Raymond Griffith, Gertrude Selby. (a.k.a. Billy's Reformation)

Knocks and Opportunities (1/26/1916) 2 rls. Cast: Billie Ritchie, Louise Orth, Reggie Morris.

Twenty Minutes at the Fair* (2/20/1916) 1 rl. Cast: Billie Ritchie, Gene Rogers, Peggy Pearce.(NFA/BFI)

False Friends and Fire Alarms (3/6/1916) 2 rls. Cast: Billie Ritchie, Gene Rogers, Peggy Pearce.

Live Wires and Love Sparks* (3/19/1916) 3 rls. Cast: Billie Ritchie, Peggy Pearce, Eva Nelson, Gene Rogers, Charles Inslee, Bert Roach, Joe Murphy.

Scars and Stripes Forever (3/22/1916) 2 rls. Cast: Billie Ritchie, Peggy Pearce, Jerry Ash, Gene Rogers, Joe Murphy.

A Friend, But a Star Boarder (3/26/1916) 1 rl. Cast: Billie Ritchie, Gene Rogers, Peggy Pearce.

A Meeting for a Cheating (4/19/1916) 1 rl. Cast: Billie Ritchie, Dan Russell.

Bill's Narrow Escape (4/26/1916) 2 rls. Cast: Billie Ritchie, Gene Rogers, Louise Orth, Eva Nelson.

Billie's Waterloo* (6/7/1916) 1 rl. Cast: Billie Ritchie, Gene Rogers, Eva Nelson. (EYE)

A Bold, Bad Breeze (7/19/1916) 1 rl. Cast: Billie Ritchie, Billy Bevan, Lucille Hutton.

His Temper-Mental Mother-in-Law (8/21/1916) 2 rls. Cast: Billie Ritchie, Lucille Hutton, Margaret Joslin, Harry Todd.

Crooked from the Start (9/6/1916) Dir: John G. Blystone. 2 rls. Cast: Billie Ritchie, Gertrude Selby, Dan Russell.

Cold Hearts and Hot Flames* (9/20/1916) Dir: John G. Blystone. 2 rls. Cast: Billie Ritchie, Gladys Tennyson, Vin Moore, Bert Roach, Joe Murphy, James T. Kelly, Monty Banks. (MoMA)

She Wanted a Ford (10/22/1916) 1 rl. Cast: Billie Ritchie, Gertrude Selby, Dan Russell.

Where is My Wife? (11/22/1916) 2 rls. Cast: Billie Ritchie, Lucille Hutton.

Scrambled Hearts (5/6/1917) 1 rl. Cast: Billie Ritchie, Anna Darling.

Foxfilm Comedy

Prod: Fox Film Corp. 2 reels.

The House of Terrible Scandals* (3/19/1917) Dir & A: Henry Lehrman. Asst Dir: David Kirkland. PH: William McGann. Cast: Billie Ritchie, Henry Lehrman, Gertrude Selby, Dot Farley, Russell Powell, Sid Smith. (EYE)

Fox Sunshine Comedies

Prod & Superv: Henry Lehrman. Dist: Fox Film Corp. 2 reels.

His Smashing Career (12/9/1917) Dir & A: Henry Lehrman. Cast: Billie Ritchie, Gertrude Selby, Billy Bevan, Victor Potel.

Son of a Gun (1/6/1918) Dir: F. Richard Jones. Cast: Billie Ritchie, Winifred Westover, Hugh Fay, Sid Smith, Princess Minnie HaHa.

Are Married Policemen Safe? (1/13/1918 or 2/17/1918) Dir: F. Richard Jones. PH: William McGann. Cast: Billie Ritchie, Winifred Westover, Charles "Heinie" Conklin, Billy Bevan, Hugh Fay, Charlotte Mineau, Guy Woodward.

A Waiter's Wasted Life (4/7/1918) Dir: Jack White & William Watson. Cast: Billie Ritchie, Lloyd Hamilton, Jimmie Adams, Eileen Percy, Anita Burrel, Tom Kennedy.

A Neighbor's Keyhole (5/5/1918) Dir: Henry Lehrman. PH: A. H. Vallet. Cast: Billie Ritchie, Winifred Westover, Fritz Schade, Hugh Fay, George Binns, Charles Dorety.

Wild Women and Tame Lions (6/2/1918) Dir: William S. Campbell. Sc: Henry Lehrman. Cast: Billie Ritchie, Ford Sterling, Ethel Teare.

Roaring Lions on the Midnight Express* (9/22/1918) Dir: Henry Lehrman. PH: Frank B. Good. Cast: Billie Ritchie, Sylvia Day, Hugh Fay, Lloyd Hamilton, Jimmie Adams, Monty Banks. (LOB)

The Fatal Marriage (12/15/1918) Dir: William S. Campbell. PH: Frank B. Good. Cast: Billie Ritchie, Sylvia Day, Hugh Fay, Minnie Goldfish, Ethel Teare.

A Lady Bellhop's Secret (5/4/1919) Cast: Billie Ritchie, Hugh Fay.

Henry Lehrman Comedies

Prod & Superv: Henry Lehrman. Dist: Associated First National.

A Twilight Baby* (12/21/1919) Dir: Jack White. PH: George Meehan. 3 rls. Cast: Lloyd Hamilton, Virginia Rappe, Billie Ritchie, Harry Todd, Charles Dorety, Lige Conley, Harry McCoy. (MoMA)

The Kick in High Life (9/13/1920) Dir: Albert Ray & Al Herman. Sc: Henry Lehrman. 2 rls. Cast: Albert Ray, Charlotte Dawn, Charles "Heinie" Conklin, Billie Ritchie, Hugh Fay.

Wet and Warmer* (11/1/1920) Dir & Sc: Henry Lehrman. PH: George Meehan & Charles Selby. 2 rls. Cast: Albert Ray, Charlotte Dawn, Billie Ritchie, Charles "Heinie" Conklin (UCLA)

For Further Research:

Nellie's Nifty Necklace (3/24/1917) Vim. Dist: General Films. 2 rls. C: Billie Ritchie, Marjorie Ray. (This item may have been produced by Henry Lehrman for L-Ko, and then taken with him when he left the company, or was something he produced between the time he left L-Ko and began working for Fox. Leading lady Marjorie Ray had appeared in some 1917 L-Kos with Dan Russell. Released through Vim and not known to exist).

ALICE HOWELL FILMOGRAPHY

Keystone Comedies

Prod: Mack Sennett. Dist: Mutual

Caught in a Cabaret* (4/27/1914) Dir: Charles Chaplin & Mabel Normand. 2 rls. Cast: Charlie Chaplin, Mabel Normand, Alice Davenport, Harry McCoy, Chester Conklin, Mack Swain, Alice Howell, Minta Durfee, Edgar Kennedy. (CQ, CUBA, DF, NFA/BFI, MoMA, MUN)

Caught in the Rain* (5/4/1914) Dir: Charles Chaplin. 1 rl. Cast: Charlie Chaplin, Mack Swain, Alice Davenport, Alice Howell, Grover Ligon. (CUBA, NFA/BFI)

The Knockout* (6/11/1914) Dir: Roscoe Arbuckle. 2 rls. Cast: Roscoe Arbuckle, Minta Durfee, Hank Mann, Charlie Chaplin, Mack Swain, Edgar Kennedy, Al St John, Alice Howell, Grover Ligon, Luke, Rube Miller, Slim Summerville, Mack Sennett. (CUBA, DF, LOC, MoMA, NFA/BFI)

Mabel's Married Life* (6/20/1914) Dir: Mack Sennett. 1 rl. Cast: Mabel Normand, Charlie Chaplin, Mack Swain, Eva Nelson, Charlie Murray, Harry McCoy, Hank Mann, Frank Opperman, Alice Davenport, Dixie Chene, Alice Howell, Grover Ligon, Wallace MacDonald.

Fatty's Finish* (7/2/1914) Dir: Roscoe Arbuckle. 1 rl. Cast: Roscoe Arbuckle, Phyllis Allen, Mack Swain, Hank Mann, Grover Ligon, Charles Avery, Ford Sterling, Al St John, Charles Bennett, Alice Howell, Harry McCoy. (LOC)

Laughing Gas* (7/9/1914) Dir: Charles Chaplin. 1 rl. Cast: Charlie Chaplin, Slim Summerville, Fritz Schade, Alice Howell, Mack Swain, Josef Swickard. (CQ, CUBA, DF, LOC, NFA/BFI, NFTS)

A Coat's Tale* (8/8/1914) Dir: Rube Miller. 1 rl. Cast: Rube Miller, Charles Parrott, Alice Howell, Harry McCoy, Bill Hauber, Virginia Kirtley, Grover Ligon, Billy Gilbert, Frank Opperman. (MoMA)

Bombs and Bangs (9/17/1914) Dir: Roscoe Arbuckle. 1 rl. Cast: Roscoe Arbuckle, Alice Howell, Rube Miller.

Lovers Luck* (9/19/1914) Dir: Roscoe Arbuckle. 1 rl. Cast: Roscoe Arbuckle, Minta Durfee, Frank Hayes, Phyllis Allen, Alice Howell, Slim Summerville, Billy Gilbert, Luke. (MoMA, NFA/BFI)

Exhibitor ad for *Balloonatics* (1917), Alice Howell's first Century Comedy.

He Loved the Ladies* (9/21/1914) Dir: Glen Cavender. 1 rl. Cast: Charlie Murray, Alice Davenport, Charles Parrott, Edgar Kennedy, Aileen Pringle, Alice Howell, Billy Gilbert, Josef Swickard, Cecile Arnold, Vivian Edwards, Bill Hauber, Ted Edwards. (MoMA)

Hello Mabel* (10/8/1914) Dir: Mack Sennett. 1 rl. Cast: Mabel Normand, Alice Davenport, Harry McCoy, Mack Swain, Charles Parrott, Alice Howell, Al St John, Minta Durfee, Phyllis Allen.

High Spots on Broadway (10/15/1914) Dir: Rube Miller. 1 rl. Cast: Rube Miller, Alice Howell.

Shot in the Excitement* (10/26/1914) Dir: Unknown (probably Rube Miller). 1 rl. Cast: Alice Howell, Al St John, Rube Miller, Josef Swickard, Edwin Frazee, Grover Ligon.

Cursed by his Beauty* (10/31/1914) Dir: Unknown. 1 rl. Cast: Charlie Murray, Alice Davenport, Alice Howell, Charles Bennett, Slim Summerville, Fritz Schade, Phyllis Allen, Harry McCoy, Charles Parrott, Cecile Arnold, Dixie Chene, Edwin Frazee.

Tillie's Punctured Romance* (11/14/1914) Dir: Mack Sennett. Dist: Alco Film Corp. A: Hampton Del Ruth & Craig Hutchinson. Based on the play Tillie's Nightmare by Edgar Smith & A. Baldwin Stone. 6 rls. Cast: Marie Dressler, Charlie Chaplin, Mabel Normand, Mack Swain, Harry McCoy, Chester Conklin, Glen Cavender, Charles Parrott, Edgar Kennedy, Alice Howell, Phyllis Allen, Minta Durfee, Charlie Murray, Bill Hauber, May Wells, Alice Davenport, Dick Smith. (LOC, MoMA, BFI, UCLA)

L-Ko Comedies

Prod: Henry Lehrman. Dist: Universal.

Father was a Loafer (2/10/1915) Dir: Henry Lehrman. 1 rl. Cast: Billie Ritchie, Alice Howell, Louise Orth, Gertrude Selby, Eva Nelson, Hank Mann.

Their Last Haul* (2/21/1915) Dir: John G. Blystone. 1 rl. Cast: Hank Mann, Alice Howell, Wallace MacDonald. (NFA/BFI)

Rough but Romantic (3/17/1915) Dir: John G. Blystone. 1 rl. Cast: Hank Mann, Alice Howell, John Rand, Gertrude Selby.

The Curse of a Name (4/21/1915) 1 rl. Cast: Harry Gribbon, Peggy Pearce, Alice Howell, Dick Smith.

A Stool Pigeon's Revenge* (5/12/1915) 1 rl. Cast: Hank Mann, Alice Howell. (UCLA)

Blue Blood and Yellow Backs (6/20/1915) 2 rls. Cast: Harry Gribbon, Reggie Morris, Gertrude Selby, Slyvia Ashton, Alice Howell.

Life and Moving Pictures (7/28/1915) Dir: Henry Lehrman. 2 rls. Cast: Billie Ritchie, Harry Gribbon, Mae Emory, Henry Lehrman, Alice Howell, Gertrude Selby, Henry Bergman.

In the Claw of the Law (8/4/1915) 1 rl. Cast: Harry Gribbon, Fatty Voss, Peggy Pearce, Alice Howell, Dick Smith.

Under New Management* (10/13/1915) Dir: Henry Lehrman. 2 rls. Cast: Gertrude Selby, Gene Rogers, Alice Howell, Raymond Griffith, Fatty Voss. (NFA/BFI)

Room and Board—A Dollar and a Half (10/20/1915) Dir: Henry Lehrman. 2 rls. Cast: Billie Ritchie, Louise Orth, Henry Bergman, Alice Howell.

Tears and Sunshine (10/27/1915) 1 rl. Cast: Gertrude Selby, Raymond Griffith, Gene Rogers, Alice Howell.

Cupid and the Scrub Lady (11/7/1915) 1 reel. Cast: Alice Howell, Fatty Voss, Billy Bevan.

Her Ups and Down (11/7/1915) 1 rl. Cast: Alice Howell, Fatty Voss.

Silk Hose and High Pressure* (11/8/1915) Dir: Henry Lehrman. 3 rls. Cast: Billie Ritchie, Gene Rogers, Henry Bergman, Alice Howell, Louise Orth, Eva Nelson, Henry Lehrman. (LOC)

Sin on the Sabbath* (12/8/1915) 2 rls. Cast: Billie Ritchie, Louise Orth, Gene Rogers, Alice Howell, Reggie Morris (MoMA)

Lizzie's Shattered Dreams (12/12/1915) 1 rl. Cast: Alice Howell, Fatty Voss, Charles Winninger.

From Beanery to Billions (12/22/1915) 2 rls. Cast: Alice Howell, Dick Smith.

Flirtation a la Carte (1/16/1916) 1 rl. Cast: Alice Howell, Dick Smith, Phil Dunham, Fatty Voss.

Her Naughty Eyes (2/9/1916) 1 rl. Cast: Alice Howell, Dick Smith, Harry Coleman.

Dad's Dollars and Dirty Doings (2/27/1916) 1 rl. Cast: Alice Howell, Dick Smith, Phil Dunham, Fatty Voss.

The Double's Troubles (4/16/1916) 2 rls. Cast: Alice Howell, Dick Smith, Billy Bevan, Harry Coleman.

The Bankruptcy of Boggs and Schultz (5/3/1916) 1 rl. Cast: Alice Howell, Dick Smith, Raymond Griffith, Phil Dunham, Anna Darling.

The Great Smash (5/10/1916) 3 rls. Cast: Alice Howell, Dick Smith, Raymond Griffith, Billy Bevan.

A Busted Honeymoon (5/24/1916) 1 rl. Cast: Alice Howell, Raymond Griffith, Fatty Voss.

How Stars are Made* (6/17/1916) Dir: John G. Blystone. 2 rls. Cast: Alice Howell, Raymond Griffith, Dick Smith, Fatty Voss. (NFA/BFI)

Pirates of the Air (6/28/1916) Dir: John G. Blystone. 2 rls. Cast: Alice Howell, Fatty Voss, Billy Bevan, Phil Dunham, Joe Moore.

Lizzie's Lingering Love (7/25/1916) Dir: Henry Lehrman. 3 rls. Cast: Alice Howell, Fatty Voss, Phil Dunham, Billy Bevan.

Unhand Me Villain! (9/9/1916) Dir: John G. Blystone. 1 rl. Cast: Alice Howell, Joe Moore, Fatty Voss. (a.k.a. The Villain Still Pursued Her).

Tillie's Terrible Tumbles (9/12/1916) Dir: John G. Blystone. 3 rls. Cast: Alice Howell, Fatty Voss, Phil Dunham.

Alice in Society (11/11/1916) 3 rls. Cast: Alice Howell, Joe Moore, Fatty Voss, Phil Dunham.

Tattle-Tale Alice (12/1/1916) 1 rl. Cast: Alice Howell.

Century Comedies

Prod: Abe & Julius Stern. Dist: Longacre Distributing Co.
Dir: John G. Blystone. 2 reels.

Balloonatics (5/1917) Cast: Alice Howell.

Automaniacs (5/1917) Cast: Alice Howell.

Neptune's Naughty Daughter* (5/1917) Cast: Alice Howell, Robert McKenzie, Eva McKenzie, Joe Moore, Fatty Voss. (DF, EYE)

Her Barebacked Career (1917) Cast: Alice Howell, Eva McKenzie. (a.k.a. *Alice of the Sawdust*)

She Did Her Bit (1917) Cast: Alice Howell.

What's the Matter with Father? (4/1/1918) Cast: Alice Howell, Eva Novak, Eddie Barry, Neal Burns, Harry Griffith.

Century Comedies

Prod: Abe & Julius Stern. Dist: Universal. 2 reels.

Oh, Baby!* (2/15/1918) Dir: John G. Blysone. Cast: Alice Howell, Bert Roach, William Irving, James Finlayson.

Her Unmarried Life (5/29/1918) Dir: John G. Blystone. Cast: Alice Howell, Hughie Mack, Bert Roach.

In Dutch* (6/26/1918) Dir: John G. Blystone. Cast: Alice Howell, Hughie Mack, Billy Armstrong, Neal Burns, James Finlayson. (EYE, LOC)

The Choo Choo Love (7/17/1918) Dir: John G. Blystone. Cast: Alice Howell, Hughie Mack, Russell Powell, Billy Armstrong, Edith Kelly, Neal Burns.

Hey, Doctor!* (8/13/1918) Dir: John G. Blystone. Cast: Alice Howell, Eddie Barry, Russell Powell, Billy Armstrong, Edith Kelly, Neal Burns, James Finlayson, Marvin Lobach (LOC as *Banana Comedy*)

Bawled Out (8/14/1918) Dir: James Davis. Cast: Alice Howell, Hughie Mack, Vin Moore, Helen Gibson.

Hoot Toot (8/28/1918) Dir: James Davis. Cast: Alice Howell.
Cupid vs. Art (9/11/1918) Dir & A: Vin Moore. Cast: Alice Howell, Hughie Mack.
Untamed Ladies (10/9/1918) Cast: Alice Howell.
The Cabbage Queen (12/18/1918) Cast: Alice Howell, Hughie Mack, Phil Dunham, William Irving.
Society Stuff (3/12/1919) Dir: Vin Moore. Cast: Alice Howell.
Behind the Front* (3/15/1919) Cast: Alice Howell, Hughie Mack. (NFA/BFI)
The Beauty and the Boob (8/9/1919) Cast: Alice Howell.

Reelcraft/Emerald Comedies
Prod: Emerald Motion Picture Co. Dist: Reelcraft Pictures Corp. 2 reels.

Cinderella Cinders* (1920) Dir: Frederic J. Ireland. Cast: Alice Howell, Dick Smith, Rose Burkhart, Frederic J. Ireland, Mattie Fitzgerald, Leo Sulky (filmed in Chicago). (GEH)
Her Lucky Day (1920) Cast: Alice Howell (filmed in Chicago).
Bargain Day (1920) Dir: Frederic J. Ireland. Cast: Alice Howell (filmed in Chicago).
Distilled Love* (1920) Dir: Dick Smith & Vin Moore. Cast: Alice Howell, Oliver Hardy, Dick Smith, Billy Bevan, Fay Holderness, Rae Godfrey (a.k.a. *A Mere Man's Love*). (LOC)
His Wooden Leg-acy (1920) Cast: Alice Howell (filmed in Chicago).
Rubes and Romance (1920) Dir: Frederic J. Ireland & Dick Smith. Cast: Alice Howell (filmed in Chicago)
Lunatics in Politics* (1920) Dir: Dick Smith. PH: Charles C. Fetty. Cast: Alice Howell, Dick Smith, Rose Burkhart, Tommy Flynn, Leo Sulky (last Emerald shot in Chicago).
Good Night Nurse (1920) Dir: Dick Smith. Cast: Alice Howell, Phil Dunham, Frank J. Coleman.
Convict's Happy Bride (1920) Cast: Alice Howell.
Squirrel Time (1920) Cast: Alice Howell.

Sunkist Comedies
Prod: Sunkist Comedy Co. Dir: Dick Smith. 1 reel.

Boulevard Profiteers (1921) Cast: Alice Howell.
Who Chose Your Wife? (1921) Cast: Alice Howell.

Feature Films

Love is an Awful Thing (8/30 or 9/15/1922) Prod: Lewis J. Selznick/Owen Moore Film Corp. Dist: Selznick Distributing Corp. Dir & Sc: Victor Heerman. PH: Jules Cronjager. 7 rls. Cast: Owen Moore, Marjorie Daw, Kathryn Perry, Arthur Hoyt, Douglas Carter, Charlotte Mineau, Snitz Edwards, Alice Howell.
Wandering Daughters (7/1/1923) Prod: Sam E. Rork. Dir & Sc: James Young. Titl: Leonore J. Coffee. PH: George Benoit. Asst dir: James Ewens & Clifford Faum. 6 rls. Cast: Marguerite De La Motte, William V. Mong, Mabel Van Buren, Marjorie Daw, Noah Beery, Pat O'Malley, Alan Forrest, Alice Howell.

Hollywood Comedies
Prod: L.K.C. Productions. Dir: Fred Caldwell. Dist: Selznick Distributing Corp. 2 reels.

The Elite of Hollywood (11/15/1923) Cast: Alice Howell, Victor Potel.

Universal Comedies
Prod: Universal. 1 reel.

Should Poker Players Marry? (3/8/1924) Dir: William Watson. Sc: Vincent Bryan. Cast: Neely Edwards, Alice Howell, Bert Roach.
Marry When Young (4/5/1924) Dir: William Watson. Au: Richard Smith. Cast: Neely Edwards, Alice Howell, Bert Roach.
Mind Your Doctor (1924) Dir: Richard Smith. Cast: Neely Edwards, Alice Howell, Bert Roach.
Spring of 1964 (4/12/1924) Dir & Sc: William Watson. Neely Edwards, Alice Howell, Bert Roach.
One Wet Night* (4/26/1924) Dir & Sc: William Watson. Cast: Neely Edwards, Alice Howell, Bert Roach, Tiny Sanford.

Why Pay Rent? (5/19/1924) Dir & Sc: William Watson. Cast: Alice Howell, Bert Roach, Harold Austin.

Rest in Pieces (6/7/1924) Dir & Sc: William Watson. Cast: Alice Howell, Billy Bletcher, Bert Roach.

Why Be Jealous? (6/23/1914) Dir & Sc: William Watson. Cast: Alice Howell, Bert Roach, Harold Austin.

Bluffing Bluffers (7/2/1924) Dir & Sc: William Watson. Cast: Alice Howell, Billy Bletcher, Bert Roach.

Patching Things Up (7/19/1924) Dir & Sc: William Watson. Cast: Alice Howell, Bert Roach, Harold Austin.

Women's Rights (7/23/1924) Dir & Sc: William Watson. Cast: Alice Howell, Bert Roach, Harold Austin.

Fair and Windy (8/4/1924) Dir & Sc: William Watson. Cast: Alice Howell, Bert Roach, Harold Austin.

Way Up North (8/18/1924) Dir & Sc: William Watson. Cast: Alice Howell, Bert Roach.

That's the Spirit* (9/1/1924) Dir & Sc: William Watson. Cast: Alice Howell, Billy Bletcher, Bert Roach, Robert McKenzie, Spencer Bell, Silas Wilcox, L.J. O'Connor. (LOC, MoMA)

The Game Hunter (9/17/1924) Dir & Sc: William Watson. Cast: Neely Edwards, Alice Howell, Bert Roach.Universal Pictures Feature

Butterfly* (10/12/1924) Dir: Clarence Brown. Sc: Olga Printzlau. PH: Ben Reynolds. 8 reels. Cast: Laura La Plante, Ruth Clifford, Norman Kerry, Cesare Gravina, Margaret Livingston, Freeman Wood, T. Roy Barnes, Alice Howell (Alice has a cameo role as an eccentric dancer at a party).

Green Tees (11/10/1924) Dir: Richard Smith. Cast: Neely Edwards, Alice Howell, Bert Roach.

Under A Spell* (1/6/1925) Dir: Richard Smith. Cast: Neely Edwards, Alice Howell, Bert Roach. (LOC)

The Lost Chord (1/21/1925) Dir & Sc: Richard Smith. Cast: Neely Edwards, Alice Howell, Bert Roach.

Papa's Pet (3/2/1925) Bull's Eye Comedy Series #2. Dir & Sc: Richard Smith. Cast: Neely Edwards, Alice Howell, Bert Roach.

Black Gold Bricks (3/9/1925) Bull's Eye Comedy Series #3. Dir: Richard Smith. Cast: Neely Edwards, Alice Howell, Bert Roach.

Tenting Out (3/23/1925) Bull's Eye Comedy Series #4. Dir & Sc: Richard Smith. Cast: Neely Edwards, Alice Howell, Bert Roach.

Sleeping Sickness (3/30/1925) Bull's Eye Comedy Series #5. Dir: Richard Smith. Cast: Neely Edwards, Alice Howell, Bert Roach.

A Nice Pickle (4/6/1925) Bull's Eye Comedy Series #6. Dir & Sc: Richard Smith. Cast: Neely Edwards, Alice Howell, Bert Roach.

Fox Comedies

Prod: Fox Film Corporation. 2 reels.

Madame Dynamite* (11/28/1926) Imperial Comedies. Dir: Zion Myers & Gene Forde. Cast: Eddie Clayton, Della Peterson, Alice Howell, Blanche Payson. (GEH)

The Society Architect (2/13/1927) Van Bibber Series. Dir: Robert Kerr. Cast: Earle Fox, Florence Gilbert, Alice Howell.

For Further Research:

Hollywood Comedies. Prod: L.K.C. Productions. Dist: Selznick Distributing Corp. Dir: Fred Caldwell. 2 reels. Alice Howell and Chester Conklin were announced as starring in this series of comedies. It's documented that Alice did appear in *The Elite of Hollywood* (11/15/1923), so it's possible that she may also have been in:

The Cream of Hollywood (1/15/1924)

The Bishop of Hollywood (2/15/1924)

THE "JOSIE" SERIES FILMOGRAPHY

Prod: Vitagraph. Dir: Lee Beggs. Writ: Kenneth S. Webb. 1 reel.

The Arrival of Josie (7/15/1914) Cast: Josie Sadler, Bernice Berner, Billy Quirk, Audrey Berry, Helen Connelly, Edna Holland, Phyllis Grey, Frank Holland.

Romantic Josie (7/25/1914) Cast: Josie Sadler, Eulalie Jensen, Billy Quirk.

Josie's Declaration of Independence (8/26/1914) Cast: Josie Sadler, Billy Quirk.

Josie's Coney Island Nightmare (8/29/1914) Cast: Josie Sadler, Billy Quirk, Denton Vane, Edna Holland, Mr. Sneeze.

Josie's Legacy (10/9/1914) Cast: Josie Sadler, Billy Quirk, Miss Allen, Mandy Wilson.

THE "JARR FAMILY" FILMOGRAPHY

Prod: Vitagraph. Dir: Harry Davenport. Writ: Roy L. McCardell. 1 reel.

The Jarr Family Discovers Harlem (3/8/1915) Cast: Harry Davenport, Rose Tapley, Audrey Berry, Paul Kelly, George Stevens, Edwina Robbins, Eulalie Jensen, Charles Eldridge, Florence Natol, Arthur Cozine, Harry Fisher.

Mr. Jarr Brings Home a Turkey (3/15/1915) Cast: Harry Davenport, Rose Tapley, Paul Kelly, Audrey Berry, Florence Natol, Ethel Lloyd, Harry Fisher, Edward Elkas, George Stevens.

Mr. Jarr and the Lady Reformer (3/22/1915) Cast: Harry Davenport, Rose Tapley, Paul Kelly, Audrey Berry, Charles Eldridge, Frank Bunny, Julia Swayne Gordon, Sabel Johnson, Jack Brawn, Roy Wilson.

Mr. Jarr Takes a Night Off (4/5/1915) Cast: Harry Davenport, Rose Tapley, Audrey Berry, Paul Kelly, Sabel Johnson, Harry Fisher, Nicholas Dunaew.

Mr. Jarr's Magnetic Friend (4/12/1915) Cast: Harry Davenport, Rose Tapley, Audrey Berry, Paul Kelly, Florence Natol, Frank Bunny,

Coming attraction slide for the Jarr Family series.

Sabel Johnson, William Bletcher, Nicholas Dunaew, Flora Finch, Harry Fisher.

The Jarrs Visit Arcadia (5/10/1915) Cast: Harry Davenport, Rose Tapley, Paul Kelly, Audrey Berry, Florence Natol, Jack Brawn, Ethel Ferguson, Frank Bunny, Charles Eldridge.

Mr. Jarr and the Dachshund (5/17/1915) Cast: Harry Davenport, Rose Tapley, Paul Kelly, Audrey Berry, Florence Natol, Harry Fisher, Joseph Halpin, Nicholas Dunaew, Bobby Huggins.

Mr. Jarr Visits His Home Town (5/24/1915) Cast: Harry Davenport, Rose Tapley, Paul Kelly, Audrey Berry, Florence Natol, Charles Edwards.

Mrs. Jarr's Auction Bridge (5/31/1915) Cast: Harry Davenport, Rose Tapley, William Shea, Helen Relyea, Eulalie Jensen, Florence Natol.

Mrs. Jarr and the Beauty Treatment (6/7/1915) Cast: Harry Davenport, Rose Tapley, Paul Kelly, Audrey Berry, Eulalie Jensen, Charles Eldridge, Josephine Earle.

Mr. Jarr and the Ladies Cup (6/14/1915) Cast: Harry Davenport, Rose Tapley, Paul Kelly, Audrey Berry, Eulalie Jensen, Charles Eldridge, Florence Natol, Harry Fisher, Billy Billings, Belle Bruce.

Mr. Jarr and Love's Young Dream (6/21/1915) Cast: Harry Davenport, Rose Tapley, Paul Kelly, Audrey Berry, Eulalie Jensen, Charles Eldridge, Florence Natol, Billy Billings, Belle Bruce, Harry Fisher, Arthur Cozine.

Mr. Jarr and the Captive Maiden (6/28/1915) Cast: Harry Davenport, Rose Tapley, Paul Kelly, Audrey Berry, Eulalie Jensen, Charles Eldridge, Billy Billings, Belle Bruce, Florence Natol, Harry Fisher, Arthur Cozine.

Mr. Jarr and Gertrude's Beaux (7/12/1915) Cast: Harry Davenport, Rose Tapley, Paul Kelly, Audrey Berry, Florence Natol, Harry Fisher, Edward Favor, Logan Paul, Jay Dwiggins.

Mr. Jarr's Big Vacation (7/26/1915) Cast: Harry Davenport, Rose Tapley, Paul Kelly, Audrey Berry, Arthur Cozine, William Shea, Francis Connelly, Harry Fisher.

Mr. Jarr and Circumstantial Evidence (8/16/1915) Cast: Harry Davenport, Rose Tapley, Charles Eldridge.

Mr. Jarr and the Visiting Firemen (8/30/1915) Cast: Harry Davenport, Rose Tapley, Paul Kelly, Audrey Berry.

Mrs. Jarr and the Society Circus (9/6/1915) Cast: Harry Davenport, Rose Tapley, Paul Kelly, Audrey Berry, Eulalie Jensen, Florence Natol, Charles Eldridge.

GALE HENRY FILMOGRAPHY

Universal Comedies

Prod: Universal. 1 reel unless noted.

The Midnight Alarm (2/7/1914) Joker. Dir: Allen Curtis. Cast: Max Asher, Louise Fazenda, Bobby Vernon, Gale Henry.

The Chicken Chasers (2/14/1914) Joker. Cast: Max Asher, Bobby Vernon, Louise Fazenda, Gale Henry, Charles McComas, Billy Franey.

The Tender Hearted Sheriff (2/21/1914) Joker. Dir: Allen Curtis. Cast: Max Asher, Louise Fazenda, Gale Henry, Bobby Vernon, Ralph McComas.

Universal Ike Has his Ups and Downs (4/7/1914) Universal Ike series. Cast: Augustus Carney, Louise Glaum, Harry Moody, Gale Henry.

Universal Ike Makes a Monkey of Himself (4/14/1914) Universal Ike series. Cast: Augustus Carney, Louise Glaum, Harry Moody, Gale Henry, Betty Gettinger.

When Universal Ike Set (4/21/1914) Universal Ike series. Cast: Augustus Carney, Gale Henry, Harry Moody.

Schultz the Barber (5/9/1914) Joker. Cast: Max Asher, Louise Fazenda, Bobby Vernon, Billy Franey, Gale Henry, Ralph McComas.

A Dream of Painting (5/15/1914) Joker. Dir: Allen Curtis. Cast: Gale Henry, Billy Franey, Louise Fazenda. ½ rl.

Universal Ike Jr. is Kept from Being an Actor (6/9/1914) Universal Ike Junior series. Cast: Bobby Feuhrer, Louise Glaum, Fred Hornby, Gale Henry, Harry Moody.

The Fatal Letter (6/17/1914) Joker. Dir & St: Allen Curtis. Cast: Max Asher, Louise Fazenda, Bobby Vernon, Gale Henry, Ralph McComas.

Love and Electricity (6/27/1914) Joker. Dir: Allen Curtis. Cast: Max Asher, Louise Fazenda, Bobby Vernon, Gale Henry, Sam Kaufman, Billy Franey. 2 rls.

Captain Kidd's Priceless Treasure (7/4/1914) Joker. Dir: Allen Curtis. Cast: Max Asher, Louise Fazenda, Bobby Vernon, Billy Franey, Gale Henry.

Love, Roses and Trousers (7/11/1914) Joker. Dir: Allen Curtis. Sc: Clarence Badger. Cast: Max Asher, Louise Fazenda, Bobby Vernon, Gale Henry, Billy Franey.

There are two Lizzie's–Gale and her auto–in this lobby card for *Lizzie's Luck* (1919). Photo courtesy of Jim Kerkhoff.

His Wife's Family (7/18/1914) Joker. Dir: Allen Curtis. Cast: Max Asher, Gale Henry, Louise Fazenda, Bobby Vernon, Billy Franey, Queenie Rosson.

The Polo Champions (7/25/1914) Joker. Dir: Allen Curtis. Cast: Max Asher, Billy Franey, Gale Henry, Louise Fazenda, Bobby Vernon, Sam Kaufman.

Wifie's Busy Day (8/1/1914) Joker. Dir: Allen Curtis. Cast: Max Asher, Gale Henry, Louise Fazenda, Bobby Vernon.

That's Fair Enough (8/8/1914) Joker. Dir: Allen Curtis. Cast: Max Asher, Louise Fazenda, Gale Henry, Bobby Vernon, Billy Franey, Sam Kaufman.

What Happened to Schultz? (8/16/1914) Joker. Dir: Allen Curtis. Cast: Max Asher, Louise Fazenda, Bobby Vernon, Billy Franey, Gale Henry, Sam Kaufman.

The Diamond Nippers (8/22/1914) Joker. Dir & Sc: Allen Curtis. Cast: Max Asher, Louise Fazenda, Gale Henry, Elsie Cort, Sam Kaufman.

Well! Well! (8/29/1914) Joker. Dir: Allen Curtis. Cast: Max Asher, Louise Fazenda, Gale Henry, Bobby Vernon.

Oh! What's the Use? (9/5/1914) Joker. Cast: Max Asher, Louise Fazenda, Bobby Vernon, Billy Franey, Gale Henry.

Jam and Jealousy (9/12/1914) Joker. Cast: Max Asher, Gale Henry, Louise Fazenda, Bobby Vernon, Billy Franey, L. Harris. ½ rl.

In the Clutches of the Villain (10/3/1914) Joker. Dir & St: Allen Curtis. Cast: Max Asher, Gale Henry, Louise Fazenda, Sam Kaufman, Billy Franey. ½ rl.

The Baseball Fans of Fanville (10/7/1914) Joker. Dir: Allen Curtis. Cast: Lyon Bradshaw, Louise Fazenda, Gale Henry, Billy Franey.

Cruel, Cruel World (10/10/1914) Joker. Dir: Allen Curtis. Cast: Louise Fazenda, Gale Henry, Billy Franey, Ed Mullaney, William Seiter.

Across the Court (10/17/1914) Joker. Dir: Allen Curtis. Cast: Louise Fazenda, Max Asher, Billy Franey, Gale Henry, Sam Kaufman.

When Their Wives Joined the Regiment (10/31/1914) Joker. Dir: Allen Curtis. Cast: Louise Fazenda, Emily Harris, Gale Henry, William A. Seiter, Billy Franey, Sam Kaufman. 2 rls. (a.k.a. *When Their Wives Joined the Force*)

The De-Feet of the Father (11/14/1914) Joker. Cast: Louise Fazenda, Billy Franey, Sam Kaufman, Gale Henry, Milburn Moranti. ½ rl.

The Battle of the Nations (11/21/1914) Joker. Dir: Allen Curtis. Cast: Louise Fazenda, Billy Franey, Sam Kaufman, Gale Henry, James Kelly.

Love Disguised* (12/12/1914) Joker. Dir: Allen Curtis. Cast: Louise Fazenda, Max Asher, Gale Henry, Billy Franey, Sam Kaufman. ½ rl. (LOC)

Hot Stuff (12/26/1914) Joker. Cast: Gale Henry, Jane Bernoudy, Billy Franey

A Mixed-Up Honeymoon (1/2/1915) Joker. Cast: Billy Franey, Gale Henry, Milburn Moranti, Elsie Cort, Ralph McComas.

Fools and Pajamas* (1/23/1915) Joker. Dir: Allen Curtis. Cast: Louise Fazenda, Gale Henry, Billy Franey, Milburn Moranti, Sam Kaufman. (MoMA)

He Fell in Love with his Mother-in-law (1/31/1915) Joker. Dir: Allen Curtis. Cast: Billy Franey, Gale Henry.

The Blank Note (2/1/1915) Joker. Dir: Allen Curtis. Cast: Billy Franey, Gale Henry, Louise Fazenda.

The Plumber Wins the Girl (2/8/1915) Joker. Dir: Allen Curtis. Cast: Billy Franey, Gale Henry, Milburn Moranti, Lillian Peacock, Ralph McComas.

Fooling Father (2/15/1915) Joker. Dir: Allen Curtis. Cast: Max Asher, Billy Franey, Gale Henry, Lillian Peacock, Ralph McComas.

Won with Dynamite (2/18/1915) Joker. Dir: Allen Curtis. Cast: Billy Franey, Ralph McComas, Gale Henry, Louise Fazenda, Sam Kaufman. ½ rl.

Love and Law (2/20/1015) Joker. Dir: Allen Curtis. Cast: Billy Franey, Gale Henry, Milburn Moranti, Lillian Peacock.

Saved by a Shower (2/27/1915) Joker. Dir: Allen Curtis. Cast: Max Asher, Gale Henry, Milburn Moranti, Billy Franey, Lillian Peacock.

The Water Cure (3/1/1915) Joker. Dir: Allen Curtis. Cast: Billy Franey, Gale Henry, Jack Francis, Louise Fazenda, Ralph McComas, Ferrie Penning.

School Day (3/8/1915) Joker. Dir: Allen Curtis. Cast: Max Asher, Gale Henry.

Back to School Days (3/8/1915) Joker. Dir: Allen Curtis. Cast: Max Asher, Gale Henry, Billy Franey, Lillian Peacock.

Schultz's Lady Friend (3/13/1915) Joker. Dir: Allen Curtis. Cast: Gale Henry, Max Asher, Billy Franey, Lillian Peacock.

The Rejuvenation of Liza Jane (3/20/1915) Joker. Dir: Allen Curtis. Cast: Max Asher, Gale Henry, Lillian Peacock. 2 rls.

Wedding Bells Shall Ring (4/5/1915) Joker. Dir: Allen Curtis. Sc: Clarence Badger. Cast: Max Asher, Gale Henry, Milburn Moranti, Billy Franey, Dolly Ohnet.

The Way he Won the Widow (4/17/1915) Joker. Dir: Allen Curtis. Sc: Clarence Badger. Cast: Max Asher, Gale Henry, Milburn Moranti, Billy Franey, Dolly Ohnet.

The Fatal Kiss (4/19/1915) Joker. Dir: Allen Curtis. Sc: Clarence Badger. Cast: Max Asher, Gale Henry, Billy Franey, Dolly Ohnet. ½ rl.

Over the Bounding Waves (4/26/1915) Joker. Dir: Allen Curtis. Cast: Max Asher, Gale Henry, Billy Franey, Milburn Moranti, Dolly Ohnet. ½ rl.

A Day at the San Diego Fair (5/17/1915) Joker. Dir: Allen Curtis. Cast: Max Asher, Gale Henry, Billy Franey, Milburn Moranti, Dolly Ohnet.

The Lady Doctor of Grizzly Gulch (5/22/1915) Joker. Dir: Allen Curtis. Sc: Clarence Badger. Cast: Max Asher, Gale Henry.

Hiram's Inheritance (5/24/1915) Joker. Dir & St: Allen Curtis. Sc: Clarence Badger. Cast: Max Asher, Gale Henry, Billy Franey, Lillian Peacock.

Lady Baffles and Detective Duck in the Great Egg Robbery* (5/27/1915) Prod: Pat Powers. Dir: Allen Curtis. Sc: Clarence Badger. Cast: Max Asher, Gale Henry, Billy Franey, Lillian Peacock. (LOC)

The Lover's Lucky Predicament (6/5/1915) Joker. Dir: Allen Curtis. Sc: Clarence Badger. Cast: Max Asher, Gale Henry, Billy Franey, Milburn Moranti, Lillian Peacock.

How Billy Got his Raise (6/7/1915) Joker. Dir: Allen Curtis. Sc: Clarence Badger. Cast: Max Asher, Gale Henry, Billy Franey, Lillian Peacock. ½ rl.

Lady Baffles and Detective Duck in the Sign of the Sacred Safety Pin (6/10/1915) Prod: Pat Powers. Dir: Allen Curtis. Sc: Clarence Badger. Cast: Gale Henry, Max Asher, Billy Franey.

A Duke for a Day (6/14/1915) Joker. Dir: Allen Curtis. Sc: Clarence Badger. Cast: Max Asher, Gale Henry.

At the Bingville Booster's Barbecue (6/19/1915) Joker. Dir: Allen Curtis. Sc: Bennett R. Cohen. Cast: Gale Henry, Max Asher, Billy Franey, Milburn Moranti, Lillian Peacock.

Lady Baffles and Detective Duck in the 18 Carrot Mystery (6/24/1915) Prod: Pat Powers. Dir: Allen Curtis. Sc: Clarence Badger. Cast: Max Asher, Gale Henry, Milburn Moranti.

When Schultz Led the Orchestra (6/26/1915) Joker. Dir: Allen Curtis. Sc: Clarence Badger. Cast: Max Asher, Gale Henry, Billy Franey, Milburn Moranti, Lillian Peacock. 2 rls.

The Mechanical Man (6/28/1915) Joker. Dir: Allen Curtis. Sc: Clarence Badger. Cast: Max Asher, "Phroso," Arthur Moon, Lillian Peacock, Gale Henry, Milburn Moranti, Billy Franey.

Right Off the Reel (7/5/1915) Joker. Dir: Allen Curtis. Sc: Clarence Badger. Cast: Max Asher, Lillian Peacock, Gale Henry, Billy Franey, Arthur Moon.

Lady Baffles and Detective Duck in Baffles Aids Cupid (7/8/1915) Prod: Pat Powers. Dir: Allen Curtis. Sc: Clarence Badger. St: Gale Henry. Cast: Max Asher, Gale Henry, Milburn Moranti, Lillian Peacock.

Freaks (7/17/1915) Joker. Dir: Allen Curtis. Sc: Clarence Badger. Cast: Gale Henry, Milburn Moranti, Billy Franey, Lillian Peacock., Arthur Moon.

Lady Baffles and Detective Duck in the Signal of the Three Socks (7/22/1915) Prod: Pat Powers. Dir: Allen Curtis. Sc: Clarence Badger. Cast: Max Asher, Gale Henry, Billy Franey, Milburn Moranti, Dolly Ohnet, Lillian Peacock.

A Duel at Dawn (7/24/1915) Joker. Dir: Allen Curtis. Sc: Clarence badger. Cast: Max Asher, Gale Henry, Billy Franey, Milburn Moranti, Lillian Peacock, Arthur Moon.

The Village Smithy (7/31/1915) Joker. Dir: Allen Curtis. Sc: Clarence Badger. Cast: Max Asher, Gale Henry, Billy Franey, Lillian Peacock, Milburn Moranti. 2 rls.

Lady Baffles and Detective Duck in Saved by a Scent (8/5/1915) Prod: Pat Powers. Dir: Allen Curtis. Sc: Clarence Badger. St: Gale Henry. Cast: Max Asher, Gale Henry, Milburn Moranti.

Their Bewitched Elopement (8/7/1915) Joker. Dir: Allen Curtis. Sc: Clarence Badger. Cast: Max Asher, Gale Henry, Milburn Moranti, Billy Franey, Lillian Peacock.

A Dip in the Water (8/14/1915) Joker. Dir: Allen Curtis. Sc: Clarence Badger. Cast: Lillian Peacock, Max Asher, Gale Henry, Billy Franey, Milburn Moranti, Arthur Moon.

Lady Baffles and Detective Duck in the Dread Society of the Sacred Sausage (8/19/1915) Prod: Pat Powers. Dir: Allen Curtis. Sc: Clarence Badger. St: Gale Henry. Cast: Max Asher, Gale Henry, Milburn Moranti, Lillian Peacock, Arthur Moon, Billy Franey.

The Bravest of the Brave (8/28/1915) Joker. Dir: Allen Curtis. Sc: Clarence Badger. St: Thomas Delmar. Cast: Billy Franey, Gale Henry, Lillian Peacock, Max Asher.

When Hiram went to the City (9/4/1915) Joker. Dir: Allen Curtis. Cast: Max Asher, Gale Henry, Billy Franey, Lillian Peacock.

At the Beach Incognito (9/11/1915) Joker. Dir: Allen Curtis. Sc: Clarence Badger. Cast: Milburn Moranti, Lillian Peacock, Max Asher, Gale Henry, Billy Franey.

He Couldn't Fool his Mother-in-law (9/18/1915) Prod: Joker. Dir & Sc: Allen Curtis. Cast: Max Asher, Lillian Peacock, Billy Franey, Gale Henry.

He Couldn't Support his Wife (9/25/1915) Joker. Dir: Allen Curtis. Cast: Billy Franey, Gale Henry, Bobby Vernon. ½ rl.

Lady Baffles and Detective Duck in the Ore Mystery (9/30/1915) Prod: Pat Powers. Dir: Allen Curtis. Sc: Clarence Badger. St: Gale Henry. Cast: Max Asher, Gale Henry, Lillian Peacock, Milburn Moranti, Billy Franey.

A Millionaire for a Minute* (10/6/1915) Joker. Dir: Allen Curtis. Sc: James Dayton. Cast: Max Asher, Gale Henry, Billy Franey, Milburn Moranti, Lillian Peacock. (LOC)

Lady Baffles and Detective Duck in when the Wets went Dry* (10/14/1915) Prod: Pat Powers. Dir: Allen Curtis. Sc: Clarence Badger. St: Gale Henry. Cast: Max Asher, Gale Henry, Milburn Moranti, Billy Franey, Lillian Peacock. (LOC)

No Babies Allowed (10/16/1915) Joker. Dir: Allen Curtis. Cast: Milburn Moranti, Gale Henry, Billy Franey.

Pete's Awful Crime (10/23/1915) Joker. Dir: Allen Curtis. Sc: Ben Cohn. Cast: Gale Henry, Billy Franey, Max Asher, Milburn Moranti.

Lady Baffles and Detective Duck in the Last Roll (10/28/1915) Prod: Pat Powers. Dir: Allen Curtis. Sc: Clarence Badger. St: Milton J. Fahrney. Cast: Max Asher, Gale Henry, Billy Franey, Milburn Moranti, Lillian Peacock.

Twentieth Century Susie (11/6/1915) Joker. Dir: Allen Curtis. Cast: Billy Franey, Milburn Moranti, Gale Henry, Charles "Heinie" Conklin, Lillian Peacock.

Chills and Chickens (11/20/1915) Joker. Dir: Allen Curtis. Sc: Gale Henry. Cast: Gale Henry, Max Asher, Billy Franey, Lillian Peacock.

Lady Baffles and Detective Duck in Kidnapping the King's Kid (11/25/1915) Prod: Pat Powers. Dir: Allen Curtis. Sc: Clarence Badger. Cast: Milburn Moranti, Max Asher, Gale Henry, Billy Franey.

Mrs. P. Rune's Boarding House (12/11/1915) Joker. Dir: Allen Curtis. Sc: James Dayton. Cast: Gale Henry, Max Asher, Billy Franey.

Slightly Mistaken (12/11/1915) Joker. Dir: Allen Curtis. Cast: Billy Franey, Lillian Peacock, Gale Henry, Max Asher, Mrs. Whistler.

Stage Struck (2/18/1915) Joker. Dir: Allen Curtis. Sc: James Dayton. Cast: Gale Henry, Billy Franey, Max Asher, Lillian Peacock. (a.k.a. The Opera Singer's Romance)

Lemonade Aids Cupid (1/1/1916) Joker. Dir: Allen Curtis. Sc: Gale Henry. Cast: Lillian Peacock, Max Asher, Gale Henry, Milburn Moranti, Billy Franey.

Those Female Haters (1/8/1916) Joker. Dir & Sc: Allen Curtis. Cast: Max Asher, Billy Franey, Gale Henry, Lillian Peacock, Milburn Moranti.

Leap and Look After (1/12/1916) Joker. Dir: Allen Curtis. Cast: Billy Franey, Gale Henry, Milburn Moranti, Lillian Peacock.

Mrs. Green's Mistake (1/29/1916) Joker. Dir & Sc: Allen Curtis. Cast: Billy Franey, Gale Henry, Lillian Peacock, Charles "Heinie" Conklin.

Wanted a Piano Tuner (2/15/1916) Joker. Dir: Allen Curtis. Cast: Milburn Moranti, Lillian Peacock, Gale Henry, Billy Franey, Charles "Heinie" Conklin.

Love Laughs at the Law (3/2/1916) Joker. Dir & Sc: Allen Curtis. Cast: Billy Franey, Gale Henry, Milburn Moranti, Lillian Peacock, Charles "Heinie" Conklin.

Muchly Married (3/19/1916) Joker. Dir: Allen Curtis. Sc: Aaron E. Bishop. Cast: Milburn Moranti, Mary Fisher, Ernest Schields, Billy Franey, Charles "Heinie" Conklin, Lillian Peacock, Gale Henry.

It Nearly Happened (3/25/1916) Joker. Dir: Allen Curtis. Cast: Billy Franey, Gale Henry, Milburn Moranti, Lillian Peacock. (a.k.a. Fifty-Fifty)

His Highness the Janitor (4/8/1916) Joker. Dir: Allen Curtis. Sc: Gale Henry. Cast: Gale Henry, Billy Franey, Lillian Peacock, Milburn Moranti, Charles "Heinie" Conklin.

Hubby Pulls One Over (4/15/1916) Joker. Dir & Sc: Allen Curtis. Cast: Billy Franey, Gale Henry, Charles "Heinie" Conklin, Lillian Peacock, Milburn Moranti.

The Jitney Driver's Romance (4/29/1916) Joker. Dir: Allen Curtis. Sc: William W. Farmer. Cast: Milburn Moranti, Gale Henry, Billy Franey, Charles "Heinie" Conklin, Lillian Peacock.

A Perfect Match, or 1 Plus 1 Equals 2 (5/6/1916) Joker. Dir & Sc: Roy Clements. Cast: Charles "Heinie" Conklin, Gale Henry, Milburn Moranti, Lillian Peacock.

A Wife for a Ransom (5/13/1916) Joker. Dir & Sc: Allen Curtis. Cast: Billy Franey, Gale Henry, Lillian Peacock, Milburn Moranti, Charles "Heinie" Conklin.

A Raffle for a Husband (5/20/1916) Joker. Dir: Allen Curtis. Sc: Gale Henry. Cast: Milburn Moranti, Gale Henry, Billy Franey, Lillian Peacock, Charles "Heinie" Conklin

A Stage Villain (5/27/1916) Joker. Dir & Sc: Allen Curtis. Cast: Gale Henry, Billy Franey, Lillian Peacock, Milburn Moranti, Charles "Heinie" Conklin.

A Dark Suspicion (6/3/1916) Dir & Sc: Allen Curtis. Cast: Billy Franey, Gale Henry, Milburn Moranti, Lillian Peacock, Charles "Heinie" Conklin.

Love Quarantined (6/17/1916) Dir & Sc: Allen Curtis. Cast: Lillian Peacock, Billy Franey, Gale Henry, Milburn Moranti, Charles "Heinie" Conklin.

The Fall of Deacon Stillwaters (6/24/1916) Dir: Allen Curtis. Sc: Aaron E. Bishop. Cast: Charles "Heinie " Conklin, Gale Henry, Lillian Peacock, Billy Franey, Milburn Moranti.

Bashful Charley's Proposal* (7/1/1916) Dir: & Sc: Allen Curtis. Cast: Charles "Heinie" Conklin, Gale Henry, Billy Franey, Milburn Moranti, Lillian Peacock. (EYE)

The Harem Scarem Deacon* (7/15/1916) Dir: Allen Curtis. Sc: Eugene B. Lewis. Cast: Gale Henry, Billy Franey, Lillian Peacock, Milburn Moranti, Charles "Heinie" Conklin. (DF)

She Was Some Vampire (7/22/1916) Dir & SC: Allen Curtis. Cast: Gale Henry, Milburn Moranti, Billy Franey, Charles "Heinie" Conklin, Lillian Peacock.

An All Around Cure (7/24/1916) Dir: Allen Curtis. Sc: William W. Farmer. Cast: Gale Henry, Billy Franey, Lillian Peacock, Charles "Heinie" Conklin, Milburn Moranti.

I've Got Yer Number (7/29/1916) Dir: Allen Curtis. Sc: Aaron E. Bishop. Cast: Gale Henry, Lillian Peacock, Billy Franey, Charles "Heinie" Conklin, Milburn Moranti

Kate's Lovers Knots (8/5/1916) Dir: Allen Curtis. Sc: Aaron E. Bishop. Cast: Gale Henry, Lillian Peacock, Billy Franey, Charles "Heinie" Conklin, Milburn Moranti. (a.k.a. Kate's Affinities)

She Wrote a Play and Played It *(8/12/1916) Dir: Allen Curtis. Sc: Ben Cohn. Cast: Gale Henry, Lillian Peacock, Milburn Moranti, Billy Franey, Charles "Heinie" Conklin. (RFA)

Soup and Nuts (8/19/1916) Dir: Allen Curtis. Sc: Ben Cohn. Cast: Gale Henry, Billy Franey, Lillian Peacock, Charles "Heinie" Conklin, Milburn Moranti.

You Want Something? (8/24/1916) Dir: Allen Curtis. Sc: Clarence Badger. St: Stella Anne Ellis. Cast: Max Asher, Gale Henry, Milburn Moranti, Billy Franey.

A Marriage for Revenge (9/2/1916) Dir & Sc: Allen Curtis. St: William W. Farmer. Cast: Gale Henry, Billy Franey, Milburn Moranti, Charles "Heinie" Conklin, Lillian Peacock.

The Elixir of Life (9/2/1916) Dir: Allen Curtis. Sc: Harry Wulze. Cast: Gale Henry, Billy Franey, Charles "Heinie" Conklin, Milburn Moranti, Lillian Peacock.

The Deacon Stops the Show (9/9/1916) Dir: Allen Curtis. Sc: Ben Cohn. Cast: Gale Henry, Billy Franey, Lillian Peacock, Milburn Moranti, Charles "Heinie" Conklin.

In Onion There Is Strength (9/16/1916) Dir: Allen Curtis. Sc: William Warren Schoene. Cast: Gale Henry, Billy Franey, Lillian Peacock, Charles "Heinie" Conklin, Milburn Moranti.

Musical Madness (9/23/1916) Dir:William Beaudine. Sc: Harry Wulze. Cast: Gale Henry, Billy Franey, Milburn Moranti, Lillian Peacock, Charles "Heinie" Conklin.

The Inspector's Double* (9/30/1916) Dir: William Beaudine. Sc: Harry Wulze. St: Charles J. Wilson Jr. Cast: Gale Henry, Charles "Heinie" Conklin, Lillian Peacock, Milburn Moranti, Harry Mann. (LOC)

Father Gets In Wrong (10/7/1916) Dir: Allen Curtis. Sc: William Warren Schoene. Cast: Billy Franey, Gale Henry, Milburn Moranti, Lillian Peacock.

Beans and Bullets (10/21/1916) Dir: William Beaudine. Sc: Harry Wulze. St: Barney Furey. Cast: Billy Franey, Gale Henry, Charles "Heinie" Conklin, Lillian Peacock, Milburn Moranti, Jack Francis.

A Crooked Mix-Up (10/28/1916) Dir: William Beaudine. Sc: Charles J. Wilson Jr. St: W.M. Baker. Cast: Milburn Moranti, Gale Henry, Charles "Heinie" Conklin, Billy Franey, Lillian Peacock.

A Shadowed Shadow (11/4/1916) Dir: William Beaudine. Sc: Jack Byrne. Cast: Milburn Mornati, Gale Henry, Lillian Peacock, Dan Duffy, Charles "Heinie" Conklin, Billy Franey.

In Love with a Fireman (11/11/1916) Dir: William Beaudine. Sc: Walter H. Newman. Cast: Billy Franey, Gale Henry, Milburn Moranti, Charles "Heinie" Conklin, Lillian Peacock.

Their First Arrest (11/18/1916) Dir: William Beaudine. Sc: Symth Addison. Cast: Billy Franey, Gale Henry, Lillian Peacock, Charles "Heinie" Conklin, Milburn Moranti.

Jags and Jealousy (11/23/1916) Dir: William Beaudine. Sc: Karl R. Coolidge. Cast: Gale Henry, Billy Franey, Milburn Moranti, Charles "Heinie" Conklin, "Snooze" Franey the dog.

A Janitor's Vendetta (11/25/1916) Dir: William Beaudine. Sc: Harry Wulze. Cast: Billy Franey, Gale Henry, Lillian Peacock, Charles "Heinie" Conklin, Milburn Moranti.

Scrappily Married (12/2/1916) Dir: William Beaudine. Sc: Harry Wulze. Cast: Billy Franey, Gale Henry, Lillian Peacock, Charles "Heinie" Conklin, Milburn Moranti.

The Tramp's Chef (12/9/1916) Dir & Sc: William Beaudine. Co-Sc: Charles J. Wilson. Cast: Charles "Heinie" Conklin, Gale Henry, Milburn Moranti, Billy Franey, Al Moranti.

Their Dark Secret (12/16/1916) Dir: William Beaudine. Sc: Harry Wulze. St: Sheeba Canne. Cast: Billy Franey, Gale Henry, Milburn Moranti, Charles "Heinie" Conklin.

The Tale of a Turk (12/1916) Dir & Sc: William Beaudine. Co-Sc: Karl Coolidge. Cast: Billy Franey, Gale Henry, Lillian Peacock, Milburn Moranti, Jack Conally.

Love in Suspense (1/6/1917) Dir: William Beaudine. Sc: Karl Coolidge. Cast: Gale Henry, Milburn Moranti, Billy Franey, Charles "Heinie" Conklin, John Cook.

Mines and Matrimony (1/13/1917) Dir: William Beaudine. Sc: Karl Coolidge. St: Irene Blake. Cast: Gale Henry, Billy Franey, Harry Mann, Charles "Heinie" Conklin, Milburn Moranti, Yvette Mitchell.

Barred from the Bar (1/20/1917) Dir: William Beaudine. Sc &St: Karl R. Cooldige. Cast: Billy Franey, Lillian Peacock, Gale Henry, Milburn Moranti.

Love Me, Love My Biscuits (1/27/1917) Dir: William Beaudine. Sc &St: Karl R. Coolidge. Cast: Billy Franey, Gale Henry, Milburn Moranti, Dolly Ohnet.

When Damon Fell for Pythias* (1/29/1917) Dir & Sc: William Beaudine. 2 rls. Cast: Billy Franey, Gale Henry, Charles "Henie" Conklin, Lydia Yeamans Titus. (LOC)

His Coming Out Party (2/3/1917) Dir: William Beaudine. Sc: Karl R. Coolidge. Cast: Billy Franey, Gale Henry, Milburn Moranti, Lillian Peacock.

Out for the Dough (2/10/1917) Dir: William Beaudine. Sc &St: Jack Cunningham. Cast: John Cook, Lillian Peacock, Billy Franey, Gale Henry, Milburn Moranti.

Mule Mates (2/17/1917) Dir & St: William Beaudine. Sc & St: Jack Cunningham. Cast: Billy Franey, Gale Henry, Fred Woodward, Milburn Moranti.

Rosie's Rancho (2/24/1917) Dir: William Beaudine. Sc & St: Jack Cunningham. 2 rls. Cast: Liilain Peacock, Gale Henry, Billy Franey, Milburn Moranti.

Passing the Grip (3/3/1917) Dir: William Beaudine. Sc: Walter H. Newman. Cast: Billy Franey, Gale Henry, Milburn Moranti, Charles "Heinie" Conklin, Lillian Peacock.

Wanta Make a Dollar? (3/10/1917) Dir: William Beaudine. Sc: Jack Cunningham. Cast: Gale Henry, Milburn Moranti, Lillian Peacock, John Cooke.

Art Aches (3/17/1917) Dir: William Beaudine. Sc: Jack Cunningham. Cast: Gale Henry, Milburn Moranti, Lillian Peacock, John Cooke, Bobby Mack, Billy Franey.

Whose Baby? (3/24/1917) Dir: William Beaudien. Sc: Jack Cunningham. Cast: Billy Franey, Gale Henry, Lillian Peacock.

What the -? (3/31/1917) Dir: William Beaudine. Sc: Jack Cunningham. Cast: Gale Henry, Billy Franey, Lillian Peacock, Milburn Moranti, Kewpie Morgan, Bobby Mack, Martha Mattox.

A Boob for Luck (4/7/1917) Dir: Dir & Au: William Beaudine. Sc: Jack Cunningham. Cast: Lillian Peacock, Billy Franey, Gale Henry, Bobbie Mack, Milburn Moranti, Billy Human.

The Careless Cop (4/13/1917) Dir: William beaudine. Sc: Jack Cunningham. Cast: Gale Henry, Billy Franey, Lillian Peacock, Milburn Moranti, R.A. Craven.

Take Back Your Wife (4/21/1917) Dir: William Beaudine. Sc: Charles J. Wilson. Cast: Billy Franey, Gale Henry, Charles "Heinie" Conklin, Lillian Peacock, Milburn Moranti.

Left in the Soup (5/5/1917) Dir: William Beaudine. Sc: Jack Cunningham. Cast: Gale Henry, Billy Franey, Milburn Moranti, Lillian Peacock.

The Man with a Package (5/12/1917) Dir: William Beaudine. Sc: C.B. Hoadley. Cast: Billy Franey, Gale Henry, Milburn Moranti, Lillian Peacock.

The Last Scent (5/19/1917) Dir: William Beaudine. Sc: C.B. Hoadley. Cast: Billy Franey, Gale Henry, Milburn Moranti, Lillian Peacock.

The Boss of the Family (5/26/1917) Dir: William Beaudine. Sc: C.B. Hoadley. Cast: Billy Franey, Gale Henry, Milburn Moranti, Lillian Peacock.

Simple Sapho (6/9/1917) Dir: Allen Curtis. Sc: Jack Cunningham. Cast: Gale Henry, Jack Dillon, Milton Sims.

One Damp Day (6/10/1917) Dir: William Beaudine. Au. Sc: Jack Cunningham. Cast: Billy Franey, Gale Henry, Milburn Moranti, Bobbie Mack, Lillian Peacock.

A Burgler's Bride (6/23/1917) Dir: Allen Curtis. Sc: Tom Gibson, Au: Jack Cunningham, W. Donnell, & Dorothy Calhoun. Cast: Gale Henry, Jack Dillon, Nellie Allen, Milton Sims.

The Twitching Hour (7/17/1917) Dir: Allen Curtis. Sc: Tom Gibson. Cast: Gale Henry, Milton Sims, Charles Haefli.

Kitchinella* (7/14/1917) Dir: Allen Curtis. Sc: C.B. Hoadley. Cast: Gale Henry, Milton Sims, Charles Haefli. (NFA/BFI)

Some Nurse (7/19/1917) Dir: Allen Curtis. Sc: Tom Gibson Au: Jack Cunningham. Cast: Gale Henry, Milton Sims, Billy Franey, Milburn Moranti.

The Soubrette (7/28/1917) Dir: Allen Curtis. Sc: Tom Gibson Au: Jack Cunningham. Cast: Gale Henry, Milton Sims, Charles Haefli, Grace Marvin.

The Stinger Stung (8/4/1917) Dir: Allen Curtis. Sc: C.B. Hoadley. Cast: Gale Henry, Milton Sims, Charles Haefli.

The Vamp of the Camp (8/11/1917) Dir: Allen Curtis. Sc: Tom Gibson Au: Jack Cunningham. Cast: Gale Henry, Milton Sims, Milburn Moranti, Charles Haefli.

Mrs. Madame Manager (8/20/1917) Dir: Allen Curtis. Sc: Tom Gibson. Cast: Gale Henry, Milton Sims, Lillian Peacock, Charles Haefli.

Busting into Society (8/27/1917) Dir: Allen Curtis. Sc: Tom Gibson. Cast: Gale Henry, Charles Dorian, Milton Sims, Charles Haefli, Mrs. George Hernandez.

A Gale of Verse (9/3/1917) Dir: Allen Curtis. Sc: Tom Gibson. Cast: Gale Henry, Milton Sims, Charles Haefli.

Back to the Kitchen (9/9/1917) Dir: Allen Curtis. Sc: Tom Gibson. Cast: Gale Henry, Milton Sims, Charles Haefli.

Nearly a Queen (9/10/1917) Dir: Allen Curtis. Sc: Tom Gibson. Cast: Gale Henry, Milton Sims, Charles Haefli.

Short Skirts and Deep Water (9/10/1917) Dir: Allen Curtis. Sc: Tom Gibson. Cast: Gale Henry, Billy Franey, Milburn Moranti.

Circus Sarah* (9/17/1917) Dir: Allen Curtis Sc: Tom Gibson. Cast: Gale Henry, Milton Sims, Charles Haefli. (NFA/BFI)

Hawaiian Nuts (9/17/1917) Dir: William Beaudine. Sc: Robert A. Dillon. Cast: Gale Henry, Billy Franey, Milburn Moranti, Milton Sims, Eddie Baker.

The Fountain of Trouble (9/24/1917) Dir: William Beaudine. Sc: Arthur F. Statter. Cast: Gale Henry, Billy Franey, Ida Tenbrook, Milburn Moranti, Nellie Allen

Marble Heads (9/24/1917) Dir: Allen Curtis. Sc: Tom Gibson. Cast: Gale Henry, Milton Sims, Billy Franey, Milburn Moranti, Tom Gibson.

The Masked Marvel (10/1/1917) Dir: Allen Curtis. Sc: Charles J. Wilson Jr. Cast: Gale Henry, Milton Sims.

Her Naughty Choice (10/1/1917) Dir: Allen Curtis. Sc: Tom Gibson Au: William Warren Schoene. Cast: Gale Henry, Billy Franey, Milton Sims, Milburn Moranti, Charles Haefli.

The Wart on the Wire (10/8/1917) Dir: Allen Curtis. Sc: Tom Gibson Au: C.B. Hoadley. Cast: Gale Henry, Billy Franey, Milburn Moranti, Charles Haefli, Milton Sims, Johnnie Cooke.

The Cross-Eyed Submarine (10/15/1917) Dir: William Beaudine. Sc: Jack Cunningham. Cast: Gale Henry, Billy Franey, Lillian Peacock, Milburn Moranti.

Who Done It? (10/15/1917) Dir: William Beaudine. Sc: Robert A. Dillon. Cast: Gale Henry, Billy Franey, Eddie Baker, Milburn Moranti, Charles Haefli, Milton Sims.

Tightwad (10/22/1917) Dir: Allen Curtis. Sc: Tom Gibson. Cast: Gale Henry, Billy Franey, Milburn Moranti.

I Quit! (10/29/1917) Dir: Allen Curtis. Cast: Gale Henry, Billy Franey, Milburn Moranti.

The Shame of the Bullcon (11/12/1917) Prod: Nestor. Dir: Allen Curtis. Au: Sc: Tom Gibson. Cast: Gale Henry, Billy Franey, Milburn Moranti.

Water on the Brain (11/26/1917) Prod: Nestor. Dir: Allen Curtis. Sc: Tom Gibson. Cast: Gale Henry, Billy Franey, Milburn Moranti, Lillian Peacock.

Secret Servants (12/17/1917) Prod: Nestor. Dir & Sc: William Beaudine. Cast: Gale Henry, Billy Franey, Milburn Moranti, Milton Sims.

Cave Man Stuff (1/7/1918) Prod: Nestor. Dir: Allen Curtis. Sc: Tom Gibson. Cast: Gale Henry, Billy Franey, Lillian Peacock, Milton Sims.

Who's to Blame (1/21/1918) Prod: Nestor.Dir: Allen Curtis. Sc: Tom Gibson. Cast: Gale Henry, Billy Franey, Lillian Peacock, Milburn Moranti.

A Flyer in Folly (3/6/1918) Prod: L-KO. Dir: Robert Kerr. Cast: Gale Henry, Hughie Mack, Bobby Dunn, Russell Powell, Katherine O'Connor.

Cooks and Crooks (3/20/1918) Prod: L-KO. Dir: James Davis. 2 rls. Cast: Gale Henry, Hughie Mack, Eva Novak, Dave Morris, Jack Connors.

Nothing But Nerve (3/25/1918) Prod: Nestor. Dir: Allen Curtis. Sc: Tom Gibson. 2 rls. Cast: Gale Henry, Milton Sims, Evelyn Selbie, Charles Haefli, Mrs. A. E. Witting.

Gowns and Girls (4/3/1918) Prod: L-KO. Dir: James Davis. 2 rls. Cast: Gale Henry, Hughie Mack, Eva Novak, Dave Morris, Walter Smith.

Saved from a Vamp (4/10/1918)Prod: L-KO. 2 rls. Cast: Gale Henry, Hughie Mack

A Rural Riot (4/24/1918) Prod: L-KO. Dir: James Davis. 2 rls. Cast: Gale Henry, Hughie Mack, Dave Morris, Katherine Young.

It's a Cruel World* (4/29/1918) Prod: Nestor. Dir: Allen Curtis. Sc: C.B. Hoadley. Cast: Gale Henry, Milton Sims, Billy Franey, Milburn Moranti. (NFA/BFI)

Her Movie Madness (5/8/1918) Prod: L-KO. Dir: Robert Kerr. 2 rls. Cast: Gale Henry, Eva Novak, Hughie Mack.

Who's Your Wife? (5/27/1918) Prod: Nestor. Dir: Allen Curtis. Sc: Tom Gibson. Cast: Gale Henry, Zazu Pitts, Milton Sims, Charles Haefli.

Butter Again! (6/10/1918) Prod: Nestor. Dir: Allen Curtis. Sc: Tom Gibson. 2 rls. Cast: Gale Henry, Billy Franey, Milburn Moranti, Milton Sims.

The Borrowed Baby (6/24/1918) Prod: Nestor. Dir: Allen Curtis. Sc: Tom Gibson. Cast: Gale Henry, Billy Franey, Milburn Moranti.

Model Comedies.

Supervised by Bruno J. Becker. Dist: Bulls Eye/Reelcraft. 2 reels.

The Wild Woman (1919) Cast: Gale Henry.

Stung (1919) Cast: Gale Henry.

The Farmerette (1919) Cast: Gale Henry.

Cash (1919) Super: Bruno J. Becker Cast: Gale Henry.

Her Honor, the Scrub Lady (1919) Cast: Gale Henry, Nelson McDowell.

The Slavey* (1919) Dir: Bruno J. Becker. Ph: Irving Ries. Cast: Gale Henry, Milburn Moranti, Hap Ward, Pearl Chapple, Richard Currier, Robert McKenzie. (LOC)

Sweet Cookie (1919) Cast: Gale Henry.

Kids (1919) Cast: Gale Henry.

Poor Fish* (1919) Cast: Gale Henry, Milburne Moranti, Eddie Baker, Hap Ward, Richard Currier. (fragment at LOC)

Pants* (1919) Cast: Gale Henry, Eddie Baker, Milburn Moranti, Hap Ward. (LOC)

Lizzie's Luck (1919) Cast: Gale Henry.

Her First Flame* (1919) Dir: Bruno J. Becker Cast: Gale Henry, Phyllis Allen, Milburn Moranti, Hap Ward, Eddie Baker. (GEH, LOC)

Her Week-end (1919) Dir: Bruno J. Becker. Cast: Gale Henry, HapWard, Bruno the Bear.

Chicken a la King (1919) Cast: Gale Henry.

Don't Chase Your Wife (1919) Cast: Gale Henry.

The Detectress* (1919) Cast: Gale Henry, Milburn Moranti, Hap Ward, Eddie Baker. (LOC)

Gas (1919) Cast: Gale Henry, Eddie Baker.
Ham an- (1919) Cast: Gale Henry, Billy Franey.
Home Talent (1919) Cast: Gale Henry.
This Way Out (1919) Cast: Gale Henry, Phyllis Allen, Billy Franey.
The Champeen (1920) Dir & Au: Tom Gibson. Ph: George Richter. Cast: Gale Henry, Billy Franey, Hap Ward, Rae Godfrey.
Heirlooms (1920) Cast: Gale Henry.
Help! (1920) Dir: Tom Gibson. Cast: Gale Henry, Billy Franey, Hap Ward, Blanche White, George Jeske.
The Movies (1920) Cast: Gale Henry.

Assorted features and shorts

The Hunch (11/28/1921) Prod: S-L Productions. Dist: Metro Pictures. Dir: George D. Baker. Ph: Rudolph Berquist. Art Dir: E. J. Shulter. 6 rls. Cast: Gareth Hughes, Ethel Grandine, John Steppling, Edward Flannigan, Harry Lorriane, Gale Henry, William H. Brown.
West is Worst (9/1922) Crescent Comedy. Prod: T.R. Coffin Prods. Dist: East Coast Productions. Dir: Bruce Mitchell. 2 rls. Cast: Jack Richardson, Eddie Barry, Gale Henry, Helen Darling, Spottiswoode Aitken.
Easy Pickin' (9/1922) Crescent Comedy. Prod: T. R. Coffin Prods. Dist: East Coast Productions. Dir: Bruce Mitchell. 2 rls. Cast: Jack Richardson, Vera Reynolds, Gale Henry, Hilliard Karr.
Night Life in Hollywood* (11/15/1922) Prod: Mrs. A. B. Maescher. Dir & Au: Fred Caldwell. Co-Dir: Jack Pratt. 6 rls. Cast: Frank Glendon, Josephine Hill, Gale Henry, J. L. McComas, Elizabeth Rhodes, Jack Connolly, Dolores Hall, as themselves—Wallace reid, Dorothy Davenport, Alice Davenport, Theodore Roberts, Sessue Hayakawa, Tsuru Aoki, William Desmond, Bryant Washburn, Bessie Love, J. Warren Kerrigan, Johnny Jones, Denishawn Dancers.
Quincy Adams Sawyer (12/4/1922) Prod: Sawyer-Lubin Productions. Dist: Metro Pictures. Dir: Clarence Badger. Sc: Bernard McConville. Ph: Rudolph Bergquist. 8 rls. Cast: John Bowers, Blanche Sweet, Lon Chaney, Barbara La Marr, Elmo Lincoln, Louise Fazenda, Joseph Dowling, Claire McDowell, Edward Conelly, June Elvidge, Victor Potel, Gale Henry, Hank Mann, Kate Lester, Billy Franey, Taylor Graves, Harry Depp, Andrew Arbuckle.

Hollywood (8/19/1923) Prod: Famous Players-Lasky. Dist: Paramount Pictures. Dir: James Cruze. Ad: Tom Geraghty. Au: Frank Condon. Ph: Karl Brown. 8 rls. Cast: The Story: Hope Down, Luke Cosgrove, George K. Arthur, Ruby Lafayette, Harris Gordon, Bess Flowers, Eleanor Lawson, King Zany. Stars and Celebrities: Roscoe Arbuckle, Gertrude Astor, Mary Astor, Agnes Ayres, Baby Peggy, T. Roy Barnes, Noah Beery, William Boyd, Clarence Burton, Robert Cain, Edythe Chapman, Betty Compson, Richardo Cortez, Viola Dana, Cecil B. DeMille, Charles De Roche, Dinky Dean Reisner, Helen Dunbar, Snitz Edwards, George Fawcett, Julia Faye, James Finlayson, Alec Francis, Jack Gardner, Sid Grauman, Alfred E. Green, Alan Hale, Lloyd Hamilton, Hope Hampton, William S. Hart, Gale Henry, Walter Hiers, Mrs. Walter Hiers, Stuart Holmes, Sigrid Holmquist, Jack Holt, Leatrice Joy, Mayme Kelso, J. Warren Kerrigan, Theodore Kosloff, Kosloff Dancers, Lila Lee, Lillian Leighton, Jacqueline Logan, May McAvoy, Robert McKim, Jeanie Macpherson, Hank Mann, Joe Martin, Thomas Meighan, Bull Montana, Owen Moore, Nita Naldi, Pola Negri, Anna Q. Nilsson, Charles Ogle, Guy Oliver, Kalla Pasha, Eileen Percy, Carmen Phillips, Jack Pickford, Chuck Reisner, Fritzi Ridgeway, Will Rogers, Sennett Girls, Ford Sterling Anita Stewart, Gloria Swanson, Estelle Taylor, Ben Turpin, Bryant Washburn, Maude Wayne, Claire West, Lawrence Wheat, Lois Wilson.

Held to Answer (11/22/1923) Prod: Metro Pictures. Dir: Harold Shaw. Ad: Winifred Dunn. Ph: George Rizard. 6 rls. Cast: House Peters, Grace Carlyle, John Sainpolis, Evelyn Brent, James Morrison, Lydia Knott, Bull Montana, Gale Henry, Thomas Guise, Robert Daly, Charles West, Charles Mailes.

A Sheik in Hollywood* (12/15/1923) Prod: L.K.C. Productions. Dist: Selznick Distributing Corp. Dir: Fred Caldwell. 2 rls. Cast: Gale Henry, Victor Potel, Fred Caldwell (a.k.a. The Sheik of Hollywood).

Changing Husbands* (8/10/1924) Prod: Famous Players-Lasky. Dist: Paramount Pictures. Dir: Frank Urson & Paul Iribe. Sc: Sada Cowen & Howard Higgins. Ph: Bert Glennon. 7 rls. Cast: Leatrice Joy, Raymond Griffith, Julia Faye, Zasu Pitts, Helen Dunbar, William Boyd, Gale Henry (in a cameo as a cross-eyed waitress).

The Fire Patrol (8/14 or 9/14/1924) Prod: Hunt Stromberg. Dist: Chadwick Pictures. Dir: Hunt Stromberg. Sc: Garrett Elsden Fort. Ph: Silvano Balboni. 7 rls. Cast: Anna Q. Nillsson, William Jeffries,

Spottiswoode Aitken, Jack Richardson, Madge Bellamy, Helen Jerome Eddy, Dick Brandon, Johnny Harron, Gale Henry, Frances Rose, Chester Conklin, Bull Montana, Charlei Murray.

Open All Night*(10/13/1924) Prod: Famous Players-Lasky. Dist: Paramount Pictures. Dir: Paul Bern. Sc: Willis Goldbeck. Ph: Bert Glennon. 6 rls. Cast: Viola Dana, Jetta Goudal, Adolphe Menjou, Maurice Flynn, Raymond Griffith, Gale Henry, Jack Giddings, Charles Puffy.

Merton of the Movies (11/3/1924) Prod: Famous Players-Lasky. Dist: Paramont Pictures. Dir: James Cruze. Sc: Walter Woods. Ph: Karl Brown. 8 rls. Cast: Glenn Hunter, Viola Dana, Charles Sellon, DeWitt Jennings, Sadie Gordon, Gale Henry, Luke Cosgrove, Elliott Roth, Charles Ogle, Ethel Wales, Frank Jonasson, Eleanor Lawson.

Along Came Ruth (11/3/1924) Prod: MGM. Dir: Edward Cline. Ad: Winifred Dunn. Ph: John Arnold. 5 rls. Cast: Viola Dana, Walter Hiers, Tully Marshall, Raymond McKee, Victor Potel, Gale Henry, DeWitt Jennings, Adele Farrington, Brenda Lane.

New Lives for Old (2/22/1925) Prod: Famous Players-Lasky. Dist: Paramount Pictures. Dir: Clarence Badger. Ad: Adelaide Heilbron. Ph: Guy Wilky. 7 rls. Cast: Betty Compson, Wallace MacDonald, Theodore Kosloff, Sheldon Lewis, Jack Joyce, Margaret Seddon, Joseph Dowling, Helen Dunbar, Gale Henry, Marvel Quivey, Ed Faust.

Declassee (4/12/1925) Prod: Corinne Griffith Productions. Dist: First National Pictures. Dir: Robert Vignola. Sc: Charles E. Whittaker & Bradley King. Ph: Gaetano Gaudio. Art Dir: J.J. Hughes. 8 rls. Cast: Corinne Griffith, Lloyd Hughes, Clive Brook, Rodcliffe Fellowes, Lilyan Tashman, Hedda Hopper, Bertram Jones, Gale Henry, Louise Fazenda, Eddie Lyons, Mario Carillo, Paul Weigel.

Youth's Gamble (7/7/1925) Prod: Harry J. Brown Productions. Dist: Rayart Pictures. Dir: Albert Rogell. Super: Harry J. Brown. Au: Henry Roberts Symonds & John Wesley Grey. Ph: Ross Fisher. 5 rls. Cast: Reed Howes, James Thompson, Margaret Morris, Wilfred Lucas, Gale Henry, William Bukley, David Kirby.

Soup to Nuts* (8/30/1925) Prod: Christie Comedies. Dist: Educational Pictures. Dir: William Watson. Sc: Hal Conklin. Ph: Paul Garnett & Alfred Jacguemin. Cartoons: Norma Z. McLeod. 2 rls. Cast: Neal Burns, Vera Steadman, Gale Henry, William Irving (DF, MoMA).

All Tied Up* (11/29/1925) Prod: Standard Comedies/Joe Rock Prods. Dist: FBO. Dir: George "Slim" Summerville. 2 rls. Cast: Frank "Fatty" Alexander, Hilliard "Fatt" Karr, Bill "Kewpie" Ross, Lois Boyd, Gale Henry.

His Wooden Wedding* (12/20/1925) Prod: Hal Roach. Dist: Pathe. Dir: Leo McCarey. Ph: Glen R. Carver. 2 rls. Cast: Charley Chase, Katherine Grant, Fred De Silva, Gale Henry, John Cossar, Lassie Lou Ahern, Al Hallett, Helen Gilmore (LOC, MoMA).

A Fraternity Mix-Up* (3/7/1926) Prod: Joe Rock/Blue Ribbon Comedies. Dist: FBO. Dir: Percy Pembroke. 2 rls. Cast: Alice Ardell, Gale Henry, Ella McKenzie, Joe Bonner, Will Hayes, Yvonne Howell, Eddie Harris, Al Ford, Jack Goodrich.

Mighty Like A Moose* (7/18/1926) Prod: Hal Roach. Dist: Pathe. Dir: Leo McCarey. 2 rls. Cast: Charley Chase, Vivien Oakland, Gale Henry, Ann Howe, Charles Clary, Malcolm Denny, Rolfe Sedan, Charlie Hall, Harry Bowen, Buddy the dog (NFA/BFI).

Galloping Ghosts*(8/20/1926) Prod: Joe Rock/Standard Comedies. Dist: FBO. Dir: Ralph Cedar. 2 rls. Cast: Frank "Fatty" Alexander, Hilliard "Fatt" Karr, Bill "Kewpie" Ross, Gale Henry (DF, MoMA, NFA/BFI).

What! No Spinach?* (8/22/1926) Prod: Joe Rock/Blue Ribbon Comedies. Dist: FBO. Dir: Harry Sweet. 2 rls. Cast: Harry Sweet, Gale Henry, Harry Martel, Marjorie Beebe.

The Vulgar Yachtsman* (11/15/1926) Prod: Joe Rock/Standard Comedies. Dir: Marcel Perez. 2 rls. Cast: Frank "Fatty" Alexander, Hilliard "Fatt" Karr, Bill "Kewpie" Ross, Lois Boyd, Gale Henry (EYE).

Break Away (1/16/1927) Prod: Christie Comedies. Dist: Educational Pictures. Dir: Harold Beaudine. Sc: Frank Roland Conklin. 2 rls. Cast: Neal Burns, Gale Henry.

Two Time Mama* (1/23/1927) Prod: Hal Roach. Dist: Pathe. Dir: Fred Guiol. Ph: Floyd Jackman. 2 rls. Cast: Glenn Tryon, Anita Garvin, Tyler Brooke, Vivien Oakland, Gale Henry, Jackie Haines, Oliver hardy, Joseph "Baldy" Belmont (MoMA).

A One Mama Man* (3/6/1927) Prod: Hal Roach. Dist: Pathe. Dir: James Parrott. Ph: Len Powers. 2 rls. Cast: Charley Chase, Eugenia Gilbert, Burr McIntosh, Gale Henry, Vernon Dent, Charlei hall, Joe Bordeaux (LOC, MAD).

Bigger and Better Blondes (5/15/1927) Prod: Hal Roach. Dist: Pathe. Dir: James Parrott. 2 rls. Cast: Charley Chase, Jean Arthur, Mario Carillo, Gale Henry, Frank Brownlee, May Wallace, Arthur Millet, George B. French, Ruth Cherrington.

What Women Did for Me* (8/14/1927) Prod: Hal Roach. Dist: Pathe. Dir: James Parrott. 2 rls. Cast: Charley Chase, Lupe Velez, Eric Mayne, Viola Richard, Gale Henry, Caryl Lincoln, May Wallace, Briderick O'Farrell, Al Hallet, Frank Whiteen, Bob Gray.

Stranded* (8/15/1927) Prod: Joe Rock/Sterling Pictures. Dir: Phil Rosen. Sc: Frances Guihan. Au: Anita Loos. Ph: Herbert Kirkpatrick. 6 rls. Cast: Shirley Mason, William Collier Jr., John Miljan, Florence Turner, Gale Henry, Shannon Day, Lucy Beaumont, Rose Gore.

Long Hose* (3/17/1928) Prod: Christie Comedies. Dist: Paramount Pictures. Dir: William Watson. 2 rls. Cast: Jack Duffy, Gale Henry, Jimmie Harriosn, Gail Lloyd, Eddie Baker.

The Wild West Show (5/20/1928) Prod: Universal. Dir: Del Andrews. Sc: John B. Cymer. Ad: Isadore Bernstein. Au: Del Andrews & Elmo ST Boyce. Art Dir: David S. Garber. 6 rls. Cast: Hoot Gibson, Dorothy Gulliver, Alan Forrest, Gale Henry, Monte Montague, Roy Laidlaw, John Hall.

All Parts (10/27/1928) Prod: Hal Roach. Dist: MGM. Dir: Hal Yates. Ph: George Stevens. 2 rls. Cast: Charley Chase, Edgar Kennedy, Nena Quartaro, Gale Henry, Max Davidson.

Ruby Lips (1/19/1929) Prod: Hal Roach. Dist: MGM. Dir: James Parrott. 2 rls. Cast: Charley Chase, Nena Quartaro, Richard Tucker, Gale Henry, Frank Austin.

The Big Squawk* (5/25/1929) Prod: Hal Roach. Dist: MGM. Dir: Warren H. Doane. Ph: Len Powers. 2 rls. Cast: Charley Chase, Nena Quartaro, Gale Henry, Edgar Kennedy.

The Love Doctor (10/5/1929) Prod: Paramount Famous Lasy Corp. Dir: Melville Brown. Ad: Guy Bolton & J. Walter Rubin. Ph: Edward Cronjager. 6 rls. Cast: Richard Dix, June Collier, Morgan Farley, Miriam Seegar, Winifred Harris, Lawford Davidson, Gale Henry (released in silent and sound versions).

Darkened Rooms (11/23/1929) Prod: Paramount Famous Lasky Corp. Dir: Louis Gasner. Ad: Patrick Kearney & Melville Baker. Ph: Archie Stout. 7 rls. Cast: Evelyn Brent, Neil Hamilton, Doris Hill, David Newell, Gale Henry, Wallace MacDonald, Blanche Craig, E.H. Calvert, Sammy Bricker (released in silent and sound versions).

Skip the Maloo* (9/26/1931) Prod: Hal Roach. Dist: MGM. Dir: James Parrott. 2 rls. Cast: Charley Chase, Jacqueline Wells, Gale Henry, Del Henderson, Eddie Dunn, Leo Willis, Fern Emmett, Harry Bernard, Jerry Mandy (remake of *A One Mama Man*).

Now We'll Tell One* (11/19/1932) Prod: Hal Roach. Dist: MGM. Dir: James Parrott. 2 rls. Cast: Charley Chase, Muriel Evans, Lillian Elliott, Gale Henry, Frank Darien, Eddie baker, Sam Harris.

Mr. Bride* (12/24/1932) Prod: Hal Roach. Dist: MGM. Dir: James Parrott. 2 rls. Cast: Charley Chase, Muriel Evans, Del Henderson, Gale Henry, Charlie Hall, Harry Bernard.

Luncheon at Twelve* (12/9/1933) Prod: Hal Roach. Dist: MGM. Dir: Charles Parrott. 2 rls. Cast: Charley Chase, Betty Mack, Billy Gilbert, Gale Henry, James Barty, Jimmie Adams, Rolfe Sedan, Harry Bernard, Sam Harris, Charlie Hall, Billy Franey.

For Further Research

One Day in Hollywood* Prod: LK Productions. Dir: Fred Caldwell. 2 rls. Cast: Gale Henry, Hank Mann, Buddy the dog. (Most likely from the Caldwell series of Hollywood Comedies, but unverified at this time).

MARCEL PEREZ FILMOGRAPHY

This a game attempt at charting Perez's prolific output. Much more information needs to be found, especially on his early European films and the period of 1917 in America.

Part One: Early European Films

The Short-Sight Cyclist* (1907) Prod: Eclipse. (MoMA, NFA/BFI)

La Police l'an 2000* (1910) (Police in the Year 2000) Prod: Gaumont. Cast: Perez, Eugene Breon, Clement Mege. (EYE)

As Robinet for Ambrosio Co. of Turin

Listed is known cast in addition to Perez.

1910

Il Capoanno di Robinet

Il Duello di Robinet (*Tweedledum's Duel*)

Frigot Impiegato Municipale

Gigetta al Reggimento (*Molly at the Regiment*) Cast: Gigetta Morano.

Gigetta si Vendica di Robinet Cast: Gigetta Morano.
Ossessione de Robinet per il Ballo
La Prima Bicicletta di Robinet* (*Tweedledum's First Bicycle*) (EYE)
Il Prurito di Robinet (*Fricot's Itching Powder*)
Robinet Ama la Figlia del Generale

1919 exhibitor ad for Perezs' Jester Comedies.

Robinet Appassionato pei Dirigibile (*Tweedledum"s Aeronautical Adventure*)
Robinet Costretto a Fare il Ladro (*Tweedledum's Forged Banknote*)
Robinet ha il Sonno Duro (*Tweedledum's Sleeping Sickness*)
Robinet ha la Mania del Savadanio
Robinet ha Perso il Treno (*Tweedledum Has Missed His Train*)
Robinet ha un Tic per il Ballo
Robinet Questerino (*Trials of Tweedledum as a Policeman*)
Robinet Studia una Parte Tragica (*Tweedledum Learns a Tragical Part*)
Robinet Vuol Fare il Jockey* (*Tweedledum wants to be a Jockey*) (EYE)
Storia di un Paio di Stivali

1911
L'Abito Bianco di Robinet* (*Tweedledum's White Suit*) (EYE)
L'Astuzia di Robinet (*Artful Tweedledum*)
L'Auto di Robinet* (*Tweedledum's Motor Car*) (EYE, MC)
Gli Auto-Scat di Robinet* (*Tweedledum's Auto-Skates*) (LOC)
Un Avventura di Robinet
La Cintura D'Oro
La Collana Rubata (*The Necklace Affair*)
La Furberie di Robinet (*Tweedledum and one of his Tricks*)
Gastone e Robinet Vogolino Prender Moglie (*Tweedledum and Frosty Want to Get Married*)
Il Pesce D'Aprile di Robinet (*Tweedledum's April Fool Joke*)
Reclame del Sarto
Robinet Ammiratore di Napoleone (*Exploits of a Napoleon Admirer*)
Robinet Arriva in Ritardo (*Tweedledum is Late*)
Robinet Aviatore* (CF, CI)
Robinet Detective
Robinet e il Monocolo della Verita Cast: Nilde Baracchi.
Robinet e L'Avventuriera (*Tweedledum and the Adventuress*)
Robinet e Troppo Timido (*Tweedledum is Shy*)
Robinet ed i Salvatori (*Tweedledum and his Rescuer*) C: Nilde Baracchi.
Robinet ha Rubato Centro Lire* (EYE)
Robinet in Bolletta (*Tweedledum's Financial Distress*)
Robinet in Societa (*Tweedledum Goes into High Life*)
Robinet Innamorato di una Chanteuse* (*Tweedledum in Love with a Cabaret Singer*) Cast: Gigetta Morano. (EYE, MC)

Robinet si Dedica Agli Sports Invernali* (*Tweedledum Tries Winter Sports*) (NFA/BFI)
Robinet Sposa un 'Americana (*Tweedledum Marries an American Girl*) Cast: Nilde Baracchi.
Robinet Tra due Fuochi* (NFA/BFI)
Robinet Vuol Diventare Eroe
Robinet Sua Moglie e il Cugino
Uno Scherzo di Robinet Cast: Nilde Baracchi.
La Scimmia di Robinet (*Tweedledum's Monkey*)
Il Sogno di Robinet* (*Tweedledum's Dream*) (DF)
Gil Stivali di Robinet (*Tweedledum's Riding Boots*) Cast: Nilde Baracchi.

1912
Un Complotto Contro Robinet
Una Dichiarazione Impossibile di Robinet* (EYE)
La Nuova Cameriera E Troppo Bella*(*The New Maid is too much of a Flirt*) Cast: Nilde Baracchi. (NFC)
L'Evasione di Robinet (Tweedeldum's Evasion) Cast: Nilde Baracchi.
Nei Lacci del Destino
Un Nuovo Furto di Robinet
L'Onomastico di Robinet Cast: Nilde Baracchi.
Le Rendite di Robinet Cast: Nilde Baracchi.
Robinet Alpino
Robinet Caricaturista Cast: Nilde Baracchi.
Robinet Commesso Viaggiatore
Robinet Contro un Rubinetto
Robinet Cycliste
Robinet Diventa un Ercole
Robinet fa il Giro D'Italia in Bicicletta
Robinet fa la Cura dei Bagni Cast: Nilde Baracchi.
Robinet fa un Allievo (*The Actor's Test*)
Robinet Falso Cow-Boy Cast: Nilde Baracchi.
Robinet Guida per Amore Cast: Nilde Baracchi.
Robinet in un Educandato* (NFA/BFI) Cast: Nilde Baracchi.
Robinet in Vacanza* (EYE, NFA/BFI) Cast: Nilde Baracchi.
Robinet Landro Inafferrabile Cast: Nilde Baracchi.
Robinet Maestro D'Equitazione (*Tweedledum's Riding School*)
Robinet Nichilista* (CI)

Robinet Operatore
Robinet Padre e Figlio* (*Tweedledum's Father and his Worthy Son*) (EYE)
Robinet Ricattatore Cast: Nilde Baracchi.
Robinet Ricco per Dieci Minuti
Robinet Scioperante
Robinet si Assicura Alla Vita (*Tweedledum Insures His Life*) C: Nilde Baracchi.
Robinet Sogna il Mare Cast: Nilde Baracchi.
Robinet Troppo Amato da sua Moglie* (*Tweedledum is Too Much Loved by His Wife*) Cast: Nilde Baracchi, Gigetta Morano. (EYE)
La Strenna di Robinet (*Tweedledum's New Year's Gift*)
Uno Zoppo chef a Strada

1913
Una Buona Giornata di Robinet
Cenerentola*
Come Robinet Sposo Robinette Cast: Nilde Baracchi.
Il Duello di Fricot Cast: Nilde Baracchi.
I Fratelli Robinet Cast: Nilde Baracchi.
Fricot Canatastorie Cast: Nilde Baracchi.
L'Idolo di Robinet
Madamigella Robinet* Cast: Nilde Baracchi. (EYE, MC)
La Madre di Robinet Cast: Nilde Baracchi.
Robinet Arma la Fioraia Cast: Nilde Baracchi.
Robinet Anarchico* (*Tweedledum as an Anarchist*)
Robinet Attaccato alla Sella
Robinet Boxeur* (CF)
Robinet Cocchiere* (CI)
Robinet Corteggiatore Tenace
Robinet e Butalin si Battono
Robinet e lo Steeple-Chase Cast: Nilde Baracchi.
Robinet Femminista Cast: Nilde Baracchi.
Robinet Guardia Ciclista* (MoMA) Cast: Nilde Baracchi.
Robinet Malato di Sonno
Robinet Poliziotto
Robinet Reporter
Robinet Sbaglia Piano Cast: Nilde Baracchi.
Robinet si da alla Malavita

Robinet Sportsman
Robinet Sposa a Vapore Cast: Nilde Baracchi.
Robinet Studia Matematica Cast: Nilde Baracchi.
Robinet Tenore
Robinet Vuol Lavorare
Robinet Vuol Piantare un Chiodo
Robinet Vuol Sposare una Dote
Robinet, Robinette Cast: Nilde Baracchi.
Una Scommessa di Butalin e di Robinet Cast: Nilde Baracchi.
La Suocera di Robinet Cast: Nilde Baracchi.

Adventure Serial for Ambrosio

Le Avventure Straordinarissime di Saturnino Farandola* (*The Extraordinary Adventures of Saturnino Farandola*) (1914) Dir: Marcel Fabre & Luigi Maggi. A: Guido Volante, from the novel by Ferdinand Robina. Ph: Ottavio De Matteis. Art Dir: Enrico Lupi & Decoroso Bonifanti. Cast: Marcel Fabre, Nilde Baracchi, Filippo Castamagna, Luciano Manara, Alfredo Bertone, Luigi Stinchi, Armando Pilotti, Dario Silvestri, Vittorio Tettoni, Oreste Grandi. (Originally released in four episodes: *The Isle of Monkeys*; *In Quest of the White Elephant*; *The Queen of Makalolos*; *Farandola Versus Phileas Fogg*). (Released in the U.S. as: *Zingo*; *Zingo and the White Elephant*; *Zingo in Africa*; *Zingo the Son of the Sea*; *Zingo's War in the Clouds*). (CI)

As Robinet for Ambrosio

1914

Amour Pedestre* (*Love Afoot*) (DF, CQ, FCA, MoMA)
L'Amore Diede la Forza a Robinet Cast: Nilde Baracchi.
Il Bastone di Robinet
Il Cavallo Fedele Cast: Nilde Baracchi.
Come Robinet Divento Comico Cast: Nilde Baracchi.
Delenda Carthago! (*The Destruction of Carthage*)
La Donne Economa Cast: Nilde Baracchi.
Duetto in Quattro Cast: Nilde Baracchi.
L'Energia di Fricot Cast: Nilde Baracchi.
Il Piccolo Fricot
Un Qui Pro Quo di Sheriff-Holfufus

Robinet alla Caccia della Volpe Cast: Nilde Baracchi.
Robinet ama Disinteressatamente Cast: Nilde Baracchi.
Robinet Cerca L'Ideale Cast: Nilde Baracchi.
Robinet Chauffeur Miope* (MC)
Robinet e Geloso* (*Robinet is Jealous*) Cast: Nilde Baracchi. (EYE)
Robinet Fotografo
Robinet ha del Crattere Cast: Nilde Baracchi.
Robinet ha il Tipo Americano Cast: Nilde Baracchi.
Robinet ha il Torcicollo
Robinet non Vuol Saperne Cast: Nilde Baracchi.
Robinet Perde e Guadagna Cast: Nilde Baracchi.
Robinet Pescatore* (EYE)
La Trovata di Robinet Cast: Nilde Baracchi.
Un Viaggio Laborioso Cast: Nilde Baracchi.

1915
La Cambiale di Robinet
La Colpe del Morto C: Nilde Baracchi.
Concorrenza Spietata
Jack Forbes Contro Robinet Cast: Nilde Baracchi.
Il Paletot a Martingala di Robinet
Quando Robinet Ama Cast: Nilde Baracchi.
Robinet Angelo Custode Cast: Nilde Baracchi.
Robinet Detective Amateur Cast: Nilde Baracchi.
Conto del Robinet e il Pranzo
Robinet Muore per Amore Cast: Nilde Baracchi.
Robinet Torna a Robinette Cast: Nilde Baracchi.
Robinette Vuol Farla a Robinet Cast: Nilde Baracchi.
Il Yacht Misterioso Cast: Nilde Baracchi.

Part Two: American Films

As Director/Actor for Joker:

A Day at Midland Beach (10/30/1915) Joker. Dist: Universal. Dir: Alan Curtis & Marcel Perez. 1rl. C: Marcel Perez.

As Bungles for Vim

Prod: Louis Burstein. Dir: Fernandea Perez. 1 reel.

Bungles Rainy Day (2/10/1916) Cast: Perez, Elsie McLeod, Oliver Hardy

Bungles Enforces the Law (2/24/1916) Cast: Perez, Elsie McLeod, Oliver Hardy, Bobby Burns, Billy Ruge.

Bungles Elopement (3/9/1916) Cast: Perez, Elsie McLeod, Oliver Hardy.

Bungles Lands a Job (3/23/1916) Cast: Perez, Elsie McLeod, Oliver Hardy.

As Tweedledum for Eagle Films

Dist: Unity Film Sales. Prod: William J. Dunn. Dir: Marcel Perez.

Torpedoed by Cupid (6/19/1916) 1 rl. Cast: Marcel Perez, Babette Perez, Rex Adams, Louise Carver, Tom Murray, Billy Slade. (a.k.a. *Tweedledum Torpedoed by Cupid*).

A Busy Night* (6/26/1916) 1 rl. Cast: Marcel Perez, Tom Murray. (a.k.a. *Tweedledum's Busy Night*) (LOC)

A Scrambled Honeymoon (7/3/1916) 2 rls. Cast: Marcel Perez. (a.k.a. *Tweedledum's Scrambled Honeymoon*).

Some Hero* (10/23/1916) 1 rl. Cast: Marcel Perez, Babette Perez, Billy Slade, Jerry Jellman, Jim McGowan, Charles Sharp. (a.k.a. *He's Some Hero*). (MoMA)

A Lucky Tramp (11/6/1916) 1 rl. Cast: Marcel Perez, Babette Perez, Melvin Andrews, Tom Murray.

Lend Me Your Wife* (11/13/1916) 2 rls. Cast: Marcel Perez, Babette Perez, Louise Carver, Rex Adams, Tom Murray. (MoMA)

A Bath Tub Elopement (11/20/1916) 1 rl. Cast: Marcel Perez, J. Malvin Ambrose, Tom Murray.

A Short-Sighted Crime (11/27/1916) 2 rls. Cast: Marcel Perez.

Somewhere in Mexico (12/4/1916) 1 rl. Cast: Marcel Perez, Billy Slade.

The Burlesque Show* (12/11/1916) (listed in film journals as both one and two reels). Cast: Marcel Perez, Babette Perez. (clips at LOC)

The Near-Sighted Auto-Pedist (12/1916) Cast: Marcel Perez, Babette Perez, Billy Slade.

As Twede-Dan for Jester Comedies:
Prod: William Steiner. 2 reels. Directed by Perez, or otherwise noted.

The Recruit (2/15/1918) Cast: Marcel Perez, Nilde Babette, Wilbert Shields.
His Golden Romance (3/15/1918) Dir: Courtlandt Van Dusen. 2 rls. Cast: Marcel Perez.
All 'Fur' Her (4/15/1918) Cast: Marcel Perez.
The Wrong Flat (5/15/1918) Cast: Marcel Perez, Nilde Babette. (a.k.a. In and Out).
This is the Life (5/1918) Cast: Marcel Perez, Nilde Babette, Thomas C. Regan. (a.k.a. *It's a Great Life*).
Oh! What a Day* (8/1/1918) Dir: William Seiter. 2 rls. Cast: Marcel Perez, Nilde Babette. (MoMA)
The Fly Ball (9/1/1918) Dir: William Seiter. 2 rls. Cast: Marcel Perez, Nilde Babette.
Ain't It So (10/1/1918) Dir: William Seiter. 2 rls. Cast: Marcel Perez.
Some Baby (11/1/1918) Dir: William Seiter. 2 rls. Cast: Marcel Perez.
Camouflage* (11/15/1918) Dir: William Seiter. 2 rls. Cast: Marcel Perez, Nilde Babette. (LOC)

Second Season as Twede-Dan for Jester Comedies
Prod: William Steiner. Dist: Territorial Sales Corp. Dir: Marcel Perez. 2 reels.

He Wins (1918) Cast: Marcel Perez, Nilde Babette.
In the Wild West (1919)Cast: Marcel Perez.
Peace and Riot (1919) Cast: Marcel Perez.
The Tenderfoot* (1919) Cast: Marcel Perez, Nilde Babette. (a.k.a. *Unidentified Jacobs and Cayton #1*) (LOC)
A Mexican Mix-Up (1919) Cast: Marcel Perez.
The Wisest Fool (1919) Cast: Marcel Perez, James Harvey Holland.
Gee Whiz (1919) Cast: Marcel Perez.
Almost Married (1919) Cast: Marcel Perez.
Business Without Pleasure (1919) Cast: Marcel Perez.
Can You Beat It?* (1919) Cast: Marcel Perez, Dorothy Earle, Flo Bailey, Pierre Collosse, Amy Manning. (GEH)
The Frame Up (1919) Cast: Marcel Perez.
In the Swim (1919) Cast: Marcel Perez.

Chicken in Turkey (1919) Cast: Marcel Perez, Dorothy Earle, Pierre Collosse.
She-Me (1919) Cast: Marcel Perez.
You're Next* (1919) Cast: Marcel Perez, Dorothy Earle, Pierre Collosse, Billy Slade. (EYE, LOC)

As Tweedy for Reelcraft

Mirth Comedies. Prod: Schiller Prods. Dist: Reelcraft. Dir: Marcel Perez. 2 reels.

Here He Is (5/16/1921) Cast: Marcel Perez.
Sweet Daddy* (1921) Ph: Herman Obrock. Cast: Marcel Perez, Dorothy Earle, Wilna Hervey, Kit Guard. (EYE, LOC)
Chick, Chick (1921) Cast: Marcel Perez, Dorothy Earle.
Vacation (1921) Cast: Marcel Perez, Dorothy Earle.
Speed (1921) Cast: Marcel Perez.
Wild (1921) Cast: Marcel Perez.
The Knockout* (1921) Cast: Marcel Perez, Pierre Collosse, Martin Kinney. (fragment at LOC)
Milk-Made (1921) Cast: Marcel Perez.
Moving (1921) Cast: Marcel Perez, Dorothy Earle, Pierre Collosse, Billy Gilbert, Billy Moran.
The Nut (1921) C: Marcel Perez.
Week End* (1921) C: Marcel Perez, Dorothy Earle, Pierre Collosse. (1st reel at EYE)
All In (1921) C: Marcel Perez.
All Around (1921) C: Marcel Perez.
Pinched* (1921) C: Perez, Dorothy Earle, Pierre Collosse, Billy Moran. (NFA/BFI)

Aladdin Comedies for Reelcraft

Prod: Schiller Prods. Dist: Reelcraft.

Shot* (1921) Dir: Marcel Perez. Ph: Herman Obrock. 1 rl. Cast: Billy Moran, Dorothy Earle, Pierre Collosse, Perez (?). (GEH)
Blowing Bubbles* (1921) Dir: Marcel Perez. Ph: Herman Obrock. 1rl. Cast: Billy Moran, Dorothy Earle.
Fireworks (1921) Dir: Marcel Perez. 1rl. Cast: Billy Moran, Dorothy Earle.

Tweedy Comedies for Sanford Productions:
Prod: Sanford Prods. Dir: Marcel Perez. 2 reels.

Fire—Fire (9/1/1922) Cast: Marcel Perez.
Take A Tip (10/1/1922) Cast: Marcel Perez.
Don't Monkey (11/1/1922) Cast: Marcel Perez.
Dog Gone It (12/1/1922) Cast: Marcel Perez.
Three O'Clock in the Morning (1/1/1923) Cast: Marcel Perez.
Friday 13th (2/1/1923) Cast: Marcel Perez.

Features as a Director:

The Way Women Love* (1920) Prod: Lyric Films/William Steiner Prod. Dist: Arrow Film Corp. Dir: Marcel Perez. Ph: William Cooper. A: Herman Landon. 5 rls. Cast: Rubye De Remer, Edward Elkas, Walter D. Greene, Thomas Magrine, Walter Miller, Rose Mintz, Hnery W. Pemberton. (LOC)

Luxury (1921) Prod: Lyric Films/William Steiner Prod. Dist: Arrow Film Corp. Dir: Marcel Perez. 6 rls. Cast: Rubye De Remer, Fredrick Kalgren, Thomas Magrine, Rose Mintz, Henry W. Pemberton.

Unconquered Women (1922) Prod: Pasha Film Corp. Dir: Marcel Perez. Ph: William Cooper. 5 rls. Cast: Rubye De Remer, Fred C. Jones, Frankie Mann, Walter Miller, Nick Thompson.

The Better Man Wins* (1922) Prod: Sanford Prods. Dir: Marcel Perez & Frank S. Mattison. 6 rls. Cast: Pete Morrison, Dorothy Woods, Gene Crosby, E.L Van Sickle, Jack Walters, Tom Bay.

Duty First (1922) Prod: Sanford Prods. Dir: Marcel Perez. 5 rls. Cast: Pete Morrison.

West vs. East (1922) Prod: Sanford Prods. Dist: Arrow Film Corp. Dir: Marcel Perez. 5 rls. Cast: Pete Morrison, Dorothy Woods, Gene Crosby, Renee Danti, Beesie De Lich, Lorenz Gillette, Robert Gray.

Pioneers of the West* (1925) Prod: William Mix Prods. Dir & A: Marcel Perez. Ph: Elmer Dyer. 5 rls. Cast: Dick Carter, Dorothy Earle, Gene Crosby, Olin Francis, Bud Osborne. (This feature has an accepted release date of 6/1/19127, but I found a review in the *Moving Picture World* of 9/19/1925. The 1927 date may be a reissue).

Lash of the Law* (1926) Prod: Goodwill Pictures, Inc. 5 rls. Cast: William Bailey, Alma Rayford, Marcel Perez, Dick La Reno, Bud Osborne, Roy Watson, Milton J. Fahrney. (No specific directorial credit is available for this film, but it was likely directed by Perez).

As Director for Joe Rock Productions:

Prod: Joe Rock/Standard Cinema Prods. Dist: FBO. Dir: Marcel Perez. 2 reels.

Hold Tight* (11/15/1925) Blue Ribbon Comedy. Cast: Alice Ardell, Joe Rock, Bobby Dunn. (NFTS)

A Peaceful Riot* (12/15/1925) Blue Ribbon Comedy. Cast: Alice Ardell, Slim Summerville, Max Asher, Leon Kent, Ethan Laidlaw, Harry Martel.

Mummy Love* (1/10/1926) Blue Ribbon Comedy. Cast: Alice Ardell, Neely Edwards, Yorke Sherwood. (GEH, LOC)

The Hurricane (4/4/1926) Blue Ribbon Comedy. Cast: Alice Ardell.

She's a Prince* (5/2/1926) Blue Ribbon Comedies. Cast: Alice Ardell, Billy Franey, Billy Engle, Dorothy Vernon.

The Vulgar Yachtsman* (11/15/1926) Standard Comedies. Cast: Frank "Fatty" Alexander, Hilliard "Fatt" Karr, Bill "Kewpie" Ross, Gale Henry, Lois Boyd. (EYE)

As Director and Writer for Universal:

Out All Night (9/4/1927) Prod: Universal. Dir: William Seiter. A: Gladys Lehman. Adapt: Harvey Thew & Marcel Perez. Titl: Tom Reed. 6 rls. Cast: Reginald Denny, Marian Nixon, Wheeler Oakman, Dorothy Earle, Dan Mason, Alfred Allen, Robert Seiter, Ben Hendricks Jr., Billy Franey, Harry Tracy, Lionel Braham.

His In-Laws (3/12/1928) Prod: Universal. Dir: Marcel Perez. A: Octavious Roy Cohen. 2 rls. C: Charles Puffy.

For Further Research:

Two of a Kind (1916) Jockey Comedy. Dist: Unicorn. Cast: Marcel Perez, Babette Perez, Rex Adams, Tom Murray.

Tweedledee and her Daughter* (ca 1916) The NFA/BFI has this listed in their holdings. It could be an alternate title for any of his American comedies, or something from his elusive Jockey/Encore films.

FAY TINCHER FILMOGRAPHY

Universal Éclair Films:

Prod: Éclair. Dist: Universal Pictures. 2 reels.

A Puritan Episode (9/24/1913) C: Julia Stuart, Alec B. Francis, Robert Frazer, Mildred Bright, Fay Tincher, Will E. Sheerer, Hal Wilson, Rose V. Koch, Clara Horton, Fred C. Truesdell.

Private Box 23 (10/5/1913) C: J.W. Johnston, Julia Stuart, Fay Tincher.

Adventures in Diplomacy (9/16/1914) Dir: O.C. Lund. A: "Illusive Isobel by Jacques Futrelle. 3 reels. C: Alec B. Francis, Fay Tincher, Edward F. Roseman, Lindsey J. Hall, Gunnis Davis.

Reliance/Majestic Films:

Prod: Reliance/Majestic. Dist: Mutual Film Corp.

Too Proud to Beg (1/31/1914) 1 rl. C: Spottiswoode Aitken, Fay Tincher.

The Battle of the Sexes* (4/12/1914) Dir & A: D.W. Griffith. Based on The Single Standard by Daniel Carson Goodman. PH: G.W. Bitzer. C: Lillian Gish, Owen Moore, Mary Alden, Fay Tincher, Robert Harron, Donald Crisp. 5 rls. (Only a fragment is known to exist) (LOC)

The Right Dope (4/15/1914) Dir: Edward Dillon. 1 rl. C: Fay Tincher.

The Quick Sands (5/1/1914) Dir: W. Christy Cabanne. A: Cabanne & Russell E. Smith. 1 rl. C: Lillian Gish, Courtney Foote, Fay Tincher, Douglas Gerrard, Robert Burns, Mary Alden.

Home, Sweet Home* (5/17/1914) Dir: D.W. Griffith. A: Griffith & Harry Aitken. PH: G.W. Bitzer. 6 rls. C: Henry B. Walthall, Lillian Gish, Dorothy Gish, Fay Tincher, Mae Marsh, Spottiswoode Aitken, Robert Harron, Miriam Cooper, Mary Alden, Donald Crisp, James Kirkwood, Jack Pickford, Courtenay Foote, Blanche Sweet, Owen Moore, Edward Dillon, Betty Marsh, Karl Brown.

Fay Tincher cartoon circa 1916.

The Escape (6/1/1914) Dir: D.W. Griffith. Based on the play by Paul Armstrong. PH: G.W. Bitzer. 7 rls. C: Blanche Sweet, Mae Marsh, Robert Harron, Owen Moore, F.A. Turner, Ralph Lewis, Tammany Young, Fay Tincher.

The Love Pirate (1/30/1915) 2 rls. C: Fay Tincher, Raoul Walsh, Elmer Clifton, Bobby Feuher.

Komic Comedies:
Prod: Reliance/Majestic. Dist: Mutual Film Corp. Dir: Edward Dillon. 1 reel except where noted.

After Her Dough (3/25/1914) C: Fay Tincher, Tod Browning, Joseph "Baldy" Belmont, Max Davidson.
Victims of Speed (4/1/1914) C: Fay Tincher, Tod Browning, Tammany Young, Joseph "Baldy" Belmont.
The Fatal Dress Suit (4/8/1914) C: Fay Tincher, Edward Dillon, James Young, Tod Browning.
Nearly a Burglar's Bride (4/22/1914) A: Anita Loos. C: Fay Tincher, Tod Browning.
The Scene of the Crime (5/10/1914) C: Fay Tincher, Tod Browning, Tammany Young.
A Race for a Bride (5/10/1914) C: Fay Tincher, Tod Browning, Tammany Young.
The Man in the Couch (5/17/1914) A: Anita Loos. C:Fay Tincher, Edward Dillon, Tod Browning.
Nell's Eugenic Wedding (5/24/1914) A: Anita Loos. C: Fay Tincher, Tod Browning, Joseph "Baldy" Belmont, Edward Dillon, Max Davidson.
An Exciting Courtship (5/31/1914) C: Fay Tincher, Tod Browning, Joseph "Baldy" Belmont.
The Last Drop of Whiskey (6/7/1914) A: Anita Loos. C: Fay Tincher, Tod browning, Tammany Young, Joseph "Baldy" Belmont, Max Davidson.
Hubby to the Rescue (6/14/1914) A: Russell E. Smith. C: Fay Tincher, Tod Browning, Max Davidson, Teddy Sampson, Joseph "Baldy" Belmont, Edward Dillon, Miss Ainslee, Charles Rice, Frank Fisher Bennett.
The Deceiver (6/21/1914) A: Anita Loos. C: Fay Tincher, Edward Dillon, Tod Browning, Joseph "Baldy" Belmont.
The White Slave Catchers (6/28/1914) A: Anita Loos. C: Fay Tincher, Edward Dillon, Tod Browning, Joseph "Baldy" Belmont, Frank Fisher Bennett, Tammany Young.
Bill's Job (7/5/1914) Bill the Office Boy series #1. A: Paul West. C: Tammany Young, Fay Tincher, Tod Browning, Andy Rice, Joseph "Baldy" Belmont, Mae Washington, George A. Beranger.
Wrong All Around (7/12/1914) C: Fay Tincher, Tod Browning, Joseph "Baldy" Belmont, Tammany Young, Mrs. Arthur Mackley, Mrs. W.H. Brown.

How Bill Squared It with his Boss (7/19/1914) Bill the Office Boy series #2. A: Paul West. C: Tammany Young, Fay Tincher, Tod Browning, Joseph "Baldy" Belmont, Mrs. Arthur Mackley, Mrs. W.H. Brown, Miss Carson, Miss Crawford.

Leave it to Smiley* (7/26/1914) A: Marc Edmond Jones. C:Fay Tincher, Tod browning, Joseph "Baldy" Belmont, Tammany Young, Max Davidson.

Bill Takes a Lady to Lunch—Never Again (8/2/1914) Bill the Office Boy series #3. A: Paul West. C: Tammany Young, Fay Tincher, Tod Browning, Mae Gaston.

Ethel's Teacher (8/9/1914) A: William J. Woodley. C: Fay Tincher, Joseph "Baldy" Belmont, Edward Dillon, Tod Browning.

Bill Saves the Day (8/16/1914) Bill the Office Boy series #4. A: Paul West. C: Tammany Young, Fay Tincher, Tod Browning, Edward Dillon.

A Physical Culture Romance (8/23/1914) C: Fay Tincher, Tod Browning, Max Stanley, Edward Dillon, Margaret Edwards.

Bill Organizes a Union (8/30/1914)Bill the Office Boy series #5. A: Paul West. C: Tammany Young, Fay Tincher, Tod Browning, "Fatty" Crane, Max Davidson, Joseph "Baldy" Belmont.

The Mascot (9/6/1914) A: Russell E. Smith. C: Fay Tincher, Tod Browning, Max Davidson.

Bill Goes into Business for Himself (9/1914) Bill the Office Boy series #6. A: Paul West. C: Tammany Young, Fay Tincher, Tod Browning, "Fatty" Crane, Paul Willis, Max Davidson. (a.k.a. *In Business for Himself*).

Foiled Again (9/20/1914) A: Russell E. Smith. C: Fay Tincher, Tod Browning, Edward Dillon.

Bill Manages a Fighter* (9/24/1914) Bill the office Boy series #7. A: Paul West. C: Tammany Young, Fay Tincher, Tod Browning, Edward Dillon, Hobo Dougherty, Max Davidson (a.k.a. *Bill Manages a Prizefighter*) (NFA)

The Million Dollar Bride (10/4/1914) A: Anita Loos. C: Fay Tincher, Tod Browning, Edward Dillon, Max Davidson.

Bill Spoils a Vacation (10/11/1914) Bill the Office Boy series #8. A: Paul West. C: Tammany Young, Fay Tincher, Tod Browning, Joseph "Baldy" Belmont, Howard Gage, Max Davidson, Maxfield Stanley.

Dizzy Joe's Career (10/18/1914) A: C. Allan Gilbert. C: Fay Tincher, Tod Browning, Edward Dillon, Joseph "Baldy" Belmont, Maxfield Stanley, Max Davidson.

Bill Joins the W.W.W.'s* (10/25/1914) Bill the Office Boy series #9. A: Paul West. C: Tammany Young, Fay Tincher, Tod Browning, Max Davidson, Mae Gaston, Edward Dillon. (LOC, AFA)

Casey's Vendetta* (11/1/1914) C: Fay Tincher, Edward Dillon, Tod Browning, Max Davidson, Sylvia Ashton. (CAN, LOC)

Ethel's Roof Party* (11/8/1914) Bill the Office Boy series #10. A: Paul West. C: Fay Tincher, Tammany Young, Joseph "Baldy" Belmont, Anna May Walthall, Mae Gaston, Maxfield Stanley, Max Davidson, Bobby Feuher (a.k.a. Bobby Ray).

Out Again—In Again (11/15/1914) C: Fay Tincher, Tod Browning, Tammany Young, Joseph "Baldy" Belmont, Max Davidson.

Ethel Has a Steady (11/22/1914) Bill the Office Boy series #11. A: Paul West. C: Fay Tincher,Tammany Young, Tod Browning, Anna May Walthall, Edward Dillon, Mae Gaston, Lucille Brown, Max Davidson, Walter Long.

A Corner in Hats (11/29/1914) A: Anita Loos. C: Fay Tincher, Tod Browning, Joseph "Baldy" Belmont, Sylvia Ashton, Tammany Young.

Mr. Hadley's Uncle (12/6/1914) Bill the Office Boy series #12. A: Paul West. C: Fay Tincher,

The Housebreakers* (12/13/1914) C: Fay Tincher, Edward Dillon, Max Davidson, Sylvia Ashton, Ed Rice. (CAN, LOC, both prints are incomplete)

Bill and Ethel at the Ball (12/20/1914) Bill the Office Boy series #13. A: Paul West. C: Fay Tincher.

The Record Breaker (12/27/1914) C: Fay Tincher, Edward Dillon, Tod Browning, Max Davidson.

Ethel Gets the Evidence (1/3/1915) Bill the Office Boy series #14. A: Paul West. C: Fay Tincher. (a.k.a. *Ethel's First Case*)

Love and Business (1/10/1915) C: Fay Tincher.

A Flyer in Spring Water (1/17/1915) Bill the Office Boy series #15. A: Paul West. C: Fay Tincher, Tod browning, Bobby Feuher, Sylvia Ashton, Max Davidson.

A Flurry in Art (1/24/1915) C: Fay Tincher.

Cupid and the Pest (1/31/1915) C: Fay Tincher, Tod Browning, Anna May Walthall, Billie West.

Bill Turns Valet (2/7/1915) Bill the Office Boy series #16. C: Fay Tincher, Tod Browning, Max Davidson, Bobby Feuher, Edward Dillon.

Music Hath Charms* (2/14/1915) 2rls. C: Fay Tincher, Augustus Carney, Tod Browning, Max Davidson, Joseph "Baldy" Belmont, Eleanor Washington. (LOC)

Ethel Gets Consent (2/21/1915) Bill the Office Boy series #17. A: Paul West. C: Fay Tincher. (a.k.a. *Ethel Gains Consent*)

A Costly Exchange (2/28/1915) A: Eugene Spofford. C: Fay Tincher, Chet Withey, Edward Dillon, Eleanor Washington, Max Davidson.

Bill Gives a Smoker (3/7/1915) Bill the Office Boy series #18. A: Paul West. C: Fay Tincher, Bobby Feuher, Edward Dillon, Max Davidson, Chester Withey.

Caught By A Handle* (3/14/1915) A: Chester Withey. C: Fay Tincher, Eleanor Washington, Max Davidson, Chester Withey. (LOC)

Ethel's Doggone Luck (3/21/1915) Bill the Office Boy series #19. A: Paul West. C: Fay Tincher, Bobby Feuher, Chester Withey, Edward Dillon, Max Davidson.

Mixed Values (3/28/1915) A: Anita Loos. C: Fay Tincher, Elmer Booth, Chester Withey.

Ethel's Deadly Alarm Clock (4/4/1915) Bill the Office Boy series #20. A: Paul West. C: Fay Tincher, Elmer Booth.

By Fair Means or Fowl (4/11/1915) C: Fay Tincher, Elmer Booth.

Ethel's New Dress (4/18/1915) Bill the Office Boy series #21. A: Paul West. C: Fay Tincher, Bobby Feuher, Chester Withey, Gladys Brockwell, Max Davidson.

Home Again (4/2/5/1915) C: Fay Tincher, Elmer Booth, Anna May Walthall, Max Davidson.

Ethel's Disguise (5/2/1915) Bill the Office Boy series #22. A: Paul West. C: Fay Tincher, Elmer Booth, Bobby Feuher.

Ethel's Romance (5/16/1915) Bill the Office Boy series #23. A: Paul West. C: Fay Tincher, Elmer Booth.

Gasoline Gus (5/30/1915) C: Fay Tincher, Elmer Booth, Chester Withey, Max Davidson, Frank Darien.

Brave and Bold (6/6/1915) A: Chester Withey. C: Fay Tincher, Edward Dillon, Chester Withey, Max Davidson.

Unwinding It (6/13/1915) C: Fay Tincher, Elmer Booth.

Where Breezes Blow (6/20/1915) C: Fay Tincher, Elmer Booth, Chester Withey, Bobby Feuher, Frank Newman, Clarence Barr.

Beautiful Love (6/27/1915) C: Fay Tincher, Elmer Booth, Loyola O'Connor, Max Davidson, Louise Aichel.

Mr. Wallack's Wallet (7/4/1915) C: Fay Tincher, Elmer Booth, Chester Withey, Max Davidson, Clarence Barr.

Beppo the Barber (7/11/1915) A: Chester Withey. C: Fay Tincher, Frank Darien, Elmer Booth, Chester Withey, Max Davidson, Louise Aichel, Edward Dillon.

A Chase by Moonlight (7/18/1915) C: Fay Tincher, Clarence Barr, Elmer Booth, Max Davidson, Louise Aichel.

Safety First (7/25/1915) A: Edward Dillon & Chester Withey. C: Fay Tincher, Frank Darien, Edward Dillon, Chester Withey, Max Davidson, Porter Strong, Bobby Feuher.

The Deacon's Whiskers (8/1/1915) A: Anita Loos. C: Fay Tincher, Max Davidson, Edward Dillon, Chester Withey, Frank Darien.

Father Love (8/8/1915) C: Fay Tincher, Frank Darien, Chester Withey, Olga Grey.

The Fatal Finger Prints (8/15/1915) A: Anita Loos. C: Fay Tincher, Edward Dillon, Max Davidson, Jennie Lee, Eleanor Washington, Frank Darien.

Faithful to the Finish (8/22/1915) A: Edward Dillon. C: Fay Tincher, Edward Dillon, Max Davidson, Chester Withey, Frank Darien, Bobby Feuher.

Shocking Stockings (8/29/1915) C: Fay Tincher, Edward Dillon, Chester Withey, Max Davidson.

Over and Back (9/5/1915) C: Fay Tincher, Frank Darien, Chester Withey, Max Davidson.

Fine Arts Film Company:

Dir: Edward Dillon. Superv: D.W. Griffith. Dist: Triangle Film Corp.

Don Quxiote* (2/27/1916) A: Chester Withey. PH: Alfred Gosden. Based on the novel by Miguel de Cervantes Saavedia. 5 rls. C: DeWolf Hopper, Fay Tincher, Max Davidson, Rhea Mitchell, Chester Withey, Julia Faye, George Walsh, Edward Dillon, Carl Stockdale, William Brown. (FAN)

Sunshine Dad* (4/23/1916) A: Tod Browning, Chester Withey & F.M. Pierson. PH: Alfred Gosdon. 5 rls. C: DeWolf Hopper, Fay Tincher, Chester Withey, Max Davidson, Raymond Wells, Eugene Pallette, Jewel Carmen, William DeWlf Hopper Jr., Leo. (LOC)

Mr. Goode, the Samaritan (5/28/1916) A: Chester Withey. PH: Alfred Gosdon. 5 rls. C: DeWolf Hopper, Fay Tincher, Edward Dillon, Chester Withey, Margaret Marsh, Lillian Langdon, Max Davidson.

The Two O'Clock Train* (5/28/1916) Triangle Komedy. A: Evelyn Kent. 2 rls. C: Fay Tincher, Jack Cosgrove, Edward Dillon, Max Davidson, Frank Bennett. (LOC as *Unidentified United Pictures Film*)
Love's Getaway (6/11/1916) Triangle Komedy. 2 rls. C: Fay Tincher, Harry Fisher, Kate Toncray, Max Davidson, Fred Warren.
Bedelia's Bluff (6/18/1916) Triangle Komedy. 2 rls. C: Fay Tincher, Max Davidson, Edward Dillon.
Laundry Liz (7/9/1916) Triangle Komedy. A: Anita Loos. 2 rls. C: Fay Tincher.
Skirts (7/30/1916) Triangle Komedy. 2 rls. C: Fay Tincher, Tully Marshall.
The French Milliner (8/27/1916) Triangle Komedy. A: Anita Loos. 2 rls. C: Fay Tincher, Kate Toncray, Max Davidson. (WT's: *Mille O'Brien* and *The Parisian Milliner*)
A Calico Vampire (9/24/1916) Triangle Komedy. A: Anita Loos. 2 rls. C: Fay Tincher, Max Davidson, Edward Dillon, Kate Toncray.
The Lady Drummer (10/1/1916) Triangle Komedy. 2 rls. C: Fay Tincher, Edward Dillon, Kate Toncray, Max Davidson.

Fay Tincher Comedy Company:
Prod: World Film Corp. Dir: Al Santell. A.D: Billy Slade. 2 reels.

Main 1-2-3 (5/27/1918) A: Fay Tincher. C: Fay Tincher.
Some Job (6/24/1918) C: Fay Tincher.
Oh, Susie, Behave (7/22/1918) A: Maie B. Havey. C: Fay Tincher.

Universal Features:

The Fire Flingers (3/31/1919) D: Rupert Julian. 7 rls. C: A. E. Warren, Clyde Fillmore, Fred Kelsey, Eva Novak, Fay Tincher, Fritzie Ridgeway, William Lloyd, Will Jeffries.

Christie Comedy Specials:
Prod: Al Christie. 2 reels.

Sally's Blighted Career (4/28/1919) D: Al Christie. A: W. Scott Darling. ST: Walter Graham. C: Fay Tincher, Harry Depp, Molly Malone, Patricia Palmer, Helen Darling, Marjorie Payne, Roscoe Karns, George B. French.

Rowdy Ann* (5/25/1919) D: Al Christie. C: Fay Tincher, Eddie Barry, Harry Depp, Al Haynes, Katherine Lewis, Margaret Gibson, Patricia Palmer, Earle Rodney, George B, French, Edgar Blue. (MoMA, LOC, CDF, AFA)

Mary Moves In (6/1919) D: Al Christie. A: W. Scott Darling. C: Fay Tincher, Eddie Barry, Harry Ham, Patricia Palmer, Katherine Lewis, George B. French, Al Haynes, Edith Clark, Ward Caulfield.

Dangerous Nan McGrew (8/1919) D: Scott Sidney. A: W. Scott Darling. C: Fay Tincher, Eddie Barry, Earl Rodney, Tom Ricketts, Jack Henderson, George George, Robert Kortman.

Wild and Western* (10/ 1919) C: Fay Tincher, Earl Rodney, Neal Burns, Eddie Barry, Gene Correy (a.k.a. Gino Corrado), Al Haynes.

Go West Young Woman (12/1919) D: Al Christie & Scott Sidney. C: Fay Tincher, Neal Burns, Helen Darling, Earle Rodney, Gene Correy (a.k.a. Gino Corrado), Ward Caulfield.

A Seaside Siren (7/1920) D: William Beaudine. PH: Edward Ullman. Dist: Educational Pictures. C: Fay Tincher, Earl Rodney, Jimmie Harrison, Virginia Ware, Eddie Baker.

Striking Models (9/19/1920) D: Reggie Morris. Dist: Educational Pictures. C: Fay Tincher.

Dining Room, Kitchen and Sink (12/26/1920) D: Scott Sidney. Dist: Educational Pictures. C: Fay Tincher, Eddie Barry, Phoebe Bassor, Francis Feeney, Andrew Arbuckle, Marion Mackay.

Universal Leather Pushers Series:

Prod: Universal. D; Edward Laemmle. 2 reels.

That Kid from Madrid (1/3/1914) Leather Pusher series #19. C: Billy Sullivan, Fay Tincher.

A Tough Tenderfoot (2/11/1924) Leather Pushers series #22. C: Billy Sullivan, Fay Tincher.

Swing Bad the Sailor (2/25/1924) Leather Pushers series #23. C; Billy Sullivan, Fay Tincher

Universal Feature:

Excitement (4/13/1924) Prod: Universal. D: Robert F. Hill. A: Hugh Hoffman. ST: Crosby George. 5 rls. C: Laura La Plante, Edward Hearn, William Welsh, Frances Raymond, Fred De Silva, Margaret Cullington, Albert Hart, Rolfe Sedan, Bert Roach, Fay Tincher, Stanley Blystone, Lon Poff, George Fischer.

The Gumps Comedies:

Prod: Samuel Van Ronkel. Dist: Universal. Based the comic strip by Sidney Smith. 2 reels.

Uncle Bim's Gift* (9/17/1923) Gumps first series #1. D: Norman Taurog. C: Joe Murphy, Fay Tincher, Jackie Morgan, Mark ("Slim") Hamilton. (GEH)

Watch Papa (10/15/1923) Gumps first series #2. D: Norman Taurog. C: Joe Murphy, Fay Tincher, Jackie Morgan.

Oh! What a Day (11/12/1923) Gumps first series #3. D: Norman Taurog. C: Joe Murphy, Fay Tincher, Jackie Morgan.

Aggravatin' Mama (12/17/1923) Gumps first series #4. D: Norman Taurog. C: Joe Murphy, Fay Tincher, Jackie Morgan.

Oh! Min! (1/24/1924) Gumps first series #5. D: Norman Taurog. C: Joe Murphy, Fay Tincher, Jackie Morgan.

What's the Use? (5/5/1924) Gumps first series #6. D: Erle C. Kenton. C: Joe Murphy, Fay Tincher, Jackie Morgan.

Andy's Temptation (6/2/1914) Gumps first series #7. D: Erle C. Kenton. C: Joe Murphy, Fay Tincher, Jackie Morgan.

A Day of Rest (7/7/1924) Gumps first series #8. D: Erle C. Kenton. C: Joe Murphy, Fay Tincher, Jackie Morgan.

Westbound (8/14/1924) Gumos first series #9. D: Erle C. Kenton. C: Joc Murphy, Fay Tincher, Jackie Morgan.

Andy's Hat in the Ring* (10/6/1924) Gumps first series #10. D: Norman Taurog. C: Joe Murphy, Fay Tincher, Jackie Morgan, James T. Kelly. (a.k.a. Andy Throws his Hat in the Ring) (MoMA)

Andy's Stump Speech* (11/3/1924) Gumps first series #11. D: Norman Taurog. C: Joe Murphy, Fay Tincher, Jackie Morgan, James T. Kelly, Charles King, Robert McKenzie, Martin Kinney. (UCLA)

Andy in Hollywood (5/12/1925) Gumps First series #12. D: Norman Taurog. C: Joe Murphy, Fay Tincher, Jackie Morgan.

Andy's Lion Tale* (10/16/1925) Gumps second series #1. D: Francis Corby. C: Joe Murphy, Fay Tincher, Jackie Morgan. (LOC, MoMA)

Chester's Donkey Party (11/2/1925) Gumps second series #2. D: Francis Corby. C: Joe Murphy, Fay Tincher, Jackie Morgan.

Dynamited (11/16/1925) Gumps second series #3. D: Francis Corby. C: Joe Murphy, Fay Tincher, Jackie Morgan.

Andy Takes a Flyer* (12/7/1925) Gumps second series #4. D: Raymond Gray. C: Slim Summerville, Fay Tincher, Jackie Morgan. (Slim Summerville is said to have replaced Joe Murphy in this short and may have played Andy in a few of the previous entires which are not available. Murphy is definitely back in the following short *The Smash Up*)

The Smash Up* (12/21/1925) Gumps second series #5. D: David Kirkland & Craig Hutchinson. C: Joe Murphy, Fay Tincher, Jackie Morgan, Dick Sutherland.

Min Walks in her Sleep* (1/18/1926) Gumps second series #6. D: Del Andrews (records say Francis Corby, but print screened with original titles said Andrews). PH: Jerry Ash. C: Joe Murphy, Fay Tincher, Jackie Morgan, Jack Gavin.

California Here We Come (2/6/1926) Gumps second series #7. D: Wesley Ruggles. C: Joe Murphy, Fay Tincher, Jackie Morgan.

Shady Rest* (2/15/1926) Gumps second series #8. D: Norman Dawn. PH: Jerry Ash. C: Joe Murphy, Fay Tincher, Jackie Morgan, Louise Carver, Robert McKenzie (in three roles), Tommy Hicks.

Min's Home on the Cliff (2/20/1926) Gumps second series #9. D: Francis Corby. C: Joe Murphy, Fay Tincher, Jackie Morgan.

Min's Away (3/1/1926) Gumps second series #10. D: Norman Dawn. C: Joe Murphy, Fay Tincher, Jackie Morgan.

Dumb Luck (3/15/1926) Gumps second series #11. D: Del Andrews. C: Joe Murphy, Fay Tincher, Jackie Morgan.

Tow Service (4/12/1926) Gumps second series #12. D: Hugh Fay. C: Joe Murphy, Fay Tincher, Jackie Morgan.

Never Again (10/18/1926) Gumps third series #1. D: Francis Corby. C: Joe Murphy, Fay Tincher.

Lots of Grief (11/1/1926) Gumps third series #2. D: Francis Corby. C: Joe Murphy, Fay Tincher.

Better Luck (11/15/1926) Gumps third series #3. D: Francis Corby. C: Joe Murphy, Fay Tincher, Jackie Morgan.

The Big Surprise (11/28/1926) Gumps third series #4. D: Francis Corby. C: Joe Murphy, Fay Tincher, Jackie Morgan.

A Close Call (12/13/1926) Gumps third series #5. D: Francis Corby. C: Joe Murphy, Fay Tincher, Jackie Morgan.

I Told You So (12/29/1926) Gumps third series #6. D: Francis Corby. C: Joe Murphy, Fay Tincher, Jackie Morgan.

Rooms for Rent (1/10/1927) Gumps third series #7. D: Erle C. Kenton. C: Joe Murphy, Fay Tincher, Billie Butts.

Up Against It (1/25/1927) Gumps third series #8. D: Francis Corby. C: Joe Murphy, Fay Tincher, Billie Butts.

Youth and Beauty (2/7/1927) Gumps third series #9. D: Erle C. Kenton. C: Joe Murphy, Fay Tincher, Billie Butts.

Broke Again (2/21/1927) Gumps third series #10. D: Erle C. Kenton. C: Joe Murphy, Fay Tincher, Billie Butts.

I'm the Sheriff* (3/7/1927) Gumps third series #11. D: Erle C. Kenton. C: Joe Murphy, Fay Tincher, Billie Butts, Bud Jamison.

Circus Daze (3/20/1927) Gumps third series #12. D: Erle C. Kenton. C: Joe Murphy, Fay Tincher, Billie Butts.

Too Much Sleep (9/17/1927) Gumps Fourth series #1. D: Francis Corby. C: Joe Murphy, Fay Tincher, Billie Butts. (Originally reviewed under the title All Wet, and shouldn't be confused with the 6/8/1930 Sid Saylor comedy).

A Battle Scared Hero (10/3/1927) Gumps fourth series #2. D: Francis Corby. C: Joe Murphy, Fay Tincher, Billie Butts.

When Greek Meets Greek (10/17/1927) Gumps fourth series #3. D; Francis Corby. C: Joe Murphy, Fay Tincher, Billie Butts.

And How! (10/31/1927) Gumps fourth series #4. D: Francis Corby. C: Joe Murphy, Fay Tincher, Billie Butts.

Ocean Bruises (11/14/1927) Gumps fourth series #5. D: Francis Corby. C: Joe Murphy, Fay Tincher, Billie Butts.

A Total Loss (11/28/1927) Gumps fourth series #6. D: Francis Corby. C: Joe Murphy, Fay Tincher, Billie Butts.

Andy Nose his Onions (12/12/1927) Gumps fourth series #7. D: Robert Kerr. C; Joe Murphy, Fay Tincher, Billie Butts.

The Mild West (12/26/1927) Gumps fourth series #8. D: Robert Kerr. C: Joe Murphy, Fay Tincher, Billie Butts.

A Case of Scotch (1/9/1928) Gumps fourth series #9. D: Francis Corby. C: Joe Murphy, Fay Tincher, Billie Butts.

Any Old Count (1/21/1928) Gumps fourth series #10. D: Francis Corby. C: Joe Murphy, Fay Tincher, Billie Butts.

The Cloud Buster (2/6/1928) Gumps fourth series #11. D: Vin Moore. C: Joe Murphy, Fay Tincher, Billie Butts.

Out in the Rain (2/20/1928) Gumps fourth series #12. D: Francis Corby. C: Joe Murphy, Fay Tincher, Billie Butts.

Al St John Silent Solo Comedies

Triangle/Keystone:

Prod: Keystone Film Corp. Dist: Triangle. 2 reels

The Moonshiners* (5/14/1916) Prod: Keystone. Dist: Triangle. Dir: Roscoe Arbuckle. 2 rls. C: Al St John, Alice Lake, Joe Bordeaux, Horace J. Haines, Mike Egan, Bert Frank. (fragment at LOC)

Triangle Films:

Prod & Dist: Triangle Film Corp. Dir: Ferris Hartman. Ph: Elgin Lessley. AD: Bert Gorman. 1 reel.

Grab Bag Bride* (1/28/1917) C: Al St John, Alice Lake, Mae Welles, Frank Hayes, Wayland Trask, Grover Ligon, Billy Gilbert. (LOC)

Her Cave Man (3/4/1917) C: Al St John, Mary Thurman, Wayland Trask, Ruth Churchill, Mae Welles.

A Self Made Hero* (3/11/1917) C: Al St John, Vera Reynolds, Nick Cogley, Mae Welles, Charles Force. (GEH)

A Winning Loser (3/18/1917) C: Al St John, Rose Pomeroy, Vera Reynolds, Al McKinnon, Mae Welles, Francis Parker.

Warner Brothers:

Prod: Warner Brothers. 2 reels.

Speed (12/4/1919) Dist: Paramount. C: Al St John, Ingram Pickett, Steve Murphy.

Cleaning Up (3/1920) Dist: Paramount. Dir: Al St John. C: Al St John, Iva Brown.

Ship Ahoy* (1920) Dist: Paramount. Dir & Writ: Al St John. Asst. Dir: Frank Griffin. C: Al St John, Iva Brown, Ingram Pickett. (Re-released as *Fired Again*) (LOC)

The Aero-Nut* (1920) Dir: Frank Griffin. 2 rls. C: Al St John. (Surviving fragment included in Robert Youngson's 1961 compilation feature *Days of Thrills and Laughter*)

Glass slide for Al St John's *The Hayseed* (1921). Photo Courtesy of Louie Despres.

Trouble* (1920) C: Al St John, Cliff Bowes, Joe Murphy (Re-released as *The Paper Hangers*) (LOC, MoMA)
The Window Trimmer* (1920) C: Al St John, Cliff Bowes, William Blaisdell, James Parrott, Ingram Pickett. (EYE)

Fox Sunshine Comedies:
Prod: Fox Film Corp. 2 reels.

The Slicker (1/1921) Dir: Al St John. C: Al St John.
The Simp (3/1921) Dir: Ferris Hartman. C: Al St John, Otto Fries.
The Big Secret (4/1921) Dir: Ferris Hartman. C; Al St John.
The Hayseed (6/1921) Dir: Ferris Hartman. C: Al St John, Alice Davenport.
Three Good Pals (6/1921) Dir: Nate Watt. C; Al St John.
Ain't Love Grand? (8/14/1921) Dir: Al St John. C; Al St John.

Al St John Fox Series:
Prod: Fox Film Corp. 2 reels.

Small Town Stuff (9/1921) Dir: Al St John. C: Al St John.
Fast and Furious (10/1921) Dir: Gilbert Pratt. C: Al St John.
The Happy Pest (11/1921) Dir: Ferris Hartman. C: Al St John, Gus Pixley, Frank Hayes, Art Rowlands.
Fool Days (12/1921) Dir: Gilbert Pratt. C: Al St John, Hilliard Karr, Ford West, Alice Davenport.
Straight from the Farm (2/1922) Dir: Gilbert Pratt. C: Al St John.
The Studio Rube* (3/19/1922) Dir: Gilbert Pratt. C: Al St John, Billy Engle, Marvin Lobach. (MoMA)
Special Delivery* (4/30/1922) Dir: Al St John. C: Al St John, Vernon Dent, Billy Engle, Tiny Ward. (MoMA)
The Village Sheik (6/4/1922) Dir: Al St John. C: Al St John.
All Wet* (9/3/1922) Dir: Al St John. C: Al St John, Otto Fries, Si Jenks, Ford West, Tiny Ward. (MoMA)
The City Chap (10/15/1922) Dir: Al St John. C: Al St John.
Out of Place* (11/19/1922) Dir: Al St John. C: Al St John, Hilliard Karr, James Donnelly, Ford West, Si Jenks, Billy Engle, Tiny Ward. (EYE, LOC)
The Alarm (12/17/1922) Dir: Al St John. C: Al St John.
Young and Dumb (1/28/1923) Dir: Al St John. C: Al St John.
The Salesman (3/11/1923) Dir: Al St John. C: Al St John.
The Author (4/29/1923) Dir: Al St John. C: Al St John, Johnny Sinclair.
Tropical Romeo (7/17/1923) Dir: Al St John. C: Al St John.
Full Speed Ahead (9/30/1923) Dir: Al St John & Benjamin Stoloff. C: Al St John.
Slow and Sure (11/18/1923) Dir: Al St John & Benjamin Stoloff. C: Al St John.
Highly Recommended (1/6/1924) Dir: Al St John & Benjamin Stoloff. C: Al St John.
Be Yourself (2/10/1924) Dir: Al St John & Benjamin Stoloff. C: Al St John.
His Bitter Half (6/15/1924) Dir: Ralph Ince. Writ: Al St John. C: Al St John.
Dumb and Daffy (7/1924) Dir: Ralph Ince. C: Al St John.
Spring Fever (1924) C: Al St John, Jean Arthur.

Tuxedo Comedies:
Prod: Reel Comedies, Inc. Dist: Educational Pictures. 2 reels.

His First Car* (7/27/1924) Dir& Writ: Al St John (uncredited Roscoe Arbuckle). C: Al St John, Doris Deane, Blanche Payson, George Davis, Leon Holmes, Donald Hughes (LOB)
Never Again* (8/24/1924) Dir & Writ: Al St John (uncredited Roscoe Arbuckle). C: Al St John, Doris Deane, Blanche Payson, George Davis, Johnny Sinclair. (LOB)
Stupid But Brave* (10/26/1924) Dir & Writ: Al St John (uncredited Roscoe Arbuckle). C: Al St John, Doris Deane, George Davis, Eugene Pallette, Johnny Sinclair, Ruth Holly (Christine Francis), "Kewpie" Morgan, Steve Murphy.
Lovemania* (12/28/1924) Dir & Writ: Al St John (uncredited Roscoe Arbuckle). C: Al St John, Doris Deane, George Davis, Johnny Sinclair, Joan Hoff. (RFA)
Dynamite Doggie* (3/22/1925) Dir: Grover Jones (uncredited Roscoe Arbuckle). C: Al St John, Ruth Holly (Christine Francis), George Davis, Pete the pup, Johnny Sinclair, Walter C. Reed, Glen Cavender. (EYE, LOB)
The Iron Mule* (4/12/1925) Dir: Grover Jones (uncredited Roscoe Arbuckle). C: Al St John, Doris Deane, George Davis, Glen Cavender, Billy Franey, Walter C. Reed, Florence Reed, Lotus Thompson, Johnny Sinclair, Buster Keaton.
Curses* (5/17/1925) Dir: Grover Jones (uncredited Roscoe Arbuckle). C: Al St John, Bartine Burkett, Walter C. Reed, Johnny Sinclair.

Biff Thrill Comedies:
Prod & Dist: Samuel Bischoff, Inc. 2 reels.

The Live Agent* (8/10/1925) Dir: Grover Jones. C: Al St John, Bartine Burkett, Johnny Sinclair. (EYE)
Service (12/10/1925) Dir: Al St John. C: Al St John, Johnny Sinclair.
Rain and Shines (1/1926) Dir: Al St John. C: Al St John, Johnny Sinclair.
His Taking Ways* (2/2/1926) Prod: Trem Carr. Dir: Al St John. C: Al St John, Charles King, Lucille Hutton, John Rand, Johnny Sinclair. (LOC)

Hal Roach Comedies:
Prod: Hal Roach. Dist: Pathe. 2 reels.

A Punch in the Nose (1/3/1926) Dir: Jay A. Howe. C: Al St John, Lucien Littlefield, Jackie "Husky" Haines, Jimmy Finlayson, Lige Conley, Kewpie Morgan, Dot Farley, Martha Sleeper, Al Hallett, Marjorie Whiteis, Janet Gaynor.

Jack White Comedies:
Prod: Jack White. Dist: Educational Pictures. 2 reels.

Red Pepper* (4/5/1925) Dir: Arvid E. Gillstrom. C: Al St John, Judy King, Babe London, John Rand, Philip Sleeman. (MoMA)

Fares Please (5/16/1925) Dir: Stephen Roberts. C: Al St John, Ruth Hiatt, Babe London, Otto Fries, Spencer Bell, Jack Lloyd.

Fair Warning* (8/27/1925) Dir: Stephen Roberts. C: Al St John, Virginia Vance, Otto Fries, Phil Dunham, Bert Young. (MoMA)

Fire Away* (11/8/1925) Dir: Stephen Roberts. C: Al St John, Lucille Hutton, James T. Kelly, Glen Cavender.

Live Cowards* (1/10/1926) Dir: Stephen Roberts. C: Al St John, Virginia Vance, Otto Fries, Eva Thatcher, Phil Dunham, Jack Lloyd, Babe London. (EYE)

Hold Your Hat (2/14/1926) Dir: Stephen Roberts. C: Al St John, Virginia Vance, Otto Fries, Eva Thatcher.

Sky Bound (3/28/1926) Dir: Stephen Roberts. C: Al St John, Zelma O'Neal, Otto Fries, Phil Dunham.

Who Hit Me* (7/11/1926) Dir: Stephen Roberts. C: Al St John, Zelma O'Neal, Otto Fries, Phil Dunham, Bobby Burns. (MoMA)

Pink Elephants* (10/2/1926) Dir: Stephen Roberts. C: Al St John, Lucille Hutton, Phil Dunham, Clem Beauchamp, Robert Graves, Spencer Bell. (LOB, UCLA)

Flaming Romance* (11/31/1926) Dir: Stephen Roberts. C: Al St John, Aileen Lopez, Otto fries, Jack Lloyd, Clem Beauchamp, Philip Sleeman, Bert Young. (LOC)

High Sea Blues* (1/2/1927) Dir: Stephen Roberts. C: Al St John, Lucille Hutton, Estelle Bradley, Phil Dunham, Clem Beauchamp, Eva Thatcher, Wallace Lupino, Al Thompson. (LOC)

Listen Lena* (2/13/1927) Dir: Stephen Roberts. C: Al St John, Lucille Hutton, Clem Beauchamp, Jack Lloyd, Glen Cavender.

Roped In (3/20/1927) Dir: Charles Lamont. C: Al St John, Lucille Hutton, Bull Montana, Robert Graves.

Jungle Heat* (4/24/1927) Dir: Stephen Roberts. C: Al St John, Lucille Hutton, Clem Beauchamp, Jack Lloyd, Glen Cavender, Phil Dunham.

No Cheating (6/26/1927) Dir: Stephen Roberts. C: Al St John, Lucille Hutton, Jack Lloyd, Blanche Payson, Phil Dunham, Clem Beauchamp.

High Spots* (7/31/1927) Dir: Stephen Roberts. C: Al St John, Estelle Bradley, Clem Beauchamp, Jack Lloyd, Glen Cavender, Michael Mann, Josephine, Elfie Fay. (LOC)

Racing Mad (1/8/1928) Dir: Stephen Roberts. C: Al St John, Estelle Bradley, Phil Dunham, Spencer Bell, Glen Cavender.

Call Your Shots (9/15/1928) Dir: Stephen Roberts. C: Al St John, Estelle Bradley, Otto Fries, Eva Thatcher, Glen Cavender.

Hot or Cold* (12/2/1928) Dir: Stephen Roberts. C: Al St John, Estelle Bradley, Harold Goodwin, Al Thompson, Eva Thatcher, Robert Graves.

Smart Steppers (3/3/1929) Dir: Stephen Roberts. C: Al St John, Adrianne Dore, Harold Goodwin, Al Thompson, Glen Cavender.

Hot Times (5/26/1929) Dir: Stephen Roberts. C: Al St John, Estelle Bradley, Harold Goodwin, Al Thompson.

MARIE DRESSLER FILMOGRAPHY

Actors' Fund Field Day* (1910) Prod: Vitagraph. Shot at the New York Polo Grounds on 10/19/1910. Cast: Harry Watson Jr., George Bickel, Bert Williams, Billie Reeves, Annie Oakley (Although Dressler is listed in this film she wasn't visible in the print available at LOC).

Tillie's Punctured Romance* (12/21/1914) Prod: Keystone. Dir: Mack Sennett. Dist: Alco Film Corp. Based on the musical play Tillie's Nightmare, book by Edgar Sloane and lyrics by A. Baldwin Sloane. 6 rls. Cast: Marie Dressler, Charlie Chaplin, Mabel Normand, Charles Bennett, Mack Swain, Harry McCoy, Chester Conklin, Glen Cavender, Nick Cogley, Charles Parrott, Edgar Kennedy,

Alice Howell, Dick Smith, Phyllis Allen, Minta Durfee, Charlie Murray, Billy Hauber, May Wells, Alice Davenport. (LOC, MoMA, BFI, UCLA).

Tillie's Tomato Surprise* (9/27/1915) Prod: Lubin Mfg. Co. Dir: Howell Hansel. Sc: Acton Davis. Asst Dir: Albert F. Mayo. 6rls. Cast: Marie Dressler, Colin Campbell, Eleanor Fairbanks, Sarah McVicker, Clara Lambert, Tom McNaughton, Jim the monkey. (LOC has a short fragment).

Tillie Wakes Up* (1/29/1917) Prod: World Film Corp./Peerless. Pres: William A. Brady. Dir: Harry Davenport. St: Mark Swan. Sc: Frances Marion. Ph: Edward Horn. 5 rls. Cast: Marie Dressler, Johnny Hines, Ruby de Remer, Frank Beamish, Ruth Barrett, Jack Brown. (ACAD, MoMA, UCLA).

The Scrub Lady* (9/1917) Prod: Dressler Producing Corp. Dist: Goldwyn Pictures. Dir & Sc: Vincent Bryan. Ph: Duke Zalibra. 2rls. Cast: Marie Dressler, Florence Hamilton, Raymonde Cacho, Fred Hallen, Harriet Ross (LOC has 2nd reel only. Em Gee Film Library also circulated a chunk as *The Love Riot*)

Fired (6/10/1918) Prod: Dressler Producing Corp. Dist: Goldwyn/World Film Corp. Dir & Sc: Marie Dressler. 2rls. Cast: Marie Dressler, William McCall, John Rand, James T. Kelly.

The Agonies of Agnes (7/8/1918) Prod: Dressler Producing Corp. Dist: World Film Corp. Sc: Marie Dressler. 2rls. Cast: Marie Dressler.

The Cross Red Nurse (1918) Prod: Dressler Producing Corp. Dist: World Film Corp. 2 rls. Cast: Marie Dressler.

The Callahans and the Murphys* (6/18/1927) Prod: MGM. Dir: George Hill. Sc: Frances Marion. Titles: Ralph Spence. Based on the book by Kathleen Norris. Ph: Ira Morgan. Art Dir: Cedric Gibbons & David Townsend. Ed: Hugh Wynn. 7rls. Cast: Marie Dressler, Polly Moran, Eddie Gribbon, Sally O'Neil, Lawrence Gray, Frank Currier, Gertrude Olmstead, Turner Savage, Jackie Coombs, Dawn O'Day, Monty O'Grady, Tom Lewis (LOC has a ten minute fragment).

The Joy Girl* (9/3/1927) Prod: Fox Film Corp. Dir: Allan Dwan. Sc: Frances Agnew. Titles: Malcolm Stuart Boylan. Adapt: Adele Camondini. Based on the story by May Edginton. Ph: George Webber & William Miller. Asst Dir: Clarence Elmer & Edmund Grainger. 6rls. Cast: Olive Borden, Neil Hamilton, Marie Dressler, Mary Alden, William Norris, Helen Chandler, Jery Miley, Frank Walsh, Clarence J. Elmer, Peggy Kelly, Jimmy Grainger Jr. (MoMA).

Polly Moran doesn't care for Marie's cooking in *The Callahans and the Murphys* (1927). Photo courtesy of Sam Gill.

Breakfast at Sunrise* (10/23/1927) Prod: First National Pictures. Pres: Joseph M. Schenck. Dir: Mal St Clair. Adapt: Gladys Unger. Sc: Fred De Gresac. Based on Le Dejeuner au soleil by Andre Birabeau. Ph: Robert B. Kurrle. 7rls. Cast: Constance Talmadge, Bryant Washburn, Alice White, Paulette Duval, Marie Dressler, Albert Gran, Burr McIntosh, David Mir, Don Alvarado, Nellie Bly Baker, Dot Farley, Bynunski Hymen, Max Asher, Joseph "Baldy" Belmont, Laurence Lacalvi (GEH, LOC).

Bringing Up Father* (3/17/1928) Prod: MGM. Dir: Jack Conway. Sc: Frances Marion. Titles: Ralph Spence. St: George McManus, based on his comic strip. Ph: William Daniels. Art Dir: Cedric Gibbons & Merrill Pye. Ed: Margaret Booth. 7rls. Cast: J. Farrell MacDonald, Polly Moran, Jules Cowles, Marie Dressler, Gertrude Olmstead, Grant Withers, Andre de Seurola, Rose Dione, David Mir, Tenen Holtz, Toto (GEH).

The Patsy* (3/10/1928) Prod: MGM. Dir: King Vidor. Sc: Agnes Christine Johnston. Titles: Ralp Spence. Based on the play by Barry

Connors. Ph: John Seitz. Art Dir: Cedric Gibbons. Ed: Hugh Wynn 8rls. Cast: Marion Davies, Orville Caldwell, Marie Dressler, Del Henderson, Lawrence Gray, Jane Winton (GEH, LOC, UCLA).

The Divine Lady* (3/31/1929) Prod: First National Pictures. Dir: Frank Lloyd. Cont: Agnes Christine Johnston. Titles: Harry Carr & Edwin Justus Mayer. Adapt: Forrest Halsey. Based on the book by E. Barrington. Ph: John Seitz. Art Dir: Horace Jackson. Ed: Hugh Bennett. Singing sequences by Vitaphone. Song: Lady Divine by Joseph Pasternac and Richard Kountz. 12rls. Cast: Corinne Griffith, Victor Varconi, H.B. Warner, Ian Keith, William Conklin, Marie Dressler, Michael Varitch, Evelyn Hall, Montague Love, Helen Jerome Eddy, Dorothy Cumming.

Hollywood Revue of 1929* (6/20/1929) Prod: MGM. Dir: Charles F. Reisner. Dial: Al Boasberg & Robert E. Hopkins. Skits: Joe Farnham. Ph: John Arnold, Irving Reis, Maximilian Fabian & John M. Nickolaus. Art Dir: Cedric Gibbons & Richard Day. Ed: William S. Gray & Cameron K. Wood. Songs: Arthur Freed, Nacio Herb Brown, Raymond Klages, Jesse Greer, Andy Rice, Martin Broomes, Joe Trent, Louis Alter, Fred Fisher, Joe Goodwin & Gus Edwards. Music Arr: Arthur Lange, Ernest Klapholtz & Ray Heindorf. Dance: Sammy Lee & George Cunningham. 13rls. Cast: Conrad Nagel, Jack Benny, John Gilbert, Norma Shearer, Joan Crawford, Bessie Love, Lionel Barrymore, Cliff Edwards, Stan Laurel, Oliver Hardy, Marie Dressler, Polly Moran, Buster Keaton, Marion Davies, Anita Page, Nils Asther, The Bronx Sisters, Natachia Natova and Co., Willian Haines, Charles King, Gus Edwards, Karl Dane, George K. Arthur, Ann Dvorak, Gwen Lee, Albertina Rasch Ballet, The Rounders, The Biltmore Quartet.

Dangerous Females* (11/16/1929) A Christie Talking Play. Prod: Al Christie. Dist: Paramount. Dir: William Watson. Sc: Florence Ryerson & Colin Clements. 2rls. Cast: Marie Dressler, Polly Moran, Frank Rice, Arthur Millet, Tom Dempsey.

The Vagabond Lover* (12/1/1929) Prod: RKO. Dir: Marshall Neilan. Ph: Leo Tover. Art Dir: Max Ree. Asst Dir: Wallace Fox. 8rls. Cast: Rudy Vallee, Sally Blaine, Marie Dressler, Charles Sellon, Norman Peck, Danny O'Shea, Eddie Nugent, Nella Walker, Malcolm Waite, Alan Roscoe, The Connecticut Yankees.

Chasing Rainbows* (1/10/1930) Prod: MGM. Dir: Charles F. Reisner. St/Cont: Bess Meredith. Dial: Charles F. Reisner, Robert Hopkins,

Kenyon Nicholson & Al Boasberg. Adapt: Wells Root. Ph: Ira Morgan. Art Dir: Cedric Gibbons. Ed: George Hively. Songs: Milton Ager & Jack Yellen. 11rls. Cast: Bessie Love, Charles King, Jack Benny, George K. Arthur, Polly Moran, Marie Dressler, Gwen Lee, Nita Martan, Eddie Phillips, Youcca Troubetzkoy.

Anna Christie* (3/14/1930) Prod: MGM. Dir: Clarence Brown. Adapt: Frances Marion. Titles: Madeline Ruthren. Based on the play by Eugene O'Neill. Ph: William Daniels. Art Dir: Cedric Gibbons. Ed: Hugh Wynn. Sound: G.A. Burns & Douglas Shearer. Gowns: Adrian. 10rls. Cast: Greta Garbo, Charles Bickford, George F. Marion, Marie Dressler, James T. Mack, Lee Phelps.

The Girl Said No* (4/4/1930) Prod: MGM. Dir: Sam Wood. Adapt: Sarah Y. Mason. St: A.P. Younger. Ph: Ira Morgan. Art Dir: Cedric Gibbons. Ed: Frank Sullivan, Tuman K. Wood & George Boemler. 10rls. Cast: William Haines, Leila Hyams, Polly Moran, Marie Dressler, Francis X. Bushman Jr., Clara Blandick, William Janney, William V. Mong, Junior Coghlan, Phyllis Crane.

One Romantic Night* (5/3/1930) Prod: Joseph M. Schenck. Dist: United Artists. Dir: Paul L. Stein. Adapt-Dial: Melville Baker. Based on The Swan by Freenc Molnar. Ph: Karl Struss. Art Dir: William Cameron Menzies & Park French. Ed: James Smith. Music Arr: Hugo Riesenfeld. Sou: Frank Maher. Asst Dir: Herbert Sutch. 8rls. Cast: Lillian Gish, Rod La Rocque, Conrad Nagel, Marie Dressler, O.P.Heggie, Albert Conti, Edgar Norton, Billie Bennett, Philippe DeLacy, Byron Sage, Barbara Leonard.

Screen Snapshots, Series 9, #14 (4/1930) Prod: Columbia. Dir: Ralph Straub. 1rl. Cast: Eddie Lambert, Calvin Coolidge, Grace Coolidge, Jack L. Warner, Mary Pickford, Dolores Del Rio, Marie Dressler, Ralph Graves, Matt Moore, Ramon Navarro, Dorothy Revier, Lowell Sherman, Eric von Stroheim.

Caught Short* (6/20/1930) Prod: Cosmopolitan Prods. Dist: MGM. Dir: Charles F. Reisner. Cont-Dial: Willard Mack & Robert Hopkins. St: Willard Mack. Ph: Leonard Smith. Art Dir: Cedric Gibbons. Ed: George Hively & Harold Palmer. 8rls. Cast: Marie Dressler, Polly Moran, Anita Page, Charles Morton, Thomas Conlin, Douglas Haig, Nanci Price, Greta Mann, Herbert Prior, T. Roy Barnes, Edward Dillon, Alice Moe, Gwen Lee, Lee Kohlmar, Greta Granstedt.

Let Us Be Gay* (7/11/1930) Prod: MGM. Dir: Robert Z. Leonard. Cont-Dial: Frances Marion. Add Dial: Lucille Newmark. Based on the play by Rachel Crothers. Ph: Norbert Brodin. Art Dir: Cedric Gibbons. Ed: Basil Wrangell. Sou: Karl E. Zint & Douglas Shearer. Gowns: Adrian. 8rls. Cast: Norma Shearer, Rod La Rocque, Marie Dressler, Gilbert Emery, Hedda Hopper, Raymond Hackett, Sally Eilers, Tyrrell Davis, Wilfred Noy, William O'Brien, Sybil Grove.

The Voice of Hollywood #14 (7/1930) Prod: Tiffany. 1rl. Cast: George K. Arthur, Barbara Stanwyck, Frank Fay, Eddie Quillan, Edmund Breese, Marie Dressler, Montague Love, Carmel Myers, James Finlayson, Vera Gordon, Ruth Roalnd, Ben Bard, Eddie Lambert.

Min and Bill* (11/21/1930) Prod: MGM. Dir: George Hill. Sc-Dial: Frances Marion & Marion Jackson. Based on Dark Star by Lorna Moon. Ph: Harold Wenstrom. Art Dir: Cedric Gibbons. Ed: Basil Wrangell. Sou: Douglas Shearer. Ward: Rene Hubert. 7rls. Cast: Marie Dressler, Wallace Beery, Dorothy Jordan, Marjorie Rambeau, Doanld Dillaway, De Witt Jennings, Russell Hopton, Frank McGlynn, Greta Gould.

Reducing* (1/31/1931) Prod: MGM. Dir: Charles F. Reisner. Dial-Cont: Wiilard Mack & Beatrice Banyard. Add Dial: Robert Hopkins & Zelda Sears. Ph: Leonard Smith. Art Dir: Cedric Gibbons. Asst Dir: Sandy Roth. Ed: William LeVanway. Sou: Douglas Shearer. Ward: Rene Hubert. 8rls. Cast: Marie Dressler, Polly Moran, Anita Page, Lucien Littlefield, Sally Eilers, William Collier Jr., William Bakewell, Billy Naylor, Jay Ward, David Morris.

Politics* (7/31/1931) Prod: MGM. Dir: Charles F. Reisner. St: Zelda Sears & Malcolm Stuart Boylan. Adapt: Wells Root. Dial: Robert E. Hopkins. Ph: Clyde De Vinna. Art Dir: Cedric Gibbons. Sou: Douglas Shearer. Asst Dir: Sandy Roth. Ed: William S. Gray. 8rls. Cast: Marie Dressler, Polly Moran, Roscoe Ates, Karen Morely, William Bakewell, John Miljan, Joan Marsh, Tom McGuire, Kane Richmond, Mary Alden, Florence Lee.

The Christmas Party* (12/17/1931) Prod: MGM. Dir: Charles F. Reisner. St: Robert E. Hopkins. 1rl. Cast: Jackie Cooper, Jerry Madden, Norma Shearer, Reginald Denny, Clark Gable, Charlotte Greenwood, Cliff Edwards, Ramon Navarro, Marion Davies, Anita Page, Lionel Barrymore, Marie Dressler, Polly Moran, Wallace Beery, Leila Hyams (Re-released the next year as Jackie Cooper's Chrsitmas Party).

Emma* (1/2/1932) Prod: MGM. Dir: Clarence Brown. St: Frances Marion. Adapt-Dial: Leonard Praskins. Add Dial: Zelda Sears. Ph: Oliver T. Marsh. Art Dir: Cedric Gibbons. Ed: William LeVanway. Sou:

Douglas Shearer. Gowns: Adrian. 8rls. Cast: Marie Dressler, jean Hersholt, Richard Cromwell, Myrna Loy, John Miljan, Purnell B. Pratt, Leila Bennett, Barbara Kent, Kathryn Crawford, George Meeker, Dale Fuller, Wilfred Noy, Andre Cheron, Dorothy Peterson.

Prosperity* (11/1/1932) Prod: MGM. Dir: Sam Wood. Sc: Zelda Sears & Eve Greene. St: Sylvia Thalberg & Frank Butler. Cont: Ralph Spence. Ph: Leonard Smith. Art Dir: Cedric Gibbons. Ed: William LeVanway. Sou: Douglas Shearer. Cast: Marie Dressler, Polly Moran, Anita Page, Norman Foster, John Miljan, Jerry Tucker, Charles Giblyn, Frank Darien, Henry Armetta, John Roche, Edward Brophy, Billy Gilbert (Original version of film was directed by Leo McCarey, but ultimately credited to Sam Wood).

Tugboat Annie* (7/28/1933) Prod: MGM. Dir: Mervyn LeRoy. Adapt: Zelda Sears & Eve Greene. Add Dial: Norman Reilly Raine. Ph: Gregg Toland. Art Dir: Merrill Pye. Ed: Blanche Sewell. Sou: Douglas Shearer. 9rls. Cast: Marie Dressler, Wallace Beery, Robert Young, Maureen O'Sullivan, Willard Robertson, Tammany Young, Frankie Darro, Jack Pennick, Paul Hurst, Willie Fung, Charles Giblyn, Marilyn Harris (Retakes directed by Sam Wood).

Dinner at Eight* (8/23/1933) Prod: MGM. Dir: George Cukor. Sc: Frances Marion & Herman J. Mankiewicz. Add Dial: Doanld Ogden Stewart. Based on the play by George S. Kaufman & Edna Ferber. Ph: Williams Daniels. Art Dir: Hobe Erwin & Fred Hope. Ed: Ben Lewis. Sou: Douglas Shearer. Score: William Axt. Gowns: Adrian. 11rls. Cast: Lionel Barrymore, Billie Burke, John Barrymore, Marie Dressler, Wallace Beery, jean Harlow, Lee Tracey, Edmund Lowe, Madge Evans, Jean Hersholt, Karen Morley, Louise Closser Hale, Grant Mitchell, Phillips Holmes, May Robson, Hilda Vaughn, Elizabeth Patterson.

Christopher Bean* (11/17/1933) Prod: MGM. Dir: Sam Wood. Sc: Sylvia Thalberg & Laurence E. Johnston. Based on the play The Late Christopher Bean by Sidney Howard. Ph: William Daniels. Art Dir: Arnold Gillespie. Ed: Hugh Wynn. Sou: Douglas Shearer. 9rls. Cast: Marie Dressler, Lionel Barrymore, Helen Mack, Beulah Bondi, Jean Hersholt, Russell Hardie, H.B. Warner, Helen Shipman, George Coulouris, Ellen Lowe.

Going Hollywood* (12/22/1933) Prod: Cosmopolitan Productions. Dist: MGM. Dir: Raoul Walsh. Asst Dir: Joe Newman. Sc: Donald Ogden Stewart. St: Frances Marion. Ph: George Folsey. Art Dir:

Merrill Pye. Ed: Frank Sullivan. Gowns: Adrian. Orch Con: Lennie Hayton. Dance Dir: Albertina Rasch. Sou: Douglas Shearer. Songs: nacio Herb Brown & Arthur Freed. 9rls. Cast: Marion Davies, Bing Crosby, Fifi D'Orsay, Stuart Erwin, Ned Sparks, Patsy Kelly, Bobby Watson, Three Radio Rogues, Sam McDaniel, Fred Toones, Sterling Holloway, Mae Clark, Robert Montgomery, Marie Dressler, Hector Sarno, Clara Blandick, The Rangers, The King;s Men.

For Further Research:

Three Dressler shorts, *Tillie's Day Off, Tillie's Divorce Case* and *Elopement*, were announced for release by the Mutual Film Corp. in 1916. The deal with Mutual fell through, so the films were either never actually made or they eventually mutated into *The Scrub Lady*, *Fired*, *The Agonies of Agnes* or *The Cross Red Nurse* and came out through Goldwyn and World.

The March of Time (1930). After *Hollywood Revue of 1929* MGM planned and shot another feature revue which was never released. Some sequences were used in later productions. Marie performed the numbers *Ballet for Marie Dressler*, *That's How It's Done on Stage*, and *Father Mustn't Know I'm Going on the Stage—He Thinks I'm a Shop Lifter*. Other performers included Joe Weber, Lew Fields, Polly Moran, Ramon Navarro, Bing Crosby, William Collier Sr., Fay Templeton, Louis Mann, DeWolf Hopper, Charles King, The Duncan Sisters, Cliff Edwards, Karl Dane, Josephine Sabel and Barney Fagin.

MAX LINDER'S AMERICAN FILMOGRAPHY

Max Comes Across* (2/26/1917) Prod: Essanay Film Co. Dir & Sc: Max Linder. Asst Dir: Leo White. 2rls. Cast: Max Linder, Martha Early, Ernest Maupain (filmed at Essanay's Chicago studio).

Max Wants a Divorce* (3/25/1917) Prod: Essanay Film Co. Dir & Sc: Max Linder. Asst Dir: Leo White. 2rls. Cast: Max Linder, Francine Larrimore, Martha Early, Ernest Maupain, Leo White, Mathilde Comont (filmed at Essanay's Chicago studio).

Max in a Taxi* (4/28/1917) Prod: Essanay Film Co. Dir & Sc: Max Linder. Asst Dir: Leo White. 2rls. Cast: Max Linder, Ernest Maupain, Martha Early, Mathilde Comont (filmed at the Thomas Ince Studio in Culver City, California).

Seven Years Bad Luck* (2/6/1921) Prod, Dir & Sc: Max Linder. Dist: Robertson-Cole. Photo: Charles Van Enger. 5rls. Cast: Max Linder, Alta Allen, Ralph McCullough, Harry Mann, Betty Peterson, F.B. Crayne, Chance Ward, Hugh Saxon, Thelma Percy, Cap Anderson.

Be My Wife* (4/2/1921) Prod, Dir & Sc: Max Linder. Dist: Goldwyn Pictures. Photo: Charles Van Enger. 5rls. Cast: Max Lindr, Alta Allen, Caroline Rankin, Lincoln Steadman, Rose Dione, Sunshine Hart, Charles MacHugh, Viora Daniels, Arthur Clayton, Pal the dog.

The Three-Must-Get-Theres* (8/27/1922) Prod, Dir & Sc: Max Linder. Dist: Allied Producers and Distributors. Photo: Max Dupont & Harry Vallejo. Asst Dir: Fred Cavens. 5rls. Cast: Max Linder, Jobyna Ralston, Caroline Rankin, Bull Montana, Jack Richardson, Bynunski Hymen, Harry Mann, Charles Mezzetti, Clarence Wertz, Fred Cavens, Jean de Limur, Lon Poff, Walt Whitman.

Linder takes Martha Early (left) and Mathilde Comont (right) for a wild ride in 1917's *Max in a Taxi.*

GEORGE ROWE FILMOGRAPHY

All films unless noted were produced by Hal Roach.

Tough Luck (12/1/1919) Dir: Fred Newmeyer. 1rl. Cast: Snub Pollard, Mildred Davis, Sunshine Sammy Morrison, George Rowe, Gaylord Lloyd.

Cracked Wedding Bells* (4/4/1920) Dir: Thomas LaRose. 1rl. Cast: Snub Pollard, Marie Mosquini, Sunshine Sammy Morrison, Eddie Boland, George Rowe, Wallace Howe.

Any Old Port* (6/27/1920) 1rl. Cast: Snub Pollard, Marie Mosquini, George Rowe, William Gillespie, Charles Stevenson, Sunshine Sammy Morrison, Noah Young, Sammy Brooks, Eddie Boland, Hughie Mack.

Call A Taxi* (7/25/1920) 1rl. Cast: Snub Pollard, Marie Mosquini, Sunshine Sammy Morrison, George Rowe, Sammy Brooks, Hughie Mack, Charles Stevenson.

Run 'Em Ragged* (8/15/1920) 1rl. Cast: Snub Pollard, Marie Mosquini, Sunshine Sammy Morrison, Hughie Mack, Wallace Howe, Charles Stevenson, William Gillespie, Mark Jones, George Rowe, Robert O'Connor. (LOC)

Money to Burn* (8/29/1920) 1rl. Cast: Snub Pollard, Marie Mosquini, Sunshine Sammy Morrison, Charles Stevenson, William Gillespie, George Rowe, Hughie Mack.

Go As You Please* (9/12/1920) Dir: Alf Goulding. 1rl. Cast: Snub Pollard, Marie Mosquini, George Rowe, Hughie Mack, Sammy Brooks, Sunshine Sammy Morrison, Gaylord Lloyd. (MoMA)

Doing Time* (9/26/1920) 1rl. Cast: Snub Pollard, Marie Mosquini, Noah Young, Charles Stevenson, Mollie Thompson, George Rowe.

Beat It* (1/9/1921) Prod: C. L. Chester. Dist: Educational Pictures. Dir: William S. Campbell. 2rls. Cast: Snookie the Human-zee, Ida Mae McKenzie, Hap Ward, James Donnelly, George Rowe, Eva McKenzie.

Open Another Bottle (2/13/1921) 1rl. Cast: Snub Pollard, Marie Mosquini, Sunshine Sammy Morrison, Hughie Mack, George Rowe.

The Punch of the Irish* (3/1921) Prod: Henry Lehrman Comedies. Dist: First National. Dir: Noel M. Smith. 2rls. Cast: Billy Engle, Virginia Rappe, Frank J. Coleman, Phil Dunham, George Rowe. (MoMA, LOC)

Make It Snappy* (3/13/1921) 1rl. Cast: Snub Pollard, Marie Mosquini, Hughie Mack, Sunshine Sammy Morrison, George Rowe. (LOB)

Ad for Snub Pollard comedies featuring Snub (left), Marie Mosquini, and George Rowe (right).

Rush Orders* (4/10/1921) Dir: Charles Parrott. 1rl. Cast: Snub Pollard, Marie Mosquini, Sunshine Sammy Morrison, Hughie Mack, George Rowe, Sammy Brooks.

Big Game* (5/22/1921) Dir: Alf Goulding. 1rl. Cast: Snub Pollard, Marie Mosquini, Sunshine Sammy Morrison, George Rowe.

The High Rollers* (6/26/1921) Dir: Alf Goulding. 1rl. Cast: Snub Pollard, Marie Mosquini, Sunshine Sammy Morrison, George Rowe, Sammy Brooks, Mark Jones, James T. Kelly.

On Their Way* (9/11/1921) Dir: Nick Barrows. 1rl. Cast: Eddie Boland, Ethel Broadhurst, George Rowe, James T. Kelly, Sammy Brooks, Tiny Ward, Bud Jamison, Wallace Howe.

The Chink* (9/25/1921) Dir: Nick Barrows. 1rl. Cast: Eddie Boland, Ethel Broadhurst, Sunshine Sammy Morrison, George Rowe. (EYE)

The Lucky Number* (10/2/1921) Dir: Erle C. Kenton. 1rl. Cast: Gaylord Lloyd, Estelle Harrison, George Rowe, Sammy Brooks, Mark Jones, William Gillespie, Charles Stevenson, Mollie Thompson.

A Zero Hero* (10/9/1921) Dir: Erle C. Kenton. 1rl. Cast: Gaylord Lloyd, Estelle Harrison, George Rowe. (EYE)

Dodge Your Debts* (10/16/1921) Dir: Erle C. Kenton. Cast: Gaylord Lloyd, Estelle Harrison, George Rowe, William Gillespie.

Never Weaken* (10/22/1921) Dir: Fred Newmeyer. Sc: Hal Roach & Sam Taylor. 3rls. Cast: Harold Lloyd, Mildred Davis, Roy Brooks, Mark Jones, Charles Stevenson, George Rowe, Marie Mosquini, Helen Gilmore, William Gillespie, Wallace Howe, Sammy Brooks.

Trolley Troubles* (10/23/1921) Dir: Alf Goulding. 1rl. Cast: Gaylord Lloyd, Beatrice LaPlante, George Rowe, Vera White, James T. Kelly.

Fifteen Minutes* (10/30/1921) Dir: Charles Parrott. 1rl. Cast: Snub Pollard, Marie Mosquini, George Rowe, Vera White, Noah Young, William Gillespie, Mark Jones.

On Location* (11/6/1921) Dir: Charles Parrott. 1rl. Cast: Snub Pollard, Marie Mosquini, Noah Young, George Rowe, William Gillespie, Tiny Ward, Mark Jones, Wallace Howe.

The Pickaninny* (12/4/1921) Dir: James Parrott & Robert Kerr. 1rl. Cast: Sunshine Sammy Morrison, Joe White, Vera White, Ethel Broadhurst, Mark Jones, George Rowe, Tiny Ward, Sammy Brooks, Eddie Baker.

Try, Try Again* (1/1/1922) Dir: Raymond Grey. 1rl. Cast: Paul Parrott, Ethel Broadhurst, Sunshine Sammy Morriosn, George Rowe, Marvin Lobach.

Loose Change* (1/15/1922) Dir: Raymond Grey. 1rl. Cast: Paul Parrott, Ethel Broadhurst, Mark Jones, William Gillespie, Charles Stevenson, Sunshine Sammy Morrison, George Rowe, Sammy Brooks, Tiny Ward.

High Tide* (3/19/1922) Dir: Nick Barrows. 1rl. Cast: George Rowe, Sunshine Sammy Morrison, Ethel Broadhurst, Mark Jones. (LOB)

Stand Pat* (4/16/1922) Dir: Raymond Grey. 1rl. Cast: Paul Parrott, Ethel Broadhurst, Sunshine Sammy Morrison, Eddie Baker, Mark Jones, George Rowe.

Light Showers* (5/14/1922) Dir: Charles Parrott. 1rl. Cast: Snub Pollard, Marie Mosquini, Noah Young, George Rowe, Mark Jones, William Gillespie, Vera White, Gaylord Lloyd. (A condensed version of this short appears in Robert Youngson's 1963 compilation feature *Thirty Years of Fun*)

The Movies* (5/28/1922) Dir: Charles Parrott. 1rl. Cast: Snub Pollard, Marie Mosquini, Noah Young, George Rowe, Charles Parrott. (A condensed version of this short appears in Robert Youngson's 1961 compilation feature *The Days of Thrills and Laughter*)

Punch the Clock* (6/4/1922) Dir: William Beaudine. 1rl. Cast: Snub Pollard, Marie Mosquini, Eddie Baker, Mark Jones, George Rowe, William Gillespie.

Hale and Hearty* (6/18/1922) Dir: Al Santell. 1rl. Cast: Snub Pollard, Marie Mosquini, Eddie Baker, George Rowe.

Friday the 13th* (7/2/1922) Dir: James Davis. 1rl. Cast: Paul Parrott, Jobyna Ralston, Eddie Baker, Mark Jones, Vera White, George Rowe, Wallace Howe.

The Dumb-Bell* (7/16/1922) Dir: Charles Parrott. 1rl. Cast: Snub Pollard, Marie Mosquini, Noah Young, William B. Davidson, George Rowe, Wallace Howe, Charles Stevenson, William Gillespie, Sammy Brooks, Lincoln Steadman. (MoMA)

The Sleuth* (7/16/1922) Dir: Raymond Grey. 1rl. Cast: Paul Parrott, Mark Jones, Beth Darlington, George Rowe, Sammy Brooks, William Gillespie, Sunshine Sammy Morrison, Charles Stevenson.

Take Next Car* (7/30/1922) Dir: Jay A. Howe. 1rl. Cast: Paul Parrott, Jobyna Ralston, Eddie Baker, George Rowe, Wallace Howe, Jack Ackroyd, Sammy Brooks.

Grandma's Boy* (9/3/1922) Dir: Fred Newmeyer. Au: Hal Roach & Sam Taylor. 5rls. Cast: Harold Lloyd, Mildred Davis, Anna Townsend, Charles Stevenson, Dick Sutherland, Mark Jones, May Wallace, Roy Brooks, Georhe Rowe, Gaylord Lloyd.

The Landlubber* (9/10/1922) Dir: James Davis. 1rl. Cast: Paul Parrott, Jobyna Ralston, Eddie Baker, Wallace Howe, George Rowe, Marvin Lobach, Sammy Brooks, Linclon Steadman.

Fire Fighters* (10/8/1922) Dir: Robert McGowan & Tom McNamara. 2rls. Cast: Jackie Condon, Sunshine Sammy Morrison, Peggy Cartwright, Farina Hoskins, Winston Doty, Weston Doty, Monty O'Grady, Dinah the mule, George Rowe, Charles Stevenson, Ernie Morrison Sr.

Out on Bail* (10/15/1922) Dir: James Davis. 1rl. Cast: Paul Parrott, Jobyna Ralston, Eddie Baker, George Rowe, Wallace Howe.

The Golf Bug* (10/29/1922) Dir: James Davis. 1rl. Cast: Paul Parrott, Jobyna Ralston, George Rowe, Eddie Baker, Marvin Lobach, Roy Brooks, Mickey Daniels. (LOC)

Young Sherlocks* (11/26/1922) Dir: Robert McGowan & Tom Mc-Namara. 2rls. Cast: Sunshine Sammy Morrison, Jackie Condon, Peggy Cartwright, Mickey Daniels, Jackie Davis, Farina Hoskins, Mary Kornman, Dinah the mule, Charles Stevenson, Dick Gilbert, George Rowe, Charley Young, Dot Farley, Ernie Morrison Sr., William Gillespie, Roy Brooks, Ed Brandenberg, Wallace Howe.

Blaze Away* (12/3/1922) Dir: Jay A. Howe. 1rl. Cast: Paul Parrott, Jobyna Ralston, Eddie Baker, George Rowe, Sammy Brooks, Wallace Howe, Mark Jones, Marvin Lobach, Sam Lufkin.

Watch Your Wife* (1/7/1923) Dir: Jay A. Howe. 1rl. Cast: Paul Parrott, Jobyna Ralston, Mark Jones, Eddie Baker, Charles Stevenson, George Rowe.

Paste and Paper* (1/14/1923) Dir: George Jeske. 1 rl. Cast: Paul Parrott, Jobyna Ralston, Eddie Baker, George Rowe.

Jailed and Bailed* (2/11/1923) Dir: Jay A. Howe. 1rl. Cast: Paul Parrott, Jobyna Ralston, Eddie Baker, George Rowe, Wallace Howe, Sammy Brooks, Marvin Lobach, Lincoln Steadman, Sam Lufkin. (MoMA)

Tight Shoes* (2/25/1923) Dir: George Jeske. 1rl. Cast: Paul Parrott, Jobyna Ralston, Eddie Baker, George Rowe, Sammy Brooks, Helen Gilmore, Mark Jones, Josephine.

Before the Public* (3/4/1923) Dir: Charles Parrott. 2rls. Cast: Snub Pollard, Marie Mosquini, Noah Young, James Finlayson, Charles Stevenson, Wallace Howe (George Rowe and Sammy Brooks appear on slides shown in a movie theatre).

Do Your Stuff* (3/4/1923) Dir: Jay A. Howe. 1rl. Cast: Paul Parrott, Jobyna Ralston, Eddie Baker, Mark Jones, George Rowe, Gaylord Lloyd. (MoMA)

Shoot Straight* (3/11/1923) Dir: Jay A. Howe. 1rl. Cast: Paul Parrott, Jobyna Ralston, George Rowe.

The Smile Wins* (4/8/1923) Dir: George Jeske. 1rl. Cast: Paul Parrott, Eddie baker, Ena Gregory, George Rowe, Sammy Brooks, Marvin Lobach, Wallace Howe, Lincoln Steadman. (LOB)

White Wings* (5/13/1923) Dir: George Jeske. 1rl. Cast: Stan Laurel, James Finlayson, Katherine Grant, Marvin Lobach, George Rowe, Vera White, Mark Jones.

Pick and Shovel* (6/17/1923) Dir: George Jeske. 1rl. Cast: Stan Laurel, Katherine Grant, James Finlayson, Sammy Brooks, George Rowe, William Gillespie.

Collars and Cuffs* (7/1/1923) Dir: George Jeske. 1rl. Cast: Stan Laurel, Mark Jones, Eddie Baker, George Rowe, Sammy Brooks, Jack Ackroyd.

The Uncovered Wagon* (7/8/1923) Dir: Jay A. Howe. 1rl. Cast: Paul Parrott, Noah Young, Katherine Grant, Mark Jones, George Rowe, Wallace Howe.

Kill or Cure* (7/15/1923) Dir: Percy Pembroke. 1rl. Cast: Stan Laurel, Katherine Grant, Roy Brooks, Noah Young, Eddie Baker, George Rowe, Helen Gilmore, William Gillespie, Sammy Brooks, Charles Stevenson.

Post No Bills* (8/5/1923) Dir: Ralp Cedar. 1rl. Cast: Paul Parrott, Marie Mosquini, Ford West, George Rowe, Helen Gilmore, Noah Young, Sammy Brooks, Mark Jones, Jack Ackroyd, Bobby Ray.

Oranges and Lemons* (8/12/1923) Dir: George Jeske. 1rl. Cast: Stan Laurel, Katherine Grant, Eddie Baker, George Rowe, Sammy Brooks, Martin "Tonnage" Wolfkeil.

Live Wires* (8/26/1923) Dir: Jay A. Howe. 1rl. Cast: Paul Parrott, George Rowe, Noah Young.

Short Orders* (9/2/1923) Dir: Percy Pembroke. Cast:Stan Laurel, Marie Mosquini, Eddie Baker, Jack Ackroyd, George Rowe, Mark Jones, Charles Stevenson.

Take the Air* (9/9/1923) Dir: Ralph Cedar. 1rl. Cast: Paul Parrott, Katherine Grant, Mark Jones, Noah Young, George Rowe, Eddie Baker, Sammy Brooks.

A Man about Town* (9/16/1923) Dir: George Jeske. 1rl. Cast: Stan Laurel, James Finlayson, Katherine Grant, Mark Jones, George Rowe, Charles Stevenson, Sunshine Hart, Eddie Baker, Sam Lufkin, Sammy Brooks. (MoMA)

Roughest Africa* (9/30/1923) Dir: Ralph Cedar. 1rl. Cast: Stan Laurel, James Finlayson, Katherine Grant, George Rowe.

Frozen Hearts* (10/28/1923) Dir: Jay A. Howe. 1rl. Cast: Stan Laurel, Katherine Grant, James Finlayson, Mae Laurel, George Rowe, Earl Mohan, Sammy Brooks, Jack Gavin.

The Soilers* (11/25/1923) Dir: Ralph Cedar. 2rls. Cast: Stan Laurel, James Finlayson, Ena Gregory, George Rowe, Mae Laurel, Eddie Baker, Billy Engle, Jack Ackroyd, Glenn Tryon, Jack Gavin, Marvin Lobach, Joe Bordeaux.

Join the Circus* (12/2/1923) Dir: George Jeske. 1rl. Cast: snub Pollard, Paul Parrott, Katherine Grant, George Rowe, Marvin Lobach, Earl Mohan, Charles Stevenson.

Scorching Sands* (12/9/1923) Dir: Robin Williamson (& Ward Hayes). 1rl. Cast: Stan Laurel, James Finlayson, Katherine Grant, Mark Jones, George Rowe, Merta Sterling, Billy Engle, Sammy Brooks.

Mother's Joy*(12/23/1923) Dir: Ralph Cedar. 2rls. Cast: Stan Laurel, James Finlayson, Ena Gregory, Mae Laurel, Jack Ackroyd, William Gillespie, Helen Gilmore, George Rowe, Charlie Hall.

The Big Idea* (1/13/1924) Dir: George Jeske. 1rl. Cast: Snub Pollard, Billy Engle, Blanche Mehaffey, George Rowe, Glenn Tryon, Jack Ackroyd, Marvin Lobach.

Smithy* (1/20/1924) Dir: George Jeske. 2rls. Cast: Stan Laurel, James Finlayson, Katherine Grant, Jack Gavin, George Rowe, William Gillespie, Glenn Tryon, Fred Karno Jr., Eddie Baker, Marvin Lobach, Sammy Brooks.

Postage Due* (2/17/1924) Dir: George Jeske. 2rls. Cast: Stan Laurel, James Finlayson, Ena Gregory, George Rowe, Eddie Baker, William Gillespie, Dick Gilbert, Martin "Tonnage" Wolfkeil, Jack Ackroyd, Charlie Hall.

Zeb Vs Paprika* (3/16/1924) Dir: Ralph Cedar. 1rl. Cast: Stan Laurel, James Finlayson, Ena Gregory, George Rowe, Eddie Baker, Dick Gilbert, Sammy Brooks. (LOB)

Friend Husband* (7/6/1924) Dir: Ward Hayes. 1rl. Cast: Snub Pollard, Louise Carver, George Rowe, Blanche Mehaffey, Billy Engle, Eddie Baker, Sam Lufkin.

Brothers under the Chin* (4/13/1924) Dir: Ralph Cedar. 2rls. Cast: Stan Laurel, James Finlayson, Ena Gregory, William Gillespie, Noah Young, Sammy Brooks, George Rowe. (LOB)

Near Dublin* (5/11/1924) Dir: Ralph Cedar. 2rls. Cast: Stan Laurel, James Finlayson, Ena Gregory, George Rowe, Jack Gavin, Mae Laurel.

April Fool* (5/18/1924) Dir: Ralph Cedar. 1rl. Cast: Charley Chase, Blanche Mehaffey, Noah Young, Jack Gavin, George Rowe, Helen Gilmore, Sam Lufkin.

Before Taking* (6/1/1924) Dir: Ralph Cedar. 1rl. Cast: Earl Mohan, Billy Engle, Ena Gregory, Gus Leonard, George Rowe, James Finlayson.

Rupert of Hee Haw* (6/8/1924) Dir: Percy Pembroke. 2rls. Cast: Stan Laurel, Billy Engle, Ena Gregory, Sammy Brooks, Mae Laurel, Pierre Coven, George Rowe, Martin "Tonnage" Wolfkeil, Al Ochs, Al Forbes, Kewpie Morgan, Jack Gavin, Irene Lentz, Gary Horton, Alith Cruze, Dick Gilbert, Pal the dog, Harry Bayfield, Charlie Lloyd, Joe Cobb, Mickey Daniels, Sunshine Sammy Morrison, Mary Kornman, Jackie Condon. (MoMA)

The Wide Open Spaces* (7/6/1924) Dir: George Jeske. 2rls. Cast: Stan Laurel, Ena Gregory, James Finlayson, Noah Young, Sammy Brooks, George Rowe. (LOB)

Short Kilts* (8/3/1924) Dir: George Jeske. 2rls. Cast: Stan Laurel, Mickey Daniels, Mary Kornman, George Rowe, Leo Willis, Ena Gregory, Jack Gavin, Martin "Tonnage" Wolfkeil, Sammy Brooks, Helen Gilmore, Patsy O'Byrne, Joy Winthrop, Ouida Wildman, Charlie Lloyd, Al Ochs, Al Forbes.

Outdoor Pajamas* (9/14/1924) Dir: Leo McCarey. 1rl. Cast: Charley Chase, Martha Sleeper, George Rowe, Leo Willis, Jack Gavin, Lyle Tayo, Beth Darlington, Jules Mendel, Charles Bachman.

Hot Heels (11/9/1924) Dir: George Jeske. 2rl. Cast: Glenn Tryon, En Gregory, James Finlayson, Leo Willis, George Rowe.

The Wages of Tin* (1/4/1925) Dir: Roy Clements. 2rls. Cast: Glenn Tryon, Billy Engle, Noah Young, George Rowe. (BFI)

The Haunted Honeymoon (3/29/1925) Dir: Ted Wilde & Fred Guiol. 2rls. Cast: Glenn Tryon, Blanche Mehaffey, James Finlayson, Yorke Sherwood, George Rowe, Helen Gilmore, Jules Mendel, Janet Gaynor.

Is Marriage the Bunk?* (3/29/1925) Dir: Leo McCarey. 1rls. Cast: Charley Chase, Katherine Grant, Marie Mosquini, William Gillespie, George Rowe, Rolfe Sedan, Sammy Brooks, Frank Terry.

Looking for Sally* (5/10/1925) Dir: Leo McCarey. 2rls. Cast: Charley Chase, Katherine Grant, Noah Young, Leo Willis, Bynunski Hymen, John Prince, Rolfe Sedan, Jack Gavin, George Rowe, Sammy Brooks, Eleanor Vanderveer, Richard Daniels, William Gillespie, Jules Mendel.

Wild Papa (5/17/1925) Dir: Jay A. Howe (& Nick Barrows). 2rls. Cast: Frank Butler, Sydney D'Albrook, Laura Roessing, Katherine Grant, Oliver Hardy, George Rowe, Jules Mendel.

Official Officers* (6/28/1925) Dir: Robert McGowan. 2rls. Cast: Mickey Daniels, Joe Cobb, Jackie Condon, Mary Kornman, Farina Hoskins, Johnny Downs, Peggy Ahern, Jackie Hanes, Jannie Hoskins, Pal the dog, Jack Gavin, James Finlayson, George Rowe, Chet Brandenberg, Dick Gilbert, Charley Young.

Isn't Life Terrible?* (7/5/1925) Dir: Leo McCarey. 2rls. Cast: Charley Chase, Katherine Grant, Oliver Hardy, Lon Poff, Leo Willis, George Rowe.

Unfriendly Enemies* (9/13/1925) Dir: Stan Laurel. 1rl. Cast: James Finlayson, Fay Wray, George Rowe, Jules Mendel, Charlie Hall.

Whistling Lions* (11/22/1925) Dir: Hal Roach. 1rl. Cast: Paul Parrott, Jobyna Ralston, George Rowe, Marvin Lobach, Wallace Howe, Eddie Baker, Sammy Brooks (Shot in August of 1922).

Tol'ble Romeo* (12/27/1925) Dir: Jess Robbins. 1rl. Cast: Frank Butler, Katherine Grant, William Gillespie, George Rowe, Helen Gilmore, Sammy Brooks.

A Punch in the Nose (1/3/1926) Dir: Jay A. Howe (& James Horne). 2rls. Cast: Lucien Littlefield, Dot Farley, Al St John, Lige Conley, James Finlayson, Martha Sleeper, Kathleen Collins, Kathleen Pickell, Harry Lorraine, George Rowe, Sammy Brooks, Betty Arlen, Janet Gaynor.

Between Meals* (1/3/1926) Dir: Raymond Grey. 1rl. Cast: Paul Parrott, Sunshine Sammy Morrison, George Rowe (Shot August and September of 1921).

Soft Pedal* (1/31/1926) Dir: Raymond Grey. 1rl. Cast: Paul Parrott, Ethel Broadhurst, Sunshine Sammy Morrison, George Rowe, Mark Jones, George Rowe, Ernie Morrison Sr., Charley Young (Shot in September and October of 1921).

The Only Son* (2/28/1926) Dir: Raymond Grey. 1rl. Cast: Paul Parrott, George Rowe (Shot in November of 1921).

The Old Warhorse* (4/11/1926) Dir: George Jeske. 1rl. Cast: Snub Pollard, Paul Parrott, Blanche Mehaffey, Billy Engle, Sammy Brooks, George Rowe, Jack Gavin (Shot in the summer of 1923).

Don Key (Son of Burro)* (5/23/1926) Dir: Grover Jones & Hal Yates (plus Jay A. Howe, Fred Guiol, & James Horne). 2rls. Cast: Max Davidson, Vivian Oakland, Stuart Holmes, Spec O'Donnell, James Finlayson, Martha Sleeper, Jackie Hanes, Jerry Mandy, Frank Butler, George Rowe, Al Hallet, Jules Mendel, Yorke Sherwood, Tyler Brooke (Shot at various times in 1925).

You're Darn Tootin'* (4/21/1928) Dir: E. Livingston Kennedy. 2rls. Cast: Stan Laurel, Oliver Hardy, Otto Lederer, Sam Lufkin, Chet Brandenberg, Christian Frank, Rolfe Sedan, George Rowe, Agnes Steele, Ham Kinsey, Charlie Hall, William Irving, Dick Gilbert, Frank Saputo.

All Washed Up* (6/2/1928) Karnival Komedies. PD: Larry Darmour. Dist: FBO. Dir: Al Herman. 2rls. Cast: Al Cooke, Barney Hellum, Spencer Bell, George Rowe.

Loose Change* (6/10/1928) PD: Al Christie. Dist: Paramount. Dir: Harold Beaudine. 2rls. Cast: Jack Duffy, Neal Burns, Lorraine Eddy, Winnie Law, Glen Cavender, Eddie Barry, George Rowe, Buddy the dog.

Two Tars* (11/3/1928) Dir: James Parrott. 2rls. Cast: Stan Laurel, Oliver Hardy, Thelma Hill, Ruby Blaine, Charley Rogers, Edgar Kennedy, Clara Guiol, Jack Hill, Charlie Hall, Edgar Dearing, Harry Bernard, Sam Lufkin, Baldy Belmont, Charles McMurphy, Ham Kinsey, Lyle Tayo, Lon Poff, Retta Palmer, George Rowe, Chet Brandenberg, Fred Holmes, Dorothy Walbert, Frank Ellis, Helen Gilmore (Many filmographies list George as a motorist but he is not visible in the released film).

Mutual
Movies
Make Time
Fly

Sources

PERIODICALS—TRADE PUBLICATIONS

The Biograph, 1914 - 1915
Edison Kinetogram, 1911—1916
Educational Film Exchange Press Sheets, 1920 - 1930
Essanay News, 1915—1917
The Exhibitor, 1924 - 1927
Exhibitors Trade Review, 1922—1924
Film Daily, 1919—1930
Fox's Exhibitor Bulletin, 1915 - 1919
Kalem Kalendar, 1914 - 1915
Loew's Weekly, 1920 - 1931
Motion Picture News, 1913—1930
Motion Picture News Blue Book, 1929 - 1930
Motion Picture News Booking Guide, 1922—1927
Motography, 1911—1917
The Movie Home Journal, 1924 - 1927
Moving Picture World, 1910—1927
Paramount Pictures Press Books, 1918 - 1923
Pathé Bulletins, 1910—1916
The Pathé Messenger, 1920 - 1922
Pathé Press Sheets, 1925 - 1929
Photoplay, 1918—1930
The Photoplayer's Weekly, 1914 - 1917
Picture-Play, 1917 - 1920
Reel Life, 1914—1916
Selig Monthly Herald, 1915
The Triangle, 1916 -1917

Universal Weekly, 1913—1930
Variety, 1930—1930
Vitagraph Life Portrayals, 1910—1916

PERIODICALS -ARTICLES

Anthony, Brian and Edmonds, Andy. *Crazy Like a Fox: The Saga of Charley Chase. Griffithiana* #48/49, 1993.

Caslavsky, Karel. *American Comedy Series: Filmographies 1914—1930. Griffithiana* # 51/52, 1994.

Doyle, Billy H. *Lost Players [Billy Quirk]*
Classic Images #160, October 1988.

____________. *Lost Players [Fay Tincher]*
Classic Images #165, March 1989.

____________. *Lost Players [Child Stars]*
Classic Images #174, December 1989.

Dunham, Harold. *John Bunny. The Silent Picture* #1, Winter 1968-9.

Farr, Robert. *Hollywood Mensch: Max Davidson. Griffithiana* #55/56, 1996.

Gill, Sam. *John Bunny: A Filmography. The Silent Picture* #15, Summer 1972.

Maltin, Leonard. *Charley Chase. Film Fan Monthly*, July-August 1969.

_____________. *The Spice of the Program. The Silent Picture* #15, Summer 1972.

Massa, Steve. *Alice Howell and Gale Henry: Queens of Eccentric Comedy. Griffithiana* #73/74, 2004.

Randisi, Steve. *The Gal who Knew the Boys. Filmfax* #40, 1993.

Roberts, Richard M. *Their Gangs: A Look at the Our Gang Spinoff Comedies of the 1920s. Classic Images* #267, September 1997.

_______________ and Farr, Robert. *Max Davidson: Papa Gimplewart Lives! Classic Images*, July 2002.

BOOKS

Anthony, Brian and Edmonds, Andy. *Smile When the Raindrops* Fall. Lanham, Maryland: Scarecrow Press, 1998.

Blum, Daniel. *A Pictorial History of the Silent Screen*. New York: G.P. Putnam's Sons, 1953.

Braff, Richard E. *The Universal Silents*. Jefferson, North Carolina: McFarland & Co., 1999.

Bruskin, David N. *The White Brothers: Jack, Jules and Sam White*. Hollywood: Scarecrow Press 1990.

Curtis, James. *W.C. Fields: A Biography*. New York: Alfred A. Knopf, 2003.

Fields, Ronald J. *W.C. Fields by Himself*. Englewood Cliffs, New Jersey: Prentice –Hall, Inc., 1973.

______________. *W.C. Fields: A Life on Film*. New York: St. Martin's Press, 1984.

Fowler, Gene. *Father Goose*. New York: Covici Friede Publishers, 1934.

Horn, Maurice. *The World Encyclopedia of Comics*. Philadelphia: Chelsea House, 1999.

Kennedy, Matthew. *Marie Dressler*. Jefferson, North Carolina: McFarland & Co., 1999.

Kerr, Walter. *The Silent Clowns*. New York: Alfred A. Knopf, 1975.

Kiehn, David. *Broncho Billy and the Essanay Company*. Berkley, California: Farwell Books, 2003.

Lahue, Kalton C. *World of Laughter: The Motion Picture Comedy Short*. Norman, Oklahoma: University of Oklahoma Press, 1966.

______________. *Mack Sennett's Keystone*. South Brunswick: A.S. Barnes, 1970.

______________., and Gill, Sam. *Clown Princes and Court Jesters*. South Brunswick: A.S. Barnes, 1970.

______________.: *Dreams for Sale :The Rise and Fall of the Triangle Film Corporation*. South Brunswick: A.S. Barnes, 1971.

Lee, Betty. *Marie Dressler: The Unlikeliest* Star. Lexington, Kentucky: The University Press of Kentucky, 1997.

Loos, Anita. *A Girl Like I*. New York: Viking Press, 1966.

Loos, Anita. *Cast of Thousands*. New York: Grosset and Dunlap, 1977.

Louvish, Simon. *Man on the Flying Trapeze: The life and Times of W. C. Fields*. London: Faber and Faber, 1997

______________. *Stan and Ollie: The Roots of Comedy: The Double Life of Laurel and Hardy*. New York: St Martin's Press, 2002.

_____________. *Keystone: The Life and Clowns of Mack Sennett*. London: Faber and Faber, 2003.

Maltin, Leonard. *The Great Movie Comedy Teams*. New York: Signet, 1970.

___________. *The Great Movie Shorts*. New York: Bonanza, 1972.

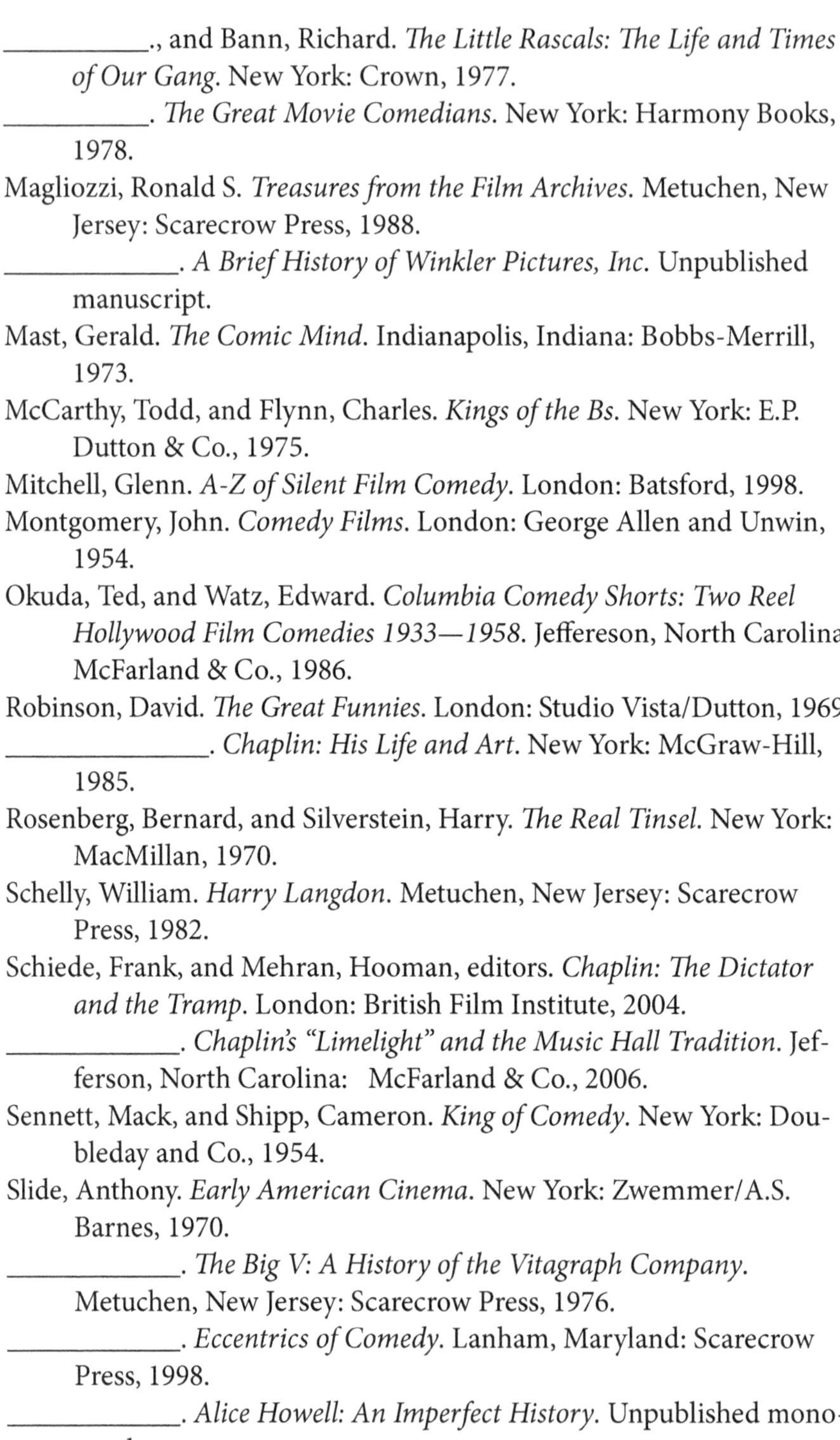

__________., and Bann, Richard. *The Little Rascals: The Life and Times of Our Gang*. New York: Crown, 1977.

__________. *The Great Movie Comedians*. New York: Harmony Books, 1978.

Magliozzi, Ronald S. *Treasures from the Film Archives*. Metuchen, New Jersey: Scarecrow Press, 1988.

__________. *A Brief History of Winkler Pictures, Inc.* Unpublished manuscript.

Mast, Gerald. *The Comic Mind*. Indianapolis, Indiana: Bobbs-Merrill, 1973.

McCarthy, Todd, and Flynn, Charles. *Kings of the Bs*. New York: E.P. Dutton & Co., 1975.

Mitchell, Glenn. *A-Z of Silent Film Comedy*. London: Batsford, 1998.

Montgomery, John. *Comedy Films*. London: George Allen and Unwin, 1954.

Okuda, Ted, and Watz, Edward. *Columbia Comedy Shorts: Two Reel Hollywood Film Comedies 1933—1958*. Jeffereson, North Carolina: McFarland & Co., 1986.

Robinson, David. *The Great Funnies*. London: Studio Vista/Dutton, 1969.

__________. *Chaplin: His Life and Art*. New York: McGraw-Hill, 1985.

Rosenberg, Bernard, and Silverstein, Harry. *The Real Tinsel*. New York: MacMillan, 1970.

Schelly, William. *Harry Langdon*. Metuchen, New Jersey: Scarecrow Press, 1982.

Schiede, Frank, and Mehran, Hooman, editors. *Chaplin: The Dictator and the Tramp*. London: British Film Institute, 2004.

__________. *Chaplin's "Limelight" and the Music Hall Tradition*. Jefferson, North Carolina: McFarland & Co., 2006.

Sennett, Mack, and Shipp, Cameron. *King of Comedy*. New York: Doubleday and Co., 1954.

Slide, Anthony. *Early American Cinema*. New York: Zwemmer/A.S. Barnes, 1970.

__________. *The Big V: A History of the Vitagraph Company*. Metuchen, New Jersey: Scarecrow Press, 1976.

__________. *Eccentrics of Comedy*. Lanham, Maryland: Scarecrow Press, 1998.

__________. *Alice Howell: An Imperfect History*. Unpublished monograph.

Spears, Jack. *Hollywood: The Golden Era.* South Brunswick: Castle Books/A.S. Barnes & Co., 1971.
Stewart, Travis D. *No Applause—Just Throw Money or The Book that Made Vaudeville Famous.* New York: Faber and Faber, 2005.
Stone, Rob. *Laurel or Hardy.* Temecula, California: Split Reel Books, 1996.
Walker, Brent E. *Mack Sennett's Fun Factory.* Jefferson, North Carolina: McFarland & Co., 2010.
Yallop, David. *The Day the Laughter Stopped.* New York: St. Martin's Press, 1976.

OTHER SOURCES

Dorward, William. *Interview with Alfred Santell.* November 1972.
Robinson Locke Collection of Theatrical Clippings 1870—1920. New York Public Library for the Performing Arts.
Nitrateville (nitrateville.com)
Silent Comedians Forum (silentcomedians.com)
Silent Comedy Mafia (silentcomedymafia.com)

Afterword by Sam Gill

Samuel Johnson may have had his James Boswell, but all of us who love silent screen comedy have our own Steve Massa. In this tour de force of a book, Steve has brought together in one place an astounding array of facts and figures, assessments and opinions, appraisals and reappraisals. It covers literally hundreds of men, women, children–and animals!–who devoted much of their lives to making films, silent comedy films, in an often thankless effort to get people to laugh or, at the very least, amused.

Most of the individuals whose work has been so entertainingly described and analyzed in this book have never been given the notice and appreciation they deserve. Thanks to Steve, many of these hardworking filmmakers are finally getting some of their long-awaited dues.

For some of these individuals–comedians such as Billie Ritchie, Harry Davenport, Marcel Perez (Tweedy), Al St John, and George Rowe–there is more detail and accurate information about them to be found here, in consistently concise and informative accounts, than most of them ever got in their own lifetimes.

And the women, the comediennes, were usually neglected even more than their male counterparts. Here, they are finally given the kind of knowledgeable attention they have never, or very rarely, been given before–Alice Howell, Josie Sadler, Gale Henry, Fay Tincher, even the better-known Marie Dressler, whose dramatic rise-and-fall-to-rise-again career Steve recounts in a very moving and thoughtful chapter, "*I'm Glad Now That I'm Homely.*"

Anyone who has even the slightest interest in silent screen comedy who would like to know more about the subject has been often faced with a daunting challenge. Simple questions that seem like they should be easily answered have often proven to be the most difficult.

A few examples: When were they born? Just where did these people come from? What kind of performers were they? What companies did they work for? How successful were they at the time? What films did they make? Do any of the films survive and, if so, what are the titles and where can I find them?

This book has set as its lofty goal to meet that challenge to answer these questions and many, many others. There is also a great need–which this book helps to meet–to provide more information regarding specific films, who appears in them, who directed and photographed them, who wrote them, where exactly they were made, and also, a surprisingly difficult question, when were they released to theatres.

This gathering of information has been supported more and more by the world's many film archives and libraries with a goal of determining the pertinent facts relating to all of the films in their collections, many of which are unidentified, or what film archivist Rob Stone has aptly described, "under-identified." Steve Massa has been at the forefront of this "movement" for many years and this book touches upon these issues on nearly every page.

Now on to a little-known secret that I'd like to share:

One of the great joys for contemporary audiences, for anyone willing to take the time to search out and watch the films described in this book, is the gradual awareness that all these extraordinary, hardworking souls, active during the silent screen era, continually crossed paths with one another, borrowed gags and bits of business from each other, and worked at the same companies or were involved with companies owned, managed, or mismanaged by the same people.

Everyone in the field seemed to know everyone else in the field and either influenced or was influenced by one another. In that fashion, they were very much like a huge extended family. So, as we today learn about them, watch their films, read a book such as this one, we can, if we let ourselves, begin to feel as if we ourselves are active members of this extremely large, sprawling, sometimes contentious, but endlessly fascinating family.

As for the super-enthusiasts among us who want to know everything that can be humanly known and conveniently gathered in one place, this book can serve as a kind of exploratory rocket running on a very high-grade fuel that will propel any of us who wish it to journey into the still largely unexplored and intriguing universe known as American silent screen comedy.

Fortunately, with Steve Massa, we have got just the exact right person at the controls to get us to our destination… and back again!

Sam Gill is co-author of the seminal Clown Princes and Court Jesters, *possibly the very first study of the rank and file performers of silent comedy. In addition to befriending and interviewing slapstick film veterans such as Babe London, Dorothy Vernon, Eddie Baker, BillyWest, Minta Durfee, and many more, Sam worked for many years at the Academy of Motion Picture Arts and Sciences' Margaret Herrick Library, where he always went way beyond the call of duty to share information with researchers, plus fostered numerous books and studies on silent film. Now retired, Sam maintains his incredible collection of photos, lobby cards, and information, works on many film projects, and continues to generously share his vast knowledge.*

Index

D

E

G

M

S

V

W

www.ingramcontent.com/pod-product-compliance
Lightning Source LLC
LaVergne TN
LVHW020517100826
845148LV00010B/1257

* 9 7 8 1 6 2 9 3 3 9 4 1 2 *